# Social Work Practice in Canada

KNOWLEDGE, VALUES, AND SKILLS

ISBN 978-1-55077-269-2

Information on how to obtain copies of this book is available at
www.thompsonbooks.com
Phone: 416.766.2763
Fax: 416.766.0398

**Library and Archives Canada Cataloguing in Publication**

Title: Social work practice in Canada : knowledge, values, and skills / Jackie Stokes, Thompson Rivers University.

Names: Stokes, Jackie, author.

Description: Includes bibliographical references and index.

Identifiers: Canadiana 20190105976 | ISBN 9781550772692 (softcover)

Subjects: LCSH: Social service—Canada—Textbooks. | LCSH: Social work education—Canada. | LCGFT: Textbooks.

Classification: LCC HV11.8.C2 S76 2019 | DDC 361.30971—dc23

**Photo Credits**

Cover: Kriachko Oleksii/Shutterstock.com; page 2: Rawpixel.com/Shutterstock.com; 28: Radachynskyi Serhii/Shutterstock.com; 54: FotoDuets/Shutterstock.com; 82: Optimarc/Shutterstock.com; 112: Monkey Business Images/Shutterstock.com; 142: Axente Vlad/Shutterstock.com; 174: Monkey Business Images/Shutterstock.com; 202: Rawpixel.com/Shutterstock.com; 230: Wellphoto/Shutterstock.com; 256: Jacob Lund/Shutterstock.com.

We acknowledge the support of the Government of Canada.

Canada

Printed in Canada.

1 2 3 4 5 6 7     25 24 23 22 21 20 19

# Social Work Practice in Canada

### KNOWLEDGE, VALUES, AND SKILLS

## JACKIE STOKES
THOMPSON RIVERS UNIVERSITY

**THOMPSON**
Toronto

# Contents

# Introduction

Field education is a core component of all social work programs. It is the time when students begin to apply their theoretical knowledge to complex, real-life situations. This book is intended to help students though their field education by introducing them to methods of approaching and providing social work practice in Canada.

Field education has a long history in Canadian social work, dating back to the early part of the twentieth century, when social work programs began to introduce both a university-based component and an agency- or community-based field component (Drolet, Clark, and Allen, 2012). It coincides with the emergence of social work as a distinct profession. The goal of field education is to promote social workers' development and competency to practise effectively. The practical component helps to ensure that new practitioners, as they begin their careers, are ready to provide effective and consistent service, based on the most up-to-date practice knowledge and skills.

## Promoting Excellence in Social Work Practice

The Canadian Association for Social Work Education–Association canadienne pour la formation en travail social (CASWE-ACFTS), founded in 1967, was established as a national body to plan, coordinate, and assess social work education across Canada. Its mission is to promote excellence in social work education, practice, and scholarly activities through the enrichment of social work education and the accreditation of social work programs. At the time of writing, the CASWE-ACFTS was reviewing and preparing amendments to its *Standards for Accreditation*, which were last issued in 2014. The CASWE-ACFTS describes field education as follows:

> The purpose of field education is to connect the theoretical/conceptual contributions of the academic setting with the practice setting, enabling the student to acquire practice skills that reflect the learning objectives for students identified in the Standards. Each program may vary its delivery of the field education component according to the nature and objectives of program and the influences of its university and local context. (CASWE-ACFTS, 2014, p. 14)

This book provides opportunities for students to apply their knowledge and skills to practice situations using a social work value system. It is a resource for students to use as they progress through field education and begin to gain an understanding of themselves as professional social workers.

## The Purpose of Field Education

Field education (sometimes referred to as "practicum," "field work," "field instruction," or "field experience") has an important place in social work education, as it provides students with valuable opportunities to apply the knowledge, values, and skills learned in the classroom to the real-life world of practice. This experience also provides an opportunity to test one's interest in the profession and, for most students, it is a valuable time to confirm their career choice.

Social work requires many different abilities for relating to individuals, families, small groups, organizations, and communities, and for advocating for social justice. Social workers have strengths in assessment and in developing intervention strategies. They also take on various helping roles such as advocate, broker, group leader, mediator, clinician, community planner, organizer, policy analyst, and researcher.

While no one agency can provide opportunities to learn every aspect of social work practice, the intent of field education is to provide the time and space to develop a repertoire of approaches. Field education in social work is not just another work experience. Instead, it is an educational learning experience designed to address unique educational needs and goals.

# CASWE-ACFTS Core Learning Objectives

The book is designed around the notion of "threshold concepts" or "meta-competencies" as the foundation of social work practice. While there is no single definitive list of meta-competencies, the ones utilized in this book emerge from the core learning objectives set out by CASWE-ACFTS:

- Identifying as a professional social worker
- Engaging in reflexive practice
- Employing critical thinking
- Ensuring professional judgements and decision-making
- Adhering to social work values and ethics
- Respecting diversity and difference
- Conducting assessments
- Developing professional relationships
- Applying knowledge of human development and behaviour
- Planning and delivering services and interventions
- Promoting community sustainability
- Advocating for human rights and social justice
- Conducting policy analysis and development
- Engaging in research and research-based practice
- Participating and leading organizational and societal system change

Discussion of these meta-competencies runs through all of the chapters in this book, but a convenient summary can be found on pages 10–11, in Chapter 1.

# Chapter Organization

This book embodies the notion that social work practice is holistic and recursive. The content design of the book falls into three broad sections: the first section relates to the social worker's "self" and professional identity; the second section relates to working with individuals and families at the micro level; and the third section relates to macro practice associated with communities and social justice.

- Chapters 1 to 4 present the grounding themes of professional identity, critical thinking, social work ethics, and cultural diversity. These themes underpin the content of subsequent chapters.

- Chapters 5 to 7 focus on the knowledge and skills associated with conducting assessments and providing services and interventions to individuals and families across the lifespan.

- Chapters 8 to 10 describe social work principles and practices in relation to community development, global human rights, social justice, and system-wide change.

# The Canadian Context

This book considers social work practice in relation to a variety of populations across Canada and it also highlights the special considerations associated with Indigenous and francophone people. The book includes a number of features on each of these populations. In some cases, a particular approach or service delivery model is examined. In others, the research of Indigenous or francophone scholars is showcased.

The emphasis on Indigenous and francophone practice and service delivery is integrated into the substance of chapters in order to underline that these populations are integral and unique to Canadian social work practice. Initially, the differences between mainstream practice and Indigenous and francophone practices may not be obvious. However, it is hoped that the importance of respecting and reconciling these different approaches will become apparent over time.

The attention given to Indigenous and francophone populations is in no way intended to detract from the unique and important work carried out by social workers and their organizations with other populations across Canada. Efforts to draw attention to those practices have been integrated throughout the chapters. It is hoped that students will be familiar with and continue to develop expertise in their own province or territory, and will also develop the capacity to work in different jurisdictions across the country.

Throughout this book, the term "service user" is used to increase the respect for personal agency and reduce the implication of power inequality that is associated with terms such as "client" and "patient."

## Mainstream and Critical Approaches

Based on the CASWE-ACFTS core learning objectives, each chapter is designed around a particular meta-competency. Within each chapter, some key summary content is provided. This is mainly designed to refresh one's thinking about the core ideas involved, and may require the student to return to academic course materials for further review.

As already described, the book pays special attention to francophone and Indigenous contexts and practices. In addition, it also covers traditional, mainstream approaches to social work practice as well as critical theory and postmodern practices.

## Practice Scenarios

Each chapter includes practice scenarios that students can work through alone, in small groups, or in a seminar setting. These practice scenarios provide an opportunity to consider, discuss, and reflect on situations that social workers have experienced in practice.

The scenarios are not designed to have a "right" answer, but to generate critical reflection and accountable decision-making in readiness for practice. In each situation, one should consider social work knowledge and values; the relevant national, provincial, or territorial codes of ethics; standards (or guidelines) of practice; and one's own experiences, biases, and perspectives.

## Social Worker Exemplars

Ultimately, this book is about preparing for practice, which entails "doing" the practice rather than just "talking" about the practice. Accordingly, in each chapter, practising social workers recall their own transformative experiences in order to demonstrate the ways in which learning has taken place for them.

Please note that while all exemplars relate real experiences in social work practice, they have been modified to ensure the anonymity of the service user. I wish to thank all of the contributors for sharing their experiences.

## Reflection, Learning, and More Practice

Field education is most effective when it is purposeful and systematic. Effective practice requires focused attention and is conducted with the specific goal of improving performance.

To this end, each chapter also includes a section entitled "Reflection, Learning, and More Practice." This section provides ideas for reflexive journalling, critical-thinking questions for small group or seminar discussion, and tangible practical ideas to ensure progress through the field education course.

# Field Education Practicalities

Each social work program has unique attributes and requirements, and each agency has different opportunities for deeper learning. It is usual to have a faculty person coordinate and oversee the student's learning in collaboration with an agency supervisor who is an active practitioner in the field. While field education programs across the country may take different forms and expose students to unique challenges, all require similar social work practice knowledge, values, and skills.

The design of the chapters is such that they can be used sequentially or referenced individually as a particular competency is focused on. However, the "Field Education Practicalities" sections have been designed to be used sequentially. In most instances, they are linked to ideas in the chapter, but in others, they are linked more to the stage one might be at in practicum.

For reference purposes, the following areas are covered in the "Field Education Practicalities" sections:

- **The First Steps in Field Placement**
  Identifying preferences, completing an interview, assessing meta-competencies (page 24)

- **Seminars, Learning Plans and Goals, and Reflexive Journalling**
  Integrating seminars, learning plans, and reflexive journalling (page 50)

- **The Ethical Responsibilities of Supervisors**
  Understanding supervisor responsibilities and student responsibilities in dual relationships and work–life balance (page 78)

- **Supervision and Feedback**
  Making the most of supervision and receiving feedback (page 108)

- **Preparing for Midpoint Assessments**
  Preparing for an assessment and reflecting on its outcome (page 138)

- **Working in Teams**
  Understanding teams, interprofessional practice, and ways of working together (page 170)

- **Working through Difficulties**
  Working with angry/hostile service users and addressing unethical practices by colleagues (page 198)

- **Staying Healthy in Social Work Agencies**
  Coping with overwhelming feelings, too much to do, and having down days (page 226)

- **Ending Relationships Successfully**
  Ending relationships with service users and agencies, and preparing for final evaluations (page 252)

- **Am I Cut Out for a Career in Social Work?**
  Understanding social work opportunities and pathways (page 280)

# The Joys and Challenges of Being a Social Worker

This book has been developed from ideas and experiences spanning over three decades in practice and teaching. Its primary goal is to introduce students to the knowledge, values, and skills associated with contemporary social work practice and to help them become thoughtful, intentional, and effective professionals.

I have thoroughly enjoyed my career as a social worker, with only minor exceptions. I have never doubted the joy that social work has provided me and the value of social work to individuals, families, and communities. I have been fortunate to have had many service users and communities teach me and inform my practice. My teaching and practice career has also been greatly enhanced though interactions with students, who have allowed me to be a lifelong learner.

To be sure, there are challenges to being a social worker. As social welfare benefits continue to diminish and agencies become increasingly bureaucratized, the emphasis of the work has changed. Many academics and social work practitioners rightly bemoan these developments. However, overall, I think the quality of social work has improved during my career. A key report influencing my early practice was the groundbreaking *Badgley Report* on sexual offences against children (Committee on Sexual Offences against Children and Youths, 1984). Today, sexual abuse reports are taken seriously and addressed. When I began my practice, many client records contained no information at all or they contained too much information that was judgemental and derogatory. With the implementation of accountability requirements and freedom of information legislation, service user records are much more respectful. As a profession, social work also advocates much more strongly for inclusionary practices. Of course, it remains an evolving profession and will continue to face challenges.

Core aspects of social work practice have not changed. One major aspect to consider is the primary population that social workers work with. Our role is to work with those who have been marginalized and oppressed, and to advocate for a fairer and more just society. The main ways of working with people and communities also have not changed. We treat all people with dignity, practise from an anti-oppressive stance, and work with people in respectful, kind, and caring ways.

I hope that the latter is the take-away message in all my classes and in this book. I maintain that, as a professional social worker, I have control over my interactions with people. I also have the awareness and training to reframe my perceptions and biases, when necessary, to see and understand someone else's situation more clearly.

Ultimately, this book is geared to supporting students as they become strong and effective social workers. Becoming a professional social worker is an exciting journey, and I hope the ideas contained in this book help guide and inspire students in their careers.

# Acknowledgements

The publisher and I would like to thank the following individuals, who kindly reviewed all or parts of this resource prior to publication:

- Sama Bassidj, MES, MSW, RSW
  Professor, Centennial College

- Janice Chaplin
  Assistant Professor and Field Education Co-ordinator, McMaster University

- Lise Milne, MSW, PhD
  Assistant Professor, Faculty of Social Work, University of Regina

- Kelly Scott
  Instructor, Faculty of Social Work, University of Manitoba

In addition to the contributions of the reviewers and social workers who shared their learning and transformative stories, this book has been greatly influenced by the leadership that Marion Bogo and her team have provided over the years relating to field education and social work competency development.

A theme throughout this book is the CASWE-ACFTS accreditation standards that inform the curriculum at social work programs across Canada. While recognizing that these standards continue to evolve, I wish to acknowledge the commission's significant accomplishments, which not only have contributed to the ideas expressed in this book, but also continue to influence the professional identity of graduating social workers across the country.

**Jackie Stokes, BSW, MSW, EdD**

Thompson Rivers University
Kamloops, BC

# Identifying as a Professional Social Worker

1

# Chapter at a Glance

# Spotlight on Social Work Luminaries
## Marion Bogo

**Marion Bogo** is a professor in the Factor-Inwentash Faculty of Social Work at the University of Toronto. She is highly regarded for her work in curriculum design for social work programs, notably in the area of field education. Her research focuses on competency for professional practice, including social work education, field education, and clinical social work supervision.

**B**eginning the social work field placement is considered by most students to be the most exciting part of their program. It is the time and place where students make substantial progress in their long and exciting journey of becoming a competent and confident practising social worker.

Many practising social workers have strong memories of their field education and can recall experiences that they still consider transformative. Those are the moments in which the academic learning, classroom reflection, and real-life experience come together in a deeper meaning and understanding. This deeper learning is described by Meyer and Land (2003) as being similar to crossing a "threshold" in which the worldview of the learner is permanently changed.

This chapter focuses on the importance of field education in becoming a professional social worker. It introduces the accreditation context of Canadian social work education and the regulatory expectations of practice, as well as the meta-competencies associated with learning and practice.

## Developing Competence as a Social Worker

Some ways to develop the meta-competency of "**identifying as a professional social worker**" are as follows:

- Ask practising social workers about transformative moments associated with the development of their professional identity.

- Examine the standards of practice associated with the regulation of social workers in your jurisdiction.

- Write a journal entry assessing your own skills and confidence in relation to the competencies required by your program of study.

- Meet with an Indigenous or a French Canadian social worker in your community and explore how different worldviews can influence practice.

**Key Concepts**

- Professional identity
- Meta-competencies
- Reflexive practice
- Learning journals
- Critical theory

Professional identity refers to the development of one's professional self-concept.

For social workers, professional identity includes one's knowledge, values, and skills in relation to social work practice.

# Developing a Professional Identity

Field education is a form of learning that prepares students to perform the role of practitioner and enables them to integrate academic theory into everyday practice. It is during the field education that most students begin to develop a real understanding of what being a social worker means and take on the roles and identity associated with the profession. Field education is often considered the signature course in social work, as it prepares students for the profession's ways of thinking, performing, and acting (Wayne, Raskin, & Bogo, 2010).

The Canadian Association for Social Work Education–Association canadienne pour la formation en travail social (CASWE-ACFTS) is an association of university faculties, schools, departments, and modules offering social work education in Canada. The association's Commission on Accreditation is responsible for accrediting social work programs. As of 2019, there were 42 programs in Canada that are accredited or have pre-accreditation status.

## What Does It Mean to Say "I Am a Social Worker?"

The CASWE-ACFTS *Standards for Accreditation* (2014) require schools of social work to support students in "identify[ing] as a professional social worker and adopt[ing] a value perspective of the social work profession." This process involves adopting the attitudes, values, knowledge, beliefs, and skills that differentiate social work from other professions. Feeling uncomfortable as one progresses through this journey is not uncommon. There may even be uncertainty about one's suitability for the profession, although this feeling usually diminishes and changes into confidence as the field education process progresses.

But what does it really mean to say you are a social worker? Of course, there is no single definition. Each social worker's understanding of what it means to be a social worker is unique to them.

**Professional identity** for social workers could be thought of as being a continuum. At one end, there is a "technical-rational" approach, which is associated with procedural knowledge and a technical application of values and skills. At the other end of the continuum is the idea of "reflexive practice," in which the complexity and uncertainty of practice is understood and appreciated (Schön, 1987). Social workers adhering to a more "technical-rational" approach are considered more "neutral" or "objective," whereas those applying a reflexive practice are seen as more active participants. Of course, social workers are never really neutral and are affected by their social location and personal experiences.

These two approaches to practice need not be mutually exclusive or necessarily in conflict, however. Marion Bogo, for example, argues that "rather than polarizing these positions, more can be gained through extracting the strengths of each so that a multi-dimensional view may emerge" (Bogo, 2010, p. 36). In her view, professional identity includes the competencies, knowledge, skills, and values associated with social work, the application of research evidence, and a grasp of the organizational context, including constraints and opportunities.

Schools of social work across Canada are required to meet the CASWE-ACFTS *Standards for Accreditation*. This framework supports the Agreement on Internal Trade (AIT), which ensures that social workers can move from province to province with degree recognition.

Mobility between Canada and the United States occurs as a result of an agreement between the Council on Social Work Education in the United States and the CASWE-ACFTS. This agreement ensures that bachelor's degrees (BSW) and master's degrees (MSW) in social work from accredited Canadian programs are equivalent to those in the United States.

## CASWE-ACFTS *Standards for Accreditation*

The CASWE-ACFTS *Standards for Accreditation* provide the framework for the curriculum offered in social work programs at accredited Canadian universities.

The first core learning objective in the CASWE-ACFTS *Standards for Accreditation* (2014) is as follows:

1. Identify as a professional social worker and adopt a value perspective of the social work profession.

   i) Social work students develop professional identities as practitioners whose professional goal is to facilitate the collective welfare and well-being of all people to the maximum extent possible.

Schools of social work are accountable to these standards, which ensures that all graduating students have the requisite knowledge, values, and skills. Each school makes it own decisions about exactly how to meet those objectives.

Advocacy for the profession occurs through provincial associations; for Yukon, Northwest Territories, and Nunavut, it occurs through the Association of Social Workers in Northern Canada. Regulation of professionals occurs through Colleges and through the Department of Health and Social Services in the Northwest Territories. Yukon and Nunavut do not currently require social worker registration to practise.

## Professional Regulation and Competency

Advocacy and regulation are two pillars of most professions, including social work. In Canada, the associations and College Registrars are provincially or territorially operated with links to national policy organizations. In most provinces, the association and the College are separate, although some are together.

The Regulatory Colleges are governed by legislation that sets out the requirements for the use of the title "social worker" as well as standards of practice. It is the Regulatory Colleges that ensure public accountability and transparency, confidence in the competency or capability of individual social workers, and a mechanism for service user complaints.

Just as the CASWE-ACFTS responded to the AIT in support of the mobility of social workers, the Canadian Council of Social Work Regulators (CCSWR, 2012) has articulated a set of entry-level competencies to harmonize the provincial requirements, differences in credential requirements, and registration requirements. This set of competencies is meant to facilitate the mobility of social workers across jurisdictions in Canada (CCSWR, 2012). These competencies represent the minimum requirements for public protection.

## Association of Social Work Boards (ASWB)

In British Columbia and all 50 US states, social work registration requires completion of a minimum competency exam. Other Canadian jurisdictions require an exam for clinical practice, and some are considering it for entry to practice.

The ASWB is a non-profit organization composed of social work Regulatory Colleges in Canada and the United States.

The ASWB North American exam is developed with input from Canadian social workers and "measures minimum competency acceptable to practice social work within a given scope of practice" (ASWB, 2013, p. 2). The exam writers are selected to reflect racial, ethnic, gender, and geographical differences, and promote principles of diversity and inclusion in social care settings. ∎

## Meta-Competencies in Social Work Practice

**Meta-competencies**

Meta-competencies are those overarching abilities that allow a social worker to adapt and anticipate responses to unique circumstances and situations. They are acquired and developed through continuously learning and reflecting on knowledge and practice.

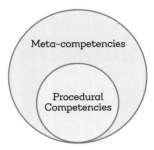

Developing an identity as a professional social worker is a required outcome for students attending schools of social work in Canada. The provincial or territorial regulatory bodies (Colleges of Social Work) set the minimum standards and requirements for practice.

The learning objectives associated with the CASWE-ACFTS *Standards for Accreditation* and the competencies associated with the CCSWR *Entry-Level Competency Profile for the Social Work Profession in Canada* are not prescriptive. Rather, they provide a framework for curriculum in schools of social work and competencies to begin practice. The attainment of these competencies enables social workers to feel confident about their ability to practise and provides safeguards for service users who can then trust they are receiving competent services based on accurate and current knowledge in the field.

### Higher Order, Overarching Qualities and Abilities

Today, social work education and practice tends to focus on "meta-competencies" (see Table 1.1 on pages 10–11) rather than technical competencies. Technical or procedural competencies refer to the discrete tasks and skills associated with a particular job (e.g., completing intake forms, carrying out a mental health assessment). **Meta-competencies** are "higher order, overarching abilities and qualities that are of a different order and nature than procedural or operational behaviours and skills" (Bogo, 2010, p. 70).

Social work education provides opportunities to learn these core skills or meta-competencies. These meta-competencies provide the foundation of social work identity and can be adapted and applied to a variety of service user contexts and agency settings.

For example, self-reflection is recognized as a core learning objective for all social workers. The CASWE-ACFTS *Standards for Accreditation* (2014) stipulate the following:

> Social work students acquire ability for self-reflection as it relates to engaging in professional practice through a comprehensive understanding and consciousness of the complex nature of their own social locations and identities. Students develop an awareness of personal biases and preferences to advance social justice and the social well-being of social work service users. (p. 10)

The CCSWR entry-level competency profile (CCSWR, 2012) also identifies a competency block for effective social work practice as including "Engaging in Reflective Practice and Professional Development." This is described as follows:

> Competencies required to monitor and manage one's own professional development, attitudes and behaviour to promote and advance the social work practice locally, nationally, and/or internationally. (p. 9)

## Reflexive Practice in Social Work

"Self-reflection" is a general term that refers to the process of self-observation, self-dialogue, and self-evaluation. It allows individuals to explore their experiences and develop new understandings and appreciations. It is an active, socially constructed process that is applied to oneself and one's practice. The purpose of self-reflection is to make sense of, or find meaning in, experiences in order to incorporate the experience into one's view of self and the world (Burr, Blyth, Sutcliffe, & King, 2016; Lam, Wong, & Leung, 2007).

During the field education component of social work education, the learning objective of self-reflection transforms into **reflexive practice**. Based on Schön's (1987) concepts of "knowing in action" and "reflection in action," social workers are understood as "reflective practitioners" who use intuitive or tacit knowledge as an essential component of practice. Reflexive practice recognizes that "knowledge and theory use is constantly being constructed in part through practitioner experiences, and also through sources such as our practice context and formal theoretical base" (Healy, 2005, p. 102).

In other words, reflexive practice, or reflexivity, is cyclical and cumulative. It requires trying to understand different perspectives and the dominant discourses related to a situation and then subjecting these knowledge claims to critical analysis in order to become aware of the dominant professional constructs influencing practice (Lam, Wong, & Leung, 2007; Payne, 2014).

## Reflexive Practice Online

Social workers are increasingly using online platforms (such as Twitter, Facebook, and blogs) to extend professional relationships. In terms of reflexive practice, online spaces—or virtual communities of practice—offer forums in which individuals can communicate with others, share links to important research, and ask questions and have them answered.

Online interaction provides a way of learning and furthering one's practice and doing the work better (Turner, 2016). For example, Ladyshewsky and Gardner (2008) described how physiotherapy students in clinical field education found that blogging was valuable as it heightened learning, built trust, and helped integrate theory into practice.

While social networking provides opportunities to reduce isolation and create learning communities, there may be ethical concerns to be aware of. For example, Hickson (2012) conducted a study on the experiences of isolated social workers who were using an online blog for reflection in a community of practice. The benefits included networking (able to hear different perspectives and opinions— locally, nationally, and globally), professional development, and self-care (an enjoyable way to express their views and reflect on their experiences). However, participants in this study also identified a number of concerns and challenges associated with using a blog for reflexive practice. These included maintaining service user confidentiality, anonymity for the blogger, and protecting the agency's confidentiality and its reputation in the community.

**Reflexive practice**

Reflexive practice is the ability to engage in a process of continuous learning by reflecting on one's beliefs and actions. It is developed by paying attention to the values and theories utilized in everyday practice.

**Table 1.1** Meta-Competencies in Social Work

While there is no definitive list of meta-competencies, a review of accreditation and regulatory standards, the IFSW's *Global Social Work Statement of Ethical Principles* (included in Appendix 1, beginning on page 285) and the broader social work literature provide support for including the following as meta-competencies. These meta-competencies frame and inform each chapter of this book.

| | |
|---|---|
| **Identifying as a professional social worker** | Social workers represent the profession, its mission, and its values. They are committed to professional conduct including reliability, integrity, and diligence in field practice, and to continuing professional development throughout their career. |
| **Engaging in reflexive practice** | Reflexive practice recognizes that broader socio-cultural structures contribute to inequitable power distributions and multiple sources of knowledge. Social workers, aware of their own social location and positionality, aim to practise using co-produced professional knowledge and power as productively as possible. |
| **Employing critical thinking** | Critical thinking requires the synthesis and communication of relevant information in all aspects of social work practice. This requires social workers to be knowledgeable of social work theory and values to contextualize practice within a socio-political organizational and cultural environment; to pay attention to the unique circumstances, histories, and experiences of the service user; and to be open to alternate meanings and understandings. |
| **Ensuring professional judgements and decision-making** | When social workers make discretionary professional decisions, they apply relevant knowledge from multiple sources and theories to their practice in order to meet the unique circumstances of the situation. |
| **Adhering to social work values and ethics** | Social workers are knowledgeable about the laws, values, ethics, and skills associated with the profession. Social workers acquire skills to monitor and evaluate their own behaviours in relation to relevant codes of ethics and to identify ethical considerations in relation to service provision. |
| **Respecting diversity and difference** | Social workers work with many populations who have been discriminated against, oppressed, and marginalized. Respecting diversity at a micro level requires mindfully respecting the dynamics of difference in cross-cultural, racial, religious, gender, sexual, age, ability, and class relationships. Social workers understand that unequal societal structures influence access to power, privilege, wealth, and resources, and they work to address and end all forms of social injustice. |
| **Conducting assessments** | Conducting an assessment is required in order to develop a complete picture of the service user's situation in order to provide the most efficacious interventions. Assessments require attention to help establish a helpful and hopeful working relationship and are completed within a culturally and service user-centred context. |

| | |
|---|---|
| **Developing professional relationships** | Professional relationships are collaborative and empowering, and conducted with respect and empathy for individual uniqueness and self-determination. Social workers use professional relationship skills in intelligent and flexible ways to enable them to navigate, mediate, learn from, and strengthen their social work practice. |
| **Applying knowledge of human development and behaviour** | Knowledge of human growth and development in the social environment includes theories of physical, cognitive, emotional, sexual, spiritual, and racial/cultural development throughout the lifespan. Social workers consider the interplay of these factors as they affect biopsychosocial-spiritual functioning. |
| **Planning and delivering services and interventions** | Following an assessment, the social worker is required to synthesize the information collected into a service plan that outlines what needs to be done and how to accomplish it. Planning and delivering services and interventions requires an understanding of the myriad of theories and techniques available, and being able to apply them in a way that is relevant to the unique situations presented. |
| **Promoting community sustainability** | Community social work involves an inclusive, collaborative, and anti-oppressive approach. It recognizes the importance of community strengths, resources, and skills as sources of social change for advancing human rights, equality, and social justice. |
| **Advocating for human rights and social justice** | Social work is a human rights profession with responsibilities to advocate for individual and collective rights and social justice globally. From this perspective, individual social problems are understood as human rights denied. |
| **Conducting policy analysis and development** | Social policy supports the well-being of citizens. Social workers advocate for inclusive and participatory policy-making that is informed by social work knowledge about the causes and interventions related to a particular social issue. |
| **Engaging in research and research-based practice** | Social workers are involved in critiquing, applying, and participating in research. Such research informs practice, service provision, policy development, and professional knowledge. |
| **Participating and leading organizational and societal system change** | Social workers are required to possess the knowledge and the interprofessional and interorganizational skills that can advance the process of organizational and system-wide change. |

# Social Worker Exemplar

## My First Job as a Social Worker

Jackie Stokes

**Transitioning from student to social worker does not happen overnight. Acquiring a professional identity is a process that goes on for many years after graduation.**

After graduation, Jackie was excited to begin her social work career as a substance-use counsellor in a small town in northern British Columbia.

She experienced anxiety, if not trepidation, as she began to develop her professional identity and understand its meaning in the context of a small, rural community. This was her introduction to the world of social work practice.

After graduating with a BSW from the University of British Columbia, I obtained a position as a substance-use counsellor in a small resource town. The position was with a non-profit society that had a part-time child-care worker and administrative assistant, and a full-time substance-use counsellor as their only employees.

Lack of experience was a problem. My final practicum had been with an employee-assistance program. Other experiences included a summer job leading an alcohol and drug evaluation project and working as a volunteer with a suicide and crisis line. Apart from a brief marriage to an alcoholic, I had little other experience to prepare me as a substance-use counsellor.

The first challenge, I thought, was the interview itself. I immediately contacted a student colleague who had a wealth of experience in the substance-use field, and we brainstormed questions that were likely to be asked.

The regional manager of Alcohol and Drug Services met me at the airport, and we began the two-hour drive to the community. This time together turned out to be an exceptional, two-way process—she got to know me, and I learned about the community and the role of the substance-use counsellor. Despite my intention to present an impression of being knowledgeable and confident, I quickly found myself telling her that I didn't have much experience. This authenticity was incredibly useful. She then proceeded to tell me more about the expectations, the regional resources, and how my past work experiences could be used in the position. By the time we arrived at the agency, I was prepped for the interview.

After pleasant and cheerful introductions, we went for lunch. It was a lovely relationship-building exercise that included all the questions I thought would occur during the interview. In retrospect, they were definitely considering capacity building and my personal and professional ability to "fit" into the community more than my content knowledge.

The result was that about two months later, I packed a pickup truck of furniture and other belongings, and moved house and home.

I was now the substance-use counsellor.

## Learning the Ropes

I still remember being terrified that first day. One step at a time, get to the office, meet the other staff, find out how the office works (I knew how to do that from multiple previous jobs). I recall, too, those first few appointments as well as my dwindling self-confidence as I was faced with situations that seemed overwhelming.

My lack of experience was compounded by not having any supervision. The competency that I could rely on most, which became a threshold crossing, was my ability to develop professional relationships. I knew I had to develop enough empathy and trust with the service users so that they would return. I also knew I would need time to seek supervision.

Over the following few days, I also realized that I had to do something to develop a network of support for myself. I realized I had to do this at two levels. One was professionally—I was out of my depth. Fortunately, I had been introduced to two services in the nearest regional centre, two hours away, during my initial interview. It was time to call them and see if I could get some supervision. I arranged to meet up with them the following week. These contacts became my "go-to" people for the next decade—and they remain friends today. They mentored me through the professional learning process of being a substance-use counsellor.

I also knew I had to look after myself. This was a very small community, but I couldn't possibly absorb all of these people's lives into my own. I started talking to other professionals in the community. Fortunately, the probation officer and public health nurse were both my age, and they also were relatively new to their jobs. They provided me with some professional and personal support (these two women continue to be my friends today). And, finally, I needed to find ways to meet my own needs, which I did through some unrelated volunteering and a non-competitive softball team.

I was starting to map out for myself how to be a holistic person in the role of a professional social worker in a small, northern BC community. ■

## Reflections on Jackie's Story

In Jackie's first days and weeks in her new role as a social worker, she began to see the importance of authenticity and genuineness. In a small community, everything seems different—even the formal interview process takes on a different form than in an urban setting.

Although she was armed with a newly minted degree, this formal "expertise" was not the most important quality that was needed. Being able to develop relationships—with service users, the non-profit board of directors, community colleagues, and practice area supervisors—was essential. This was her strongest asset, and it served her well in those early days.

### From Theory to Practice

As you reflect on Jackie's story, give some thought to the following points:

1. What are some of Jackie's thoughts, feelings, and actions that provide insight into her professional identity development?

2. Describe some of the meta-competencies that Jackie was practising, either in an elementary or a more advanced way?

3. Was Jackie using self-reflection or reflexivity? If so, how?

4. Think of a situation in which you would be asked to practise outside of your confidence area. What are some of the key meta-competencies (personal or professional) that you could draw upon?

Learning journals are a way of documenting day-to-day practice experiences and how the social worker is interpreting and responding to them.

Learning journals can serve as a record as well as a chronology of one's thinking over time.

# Developing Reflexivity in Practice

Reflexive practice requires social workers to "critically review their day-to-day analysis and practice in order to reveal their own social, intellectual and professional values and assumptions, as well as their less conscious motivations" (Lam, Wong, & Leung, 2007, p. 96). A **learning journal** can provide a way of formally integrating reflexivity into everyday practice situations and is often a required component of field education.

A reflexive journal entry begins with the identification of a notable experience (positive or negative) that one has encountered in a field agency. One then self-reflects on the experience and goes on to think critically about the wider issues involved.

Constable (2013) recommends that journalling involves the following three-step process:

- **Stage 1: Identify a notable experience.** Describe an experience, issue, or concern that you have. This should be done in an unstructured manner to capture your thoughts spontaneously.

- **Stage 2: Self-reflect on the experience.** Reflection includes making sense of one's experiences through self-knowledge and awareness of one's own worldview as well as examining the experience within the knowledge and values associated with formal learning. Constable suggests reflecting on the issue or concern by asking yourself the following questions:

  - What is going on here?
  - What assumptions am I making?
  - What do the assumptions tell me about my beliefs?
  - Are there other ways of looking at this issue or concern?

- **Stage 3: Think critically.** The final stage is to become reflexive. This means going beyond simply analyzing what was done and how the experience was perceived and understood. It requires thinking about dominant professional constructs influencing practice. It becomes a process of "thinking about thinking." During this process, social workers ask critical questions, such as the following:

  - What are the assumptions generated by formal and practice theories?
  - What are the wider socio-cultural contexts of this experience?
  - How are the multiple inter-relationships between power and knowledge being addressed?
  - How are multiple sources of knowledge (including self and service user) being used in the process of knowledge creation?

Using a learning journal in this way introduces an element of uncertainty to practice—it forces one to challenge dominant assumptions and discourses. There is an active attempt to generate generalizable knowledge about self and about the profession in the context of dealing with dynamic and unique practice situations.

The CASWE-ACFTS has long recognized the complexity of Canadian society and the special dynamics affecting Indigenous peoples.

Principle 10 of the CASWE-ACFTS *Standards for Accreditation* (2014) states the following:

**10.** Social work programs acknowledge and challenge the injustices of Canada's colonial history and continuing colonization efforts as they relate to the role of social work education in Canada and the self-determination of the Indigenous peoples.

## Truth and Reconciliation

Generally speaking, Canadian social work has a proud history of social justice-oriented activities. However, in the past, the profession had participated in, rather than challenged, oppressive colonial practices. Most notably, this occurred when Indigenous people were being decimated through forced removals from their families and communities into residential schools and the child welfare system.

In 2018, the CASWE-ACFTS, the Canadian Association of Social Workers (CASW), and the CCSWR celebrated National Social Work Month by presenting a joint statement on the theme of "Bringing Change to Life" in order to open space for the social work profession to reflect and act on truth and reconciliation. The statement committed the profession to the following goals:

- Continuing to provide ethical, responsible, and high-quality service;

- Supporting schools of social work in Canada in making truth and reconciliation a priority in shaping the next generation of Canadian social workers;

- Bringing humility and accountability to social justice efforts; and,

- Recognizing social work's role in Indigenous people's lives.

## The Truth and Reconciliation Commission's Calls to Action

The final report of the Truth and Reconciliation Commission of Canada (TRC) included 94 calls to action for Indigenous and non-Indigenous Canadians to come together in a concerted effort to help repair the harm caused by residential schools and move forward with truth and reconciliation. These calls to action have implications for social work in many areas, most notably in the fields of child welfare, health, human rights, legal equity, youth programming, and missing women and children.

Nowadays, social work programs throughout Canada provide courses to ensure a strong understanding of the history and treatment of Indigenous peoples. One challenge for social workers as they honour Indigenous knowledge is to safeguard against appropriation and misappropriation of knowledge and Indigenous culture and practices (Baskin, 2016).

In order for non-Indigenous social workers to take up Indigenous ways of helping, Baskin (2016) suggests concentrating on Indigenous worldviews rather than on specific cultures and spiritual practices. She states that

much of Indigenous worldviews—such as a holistic approach, connection to the land, a focus on the family and community rather than the individual, healing instead of punishment, and the inclusion of spirituality—are universal for many peoples of the world. (p. 17)

Baskin observes further that self-reflexivity will help to redress the power imbalance. She recommends that social workers not only ask questions of Indigenous service users, but reciprocate by inviting service users to ask questions so as to make visible the social worker's perspectives and understandings. ■

## Understanding "Self"

During field education and early into their careers, social workers can be thought of as being on a journey of self-discovery. The term "journey of self-discovery" refers to a person's attempt to determine how they personally feel about issues or priorities rather than simply following along with family, friends, or colleagues. It involves a heightened awareness of how one's social location, positionality, and intersectionality affects their perceptions and the meanings that they attribute to their experiences.

- **Social location.** Social location refers to the social groups that people belong to in society, based on such things as their gender, ethnicity, race, social class, age, ability, religion, sexual orientation, or geographical location. Group membership confers a certain set of social roles and rules that heavily influence people's identity and worldview.

- **Positionality.** Positionality is similar to social location but subsumes the notion of power. It refers to the different levels of power that occur based on one's social position in relation to others (Al-Krenawi, Graham, & Habibov, 2016).

- **Intersectionality.** Intersectionality points to the idea that all aspects of social location contribute to the unique person that each of us is, as well as to the subjectivities with which we understand ourselves and by which others understand us (Al-Krenawi et al., 2016).

Moving from self-reflection to reflexivity in learning requires critically analyzing social exclusion and the unequal distribution of power. Critical reflection requires unpacking, identifying, and exploring the behaviours, structures, processes, practices, and policies that create and sustain such exclusion (Yee & Dumbrill, 2016).

## "Self" and Self-Care

Many students experience excitement, tinged with anxiety, as they prepare for field education. Learning to manage troublesome emotional encounters is a skill to be developed as new situations, contexts, or responsibilities arise. Field education can be a time to practise this skill. This involves using or adapting self-care strategies that have already been shown to be helpful and developing more self-care strategies as they become necessary.

Mindfulness, for example, is a great stress-reduction strategy. An exercise that can be incorporated easily and quickly into daily interactions is the "**STOP**" strategy:

- **S:** Stop what you are doing;

- **T:** Take deep and/or mindful breaths;

- **O:** Observe your experience in the moment—your thoughts, feelings, and emotions; then,

- **P:** Proceed with activities (such as seeking social connections) that will support you in the moment (O'Hara, Weber, & Levine, 2016, p. 52).

# Francophone People in Canada
## Respecting and Strengthening Unique Identities

Canada is a bilingual country, with Quebec being the biggest province and the biggest French region in the world outside of France (Zhang, 2016).

The CASWE-ACFTS *Standards for Accreditation* (2014) recognize and respect the unique position of francophone people in Canada, and the importance for social work students across the country to recognize and respect francophone people's unique history and culture within Canada. Principle 11 states the following:

**11.** Francophone people are specifically highlighted as constituents of Canadian history and identity, and social work education programs ensure representation of related concerns and issues.

Québécois identity and francophone identity throughout Canada continue to go through intense debate and interrogation involving a process of self-interpretation and re-narration (Maclure, 2003).

### Linguistic Identity

Francophone identity in Canada is shaped by a range of historical and contemporary factors, including globalization and Quebec's status within the federation (Maclure, 2003). Québécois identity is a "live concern that cuts across class, sex, and generational barriers, affecting every citizen who has to live with identity indeterminacy on a daily basis" (Maclure, 2003, p. 4). For most Quebecers, their Canadianness is not in question, but the primary object of allegiance is in their Quebecers' hearts (p. 6).

Legislation in the 1970s established French as the dominant language in Quebec. More than 30 years later, the proportion of French speakers among residents whose mother tongue is not French is high. However, in other provinces of Canada, the proportion of the population who speak French is decreasing (Zhang, 2016).

### The Strength of Francophone Identity Today

French Canadians no longer think of themselves as a racialized group, even though they were once considered by nineteenth-century Anglo-Saxons as "not quite white." Today, French Canadians consider themselves as a distinct population within a modern, Western country (Scott, 2016).

While the relationship between historic narratives and ethnic identity has been explored, few studies have investigated how young French Canadians interpret Canadian history and its impact on their identity (Lévesque, 2017). However, two recent studies have looked at this question.

Lévesque (2017) examined the francophone identity of French Canadian students in two high schools and a university in Ottawa. While the students could reconstruct Canadian history in many ways, the majority preferred to structure their narrative along the storyline of French Canadian collective memory. This perspective is likely to have been influenced by the explicit requirements of the Ministry of Education in Ontario to promote francophone culture and identity-building in the curriculum.

As students complete high school, decisions about career development are typically difficult and challenging. The research question for Sovet, DiMillo, & Samson (2017) was whether students with a francophone identity but educated within English Canada had greater difficulties making career decisions. The findings from their study of almost 1,000 students attending French-language secondary schools in Ontario was that francophone students were less inclined than other linguistic groups to report career decision-making difficulties. The Franco-Ontarian students in this study were able to maintain a strong linguistic identity even within the Anglo-dominant socio-economic context.

These studies underline the depth of francophone culture and the enduring importance of the francophone identity in Canada today. ■

# Critical Theory and Field Education

**Critical theory**

While critical theorists emphasize the importance of structural analysis and broad-based solutions, they also stress the need to understand the unique ways in which individuals understand their situations and the role human agency plays in bringing about personal and social change.

Nowadays, social work education includes a strong critical theory perspective. The focus of critical theory is to shift the explanation of social issues away from individuals and families to the "less visible" social conditions. The focus is on making social change at the broader societal level in order to reduce individual distress.

**Critical theory** views individual problems in the context of oppression and injustice, such as income inequality, racial and gender discrimination, and abuse and exploitation. It builds on radical traditions that include feminist theory, anti-racist theory, and post-colonial theory in order to inform an anti-oppressive social work practice. Anti-oppressive practice is about ensuring that social work practice does not replicate and reproduce existing inequalities.

## Field Education—Does It Replicate the Status Quo?

Schools of social work make student admission decisions, curriculum design, and field placement choices. Typically, field placements occur in an agency setting. They entail working with a particular population or in a specific geographical location, with the student engaging in program-based tasks and activities to gain specific learning experiences. This agency-based model focuses primarily on providing services and replicates the work environment that new graduates likely will enter. The question is whether this type of field education is simply replicating the status quo.

Preston, George, and Silver (2014) argue that the predominant agency-based model of field education largely ignores social work's commitment to social justice goals (p. 63). Given the centrality of field education in preparing students for social work, they argue that this omission jeopardizes the commitment to educating students for critical social work. They ask, "Is the role of social work education to simply support students in passing registration exams and to prepare students for work in an agency setting? Or is it also to educate future social workers to be critical and to challenge and change how social work is done?" (p. 63).

Within social work curriculum and scholarship, there are commitments to social justice and equity. However, in the standards of social work practice, there remains a strong emphasis on service delivery with an intent of optimizing psychosocial and social functioning. This signals a primary focus on individual change rather than societal change. Preston et al. (2014) argue that, in this context, the "complexity of social work practice becomes reduced to simple answers and short-term solutions that focus on minimalist service provision, specialization, and fragmented services that address only surface and thus decontextualized issues in the lives of services users" (p. 59).

By contrast, anti-oppressive social work practice, which is taught in many social work programs across Canada, seeks to build alliances, embrace participatory models, and infuse an understanding of oppression and dominance in all aspects of social work practice.

## Transforming Field Education

While the CASWE-ACFTS *Standards for Accreditation* (2014) have moved toward an anti-oppressive perspective that stresses critical analysis, diversity, and community needs, Preston et al. (2014) suggest that this perspective is not reflected in the field education component.

Field education, they maintain, is focused mostly on the number of hours in placement, the qualifications of field instructors, and evaluation processes. To bring field education more in line with current curriculum trends, these authors recommend a shift away from agency-based placements toward field placements in which communities and broader social issues are the focus, thereby potentially bridging both service delivery and activism.

Their approach specifically envisions field placements based in real communities rather than in specific social work agencies, with the field education office acting as a hub for dialogue, collaboration, and action. Preston et al. (2014) argue that "we need to reimagine field education creatively, thinking outside the box in ways that exposes and unsettles current practices" (p. 67). This model of field education would more effectively link agencies and practitioners to issues that are relevant to members of marginalized communities.

## Competency and Regulatory Frameworks in Social Work

Some academics have critiqued the use of competency frameworks. Their concerns are that competency frameworks can undermine professional judgement and reduce complex decision-making to mechanistic technical skills. Further, they argue that the social justice aspects of social work, along with the responsibilities to examine and critique broader government policies, are minimized or made more invisible when applying a competency framework to practice.

Proponents of competency frameworks argue that the frameworks are blueprints, rather than directives, and provide transparency to students about what they are expected to learn in order to practise responsibly and with intentionality. The competencies are holistic principles that are enacted through critical thinking within social policy constraints and within organizational and cultural contexts. Given that social workers' practice is governed by legislation in order to protect the public, these blueprints represent one element of accountability to the public and provide transparency for practising social workers when disputes about practice occur.

The tensions between educators and regulators in this regard came to the forefront in British Columbia in 2015 when all new applicants to the BC College of Social Workers had to complete a formal licensing exam. There was understandable fear and angst about this process. The primary concerns were the relevancy of the licensing exam to the Canadian context and, in particular, whether it adequately captured the practice of Indigenous social workers. Since 2015, and as of 2018, the applicants have shown high levels of success, with a first-time pass rate of 92% when writing the bachelor's exam.

# Social Worker Exemplar

# Transforming My Worldview

**Ralph Tarlit**

**Many social workers remember field education fondly as a "transformational" experience. For many, it is a time when they begin to view themselves and the world differently.**

Ralph is a compassionate and kind man who experienced many forms of adversity and marginalization in his young life.

As he progressed through his practicum, Ralph's new learning confirmed his own personal experiences of injustice and inequality and contributed significantly to the development of his professional identity as a Canadian social worker.

Because I had always considered myself a caring person and a good communicator, I always thought that social work would suit me quite well as a career. What I did not realize was the wide range of other skills that were needed to be a well-rounded and effective practitioner.

I am a racialized, 36-year-old male. My family came here from the Philippines, but I was born in Canada. I am also a gay man and a cancer survivor. During my social work education to date, I transformed personally in so many ways. This transformation has been a life-changing event in my life. My personal and professional values are now more congruent—something that is so important to being an authentic professional.

On one of my trips to visit friends in Vancouver, I suddenly realized how much my worldview had changed. I thought that I had a clear vision of what my future would look like—a fancy apartment, a nice car, and the glitz of downtown living. My priorities were simply to make sure that I looked good and integrated into an urban lifestyle.

On that eventful trip, my friends had organized a welcoming party for me—just like the good old times, we were together enjoying one another's company. But something was different. I wasn't laughing at the jokes, and I cringed at some of the oppressive language being used (which once seemed like no big deal). Although I still loved my friends dearly, I knew I had changed. Being aware of poverty and privilege changed my sense of priorities, making it more difficult to engage in the old ways.

The new ideas I had been introduced to—professional values, ethics, colonization, interpersonal communication, self-awareness, critical reflection, trauma-informed care, self-care, and many more—have been invaluable sources of knowledge and have contributed to my professional development. They have facilitated so much personal growth and, ultimately, have affected the way I view the world and how I now approach other individuals. Learning about the colonization of Indigenous people has exposed and challenged previous biases that I had. Learning about substance-use theory has broadened my thinking, allowing me to humanize experiences.

## Reframing Personal Struggles

Another example of my change in outlook occurred when I drove down East Hastings Street for the first time in years. Previously, I had believed that the people in the Downtown Eastside were there because of personal shortcomings, that they could always just get a job and better their lives. In the past, not only did I feel uneasy about being in this part of town, I also was ignorant to their living conditions and the circumstances that resulted in them being there.

With the new learning that I've acquired, I now feel a greater sense of empathy for the vulnerable position of persons on the Downtown Eastside. Learning about the structural factors and other influences on their lives has had a profound effect on me.

One of the most significant changes relates to my ability to reframe my own personal struggles. I now have a better appreciation of all of the adversity I experienced—cancer, a heart attack, drug use, and sexual identity issues. These events caused a lot of heartache and damage, but I now know that they also have enriched my professional self. I can now see that the very struggles that tormented my life are now assets in my professional practice.

Being enrolled in the human service program has transformed my personal and professional life. Not only have I learned many different skills and expanded my professional repertoire, but the program has also allowed me to engage in self-reflection.

As a result of all this, I feel I can be more effective as a professional social worker and that I am better equipped to live my life in a positive way. ■

# Reflections on Ralph's Story

Through a process of self-reflection, Ralph came to recognize how his own social location and experiences had influenced his worldview. New knowledge and experiences gained during field education challenged his perceptions of injustice and power, and ended up transforming his whole life.

As Ralph's professional identity developed, so too did his appreciation of self. As a result, he feels he will be an effective social worker and better able to live a happier and more productive life.

## From Theory to Practice

As you reflect on Ralph's story, give some thought to the following points:

1. How did Ralph's self-identified social location and intersectionality inform his worldview? How did marginalization and dominance influence his worldview?

2. Describe the meta-competencies that Ralph was expressing as he reflected on his personal transformation?

3. Is Ralph's account consistent with Constable's framework for writing a reflexive journal (see page 14)? What additional ideas or thoughts could be added to Ralph's account to indicate more reflexivity?

4. Think of a situation that you have been involved in, either personally or during field education, that resulted in a personal and professional transformation or new awareness. Write a reflexive journal entry that provides insight about this transformation for other social work students in your program.

# Practice Scenarios

The development of an identity as a professional social worker is unique to each individual. It does not happen overnight, but emerges as individuals expand their values, knowledge, and skills throughout their education and subsequent career. During field education there will be many times when you ask yourself "How do I think as a social worker?" "What is expected of me as a social worker?" or "What kind of social worker do I want to be?"

The practice examples below typically arise as one enters the social work field. As you read through these examples, consider how the person involved could be reflexive. Also consider how thinking about broader social work meta-competencies may contribute to the successful development of a professional identity. Having a positive attitude, in general, and an appreciation of the university faculty and your agency supervisors, in particular, are often the keys that will open doors for enhanced opportunities for work and learning.

---

## 1.1 Developing Flexibility

As long as you can remember, you have wanted to be a social worker and practise in the area of substance use. During your coursework, you have also developed an interest in mental health and have a vision of yourself as a "therapist." You identified these goals with the field education coordinator, but have just been told that your placement will be with a local women's shelter. The coordinator described the rationale, saying that there were multiple people at the shelter experiencing mental health and substance-use issues, and so you would be exposed to learning in this clinical area. The coordinator believed there was a benefit to broadening your experiences beyond "individual clinical" work to developing an understanding of the broader structures that impact individuals' lives.

1. What are some meta-competencies that could be developed at a women's shelter?

2. How can the skill of reflexive practice assist you in reframing disappointment about a field education assignment?

3. In this situation, you had a perception of your social work identity as a therapist. Is this perception consistent with a social worker's professional identity? If this perception is one strand of an identity, how does one broaden one's scope?

4. What are some ways of reframing a decision in which one feels powerless?

---

## 1.2 Preparing for Diversity

You have lived in the city your university is in for just one year, and you are not very familiar with many of the cultural and ethnic populations living in the region. On your second day in practicum, you are invited by another social worker to visit a family living in one of the outlying communities you are not familiar with. You are excited about getting out of the office and doing "real" social work, but wonder about how you will experience the differences.

1. In preparation for meeting with people from a community different from your own, what steps can you take to ensure openness and respect for any differences?

2. Think of an example in which you have learned something new about someone else who has a different social location than you (e.g., a grandparent, a child with diverse abilities, an immigrant). How can that learning help you in this situation?

3. How may the social work knowledge you have gained from a white hegemonic paradigm further oppress and be divisive?

4. Explain how you would answer the following question from a family member: "What do you know of my world? You are a fancy university student with so many advantages."

## 1.3 Managing Humility

After your initial interview at an agency that coordinates volunteers in your community, you raised some concerns with your faculty liaison about how much social work would occur. Your instructor reminded you that learning occurs in multiple ways, and that each task is an opportunity for learning, if one is open to it and has a positive perspective. During the first week, you have been asked to answer phones, help with some filing, and clean out a cupboard of resources. You have also been told that the agency would like your assistance with developing a board training manual. You have been disappointed with these initial tasks.

1. What are some self-care strategies that can assist you in positively framing your field education to date?

2. How do these tasks contribute to your identity as an emerging social worker?

3. Can you identify how these tasks move beyond the technical capacity to contribute to the development of one or more meta-competencies?

4. What problem-solving strategies can you put into place to ensure that your experiences broaden to be more student-learning-centred than volunteer associated?

# Field Education Practicalities
## The First Steps in Field Placement

Students enter field education with a wealth of experiences and hopes. Many have already identified populations they would like to work with or issues of particular interest. This is the beginning of the formation of a professional identity.

As you go through the first steps of field education, remember that it is important to be flexible and that learning comes in unexpected ways.

Each school of social work has slightly different processes for obtaining field education sites and matching students. In most cases, students have some input into identifying an agency or population of interest.

### Identifying Preferences in Field Education

If there is an opportunity to identify preferences for a field education site, it is helpful to have thought through both learning goals and pragmatics.

Some students enter a social work program because of a strong desire to work with a particular agency or population. This may be due to prior experiences—that is, personal, volunteer, or work experiences. It is important to try and articulate the importance and reasons for your preference to your school field coordinator. In some situations, the outcome may be met; in others, the field coordinator may recommend expanding your experiences to develop further competencies and generalist social work practices.

In the initial stages of identifying a potential field agency, other pragmatic issues may also be raised. This includes identifying any required accommodations relating to equity concerns.

While there are good reasons to be open to a variety of experiences, there are also times to be clear about the boundaries required to ensure a safe environment for good learning. For example, if you do not have a vehicle, is the agency on a public transit route or within reasonable walking distance? If there are constraints on your time, how can these be accommodated?

Many field education sites have minimal staffing and may require someone who is self-directed. Do you prefer closer supervision, or do you consider yourself more of an independent learner?

Are there any potential value conflicts that may arise for you? Some agencies have a stated religious foundation to their work; other agencies may work from an ideological stance that may be different from yours. For example, an agency may promote reproductive choice, while your personal value stance may differ. Another agency may work with convicted sex offenders. If you have concerns about any personal conflicts, be sure to speak with the field coordinator and agency supervisors about them.

### Completing an Interview

An interview may or may not be required, and it may take the form of an informal conversation or a more formal panel interview. Preparation is important—it is the moment of first impressions, for both you and the agency staff and/or board.

Prior to the day, some preliminary homework is useful. Update your resumé and learn as much as you can about the agency and the population it serves. Then locate the address and identify the pragmatics of transportation—Where is the parking? How long will it take to get there? etc.

Often students ask about dress code. In most social work agencies, appropriate dress is semi-casual (conservative but not too formal or informal), clean, and non-revealing. Walking by the agency or asking colleagues can be helpful in ascertaining this information.

Although all interviews are different, some expected questions (that you can prepare for) include the following:

- What is your interest in this agency and/or population?
- What are your qualifications or prior experiences that prepare you for field education at this agency?
- What type of supervision do you find helpful?
- Can you give an example of being a member of a collaborative team?
- Can you describe a time you had a conflict and how you managed it?
- Would you experience any specific challenges working with this population?

## Assessing Meta-Competencies

Self-assessment, combined with faculty and field supervisors' feedback, is important in the development of professional identity and conduct. Skills and the development of meta-competencies evolve over time. Furthermore, the development of each meta-competency does not occur simultaneously.

As you prepare for the initial interview and collate your learning and knowledge to date, it can be useful to self-assess your practice skills in each of the meta-competencies.

The following descriptors may be useful in assessing your skill level:

- **Introductory level.** Is aware of the meta-competency, but does not know how it would be used in practice situations.
- **Basic level.** Can use knowledge, values, and skills when asked, but does not take them into account in practice or in professional relationships (needs to be reminded).
- **Intermediate level.** Is conscious of knowledge, values, and skills in professional relationships, but these elements don't always affect behaviour in practice situations.

- **Advanced level.** Is conscious of using knowledge, value, and skills in professional relationships, and can quickly adapt to different situations as necessary.

## Self-Assessment in Practice

For each of the meta-competencies associated with your school's field education program, identify your current skill level and identify some experiences you are hoping to gain as you enter field education in order to progress further. This process may be useful as you develop a learning plan, and as you undertake midpoint and final evaluations to show strengthened practice. ■

## Field Education Practicalities

1. Each university and college will have its own processes for assigning and connecting students to a field agency. Many will require a student to have an initial interview with the host field site. In preparation for this interview, review your resumé and cover letter, which serve as your formal introduction to the agency. Do your resumé and cover letter represent your emerging professional self? Or are they more reflective of the requirements for an entry-level non-professional job?

2. As you prepare for the interview, you may want to rehearse some potential interview questions, such as those on your strengths and competencies; knowledge of the agency and population served; interest and suitability for a practicum in this particular agency; or social location and privilege. Of course, you might also want to do some homework regarding appropriate dress, the location, and the time it will take to get there.

## Journal Ideas

1. Reflect on the placement decisions that are occurring for you.

2. How is your social location reflected in you and your social work practice?

3. Identify the privileges you experience in society. How do they affect your perspective of service users?

4. Create a list of strategies or activities that you are already using as a source of energy renewal. Are there others you would consider adding in order to support your self-care through your practicum and beyond?

## Critical-Thinking Questions

1. How would you describe professional identity in social work? Is it important? Why or why not?

2. Compare and contrast the factors that lead to differing professional identities among those in social work compared with those in other disciplines, such as nursing?

3. Describe some of the differences between the competencies required by the code of ethics and standards of procedure in your province or territory and those set by ASWB.

4. The CCSWR competency profile and the ASWB competencies are not universally accepted by academics and Canadian schools of social work. What are the arguments for and against regulatory authorities listing competency requirements? Why do you think academics support educational accreditation and may not support competencies to protect the public?

5. Would you describe field education as an opportunity to learn the tasks associated with being a social worker or as an opportunity to reflect critically on how social work is done? Are these two approaches necessarily in conflict with each other?

6. How does field education in your college or university reflect community or activist approaches to social work?

# Chapter Review

Developing an identity as a professional social worker begins in social work coursework and becomes clearer through field education. This is a dynamic process. While there are many requirements associated with professional identity, exactly how they are incorporated and understood in each context is unique.

Throughout a social worker's career, "**engaging in reflexive practice**" is a core meta-competency. Reflexive practice ensures that social workers are aware of how their personal beliefs, biases, and social location influence their practice with individuals, families, and communities, and advance social justice.

Students develop a sense of professional identity in different ways. For Ralph, whose experiences are profiled in this chapter, a starting point was self-awareness of his changing worldview. For other students, prior work experiences in health and social care environments may be important. For still others, the relationships with faculty and agency supervisors or even the type of agency that one is working in may be important.

Increasing self-awareness and facing field education challenges can be stressful. Developing a range of self-care strategies can set the foundation for managing the ongoing emotional and personal toll social work can take.

The brief practice scenarios described on pages 22 and 23 will also help in the development of professional identity. They challenge students to reframe their expectations and to develop reflexive practice skills, respect diversity and difference, and employ critical thinking.

At this stage, you are likely to have secured your field placement and are in the process of preparing your self-assessments in order to begin the next stage of developing a learning plan.

## Identifying as a Social Worker in Practice

This chapter outlines numerous ways in which students can develop their professional identity as social workers. Here are some highlights and further suggestions:

- Talk with other social workers about how they make meaning of their own professional identity.

- Know the accreditation standards and frameworks of practice.

- Use self-reflection to develop an awareness of personal bias and worldviews.

- Use online communities to extend professional relationships and to support the integration of theory and practice.

- Develop professional networks for supervision and reflection, and personal networks for support and self-care.

- For non-Indigenous students, concentrate on learning about Indigenous worldviews.

- Develop safe spaces to reflect on social work's role in Indigenous peoples' lives and on the process of truth and reconciliation.

- Critically reflect on the inter-relationship of power and knowledge in people's lives and in your own practice.

- Pay attention to the linguistics and social identity of French Canadians.

- Develop a congruence between personal and professional values in your daily life.

- Commit to adopting a critical theory approach to societal change through examining issues in a social justice and equity framework.

- Adopt problem-solving strategies, engage support, and reframe expectations.

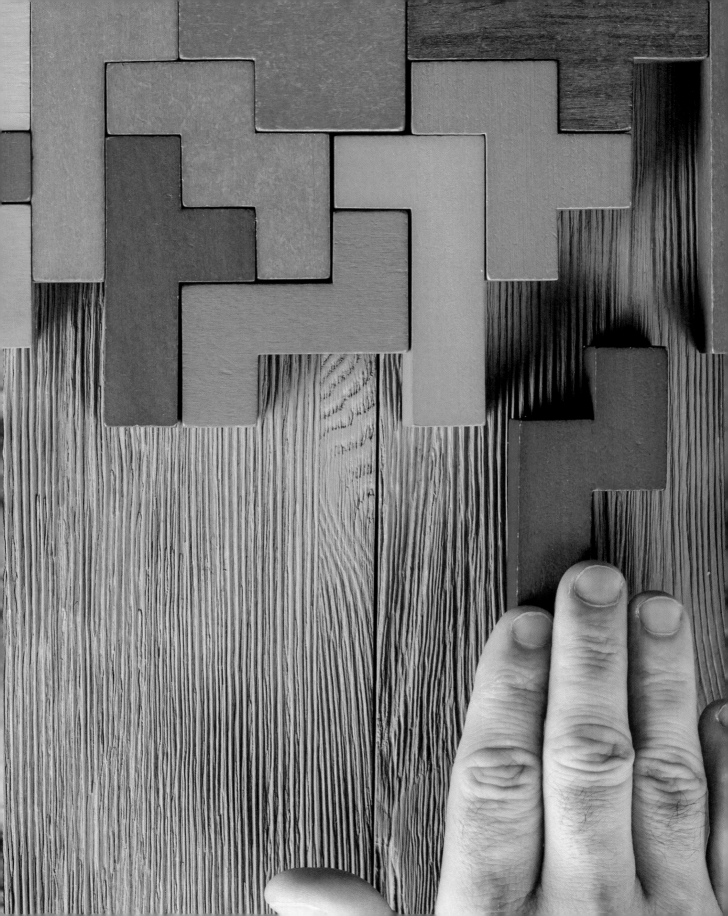

# Employing Critical Thinking

# 2

> *Knowing a great deal is not the same as being smart; intelligence is not information alone but also judgment, the manner in which information is collected and used.*
>
> —**Carl Sagan** (1922–1996), American astronomer, astrophysicist, and science popularizer

# Chapter at a Glance

# Spotlight on Social Work Luminaries
## Gabor Maté

**Gabor Maté** is a physician whose harm reduction work in the Downtown Eastside of Vancouver informed his beliefs about the connections between childhood trauma, neurobiology, and mind–body health. He has been a strong defender of InSite, the first legal supervised drug injection site in North America, and is the author of *In the Realm of Hungry Ghosts*.

**S**ocial work theory is the foundation of practice, but the connection between theory and practice is not a simple one. Real-life situations are often too complex for easy, formulaic answers. The meta-competency of **"employing critical thinking"** is required in order to be able to apply multiple sources of knowledge and theory to the diverse situations that social workers respond to every day.

Field education is the time to begin to reconcile what has been learned in school with the often messy and complicated world of practice. During this time, some things learned in the classroom are reinforced, while others are modified and adapted, or even discarded. Based on these experiences, social workers develop a unique approach to social work practice that strengthens their professional identity.

This chapter focuses on knowledge utilization and the importance of critical thinking. A high value is placed on transparency—the ability to articulate the decision-making process, both verbally and in writing, in a way that is consistent with social work values and principles.

## Developing Competence as a Social Worker

Some ways to develop the meta-competency of **"employing critical thinking"** are as follows:

- Consider the theoretical and knowledge base prevalent in your field site and think about how that knowledge base privileges some theories and sources of knowledge over others.

- Identify one peer-reviewed research article that is consistent with your field site's population and approach, then discuss it with your field supervisor or write a reflexive journal entry on how this source could be integrated with actual practice in your agency.

- Using either the integration of theory and practice (ITP) loop or complex practice behaviour model, write a reflection journal on a situation that you are experiencing (observing or participating in) in the field agency.

**Key Concepts**

- ITP loop
- Complex practice behaviour model
- Evidence-based practice (EBP)
- Postmodern theory

# Social Work Theory

The terms "theory" and "knowledge" refer to different things in social work. Social workers typically use the term "theory" to capture or convey their understanding of a specific situation or problem. On the other hand, "knowledge" refers to a more complex enterprise that is inclusive of multiple perspectives and a variety of theories so as to build a fuller understanding (Trevithick, 2008).

## The Social Construction of Theory

Social work is an applied field in which theory and knowledge are evaluated in terms of their usefulness for practice and policy development. Like other helping professions, social work draws heavily on interprofessional research and theory. The most notable disciplines among these are sociology, psychology, political science, public health, and community development. These disciplines inform the theoretical base of social work, and in turn shape how social workers construct and interpret service user needs.

There are different approaches to research in the field of social work. Research, as one component of social work theory, may be either "instrumental" or "conceptual." For example, a study by Kreisberg and Marsh (2016) found that research conducted in the United States was quite different from that in Europe. The United States had a strong instrumental focus (e.g., to increase practice effectiveness), whereas European research was more conceptual.

Likewise, Holland and Scourfield (2015) describe similarities and differences in the approaches to professional knowledge between social work and the health-care professions. For example, the field of public health and social work share a socio-ecological approach to intervention. However, they are distinguished from one another insofar as public health favours medical models and population-level interventions, whereas social work tends to emphasize human rights and social justice concerns.

Similarly, counselling and psychology share with social work ethical concerns and processes, such as unconditional positive regard, confidentiality, and informed consent. However, counselling and psychology typically focus on the individual's level of functioning, while social work focuses on the person-in-environment. Community development and social work emphasize group self-organization and collective development. By contrast, social work frequently focuses on individual case work and high-risk individual situations.

The challenge for social workers, and social work students, is to draw on multiple sources of research and theory in order to apply the most appropriate knowledge to what are often unique and highly complex situations. An important emphasis in social work theory and practice, and something that distinguishes it from other professions, is that service users' understanding of their situation and problems figures prominently when it comes to working toward lasting solutions.

Critical thinking requires the synthesis and communication of relevant information in all aspects of social work practice. It requires social workers to be knowledgeable about social work theory and values, and to contextualize practice within a socio-political, organizational, and cultural environment. It also requires social workers to pay special attention to the unique circumstances, histories, and experiences of each service user.

## CASWE-ACFTS *Standards for Accreditation*

The importance of linking multiple sources of knowledge to practice and applying critical-thinking skills are highlighted in principles 2 and 4, and in the core learning objective 5 of the CASWE-ACFTS *Standards for Accreditation* (Canadian Association for Social Work Education–Association canadienne pour la formation en travail social [CASWE-ACFTS], 2014):

**Principle 2.** Social work education links together the interdisciplinary theoretical knowledge base of social work and professional practice.

**Principle 4.** The integration of knowledge, values, and skills in the context of field education is a critical and distinctive aspect of social work education; therefore, field education is considered the central component of social work education.

**Core learning objective 5.** Employ critical thinking in professional practice

i) Social work students develop skills in critical thinking and reasoning, including critical analysis of assumptions, consistent with the values of the profession, which they apply in their professional practice to analyze complex social situations and make professional judgments.

ii) Social work students are able to apply critical thinking to identify and address structural sources of injustice and inequalities in the context of a Canadian society.

iii) MSW students are able to apply knowledge of a variety of social work theories and perspectives to critically analyze professional and institutional practices.

## Professional Regulation and Competency

The Canadian Council of Social Work Regulators (CCSWR) *Entry-Level Competency Profile* (CCSWR, 2012) likewise identifies the integration of knowledge and practice as a foundation of, and implicit in, many of the competency blocks.

For the CCSWR, this includes the practice of conducting assessments, planning interventions, and delivering services.

## Association of Social Work Boards (ASWB)

The ASWB is a non-profit organization composed of social work Regulatory Colleges in Canada and the United States. The ASWB competency requirements for entry-level practice include demonstrating sound knowledge and critical-thinking skills in the following areas:

- Child behaviour and development
- Family theories and dynamics
- Systems and ecological perspectives
- Social change and community development theories
- Determining which individual, family, group, or combined modality meets the needs of service users' systems ■

The integration of theory and practice (ITP) loop is a model for understanding the relationship between theory and social work practice.

First developed by Bogo and Vayda (1998), the ITP loop involves retrieval of all the facts, reflection on the overall situation, linking back to existing knowledge and theory, and then finally deciding on a professional response or intervention.

# Integrating Theory and Decision-Making in Practice

In social work, applying theory to practice is not a straightforward, linear process. Rather, the process is circular, cumulative, and inclusive of alternate forms of knowledge and awareness of self.

Marion Bogo and her colleagues have undertaken decades of research with social work students and provided leadership to countless scholars in relation to the complex practice of integrating both theory and practice in a social work context. They have developed a model that describes the integration of theory and practice (ITP), which they refer to as the *ITP loop*.

## The ITP Loop

The **ITP loop** starts with retrieving the salient facts and gaining an understanding of the situation, and then personally reflecting on these in light of one's own experiences and social location. Those ideas are then linked to knowledge bases and theoretical understandings in order to provide a response or action (see Figure 2.1). As new ideas emerge, one's practice perspectives continue to evolve and adapt.

Bogo (2006) describes the four phases of the ITP loop as follows:

1. **Retrieval.** Retrieve and recall the relevant facts in the practice situation.
2. **Reflection.** Reflect on your reactions to the experience and become aware of your personal reactions, beliefs, and attitudes in relation to the situation.
3. **Linkage.** Link the experience and reactions to concepts, theories, knowledge, and skills discussed in courses, reading, and the field. Explain the situation you have observed using one or more theoretical perspectives.
4. **Professional response.** Identify a professional response, which could include needing more information, knowledge, or advice, to make the decision. Analyze what you should do next in this situation, and identify the response options that might apply under similar circumstances in the future.

**Figure 2.1** The Integration of Theory and Practice (ITP) Loop

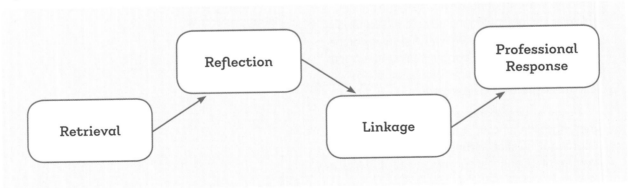

**Source:** Bogo (2010); Bogo and Vayda (1998).

## Critical Thinking and Complex Practice

In the **complex practice behaviour model** developed more recently by Marion Bogo and her colleagues, complex practice behaviour is summarized as follows:

> At the heart of any view of competence is the recognition that practitioners are engaged in carrying out complex practices and practice behaviors. A range of skills is used by social workers, including interviewing and interpersonal communication skills. However, the enactment of these practices is a product of the integration of many components. [Figure 2.2 below] illustrates this perspective: Social workers use knowledge and skills guided by the way in which they engage in critical thinking to understand the situations they confront. They draw on theoretical and empirical knowledge as well as tacit knowledge derived from their lived experiences, both personal and professional. Professional judgement is based on the links between a practitioner's thoughts and feelings and the reflective and critical thinking she or he brings to the judgements and decisions made. Therefore, competence involves awareness of our emotional states, feelings, and reactions and the use of reflection and self-reflection to understand, manage, and work productively in practice. (Bogo, Rawlings, Katz, & Logie, 2014, pp. 9–10)

Complex practice behaviour occurs within a broader organizational, community, and professional context. Social workers respond intentionally (rather than simply reactively) to situations. They do this by drawing on knowledge and theories, and considering their assumptions and biases in order to enact an intentional and deliberate action (or skill).

**Complex practice behaviour model**

The complex practice behaviour model recognizes that decision-making in social work is influenced by the worker's professional knowledge and skills and also by their emotions, ability for self-regulation, and their personal biases and assumptions.

**Figure 2.2** A Model of Holistic Competence in Social Work

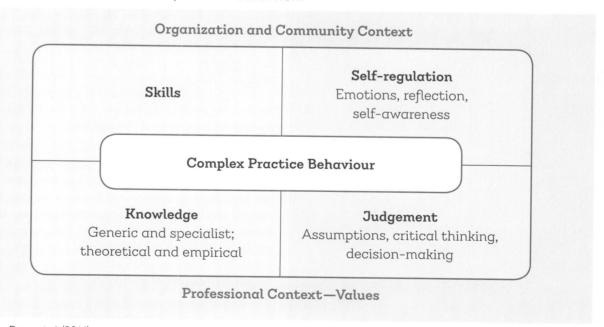

**Source:** Bogo et al. (2014).

# Linking Theory to Practice

Fran Harvey

**Fran was working in a non-profit community agency that provided short-term counselling when she encountered Elaine and her son, Austin.**

Fran has an MSW and almost 20 years of social work experience in the areas of children's mental health and child welfare. She is also a single parent with two teenage boys.

Although Fran had much practice experience assessing and planning treatment and interventions, this was a complex and memorable family.

She felt the need to be reflexive about the situation and how she was interpreting the issues.

Elaine, was in her mid-40s when she attended counselling, ostensibly for concerns related to her 16-year-old son, Austin, who excelled academically but was showing increasingly worrisome behaviours. Elaine was separated but co-parenting. Austin and his sister were both adopted from an international orphanage at the ages of three and one, respectively.

Lately, Austin was having outbursts at school, had threatened a teacher, and was also being increasingly violent with his younger sister. Elaine had also recently received a call from Austin's teacher informing her that his English essays, while fine grammatically, included violent fantasies.

Austin was forthcoming during his interview. He mirrored the information his mother had provided and talked openly about his parents' separation and its effect on him. He said that he liked school and did well academically. He hoped to be a forensic psychologist one day. Austin acknowledged his Chinese ethnicity but rarely wondered about his heritage or relatives. He had no memories of his early childhood. He was appreciative of being adopted and knew that his parents loved him greatly. He had one good friend in school, but shared that he was seen as a bit of a "nerd" and didn't really fit in. This didn't bother him, as he "didn't really like those kids anyway."

Austin understood why the teacher had contacted his mother, but he did not see a problem with his fascination with killings and death. He saw this fascination as similar to being interested in TV shows such as *CSI* and *NCIS*, and novels by Stephen King. When asked, he showed no empathy for any victims depicted in his stories or in the shows.

He admitted to being mean to his sister and to frightening her—pulling her hair, twisting her arm behind her back, and once punching her in the stomach severely enough that she fell to the ground. He also shared that he had enjoyable memories as a three- or four-year-old of catching frogs and pulling their legs off. Austin denied using alcohol or any type of licit or illicit drugs, denied feeling depressed, and had never had thoughts of suicide.

This was an evening appointment, and at the end of the session, I walked him to the front door of the building where his mother was waiting.

### Awareness of "Self"

Throughout the interview, the information itself was troubling, but the emotional effect on me was even more troubling. I could not detect any compassion or empathy from Austin, and his non-verbals were almost completely flat. I also felt that Austin was looking right through me, and somehow daring me with his eyes to show my own incompetence and/or fear.

I had seen many troubled young people, and many young people who were considered "nerds" and had poor interpersonal relationships. Many were angry and had violent thoughts, and hurting animals was not uncommon for them. Plus, I was used to having teenagers in my own home. But, my emotional reaction here was different. I asked myself why I had escorted him out of the building, since this was not my usual practice.

My instincts told me that there was something pretty serious going on with Austin. Despite many years of work experience, I felt that I needed advice, so I connected with a colleague to consider next steps. My colleague encouraged me to pay attention to my intuition, while continuing to collect more information for decision-making.

At the following meeting, I told Austin and his mother separately that I was concerned, that I had read Austin's writings and found them deeply troubling. The school confirmed that his writing was articulate, but that the content was unusual and of concern. A referral was made to Children's Mental Health. Subsequently, Elaine told me that Austin was immediately hospitalized.

The following months were even more chaotic for Austin and his family. Austin was charged with assault following a physical altercation with a nurse and spent a night locked in a correctional facility. Concerns had also been raised that Elaine could not protect her younger daughter if Austin was returned to their home.

An interprofessional team meeting was called at the hospital in order to assess the situation and make recommendations. Elaine asked me to attend the meeting as her support and her advocate. ∎

### Reflections on Fran's Story

This was a complex and challenging family situation. Fran used multiple sources of knowledge in her efforts to understand Austin's situation and decide on the appropriate response. In particular, she used her awareness of "self" and her own experiences of being a single parent with adolescent children.

Fran tried to put herself in both Austin's and his mother's shoes. She used multiple skills, including developing a personal relationship, providing authentic feedback to Elaine and Austin, and paying attention to non-verbal reactions.

In the end, she also recognized her own professional limitations. Seeking advice, even as an experienced social worker, seemed necessary for personal confidence, emotional support, and professional wisdom.

### From Theory to Practice

As you reflect on Fran's story, give some thought to the following points:

1. What theories or knowledge sources was Fran using to make decisions in this situation?

2. One of the decisions Fran made was to walk, or escort, Austin out of the office. What may have been the assumptions or self-awareness that contributed to this decision?

3. Fran saw herself as a generalist social worker. How did she reach the conclusion that there was a need for specialist knowledge and services? How do you know when your own expertise does not match the service user needs?

4. How does seeking advice and supervision fit within the complex practice behaviour model?

# Evidence-Based Practice

Complex practice in social work is more than the simple application of formal theory. The decision-making associated with practice requires bringing the best available research evidence to bear on the problem.

The idea of **evidence-based practice (EBP)** emerged in the 1990s from the field of medicine. EBP can be described as "the conscientious, explicit and judicious use of current best *evidence* in making decisions about the care of the individual patient" (Sackett, Rosenberg, Gray, Haynes, & Richardson, 1996, p. 71; italics added). In order to be more reflexive and consistent with social work values, Edmond, Megivern, Williams, Rochman, and Howard (2006) expanded on this definition. They describe EBP as "the conscientious and judicious use of current best *practice* in decision-making about interventions at all system levels" (p. 384; italics added).

An important source of knowledge that contributes to social work decision-making is service users themselves. EBP includes understanding their perceptions of the cause and possible solutions to the issues they face. It also requires taking into account service user characteristics. For example, children in foster care have different needs than children in intact family homes. Likewise, individuals in Indigenous communities may prefer holistic understandings and interventions that take into account cultural traditions and practices.

Shlonsky and Benbenishty (2014) argue that EBP is inclusive of all sources of information, with a central issue being how to weigh each source in terms of its quality and applicability to a specific and unique situation.

**Figure 2.3**
The Components of
Evidence-Based Practice
in Social Work

**Source:** Adapted from Regehr, Stern, and Shlonsky (2007).

# Quebec Guidelines on Evidence-Based Practice
## Fostering Knowledge Transfer and Clinical Excellence

Practice guidelines are typically developed by professional associations on behalf of their members as a way of promoting effective practice. According to Rosen and Proctor (2003), practice guidelines serve to "increase the predictability of practice behaviours, and enhance service user confidence in treatment as meeting professional standards" (p. 1).

Rosen and Proctor (2003) define "practice guidelines" as follows:

> a set of systematically compiled and organized statements of empirically tested knowledge and procedures to help practitioners select and implement interventions that are the most effective and appropriate for attaining the desired outcomes. (p. 1)

### Promoting Clinical Excellence

As in other jurisdictions, Quebec has studied how to implement EBP in the social services. The province's Institut national d'excellence en santé et services sociaux (INESSS) is mandated to promote clinical excellence and the efficient use of resources in the health and social service sectors. In the absence of validated processes to develop practice guidelines in the social and human sciences, INESSS set up a task force to review the literature and define a process for the development of such guidelines.

In 2010, INESSS created the Committee for the Development of Practice Guidelines in Social Care to optimize practice guidelines in psychosocial practices. This committee included representation from the social work field.

In 2012, the committee's recommendations were published in a preliminary report, which were summarized in an article by Beauchamp, Drapeau, and Dionne (2015).

### INESSS Committee Recommendations

The committee recommended that practice guidelines should be transparent and based on a synthesis of scientific data supported by exhaustive contextual data and expert knowledge. It also recommended that practice guidelines be developed through interdisciplinary collaboration so as to include many different points of view and diverse knowledges and experiences.

In response to the question of which data to use to inform the guidelines, the committee concluded that it is important to establish the relevance of a study based on its ability to answer one or more research questions relevant to the guideline being developed.

It recommended that practice interventions be weighted on a scale (established, emerging, not established, ineffective, or harmful). After scaling the quality of the research study, attention turned to whether the study was supported by contextual (the socio-political-economic organization environment) and experiential data (expert knowledge). It was this triangulation of various data, drawn from multiple sources (scientific, contextual, and experiential), that determined whether an intervention was included in practice guidelines.

Although multiple barriers exist to integrating evidence into practice and reducing the knowledge–practice gap, practice guidelines are important. They provide a framework that can help social workers make complex decisions with the confidence that a particular intervention will result in more good than harm in a given context. ■

# Influences on Decision-Making

Decision-making by social workers occurs within an organizational context and a broader socio-political environment. Baumann, Kern, and Fluke (1997) first described a Decision-Making Ecology (DME) framework in the mid-1990s. The DME framework has subsequently been adapted by Smith, Fluke, Fallon, Mishna, & Decker Pierce (2018).

Using decision-making in the field of child welfare as an example, the DME framework can be used to consider the extent to which decisions are based on the peculiarities of the case (e.g., type and severity of maltreatment, risk, poverty), the characteristics of the decision maker (e.g., experience, values), the organizational setting (e.g., policy, workload, resources), and external characteristics (e.g., critical events, funding).

The DME framework has been useful in looking at the factors associated with social work decision-making. For example, Smith et al. (2018) found that workers in a specialist service in child welfare were less likely than workers in multiservice agencies to make referrals. However, the case factors were more important when making decisions about in-home supports compared to out-of-home care. Similarly, in relation to service provision in the substance-use field, Stokes (2019) found that case factors were more important in decisions about assessing substance-use severity, whereas organizational characteristics influenced decisions about service provision.

**Figure 2.4** Decision-Making in Social Work Practice

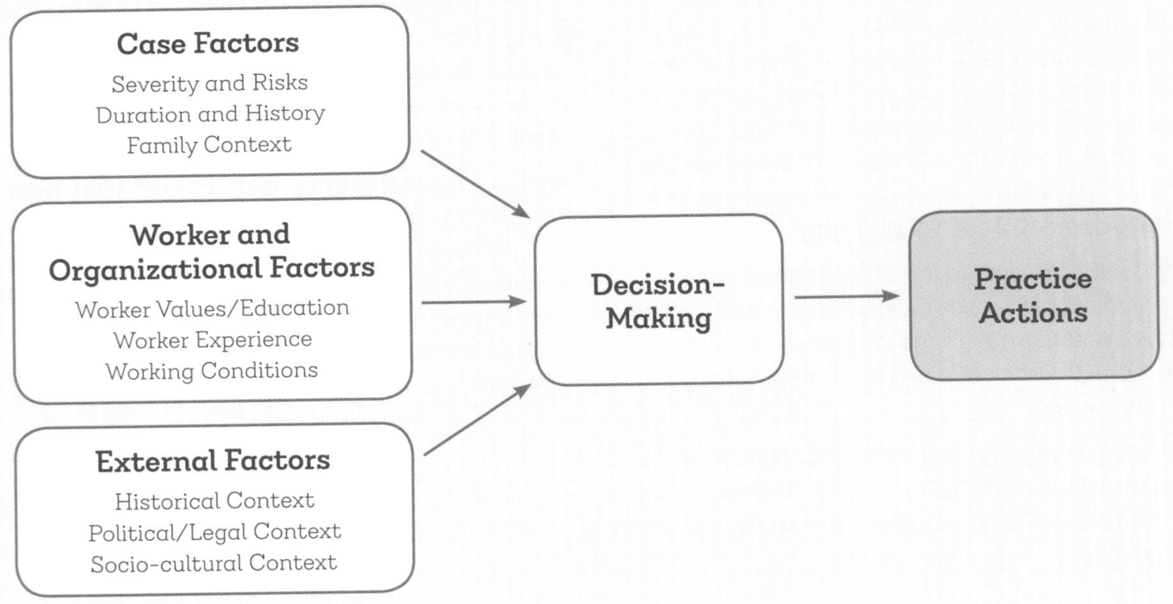

**Source:** Adapted from Smith et al. (2018).

## Practice Models in Social Work

Practitioners often criticize formal theory as having been developed in isolation from the complexities of practice; as too time-consuming to research, given the large caseloads and heavy record-keeping requirements of practitioners' jobs; as too difficult to adapt to emerging programs and needs; and as too challenging to implement if it doesn't correspond with an organization's philosophy (Larsen, 2012).

Indeed, the range of theories and practice models that a social worker might encounter can be overwhelming. They include the following:

- Anti-oppressive theory; attachment theory; behavioural theory; cognitive theory; critical theory; ecological theory; existential theory; feminist theory; human development theory; humanistic theory; psychoanalytic theory; strengths-based theory; structural theory; systems theory.

- Anti-racist practice; cognitive-behavioural therapy; creative arts therapy; digital storytelling; Indigenous practice; mindfulness-based practice; multi-cultural practice; narrative therapy; spirituality practices; task-centred therapy; solutions-focused practice; play therapy.

Decision-making in social work is seldom a straightforward application of a particular theoretical strand (Heinsch, Gray, & Sharland, 2016). Theories, as taught in the classroom, are typically presented as being relatively clear-cut. In practice, the situations are usually very complicated, and there are tensions between the use and application of knowledge and evidence. For this reason, it is recommended that social workers have a systematic and intentional way to work through, and make visible their decision-making and practice actions.

## The Importance of Practice Wisdom

A good deal of social work decision-making is unconscious and hands-on. Social workers make many decisions in a day, and, in the course of doing so, they often develop shortcuts to become quicker and more efficient decision-makers.

This kind of tacit or intuitive knowledge is developed over time through experience. Although this knowledge may be difficult to replicate or understand, it is well understood that it plays an important part in the decisions social workers make everyday.

Ultimately, practice knowledge involves critically thinking through and weighing multiple sources of experiential and research evidence, taking into account the particular circumstances and needs of the service user, and being aware of the constraints and opportunities inherent in the organizational context.

Of course, none of these points change the fact that social workers are responsible for being analytical about their decisions and transparent in their practice. At any time, they may be called upon to identify and explain the underlying assumptions and theoretical frameworks associated with their work—to service users, managers, or even judicial inquiries.

# The Role of Emotions in Decision-Making

Social work practice is often emotionally charged, both for the service user and the social worker. Research supports the idea that emotions, or the use of "self," play a major role in decision-making.

Modern neuroscience research suggests that affective and subjective reactions are, in fact, integral to all cognitive processes, personal and professional (Immordino-Yang & Damasio, 2007; Kahneman, 2011). For this reason, developing emotional self-awareness and self-regulation could be as important a practice competency for beginning social workers as understanding one's social location or having a sound grasp of multiple theories and practice models.

**Emotional Awareness and Professional Judgement**

It is important to understand that subjective thinking, personal feelings, and emotional reactions all contribute to how situations are perceived and how decisions are made. Emotional awareness is part of professional judgement, as Bogo et al. (2014) note:

> Professional judgement is based on the links between a practitioner's thoughts and feelings and the reflective and critical thinking she or he brings to the judgements and decisions made. (p. 10)

Keinemans (2015) goes so far as to suggest that deliberate and conscious reasoning (i.e., sound judgement) is insufficient on its own for complex decision-making. She suggests that social workers should go even further and consciously develop and use human emotions in order to become even more effective in serving the interest of service users.

Learning to manage emotions—to show genuine interest and emotional warmth and provide emotional support—is a core skill in communicating with service users. This skill includes the ability to show empathy.

Empathy is the ability to identify intellectually with the feelings, thoughts, and attitudes of another person. It is easier to feel empathy toward an individual we can relate to or a situation we can appreciate and understand. Therefore, in order to enhance empathy and practise compassion, it is necessary to be able to relate to and identify with others, including those from different social locations and social circumstances.

Developing a deeper understanding of a particular situation can have a significant emotional impact on a social worker. Practising self-awareness and self-regulation will help the social worker relate to the service user compassionately while avoiding personal triggers or internalizing the service user's emotions.

# Indigenous Healing Practices
## Spirituality and a Sense of Interconnectedness

**S**ocial work is increasingly including spirituality in practice as a counterweight to the technologization, managerialism, and medicalization of mainstream models (Wong & Vinsky, 2009). Spirituality emphasizes a search for meaning, which accepts alternative knowledge systems and the sharing of knowledge.

The inclusion of spirituality in social work discourse taps into non-Western modalities of social work practice and into Indigenous wisdom and resilience:

> Traditional Indigenous healing practices are embedded in a spiritual sense of interconnectedness which is fundamentally different from the dominant Western paradigm. (Coates, Gray, & Hetherington, 2005, p. 393)

Further, the "need to respect Indigenous spirituality in its own right" is identified in the 94 calls to action (#60) included in the Truth and Reconciliation Commission of Canada report of June 2015.

### "All Our Relations"

A traditional Indigenous perspective is one where spirituality is intrinsically linked to beliefs and daily living.

"All Our Relations" (a belief that all individuals are related and must live harmoniously with each other and with all animate and inanimate forms) and the "Sacredness of Life" (the belief that is expressed in honouring ceremonies at sunrise and sunset, through sun dances, smudges, and sweat lodges) are some key concepts that underpin Indigenous perspectives (Coates et al., 2005).

Faith and spirituality are important aspects of making meaning of the struggles individuals face. Including and acknowledging the significance of spirituality can assist in understanding an individual's strengths and ability to practise resilience (Darrell & Rich, 2017).

### Respecting Traditional Ways of Healing

Working with photographer Philomena Hughes, Joanna Palmer (2018) interviewed Indigenous people in northern British Columbia who were involved in supporting the health and well-being of communities in the region.

Here are some of their views on working with Indigenous communities in ways that align with and respect Indigenous approaches to well-being and healing:

> "As a passionate advocate, I work closely in partnership with provincial, federal, and Indigenous levels of government to inform innovative and transformative health-care practices across the lifespan, to advance self-determination, governance and individual capacity for the Carrier Sekani Family Services Member Nations and their people."
> —Warner C. Adam, CEO, Carrier Sekani Family Services (Palmer, 2018, p. 1660)

> "I work with patients to find ways to release pain [associated with various traumas] from their spiritual/mental/emotional/physical bodies. We do this through talking, art, traditional practices, education movement, and various ceremonies."
> —Jane Inyallie, wellness counsellor, Central Interior Native Health Society (Palmer, 2018, p. 1662)

> "It is important and motivates me to see Indigenous cancer patients and their families receive culturally relevant and safe care that honours and respects traditional ways of healing and creates the space within the current system to guide and teach cancer agency staff the importance of building meaningful relationships and incorporating traditional practise in the care and treatment of and with Indigenous people."
> —Preston B. Guno, provincial director, Indigenous Cancer Care (Palmer, 2018, p. 1663)

> "[Guided by Elders, my role is to] assist with navigating the health-care system to enable participants to address their health-care needs in a safe and respectful process."
> —Sharon A. Springer, Cedar research nurse at Cedar Project (Palmer, 2018, p. 1666) ■

# Social Worker Exemplar

## Unconditional Positive Regard

Kelly Cunningham

**Social workers are taught to document their assessments and their treatment recommendations in writing. They are also taught always to guard and respect a service user's confidentiality and privacy.**

In this transformative and memorable story, Kelly's practicum supervisor taught her important lessons about always being non-judgemental and authentic in relation to service users.

Kelly learned to be cautious about her interpretation of what is written in files, as well as thoughtful about her own file recording. She also learned the importance of being open-minded and present-focused in order to form positive professional and non-judgemental relationships.

Before deciding to move from the West Coast to the East Coast of Canada, I had been working in Community Living for a few years after graduating with my BA in Sociology. I was supporting adults and youth with physical and developmental disabilities. I loved the work I did, but decided I wanted more substantial guidance in my professional life. I wanted to be a social worker.

I moved across the country to live in the Maritimes and to study social work. I was 26 years old at the time. After two semesters, my fellow classmates and I began our first field placements. I chose to work at a small non-profit agency in the community, working with adults in various stages of life. My time in placement focused on being an outreach worker in the community. I was involved in supporting people in their personal goals to secure and maintain safe and affordable housing.

My supervisor, Kathy, was a seasoned outreach worker who spent her working days advocating and supporting adults with mental health and substance-use issues attain affordable housing. I spent the majority of my time working with her. Most of the people Kathy and I worked with were single men over the age of 50. One memorable experience stands out.

The man's name was Calvin. Kathy introduced Calvin to me at the community soup kitchen one afternoon. At the time, he was having difficulty receiving his social assistance cheque and was worried about losing his housing.

Over the following few weeks, Kathy and I met with him a few times to support him in getting things sorted out. During this time, I found Calvin a pleasure to work with. He was in his late 60s and lived alone, and he had no family nearby. I enjoyed having conversations with him and genuinely cared for his well-being. I worked hard on his behalf.

It wasn't until near the end of my field placement that my supervisor gave me some background information on Calvin. Kathy told me, for example, that Calvin had previously served several years in an American prison for child sexual abuse. She told me that she hadn't mentioned it to me earlier because she didn't think it was relevant to my work with him and that knowing his background may have influenced my ability to form a positive relationship.

## Authenticity and Transparency in Practice

When Kathy gave me this information, I remember feeling shocked and disgusted. Part of me wished I had known. But as I let it sink in and processed it further, I wondered if it would have made a difference. Would I have been less friendly to him? Would that information have made me a better social worker? I wasn't sure.

But then I realized that Kathy had taught me a valuable social work lesson. Withholding that part of Calvin's past enabled me to form a working relationship with him based on who he was at that moment. It taught me that each person I will end up working with has a history and a past.

Relationships are what social work is all about. Knowledge, feelings, and beliefs related to a person's past can detract from one's ability to build relationships. This experience taught me about the practical significance of being self-aware and non-judgemental.

As a social work student, this experience taught me that concepts such as unconditional positive regard are easy to talk about in the classroom but are more difficult to apply in practice. If I had known Calvin's past, I may not have been able to see the good that was there. I may not have been very helpful to him.

Years have now passed since my practicum and this experience. I am now back on the West Coast working in child protection, but my experience with Calvin has always stuck with me—it was transformative learning.

In my practice, I am careful and thoughtful when reading the files of service users. I remind myself that every person I work with has a past and that my interpretation of that past may trigger an emotional reaction in me that could detract from building a positive relationship in the present and seeing the person as they are now.

This learning continues to influence me as I recognize how my current recording of service users' situations may influence the judgement of subsequent social workers who will meet those service users. I strive to continually practise anti-oppressive, collaborative, and respectful recordings. ■

## Reflections on Kelly's Story

Students and social workers are ethically bound to be transparent and authentic in their interactions with service users. In Kelly's situation, information was contained in the running record that could have negatively influenced her working relationship with Calvin.

Kathy, her experienced field placement supervisor, taught her a lesson in transparency, authenticity, and service user rights to privacy.

### From Theory to Practice

As you reflect on Kelly's story, give some thought to the following points:

1. What do you think of the supervisor's decision to withhold the information that Calvin had a prior conviction for child sexual abuse? If you were the supervisor, would you have withheld this information from Kelly?

2. Does the supervisor's approach align with basic social work principles and values? What are these values?

3. Under what conditions might it be permissible for a supervisor to withhold information?

4. Kelly recognizes that her empathy for Calvin may have been affected by her emotional response to knowing about his past. How do you self-regulate your emotions in order to ensure unconditional positive regard for those you work with?

5. Can you think of a situation in which someone has withheld information from you? What was that person's reasoning? Did it really matter?

6. As you read written records in your field site, what are some of the recording practices that influence you, either positively or negatively?

7. What are some of the practices you can instill in your written recordings to reflect anti-oppressive practice?

## Postmodern theory

Postmodern theory calls attention to the contingent or socially conditioned nature of knowledge. Knowledge and values are seen as products of particular political, historical, or cultural discourses and hierarchies.

For example, postmodern theory focuses on deconstructing common beliefs and questioning accepted definitions. The relationship between the service user and social worker is therefore highly collaborative. Change comes about primarily through dialogue.

# Postmodern Contributions to Social Work Practice

Postmodern theory has contributed significantly to the knowledge base at the heart of social work practice and is increasingly being used in practice situations to understand the complexities of power, identity, and change. Postmodernist thinkers insist that traditional frameworks are no longer relevant and that we must acknowledge the existence of diverse and multiple frameworks or discourses (Fook, 2016).

### Including Narratives That Speak to Identity

**Postmodern theory** challenges the use of binary ideas in social work (e.g., normal/abnormal, true/false, male/female, right/wrong). The term that is used—"deconstruction"—refers to the "breaking apart of the dualisms to show a range of positions that lie within and beyond opposed entities" (Healy, 2005, p. 205). For example, there are as many variations in the duality of "working class" and "middle class" as there is in the states of "powerful" and "powerless"—they are merely two extremes on a continuum.

Postmodern theorists also question narrow definitions of "truth," "reason," and "rationality," arguing that such terms can limit one's ability to understand and respond to cultural contexts that are typically marked by uncertainty and change. They maintain that positivistic knowledge—the view that only "factual" knowledge gained through observation (the senses) and measurement is trustworthy—subverts other forms of knowledge, such as emotional or tacit knowledge, that can provide important practice insights.

Narrative practice models in social work use postmodern methods. Narrative practice centres on the following:

> the idea that narratives we, and others, construct about us actively shape our experiences, our sense of self, and our life options. We are constrained by harmful narratives, and so intervention is focused on understanding and transforming those narratives from constraint to honouring the person's capacity. (Healy, 2005, p. 206)

At its core, social work is a field of activity in which the importance of discretion and judgement cannot be discounted (Humphries, 2003). Postmodernists underscore this point.

While there is considerable tension within social work about the role and nature of "evidence" and theory, for postmodern theorists, this dichotomy is largely definitional and ideological. The dichotomy between quantitative and qualitative methods is also portrayed as a false one. Webb (2001) argues that the tendency to separate "facts" and "values," which often is implicit in discussions of EBP, can undermine professional judgement and discretion. Postmodern thinking does not eschew facts and scientific understanding, but seeks to add a richer layer by expanding the definition of evidence to include narratives that speak to identity and are reflective of the uniqueness of individuals and individual situations (Dybicz, 2015).

## Post-colonial Theory and Indigenous Knowledge

Proponents of anti-oppressive, structural, and postmodern theory maintain that marginalization and inequity result from social organization rather than individual deficiencies. While these anti-oppressive theories can help uncover the roots of oppression for Indigenous peoples, Baskin (2016) critiques them as nevertheless being grounded in Western worldviews that do not allow for the importance of Indigenous worldviews and values.

The "Indigenization" of social work practice has largely involved adapting Western models or theories to fit non-Western contexts. However, more recent "post-colonial" understandings hold that "social work knowledge should arise from within the culture, reflect local behaviours and practices, be interpreted within a local frame of reference and thus be locally relevant" (Gray & Coates, 2010, p. 3). The term "post-colonial" is now used to describe non-Western theory and knowledge more generally.

Post-colonial theory looks at patterns among colonized peoples around the world and provides a message that Indigenous peoples are not alone in their struggles to decolonize (Baskin, 2016). It opens space and credibility for Indigenous knowledge and brings the values and beliefs associated with an Indigenous worldview from the margins to the centre. The theory is not simply associated with a period of time, but also with the discourse associated with colonization that did not stop when the colonizers went home.

Compton-Osmond (2017) describes a true and anti-oppressive Indigenous approach to social work practice as one that reflects the community's beliefs, values, needs, and wishes—as determined by them. She notes that what works for one Indigenous community or family may not work for another, and suggests that respectful and anti-oppressive practice starts by simply asking questions such as the following:

- Can you help me learn about your culture and traditional beliefs?

- How would you like to incorporate your cultural practices and beliefs into our work together?

- Let's agree to be open and honest at all times. If you'd like to do things differently or something doesn't feel right to you, let me know about it.

Post-colonial theory underlines how colonization has harmed, and continues to harm, Indigenous peoples and the relationships between colonized and colonizing peoples. It requires working in partnership with Indigenous peoples and other groups to help professionals work toward a true process of decolonization (Baskin, 2016).

# Practice Scenarios

During field education, and later in practice, you will be exposed to many new situations, for which you will only have been given minimal information. Preparing yourself is important. This means thinking about the theories and skills that you may want to use, finding out from your supervisor how their experiences and knowledge strengthen their understanding (or contextualize a situation or response), and reminding yourself to incorporate the service user's understanding of the situation.

As you begin to work through the practice scenarios below, think about the types of evidence that you are using. What priority do you give to the service user's needs and preferences? How does your own experience contribute to your decision-making? What theoretical knowledge and approach are you likely to use in your response? And how can you ensure that you always reflect social work values and knowledge?

## 2.1 Meeting Basic Needs and Self-Worth

You are shadowing a psychiatric nurse who is completing an intake process with Camille. Camille is 42 years old and was admitted three days ago with schizophrenia. She is married, has one child (age 14), and usually lives in a community approximately 10 hours away. She is calm and coherent and wants more intensive help than she has been receiving at home.

During the intake process, she describes how she does not have any personal ID as she lost it many years ago. She says that she has no SIN card, no driver's licence (although she is eligible for one), and no medical card. She also describes how this is a problem when doing daily tasks. The psychiatric nurse introduces you as a social work student, and asks Camille if she would like your help to get her ID back.

1. What is your first reaction to being asked to assist Camille with her ID?
2. What, if any role, does assisting Camille getting her ID have to do with her psychiatric treatment?
3. Is accessing Camille's ID with her an appropriate role for a social worker?
4. From which theoretical perspectives would you approach this task?
5. What are your next steps?

## 2.2 Emotional Awareness and Assisted Dying

Your social work placement is in a long-term care facility. You have worked there for several weeks and are developing close relationships with several of the residents. Katy, age 78, was trained as a nurse and worked full-time for most of her life. Her husband died three years ago, and she has two daughters and four grandchildren.

One daughter lives close by and visits once or twice a week. Katy was diagnosed with Parkinson's disease five years ago, and she was able to live independently until about six months ago. Katy has increasing tremours and significant muscle stiffness, which is affecting her movement as well as her ability to feed herself and maintain her personal hygiene. Katy accepts staying in the long-term care facility, but she is very concerned about the burden she is placing on her daughter. She is also concerned about her mental state, which seems to be rapidly deteriorating. This morning she asked you if you could spend some time talking with her about assisted dying.

1.  How do your own experiences and values inform your personal perspectives on assisted dying?

2.  What social work principles and values would be important to consider? Which social work theories would inform your next steps?

3.  What would be your role in this situation? Is there any other information, or resources, that you would require to respond to Katy's request?

## 2.3 Self-Determination and Cognitive Impairment

Your social work placement is in a non-profit society providing community services to people who have brain injuries. Kevin is 35 years old and has a brain injury as a result of a drug overdose. He continues to live independently, attends counselling with a mental health and substance-use counsellor regularly, receives a disability pension, and enjoys the social activities at the centre. He has a noticeable slur to his speech and at times has inappropriate vocalizations. He particularly enjoys reading the local newspaper and getting into discussions (sometimes heated) with other participants. This week he was reading about the local elections and has informed you that he is intending to register to run as a city councillor.

1.  What are your initial thoughts about this?

2.  How does your social location impact your perspective on his decision?

3.  Which values and principles in social work inform your perspectives?

4.  What theories would inform your next steps with Kevin?

# Field Education Practicalities
## Seminars, Learning Plans and Goals, and Reflexive Journalling

Most social work programs include a seminar as a component of field education. While the format of seminars may vary, their general goal is to provide a collegial forum for students to reflect on practices they are seeing and undertaking. As well, seminars are an opportunity to analyze practices from the perspectives of oppression, equality, and social justice.

Reflexive journalling is a tool for describing, analyzing, and understanding practice. While a *reflective* journal describes events and their meaning, a *reflexive* journal connects theory and practice (including contextual influences) to develop and extend one's practice competence. Reflexive journalling is also a tool for self-care and to work through emotionally charged experiences.

Students will have varying experiences in their field placements. At least some of the time, the tasks may seem mundane and more like those assigned to a volunteer (e.g., answering the telephone, attending an open house, greeting service users). At other times, one may be expected to act more like a staff member (e.g., taking minutes at a meeting, networking with other agencies, or speaking at a forum). However, regardless of the task assigned, the primary purpose of field education is learning to practise as a social worker, which includes thinking from a social work perspective and acting professionally.

All jobs have a mix of activities associated with them, and each person finds some activities more interesting or appealing than others. However, learning can happen in every task through reflexive learning. You could reflect on questions such as these:

- How does engagement in the first phone contact with a service user provide the foundation for effective practice?
- How do the minutes I took reflect a social work bias or perspective?
- How can follow-up contacts impact service delivery?

### Integrative Seminars

Most social work programs will have a form of integrative seminar associated with field education. A seminar may be run as a class group, a virtual group, or sometimes on a one-to-one basis. The purpose of these seminars is in part for faculty liaisons to have contact with students to ensure that the field component is running smoothly. More importantly, these seminars provide an opportunity for students to ask for information or assistance when difficulties arise. In most cases, they are valuable opportunities for students to share their experiences, in a reflexive way, and learn from one another's practice.

Seminars, as a component of field education, are considered to be an important element of practice learning. Thus, social work values such as confidentiality and integrity remain paramount. Students are required to speak about service users, agencies, or community practices in ways that provide opportunities for learning, but protect the anonymity and privacy of those directly involved.

## Learning Plans

The primary goal in a student placement is learning. This includes learning why a task is done, understanding its purpose, and connecting it to a larger picture within the agency, the community, or social welfare initiatives. In addition, students are required to reflect critically and analyze situations within the theoretical lens they have been taught and within the current socio-political climate.

In most situations, students will begin their skill development through initial observation. During this time, students should identify skills that social work employees use, by connecting what they see to what they have learned, and asking questions at appropriate times. Once a trusting relationship between the students and supervisors has been developed, there is an opportunity to practise specific skills while being observed. In general, independent work is the final stage.

There are many factors associated with independent work with service users, but this only occurs in situations of low risk and when the agency supervisors are confident in the values, skills, and knowledge of the student.

Most schools require a learning plan, which identifies a conscious desire to seek knowledge and learning in specific areas and competencies. The learning plan may identify existing knowledge, values, and skills in order to identify further development particular to the field agency. Learning plans and goals may be particular to the school or setting, and will differ slightly from student to student. However, a starting point is to review the curriculum requirements of field education in your school, to review the standards of practice in your province, and to reflect on the meta-competencies introduced in Chapter 1. The final learning plan is usually developed by the student and approved by the agency supervisor and faculty liaison.

A learning plan (or learning contract) is simply a framework with mutually agreed upon performance standards. It should align with broader social work meta-competencies and specific learning goals associated with the student, the educational institution, and the field agency.

## Learning Goals

Learning goals outline what one intends to do, provide examples of tasks or activities that will be undertaken to achieve the goals, and identify the method that will be used to evaluate the goals. For example:

- **Goal 1:** Conduct myself as a professional social worker.
  - Dress appropriately, have a professional demeanour, and use social media appropriately.
  - Participate in self-reflection through journalling and agency supervision.
  - Establish boundaries appropriately.

  *Evaluation:* Agency supervisor, journal entries, examples of boundary setting

- **Goal 2:** Advance human rights and social justice initiatives.
  - Participate in the community's "16 days of activism against gender-based violence."
  - Identify examples of micro-level work that could be framed as a human rights violation.

  *Evaluation:* Information presented in seminar on "16 days" and journal entries

## Reflexive Journalling as Self-Care

In Chapter 1, the value of starting a learning journal, or reflexive journal, as a way of deepening learning and understanding was introduced. Some schools of social work require a learning journal, and may provide some guiding questions, while others recommend one. In both cases, confidentiality guidelines should be adhered to. Journalling provides an insightful and powerful means of fostering understanding, applying concepts, enhancing critical thinking, improving achievement and attitudes, and changing perceptions (Dunlap, 2006).

Many social workers use journalling throughout their career as a component of an ongoing wellness and self-care plan. Identifying positive experiences in your journal can build confidence and strengthen your practice. These are reflections that you can return to on "down days." Seeing self-growth can also help reduce stress and anxiety in more challenging times. It is important to ensure the journalling is a "letting-go" process, one that provides space for positive growth and contentment. ■

# Reflection, Learning, and More Practice

## Field Education Practicalities

1. In preparation for developing your learning plan, locate the learning contract outline for your program and review the learning goals associated with field education. It is also a good idea to review the evaluation tool that will be used in your field education.

2. Write out two or three learning goals that you would like to discuss with your field education supervisor.

3. As you enter your field agency, review your existing social work knowledge and the theories you encountered during your formal education.

## Journal Ideas

1. Spend some time making notes on your emotional responses to external events, and write a journal entry on your reflections. Under what circumstances were you aware of your emotional self-regulation? Conclude with thoughts on how to use emotions in decision-making.

2. Review some of the social work textbooks you have used in the past, and make a list of the theories that you have covered. Write a brief summary of each theory.

3. Recall a recent practice experience (from previous practicum or volunteer experience) where you felt positive about your work. (Or choose a situation that is troubling you.) In your learning journal, complete an ITP loop (retrieval, reflection, linkage, and professional response).

4. identify a situation you have experienced and write a journal entry, ensuring explicit linkage to theory.

## Critical-Thinking Questions

1. Describe how a social work perspective toward individuals in need differs from a psychological or counselling perspective. What are the similarities and differences between social work and psychology?

2. What is it about social work that appeals to you and your professional goals?

3. If a person is seeking help for anxiety and depression, how would the approach by a social worker be similar to, or different from, that of a psychologist?

4. Could a public health approach to the current opioid crisis be helpful? What would that look like?

5. Review the DME framework. Debate its strengths and weaknesses with a colleague or your field supervisor. Discuss the ability of this framework to incorporate multiple sources of "evidence."

6. Many provincial and territorial jurisdictions have undertaken, or are in a process of developing, practice guidelines. Review the practice guidelines in your province or territory, and identify strengths and gaps.

7. What are some of the practices you have witnessed or read about that would seem to reflect the application of post-colonial theory with Indigenous peoples?

# Chapter Review

Social work students develop the competency of critical thinking as they adapt their classroom knowledge to unique service users in a myriad of practice settings. Choosing a particular intervention for a given situation is not easy, given the huge range of theories that students are introduced to.

There are multiple ways of developing critical thinking as a meta-competency. However, they all require reflexivity about choosing the theory and knowledge most suitable for a specific set of circumstances in practice. Ultimately, social work practice is complex and requires an integration of skills, knowledge, values, self-awareness, and self-regulation.

Social workers and students develop critical thinking in different ways. Fran recognized her unconscious emotions as a trigger to paying attention to the theories she was applying to Austin's situation. Kelly was given the freedom by her agency supervisor to develop a professional relationship without background knowledge that may have impeded her relationship-building skills.

The practice of reflexive journal writing develops critical thinking as one explains one's practice. It can also be beneficial to develop resilience and self-care in relation to the emotional demands of the job.

In the practice scenarios in this chapter, critical thinking emerges in different ways. In each of the situations, a variety of responses are possible, depending on one's approach. But in each situation, one has to pay attention to one's own biases and values, and the underlying theoretical perspectives, in order to make a decision about the most appropriate practice.

By now, you are probably feeling more comfortable with your field agency, and you should be thinking about your own learning goals and starting your learning journal.

## Employing Critical Thinking in Practice

This chapter outlines numerous ways in which students can employ critical thinking in practice situations. Here are some highlights and further suggestions:

- Recognize the recursive relationship between theory and practice.

- Understand that social workers weigh the relative importance of multiple sources of knowledge in practice decision-making.

- Be prepared for emotional responses to service situations.

- Understand how multiple factors, including the organizational context, influence decisions about service delivery and referrals.

- Consider the pros and cons of reading written reports prior to meeting a service user.

- Review written reports in order to become aware of inherent bias and for examples of anti-oppressive recordings.

- Pay attention to tacit or intuitive knowledge and unconscious emotions in practice.

- Recognize the importance of spirituality as an aspect of connected practice.

- Practise in anti-oppressive ways in Indigenous communities by adopting the stance of a learner in relation to cultural and traditional beliefs.

- Examine the use of "evidence" in practice guidelines.

- Pay attention to discourse that uses dualisms (e.g., normal/abnormal), and understand that such discourse presents two extremes on a continuum of multiple diversity.

# Adhering to Social Work Values and Ethics

## 3

> *Real integrity is doing the right thing, knowing that nobody's going to know whether you did it or not.*
>
> —**Oprah Winfrey,** American media executive, television host, publisher, and philanthropist

# Chapter at a Glance

# Spotlight on Social Work Luminaries
## Bridget Moran

**Bridget Moran** (1923–1999) was a prominent social activist in British Columbia, best known for her award-winning biography *Sai'k'uz Ts'eke: Stoney Creek Woman* and her memoir *A Little Rebellion*, which recounts her disputes with government and her advocacy for children as a child-protection social worker.

C odes of ethics unify a profession and at the same time provide assurances of competency to the public. At the centre of social work practice and decision-making in Canada is the Canadian Association of Social Workers (CASW) *Code of Ethics* (2005a). This code provides a framework to ensure that all social workers practise from a core set of values and principles, even though specific areas of practice may vary. The CASW *Guidelines for Ethical Practice* (2005b), a companion document, provides further clarity on decision-making.

Students graduating from an accredited Canadian social work program are expected to demonstrate the capacity to incorporate values and ethical standards into their professional interactions. Field education provides a real-life opportunity in which to begin to think through ethical issues in a practice context.

This chapter focuses on the application of ethical principles in social work practice. These principles include the centrality of the professional relationship and key values such as self-determination, confidentiality and privacy, and cultural safety. Common issues of boundary violations, reporting child maltreatment, and the use of technology are also discussed.

**Key Concepts**

- CASW *Code of Ethics*
- CASW *Guidelines for Ethical Practice*
- Right to self-determination
- Confidentiality and privacy
- Boundary violations
- Ethical transgressions
- Ethical decision-making models

## Developing Competence as a Social Worker

Some ways to develop the meta-competency of "**adhering to social work values and ethics**" are as follows:

- Identify the kinds of ethical dilemmas and tensions that are typical in your field practice area, and discuss with a field supervisor how competing decisions and actions are managed within the agency.

- Be conscious of offering all the choices and options available in a situation (including ones you are biased against) as a way of ensuring self-determination for the service user.

- Identify and discuss with field colleagues any ethical dilemmas or tensions that arise.

- Practise using a formal ethical decision-making model.

- Develop a self-care plan to manage the emotional complexity of work–home stressors and dilemmas.

# Ethical Dilemmas in Everyday Practice

The principles of ethical practice are outlined in the **CASW *Code of Ethics*** and the **CASW *Guidelines for Ethical Practice***. At their core is the development of a professional relationship between the social worker and the service user. Depending on the type of practice and the nature of this relationship, social workers may need to make difficult choices between competing ethical imperatives. Three common ethical dilemmas in social work are described below.

### 1. Involuntary Service Users

Many social workers practise in child welfare, justice, or adult guardianship. These are areas in which an individual is required by law to engage with a social worker. Ethical dilemmas can arise with these "involuntary users." In some cases, they may be resistant or lack motivation to change, or even be openly hostile. In these situations, the social worker has a dual role to navigate—a legalistic or surveillance role and a helping, therapeutic, and problem-solving role (Trotter, 2015).

Balancing and coming to terms with these potentially conflicting demands can be especially challenging from an ethical point of view.

### 2. Voluntary Service Users in Crisis

Another type of ethical dilemma can arise when an individual in crisis exhibits panic, dread, or pressure that results in a heightened emotional state in the social worker. This heightened emotional state may affect the social worker's ability to make sound judgements and take appropriate actions.

For example, a service user in crisis shows extreme anger and frustration about not getting enough help. In such a situation, some social workers may respond through a "power" lens, simply stating that agency policy prohibits them from providing a particular resource at this time. Still others may respond more empathetically, understanding that the service user's anger is likely a response to lack of control, and decide to use a problem-solving model to look at the options available. Or, the social worker may use a crisis-intervention approach and, after assessing imminent danger, move to build a more collaborative relationship with that individual and evaluate possible coping strategies (Taylor, 2010).

### 3. Voluntary Service Users in Need

A different kind of ethical dilemma can arise when providing personal services to a service user on an individual basis, knowing full well that broader social injustices are the ultimate source of the problem. For example, social workers frequently find themselves distributing food at food banks. Most would argue that the solution is for there to be a food security program for everyone. On the other hand, providing food basics to people is often a matter of urgency. The natural response to help individuals meet their physiological needs is consistent with Abraham Maslow's hierarchy of needs, but it could also be viewed as being in conflict with the guiding ethical principle of confronting social injustice (Taylor, 2010).

The importance of being able to apply the social work CASW *Code of Ethics* (2005a) is underscored in the second core learning objective of the CASWE-ACFTS *Standards for Accreditation* (Canadian Association for Social Work Education–Association canadienne pour la formation en travail social [CASWE-ACFTS], 2014):

2. Adhere to social work values and ethics in professional practice.

i) Social work students have knowledge of the relevant social work codes of ethics in various professional roles and activities and institutional contexts, with a particular emphasis on professional responsibilities towards vulnerable or disadvantaged groups.

ii) Social work students acquire skills to monitor and evaluate their own behaviours in relation to the relevant codes of ethics.

## Professional Regulation and Competency

The Canadian Council of Social Work Regulators (CCSWR, 2012, p. 10) competency profile includes the following competency block on "applying ethical standards":

1. Identify ethical considerations related to the problem or needs being addressed.

2. Determine whether a planned course of action is consistent with professional ethics.

### Act ethically:

3. Act in accordance with the regulatory framework for social work practice.

4. Evaluate professional and organizational policies, procedures, and materials to assure adherence to social work ethics.

5. Follow appropriate protocols for seeking assistance when facing conflict in the workplace.

6. Ensure the proper handling and storing of information (including information transmitted electronically) to protect confidentiality.

7. Recognize and manage personal values in a way that allows professional values to guide practice.

8. Identify and manage conflicts of interest and/or dual relationships with service users or former service users.

9. Establish and maintain clear and appropriate boundaries in professional relationships.

### Bring ethical transgressions to the attention of relevant parties:

10. Address conflicts of interest with relevant parties.

11. Inform service users when a real or potential conflict of interest arises, and take reasonable steps to resolve the issue in a manner that makes the service user's interests primary.

12. Report alleged abuse and neglect in compliance with laws and social work ethics.

13. Identify and address inappropriate behaviour or discriminatory practices.

14. Identify ethical violations and take appropriate action.

### Advocate for and engage in practices to further human rights and social justice:

15. Advocate for service users' right to autonomy and self-determination.

16. Protect individuals from the undue influences and abusive use of power.

17. Identify linkages between situation/problem and life conditions, with particular attention to issues of oppression and discrimination.

18. Analyze, formulate, and advocate for policies that advance social justice and well-being.

19. Advocate for policies and services sensitive to diversity issues.

20. Advocate for the equitable access of all persons to resources, services, and opportunities.

21. Advocate for appropriate resources.

22. Identify how a culture's structures and values may oppress, marginalize, alienate, or create or enhance privilege and power.

## Association of Social Work Boards (ASWB)

The ASWB is a non-profit organization composed of social work Regulatory Colleges in Canada and the United States.

The ASWB BSW exam is required to show minimum competency in some jurisdictions.

The exam has 19% of its weighting on professional relationships, values, and ethics. It comprises (a) ethical responsibility to the service users and profession; (b) confidentiality, and (c) the service user's right to self-determination. ∎

# The Ethical Foundations of Social Work Practice

**Right to self-determination**

Self-determination is an ethical principle that requires respecting and promoting the rights and needs of service users to be free to make their own decisions.

Social workers promote this right by assisting service users in their efforts to identify and clarify their goals.

The core ethical values of social work are introduced in the early stages of social work education and seem relatively simple to understand, at least in theory. As one progresses through field education and into career pathways, the nuances and complexities of ethical practice become more pronounced.

## Self-Determination

The ethical principle of a person's **right to self-determination** (the right to make their own decisions) is ingrained in social work values. Although seemingly straightforward, the concept of self-determination is often ambiguous in everyday practice, and in recent years increasingly so (O'Hara, Weber, & Levine, 2016).

Practitioners are challenged to respect and uphold the principle of self-determination when working with service users whose concept of what is good for them differs from that of social workers (Dolgoff, Harrington, & Loewenberg, 2012). Self-determination becomes even more complex when providing services to minors, or vulnerable populations, and when the administrative or organizational policies and context are factored in.

Dolgoff, Harrington, & Loewenberg (2012) suggest that professionals can only truly promote individual freedom, autonomy, and the right to self-determination if the following conditions exist:

- The context provides more than one option from which a person can make a choice;
- There is no coercion on the person from any source to choose one or another option;
- The person is aware of all the available options;
- The person has accurate information about the cost and consequences of each option so that they can assess them realistically;
- The person has the capacity and/or initiative to make a decision on the basis of this assessment; and,
- The person has an opportunity to act on the basis of his or her choice (p. 100).

An emerging challenge for social workers is respecting self-determination when working with end-of-life decisions. Social workers have long been at the forefront of hospice and palliative care, and have supported individuals and families in the grieving and loss associated with end of life. With physician-assisted dying now legal in Canada, social workers may find that they have substantial roles to play in working through such situations with service users and their families, and their physicians and health advocates.

Social workers practising in this area have to balance their personal values with those of the service user and family to ensure that the ethic of self-determination is upheld in a non-coercive and non-manipulative way.

# Indigenous Worldviews, Values, and Ethics
## "Everything Is Shared"

Practising in respectful and culturally safe ways with Indigenous service users requires social workers to recognize that Indigenous values and practices are unique and often different from Western values and practices.

For example, values associated with Indigenous worldviews include community (taking care of one another); viewing time as relative; respect for age (Elders); cooperation; patience; listening, generosity, and sharing; living in harmony; giving indirect criticism; humility; spiritual existence, intuition; and the interconnectedness of the mind, body, and spirit (Baskin, 2016). In addition, Indigenous worldviews recognize that all animate and inanimate beings have a spirit, and therefore respect for the environment around us is a moral responsibility.

These values can contrast sharply with the more prevalent Western values and practices of individualism (taking care of oneself); timeliness; competitiveness; aggressiveness; speaking up and being heard; materialism; conquests over nature; giving direct criticism; self-attention (egocentrism); and the separation of the mind, body, and spirit.

### The Principle of Non-interference

Mainstream social work practice is about interfering or intervening. People are often told what services to access, how to care for themselves, how to raise their children, and how to manage their relationships.

On the other hand, non-interference is a value associated with Indigenous peoples. It is about

> not getting in the way of another person's journey or process or preventing someone from doing something simply because we do not agree with it. It means not giving advice, not being directive, and not participating in another person's process unless invited to do so. (Baskin, 2016, p. 129)

### The Principle of Generosity and Sharing

Individualism is a core value in Western social work practice—a person's difficulties are associated with the individual person or family, and the solution involves working one-on-one to get that individual or family back on the right track.

By contrast, Indigenous perspectives view practice that focuses on one person or family as reinforcing isolation. Baskin (2016) points out that mainstream practice reinforces conditions of isolation (which is often a larger part of the problem) and, further, puts the wider community at risk. She argues that "by not bringing the collective together, we are missing out on many helpful possibilities, suggestions, and opportunities that might help us to assist one another" (p. 129).

### The Principle of Self-Determination

The principle of self-determination likewise has a different meaning in the Indigenous context.

In a personal communication to the author, Dionne Mohammed, an Indigenous colleague explains the complexity of applying the value of self-determination in Indigenous communities:

> An Indigenous person's place in the community is determined by how their strengths can be utilized to aid the community as a whole—not just oneself. The adults and Elders notice the strengths in the young and then guide them into areas where they can contribute to the community and mature.

In other words, the "self" part of self-determination does not align with ethical protocols in Indigenous communities. Dionne pointed out that seeking to enforce the principle of self-determination may well be met with resistance, if not perplexity. ■

Confidentiality and
privacy

Confidentiality is an
ethical responsibility
to not divulge personal
information; privacy is a
right entrenched in law to
ensure that service users
control how their personal
information is collected,
used, and disclosed.

## Confidentiality and Privacy

The ethical concept of **confidentiality and privacy** applies to all health and social service professions. As service users share personal information, the responsibility for maintaining confidentiality and privacy increases. The safeguards around privacy have become increasingly complex, as many agencies and organizations now have interconnected databases of service user information that many professionals have access to.

To ensure there is respect for the service user's rights to confidentiality and privacy, Schulz (1994) recommends remembering the three Rs:

- **Rapport.** Developing and maintaining good working relationships with service users not only helps with decisions regarding how to deal with a problem at hand, but also can provide some immunity to problems related to confidentiality. If the social worker is able to build genuine trust with the service user, then that is half the battle.

- **Reasonable behaviour.** There may be situations where a social worker must break confidentiality and consult with colleagues and supervisors. In its simplest form, "reasonable behaviour" is consistent with the norms of practice—other practitioners would perform similarly in the same situation.

- **Rights and duties of informed consent.** The rights and duties of informed consent build on the freedom of service users to make choices that directly affect them. Service users should be made aware of those rights and duties at the beginning of any professional relationship.

The issues of confidentiality and privacy have become especially prominent in recent years, due to the widespread capture of private information and the ubiquitous use of information technology. With the troubling releases of vast quantities of personal information from government databases and web platforms to private agents, confidentiality and privacy may have become the most important ethical concern of the day. Social workers have a duty to disclose their policies related to privacy and confidentiality to services users.

Social workers providing any electronic services (e.g., Internet, social media sites, text messaging, websites, and videoconferencing) must strictly adhere to privacy and confidentiality guidelines and maintain all proper electronic safeguards. These safeguards include securing data through the use of firewalls, encryption software, and password protection. Then there is also the broader issue of informing service users of any third-party services that may have access to their information and being aware of the implications of laws such as the US Patriot Act in the case of cloud-based storage servers. It is good practice to seek guidance from information technology (IT) specialists on such matters. Social workers who develop professional websites have a special responsibility to ensure that the privacy of service user information is strictly maintained.

In addition, all social workers who access search engines regarding any aspect of the service user's care must document such research in the service user's record.

# "Informed Consent" in Quebec
## Supporting Persons with Intellectual Disabilities

The ethical principle of "informed consent" is entrenched in Quebec health-care law, which includes informed consent for people with intellectual disabilities.

The issues and concepts in relation to obtaining consent to care for persons with intellectual disabilities are vast and numerous, although there is minimal research and few practice guidelines that social workers can draw upon to guide their decision-making.

Informed consent is concerned with voluntariness and capacity. In some situations, services may be provided without consent. In these cases, the "Nova Scotia Criteria" have been recognized by the Supreme Court of Canada and, in Quebec, by the Court of Appeal of Quebec as criteria for court-ordered mental health treatment. These criteria appear in the Involuntary Psychiatric Treatment Act (2007) of Nova Scotia.

### The Nova Scotia Criteria

According to Nova Scotia Mental Health Services (2017):

> The Act is about making sure that those who are unable to make treatment decisions, due to their severe mental illness, receive the appropriate treatment. . . . The Involuntary Psychiatric Treatment Act is appropriate when someone with a mental disorder:
>
> - as a result of the mental disorder
>   - is threatening or attempting to be or has recently been a danger to him/herself or others; or
>   - is likely to suffer serious physical impairment or serious mental deterioration or both;
> - lacks capacity to make decisions about his or her care,
> - requires care in a psychiatric facility and cannot be admitted voluntarily.

### Capacity, Consent, and Refusal

In many parts of the world, persons with intellectual disabilities are discriminated against in terms of their right to make decisions for themselves regarding their health, wellness, and living environment.

In 2012, a Clinical-Legal Intervention Committee (CLIC) was established at the largest rehabilitation centre for people with intellectual disabilities in Quebec. The committee's purpose was to guide and support clinical teams with respect to situations where capacity, consent, and refusal constitute a major issue for the person with intellectual disabilities.

As with all ethical principles, informed consent for persons with intellectual disabilities must take into account the context. Caux and Lecomte (2017) caution about applying the Nova Scotia Criteria in a general manner, as it lacks nuance. They suggest that the capacity to consent to care must be adapted to each different context or intervention:

> The fitness of people with ID [intellectual disabilities] to consent to care, especially in the case of psychosocial care, can vary according to the person receiving the care, the person offering it, or even to the time of day the care is offered. (p. 464)

For example, a person with intellectual disabilities may be deemed incapable of making decisions in certain areas of civilian life, but be perfectly capable of consenting (or not) to psychosocial interventions such as moving to a new residential resource or accepting a new support service.

Furthermore, while people with intellectual disabilities may be unable to consent to care by themselves, they may be perfectly fit to do so with the support of a significant friend or family member. ■

## Boundary violations

Crossing boundaries in professional relationships usually occurs insidiously and without mal-intent. Social workers who practise by always focusing on the service user's well-being have less risk of violating professional boundaries. Of course, any form of sexual interaction with service users is a clear boundary violation.

## Boundary Violations, Dual Relationships, and Conflicts of Interest

The ethical principle to maintain clear and unambiguous boundaries with service users is thoroughly taught in schools of social work. However, like many other ethical principles, it can become more difficult to implement in practice.

**Boundary violations** refer to a wide range of behaviours that breach the core intent of the relationship with the service user and become coercive, manipulative, deceptive, or exploitative. Dual relationships involve boundary violations in which the professional exploits the relationship to meet personal needs rather than service user needs (Reamer, 2013).

It is often difficult to avoid dual and multiple relationships completely, particularly in small, remote communities. Examples in remote community practice settings might include:

- Calling a mechanic service to your home for a car problem, and the mechanic is a current service user

- Being the only counsellor in town, and your partner's colleague requests an appointment

- Being in hospital yourself, and the nurse assigned to you is a service user

- Volunteering in an after-school social group for elementary children, and one of the children also attends professional counselling with you

Reamer (2013) refers to this as "boundary crossing" or "boundary bending," which he describes as a social worker's involvement in a dual relationship with a service user that is not necessarily coercive, manipulative, deceptive, or exploitative, and not inherently unethical.

Reamer (2013) describes some of the more common boundary violations from which social workers can personally benefit. They include marketing personal care or other therapeutic services to service users; making oneself too available to service users in order to better cope with one's own personal feelings of social isolation or loneliness; and allowing altruistic feelings to override therapeutic needs, such as by giving service users one's home telephone number, gifts, or personalized and affectionate notes.

Of course, maintaining boundaries in the digital age is even more complex. For example, social workers using digital technology need to be forthcoming with service users about their policies related to electronic communication between formal appointments, after normal working hours, during emergencies, and during their vacations.

Additionally, social workers have a responsibility to take reasonable steps to prevent service user access to their personal social networking sites. To this end, social workers should maintain separate professional and personal social media and websites, including separate email addresses that are not work-related, in order to establish clear personal–professional boundaries and avoid inappropriate dual relationships.

## Ethics and Diversity

It is only recently that ethical standards have incorporated principles related to social and cultural diversity. Social workers now recognize that key ethical concepts (such as privacy, self-determination, boundary violations, and informed consent) may vary depending on the specific context and on the ethnic and cultural groups involved. Attending to such differences is a continuously reflexive process.

Reamer and Nimmagadda (2017) provide a good example of the cultural and ethical differences associated with social work in India, which in turn can inform working with South Asian populations in Canada. In India, social work is rooted in cultural values of *Rgveda* (the idea that a cosmic order stands for harmony and balance in nature and in human society), the idea of *Dharma* (ethical concepts of duty, obligation, and righteousness), and the core values of *Bhakti* (humanism and individual worth and dignity), *Sarvodaya* (value of equity, justice, and empowerment) and the spirit of *Swarajya* (promotion of self-governance). These values resonate with traditional social work values.

However, the Western notion of a democratic partnership between provider and service user can become confusing when service users place social workers on a proverbial pedestal. For example, the principle of self-determination can be confusing in a society like India where the social worker is expected to offer advice as opposed to following the service user's leads and wishes.

Issues of confidentiality can become even more complex within a cultural context. Reamer and Nimmagadda (2017) provide the example of a social worker in India being asked whether a particular male, a potential marriage partner, is of "good character." The social worker, in this situation, is caught between the duty to the service user and the protection of a third party (the potential bride).

Boundary issues and dual relationships may also become more complicated in a cultural context. Social workers in an Indian context may receive invitations to social, religious, and life-cycle events. Not accepting such invitations may be seen as disrespectful. Social workers need to have a more flexible and subtle approach when faced with such situations.

Racialized social workers and racialized social work students, who may have been constituted as "other" by society at large, can experience unique dilemmas and tensions in practice (Badwall, 2014). They may experience blatant racism; for example, when a service user refuses to work with them or makes racist comments during an appointment. Such shocking and painful moments can be made worse by a colleague's unsupportive response to stay "client-focused, empathic, and critically reflexive about their professional power" (p. 2). An ethical dilemma arises when the imperative to be "empathic and client-centred" takes precedence over addressing overt racism, especially when social work education stresses the importance of practice being firmly rooted in the pursuit of social justice (Badwall, 2014).

# Social Worker Exemplar

# Reporting Child Abuse

## Connie Macadam

**A common dilemma for social workers is whether or not to report suspected child harm to a statutory authority.**

Connie is a social worker with 12 years of experience under her belt. She has seen a lot and helped a lot of individuals and families in the course of her career.

In this instance, Connie had a good professional relationship with multiple members of a family. However, the stepfather had serious substance-use issues, which on occasion had led to family violence. Making a child-abuse report may have serious consequences for her ability to provide ongoing services to the family.

What was she to do?

I first met the Andrews family when Grace came in due to concerns about her substance-using partner, Ed. Grace and Ed were in their 50s, both working at a local mine. Both had their own children.

Ed's children did not live with them, but Grace's daughter (Stephanie) did. Grace did not use psychoactive substances of any kind and was increasingly frustrated at Ed's drinking and recreational drug use. For his part, Ed did not acknowledge having any problems, and told Grace repeatedly that "if she was just a little less aggravating, and would stop pushing his buttons, then his drinking would reduce."

After about three months, Grace dropped out of counselling, only to reappear a year later. Meanwhile, Ed's heavy drinking continued. The previous week, she and Ed had a physical altercation that resulted in the police being called and Ed being removed from the house for the night. Grace said that this was not the first time, but it was the worst. She was particularly worried because Stephanie, who was 14 at the time, was home and heard it all.

Grace was also concerned about Stephanie, then in grade 8, who was getting into trouble at school. Stephanie had aligned herself with a group of known drug users. Her grades had begun to slip, and she was increasingly defiant toward her mother and Ed.

I met with Grace several more times. Against my recommendations, she chose to have Ed return to the house. One condition of Ed's return was that he attend counselling, which he promptly started. He joined AA and was having some success, both with his sobriety goals and anger management.

About a year later, Grace returned with Stephanie. Stephanie was now 15 and in grade 9, but had been suspended for smoking marijuana. Stephanie agreed to see me individually and indicated that she wanted to attend a youth treatment centre. She ended up attending a 30-day program, and her after-care plan included continuing with family counselling.

Grace and Ed had attended the final week of the treatment program with Stephanie, and all three had made remarkable changes. All were hopeful. I saw them as a family group, and I also saw Stephanie separately for a short time. Then I lost contact again.

## An Obligation to Protect

Some months later, Stephanie returned. She was using substances again, although maintaining her grades at school and not in trouble with the police or school. However, this time Stephanie was concerned about her mother and Ed, who was also using again and becoming increasingly violent.

During the interview, I asked Stephanie whether Ed had assaulted her. Her teary response was that he had. She had been the brunt of a lot of verbal abuse from Ed for many months, and he had now turned to physical abuse. The previous night, she received a black eye while trying to prevent Ed from punching her mother.

I remember feeling emotionally devastated on hearing all this. I had grown close to the family and the progress I felt they had made. Obviously, I was sad to hear about the violence and Stephanie now being a victim. I was sad to hear that Ed had lost his sobriety yet again. And I was sad for Grace, who was once again in the throes of family violence and chaos.

This was clearly a serious issue that could not be taken lightly. Both the substance use and family violence were increasing in quantity and intensity. Stephanie, along with other family members, had previously signed informed consent forms multiple times (although all except Stephanie's had expired once the files were closed). Stephanie signed a new informed consent form that day.

Legally, Stephanie was a minor, and this was clearly child abuse. It had to be reported. However, I also knew that a report can create more chaos for everyone, at least in the short term. Stephanie did not want a report to be made to the children's ministry and became visibly upset when this was raised. I was fairly sure that I could assume that neither Grace nor Ed would want it reported.

A professional report to child protection was required by law. I wanted to make a decision that incorporated Stephanie's self-determination. At the same time, I needed to address the risks to her safety and the legal responsibilities placed on me as her social worker.

The decision to submit a report to child protection was difficult, but it was one I had to make nevertheless. ∎

## Reflections on Connie's Story

This was a situation where personal and professional relationships were confounding decision-making. The file was formally closed, but that didn't take away from the emotional relationship already established with the family.

In reviewing this situation, there were a number of ethical principles to consider. Stephanie had the right to self-determination, and did not want a report made. She trusted Connie to help and didn't believe that a report to the ministry would assist her.

In terms of confidentiality and privacy, however, Stephanie had signed an informed consent form that included reporting harm to children. Since Stephanie was formally the only service user of three involved with agency at the time, Connie had to ensure that no information from the work with Grace and Ed would be disclosed in any reporting to the ministry.

### From Theory to Practice

As you reflect on Connie's story, give some thought to the following points:

1. Was Connie in a dual relationship or bending boundaries? How does one manage dual relationships in family work when there are multiple individuals?

2. In what way was Connie using a complex practice model, intentionally or not, to work through the underlying issues in this situation (integrating theory/knowledge, self-regulation, skills, and judgement)? See the discussion of complex practice behaviour models on page 35 for reference.

3. Do you think you would have felt an ethical dilemma if you had been in this situation? If so, which ethical principles do you think were in conflict?

4. Was there anything Connie could have done earlier on in the relationships with this family to minimize the conflicts she ended up facing?

# Ethics and Technology

Social workers today are living in an age characterized by massive computerization of information and a plethora of ways to stay informed and connected. The use of electronic technology has changed the way in which social workers practise in virtually every area.

Nowadays, social workers can provide services to service users through online counselling, telephone counselling, video counselling, cybertherapy (avatar therapy), self-guided web-based interventions, social networks, email, and text messages. The possibilities are endless, as are the risks.

## Weighing Risks and Benefits

While technology offers many benefits to service users, particularly in relation to accessibility, its use is fraught with ethical risks and challenges. Indeed, the use of social media today is so integrated into one's personal and professional life that, even when there is an awareness of the risks involved, ethical breaches can be made unwittingly.

Consider, for example, the following online activities by students:

- A student attends the practicum orientation interview and posts on Facebook that it was awful.
- A student is dismayed about a mark on a recent paper and posts on Facebook that she wishes the instructor were dead.
- A student takes a Snapchat video during a classroom presentation and sends it to friends with a humorous commentary.

All of these posts were seen by the victims and/or instructors within 24 hours and had serious ramifications for the students involved. Before you post online, ask yourself these questions: Would I want someone to post this about me? Would I be okay if my mother saw this? Would I want this picture to appear in the news?

Social workers will encounter many such dilemmas throughout their practice. Despite their best efforts to be ethical in every situation, all social workers will contravene their code of ethics from time to time. Typical examples include speaking about a service user to a social work friend, inadvertent administrative fraud, such as taking office supplies home, calling in sick when not too sick, and not respecting a service user fully. In most cases, these are lapses in judgement that can, and should, be self-regulated so as to be non-recurring.

Sometimes, however, a transgression may have deeper roots, such as "compassion fatigue" or burnout. In this case, the inappropriate ethical behaviour or misconduct may continue over time and require supportive intervention by supervisors and colleagues.

Although rare, egregious acts of unethical conduct may warrant disciplinary action.

## Avoiding Ethical Transgressions

**Ethical transgressions** can occur inadvertently, but social workers are nevertheless accountable to their supervisors, managers, their professional associations, and even judicial inquiries. It is important, therefore, to have a systematic and deliberate way of working through ethical issues and risks.

Typical challenges include deciding how to respond to a request to "friend" or follow a service user on a social media platform, deciding whether to post information related to work with service users on a blog, and deciding whether to use service user exemplars on a workplace website (CASW, 2014).

Ethical transgressions online, particularly through social media, could affect one's employment and even one's social work career. To reduce the ethical risks in using social media, the CASW (2014) recommends these steps:

- **Consultation.** Discuss with colleagues the ethical challenges of using social media, and consider different strategies to mitigate risks. These strategies should always prioritize the best interests of the service user.

- **Privacy and confidentiality.** Recognize the responsibility of maintaining service-user privacy when any information shared on social media is part of the public domain.

- **Models for ethical decision-making.** Explore the various models of ethical decision-making and make use of them as necessary.

- **Policies and guidelines.** Become familiar with relevant provincial/territorial standards on social media use in practice.

- **Social media operations.** Become familiar with operational policies of websites and social media sites, and ensure your own privacy settings are set to the highest levels.

- **Documentation.** Document conversations with service users pertaining to social media.

- **Boundaries.** Recognize when boundaries are being challenged when using social media.

- **Informed consent.** Inform service users about your organization's professional social media policy.

- **Explore your online identity.** Find out what information may be available about you online by periodically engaging in an Internet search.

- **Develop your own risk management guidelines.** It is important to stay current with social media platforms as they evolve and change.

These recommendations are not intended to be exhaustive, or entirely prescriptive. Instead, they seek to provide social workers with a degree of clarity on how to interpret and apply ethical values and principles in relation to social media, and how to avoid unnecessary risks.

Social workers are encouraged to consult their provincial/territorial regulatory body or professional association for specific guidelines on the use of social media and information technology in general in their jurisdiction.

**Ethical transgressions**

Rarely does an individual engage in a major act of unethical behaviour without making smaller ethical transgressions along the way. Ethical social workers take a preventive approach by recognizing the "slippery slope" conditions, experienced in everyday practice, associated with ethical misconduct.

Ethical decision-
making models

Ethical decision-making
models provide a
framework, or process,
to engage in when one
is faced with an ethical
dilemma or conflict.
Social workers in practice
tend to use a variety of
models heuristically.
However, the more
challenging the situation,
the more important
it is to use a formal
decision-making model.

# Ethical Decision-Making Models

Ethical issues, as taught in the classroom, are typically presented as being relatively clear-cut; in practice, they are usually much more complicated. For this reason, it is recommended that social workers have at hand a deliberative and more systematic way to work through their reactions and biases as they seek to resolve ethical dilemmas.

For help in this regard, a number of scholars have come up with **ethical decision-making models** that can provide a more structured way of working through an ethical dilemma.

### Reamer's Ethical Decision-Making Model

Reamer's ethical decision-making model (2013) draws on the arguments of moral philosophy, stressing the fundamental right of all human beings to freedom and well-being. This model is used, for example, by the Newfoundland and Labrador Association of Social Workers (2018). Briefly, the steps are as follows:

1. Define the problem and state the "dilemma equation" in terms of which values are in conflict.
2. Gather information from the code of ethics, agency policy, laws, research.
3. Consult with supervisors and colleagues, and perhaps receive legal recommendations.
4. Identify the available options and choices and the reasons in favour of, or against, each course of action.
5. Examine the context, cultural considerations, and impact on the professional relationship.
6. Make a decision and document the decision-making process (Reamer 2013).

### Mattison's Ethical Decision-Making Model

Mattison's ethical decision-making model (2000) includes a discretionary component. This model takes into account that social workers are influenced by their professional roles, practice experiences, individual perspectives and preferences, and cultural context. Her process for working through an ethical dilemma is as follows:

1. Fully explore the case details and gather needed information to understand the situation holistically.
2. Pay attention to ethnic-based traditions and the ways in which members of a group are likely to define and cope with problems.
3. Distinguish the practice aspects of the case from the ethical considerations.
4. Explicitly identify the value tensions (e.g., adolescent's right of self-determination or autonomy versus the parents' right to know).
5. Weigh and measure the possible courses of action that seem reasonable and the potential consequences of these.
6. Choose your course of action, document the decision, and be prepared to justify the decision.

## A Reflective Framework for Ethical Decision-Making

Of course, ethical decision-making requires reflection, as there is often much ambiguity and uncertainty when working with individuals, families, and communities. For this purpose, Beverley Antle, author of the CASW *Code of Ethics* (2005a), developed a reflective model for ethical decision-making centring around the concepts of risk and risk tolerance (Antle, 2005; Bridgeman & Johns, 2015).

The Antle (2005) model depicts how social workers continuously evaluate risks in the areas of service user self-determination, informed consent, capacity for decision-making, best interest of the service user, human rights, and legal and legislative responsibilities. Encouraging dialogue and discussions on risk and risk tolerance in these areas fosters reflection and critical thinking, which in turn can help both social workers and service users navigate the ethical complexities that seem to be inherent in social work practice.

Antle's reflective framework for ethical decision-making in social work practice is depicted in Figure 3.1.

**Figure 3.1** A Reflective Framework for Ethical Practice

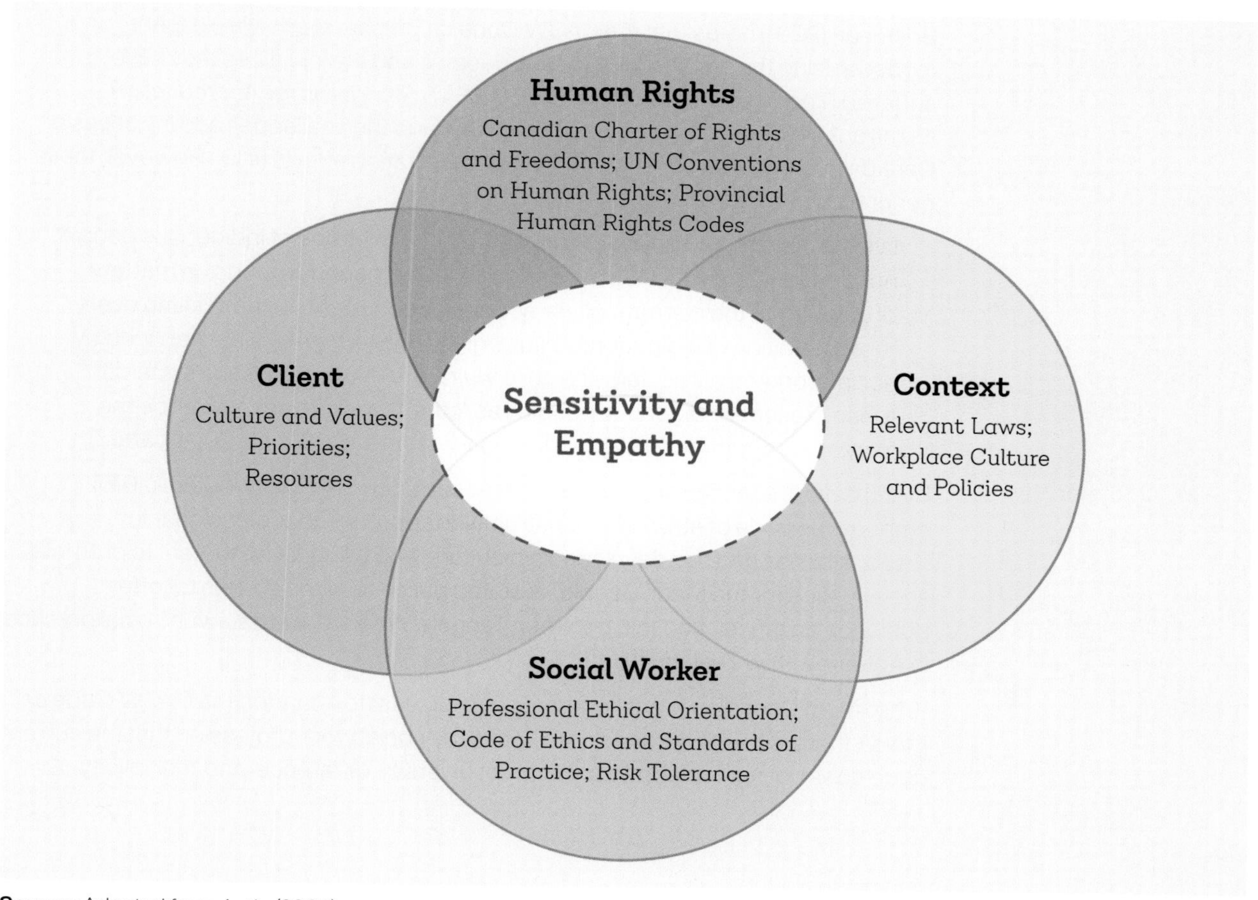

**Source:** Adapted from Antle (2005).

# Critical Practice and Codes of Ethics

The CASW *Code of Ethics* (2005a) is at the core of professional identity and decision-making in Canadian social work. However, for many practising social workers, the code does not fully represent the postmodern emphasis on power relations, difference, and diversity (Briskman, 2001).

### Power, Difference, and Diversity

The traditional approach to ethics has been between Kantian (principle-based) ethics and utilitarian (outcomes-based) ethics, both of which focus on universalistic principles. Banks (2008) argues for newer approaches, such as virtue ethics (focusing on qualities of character); ethics of care (focusing on caring relationships); communitarian ethics (focusing on community, responsibility, and cooperation); and pluralist, discursive, postmodern, or anti-theory approaches to ethics that eschew single, all-embracing theories. Banks (2008) suggests that social work ethics be informed by radical, transformative, and anti-oppressive approaches that take into account the full organizational, policy, political, and social context.

The shortcoming of traditional ("universalist") approaches to ethics and ethical decision-making is particularly poignant with respect to Indigenous peoples. Briskman (2001) notes that the CASW *Code of Ethics* is silent with respect to recognizing the rights of Indigenous peoples and the injustices they have suffered. The principles of the CASWE-ACFTS *Standards for Accreditation* (2014) acknowledge Indigenous peoples (#9) and the challenges and injustices of Canada's colonial history and continuing colonization efforts (#10). However, these general statements do not

> lament the place social work has had in the oppression of Indigenous people; nor does it specify the need to consult with Indigenous groups on matters of concern to their communities; nor does it comment on the existing over-representation of Indigenous children in the systems which are serviced by social workers, particularly the child welfare and juvenile justice systems. It also presents Indigenous peoples as "other," failing to acknowledge the increasing number of Indigenous social workers. (Briskman, 2001, para. 7)

By contrast, the Aotearoa New Zealand Association of Social Workers (2015) embeds the code of ethics in a constructivist approach to professional responsibilities and has developed a bicultural and bilingual document to promote social justice for the Maori people. A stated purpose of the code is to "offer guidance on the relationship between Tangata Whenua and Tauiwi in social practice in Aotearoa New Zealand" (p. 6).

While most Canadian practitioners would not want to abandon the CASW *Code of Ethics*, there is a widespread sense within the social work profession that the current code does not fully celebrate and accept diversity, difference, and multiplicity.

## The Complexity of Applying Ethical Decision-Making in Practice

The real-life application of ethical principles is highly complex and uncertain. This has led postmodern theorists to call into question the very idea of "universal values" and "all-embracing theories" (including ethical theories). By its very nature, they argue, ethical decision-making in social work is fraught with complex economic, political, organizational, and interpersonal issues.

A number of scholars have attempted to assess the role ethical concerns play in everyday social work practice. For example, Rossiter, Walsh-Bowers, and Auclair (1998) interviewed Canadian social workers about the use of ethics in their practice and found "that workers have very little time in which to discuss ethical questions. Moreover, even when practitioners do have the time, many are anxious about being judged as professionally inadequate by their superiors once they acknowledge ethical misgivings" (p. 6). Social workers seemed to have a tacit belief that they were expected to know how to answer ethical questions and, furthermore, that it was taboo to raise ethical concerns. Participants wanted safe spaces in which to discuss their ethical concerns. Rossiter and her colleagues also found that in practice, social workers didn't use ethical decision-making models, which may be related to time constraints in applying a step-by-step model.

In a more recent study, Marshall Fine and Eli Teram (2009) of Wilfrid Laurier University in Waterloo, Ontario, undertook research to gain a better understanding of the lived experiences of social workers in the course of making ethical decisions. Their respondents were grouped into two categories: the "Believers" (who used principle-based ethics) and the "Skeptics" (who used virtue-based ethics). The study found the following:

- **The Believers** generally abided by the code of ethics, even when they didn't agree with a particular principle.
- **The Skeptics** were more leery of the code of ethics, and took the position that the facts of the situations had to be viewed in context.

Not unexpectedly, the social workers who participated in the study were found to be thoughtful and caring. They reflected critically on their behaviours and were concerned about the welfare of service users. However, similar to the Rossiter et al. (1998) study, these social workers also noted their fear of dialogue, and of potential censure, around ethical issues and decision-making. Social workers in both groups found adhering strictly to the code of ethics difficult at times, and they identified the need for greater consultation and supervision on ethical issues.

Clearly, ethical decision-making (much like social work practice itself) occurs within a complex climate, with each situation raising unique concerns. Therefore, ethical decision-making is not simply a detached, problem-solving exercise. Instead, it is fundamentally a communicative process of understanding the applicability of ethical principles, values, and standards, for which consultation with colleagues is essential.

# Acknowledging Dual Relationships

Erika Picton

**Erika reflects on ethical dilemmas that she confronted in each of her two practicums, and draws important lessons for her future practice.**

Erika had to complete two practicums as part of her program. Little did she suspect that she would be faced with significant ethical dilemmas in each of the field placements.

Erika displayed honesty and integrity in both instances, and she was able to learn from her encounters and move on in her career.

Erika was hired immediately upon graduation.

Within the first three weeks of my first practicum, I was asked to visit a number of other agencies that my field agency regularly networked with in order to become familiar with their work. At one agency, I encountered a fellow student and then realized he was there as a service user. He clearly did not want to be seen. I smiled and gave the familiar head nod, but he did not return the greeting.

Although I understood the confidentiality guidelines, and that it was inappropriate to approach service users in public, I was concerned about my relationship with this student, particularly if we were likely to work on projects together. Coming from a place of genuine compassion and caring, I found an opportunity, when no one else could overhear us, to let him know that I would not disclose to anyone else that I had seen him in the other agency. He was very upset with me and later reported my ethical infraction to faculty. I realized that I had made a critical mistake.

I was reprimanded by faculty and had to issue an apology to both my own field agency and the one I had been visiting. I felt horrible, and I deliberated whether I had chosen the right profession. For months afterwards, I felt the sting, and it was a lesson I took seriously.

## My Second Practicum

The following year, I started my second practicum and was thrilled that I was placed at North Meadows, the psychiatric facility that I had wanted. As luck would have it, within the first week, I was confronted with yet another "dual relationship" situation.

Walking through the buildings, I saw Jenn, who was one of my best friends while growing up. Her mother and older sister had both tutored me in music lessons. I joined their family band and spent many Friday nights jamming at their house, and then spending the weekend with them. I even dated Jenn's older brother briefly. To this day, I call their mother "Mama."

I knew of Jenn's past traumas and subsequent concurrent disorder, and I was aware of her previous stays at North Meadows. I had even suspected that I would run into her. But I was still seriously taken aback seeing her at my field site on my very first day. This was not just anyone—it was a very close friend, and it posed a major ethical dilemma.

## Honesty and Openness Prevail

When I first saw her, I was at a momentary loss of what to do, but I quickly avoided contact. I struggled throughout the day. Would I be forced to step down from my position at the one place that I had really wanted to complete my practicum?

My previous experience added to my anxiety. I did not want to recreate issues that I had dealt with during my first practicum. If my presence were to detract from Jenn's recovery, then removing me from the situation would be a logical and correct move. How could I navigate this situation without jeopardizing my placement, not to mention my relationships with Jenn and her family?

I reminded myself about the CASW *Code of Ethics* and decided that transparency would be the proper course of action, even if it meant losing my practicum spot. Full disclosure was the only ethical thing to do. I did not want my integrity to be called into question again. Although Jenn had yet to discover that I was at North Meadows, I knew that an encounter could not be avoided, so I decided to face it head on.

I arranged to meet with my faculty liaison. Part of my dilemma was that I realized I would also need to disclose my previous year's experience, which she didn't know about. The faculty liaison talked frankly with me, and we decided that I would raise the issue the following week, when she and I would be attending the first orientation meeting.

At the orientation meeting, the field supervisor was also great. She asked some questions about what I would like to do, and we came up with a plan. The field supervisor and I met with Jenn to ascertain any concerns on her part. We also reviewed Jenn's rights to confidentiality and privacy.

Thankfully, the results were optimal. Jenn, too, was accommodating. So long as I was able to maintain confidentiality and transparency, I could continue my practicum at North Meadows.

I drew valuable lessons about honesty and transparency from my field experiences that remain with me to this day. ∎

## Reflections on Erika's Story

As an aspiring social worker, Erika believed that she was doing the right thing by building positive collegial relationships. However, others in her agency thought she might be very close to crossing the line.

These were challenging times for Erika, so early in her career. However, she realized that by being honest and transparent, she might find ways to mitigate risks and avoid ethical violations, and she did.

She also found out that working as a part of a team brings additional advantages. Her team members identified options that she may not have thought of on her own.

### From Theory to Practice

As you reflect on Erika's story, give some thought to the following points:

1. Erika also has a rights to privacy as a student. Did she have to disclose her experience in the earlier practicum, during which she was seen as demonstrating unethical conduct?

2. How would you describe Erika's dilemmas? Were they caused by dual relationships? Were they boundary violations? Were they simply cases of "boundary bending?"

3. What were Erika's ethical responsibilities to faculty and field education supervisors, and vice versa?

4. Using one of the ethical decision-making models described in this chapter, work through each of Erika's dilemmas. What conclusions did you reach?

# Practice Scenarios

Social work values and ethics underpin all decision-making in professional practice. Developing competence in applying these values and ethics is essential, regardless of the area of practice that you are involved in. The examples include important ethical tensions that are commonly found in practice, and need to be taken into account before action is taken.

In the practice examples below, think about practice considerations, the ethical dilemmas involved, and possible decision options. Work through the ethical dilemmas using a formal ethical decision-making model. None of these situations has one right answer. At the same time, none should be decided on quickly and lightly. These examples include important ethical dilemmas and tensions that need to be taken into account before action is taken.

## 3.1 Reporting to Legislative Authorities

A service user has been referred by the courts for treatment at your non-profit agency. As one of the conditions of probation, the service user is required to see the counsellor once a week. The problem is that the service user doesn't. Sometimes, the service user is very faithful to the schedule; other times, the service user disappears for a few weeks, but always returns. Under the agreement the agency has with the courts, and the informed consent form signed by the service user, the probation officer is supposed to contact the counsellor for regular updates, but has never done so. Do you contact the probation officer?

1. Identify your initial response to the question.

2. Identify the competing tensions, or dual role, that you have in this situation.

3. What are the underling structural values associated with voluntary agencies reporting to legislative authorities?

4. How do the CASW *Code of Ethics*, the CASW *Guidelines for Ethical Practice*, agency policy documents, and the signed informed consent form affect your decision-making?

5. Does it make a difference whether the service user is likeable or has been challenging and openly hostile?

6. Write out your decision and the factors that were taken into consideration.

## 3.2 What Is in the Best Interests of the Child?

Pam is an Indigenous 14-year-old who has been living in a group home for children with diverse abilities for the last year. She has poor impulse control, explosive anger, and limited life-skills functioning. She is scheduled to attend school for half a day at a time, but frequently only attends for two or three days per week. The children's mental health assessment team recommends that she return to her home.

Pam's father is employed as a construction worker, and her mother is a part-time cashier. They live in a small apartment with their son, Brian, who is 11. The family meets with Pam at least once a week and have taken her out for the day twice in the last month. The visits have been exhausting for the parents, but they are satisfied with the arrangements. They do not agree with the recommendation for Pam to return home, in part because of fears for the safety of their son.

1. As the child-protection social worker on the mental health team, what are the practice considerations and ethical tensions?
2. How does one consider the cultural context in this situation? What are the considerations from the code of ethics?
3. Who else should be involved in the decision-making?
4. Write out your decision and the factors that were taken into consideration.

## 3.3 Assessing for Harm to Self and Others

You have been working with a 15-year-old boy for the last six months, and a component of your work has been using text messages as a means of communication. You have become very concerned about his increasingly dangerous drug use. He frequently buys street drugs, and has had one fentanyl overdose. His friends had a naloxone kit and used it on him. He now carries one himself. He has also disclosed that he has, on two occasions, had sex with older men as a trade for the drugs. He lives with his mother and her boyfriend, and does not want you to tell his mother. At 9:00 p.m. tonight, you received a text indicating that he was very high and was going to go onto the street for the first time to make some money. Twenty minutes later, you received this text: "Oops, sorry, sent this wrong. I'm ok." How do you respond?

1. What are the ethical values and practice issues to take into consideration?
2. How does the context (e.g., time of night, use of texting, his age) affect your assessment of the situation?
3. What are the risks? Who is taking them? What is your role in relation to these risks?
4. How do boundary and relationship issues contribute to your decision-making?
5. What are the options in this scenario?
6. Write out your decision and the factors that were taken into consideration.

# Field Education Practicalities
# The Ethical Responsibilities of Supervisors

Social work mentors, either in the field or in academia, have multiple responsibilities toward social work students. These responsibilities include maintaining appropriate boundaries in relationships and ensuring competence in their knowledge transmission, mentoring, and interactions.

Underlying these responsibilities is recognition of and respect for the inherent power differentials associated with the instructor/supervisor–student relationship.

The CASW *Guidelines for Ethical Practice* (2005b) outlines a number of ethical principles for field education supervisors. For example, section 2.6.3 states:

Social workers do not engage in a romantic relationship, sexual activities or sexual contact with social work students whom they are supervising or teaching.

## Field Education Supervisor Responsibilities

In addition to the prohibition of intimate and sexual relationships with students, field instructors and social work faculty have the following responsibilities to students:

**3.5.1**  Social workers provide instruction only within their areas of knowledge and competence.

**3.5.2**  Social workers endeavour to provide instruction based on the most current information and knowledge available in the profession.

**3.5.3**  Social workers foster in social work students' knowledge and understanding of the social work profession, the *Code of Ethics* and other appropriate sources of ethical practices.

**3.5.4**  Social workers instruct students to inform clients of their student status.

**3.5.5**  Social workers inform students of their ethical responsibilities to agencies, supervisors and clients.

**3.5.6**  Social workers adhere to the principles of privacy and confidentiality in the supervisory relationship, acknowledging with students any limitations early in the professional relationship.

**3.5.7**  Social workers recognize that their role in supervising students is intended to be educational and work-focused. In the event that a student requests or requires therapy, the instructor refers the student to another competent practitioner.

**3.5.8**  Social workers evaluate a student's performance in a manner that is fair and respectful and consistent with the expectations of the student's educational institution.

**3.5.9**  Social workers do not engage in any dual or multiple relationships with students, in which there is a risk of exploitation or potential harm to the student. Social work educators and field instructors are responsible for setting clear, appropriate, and culturally sensitive boundaries.

## Student Responsibilities in Dual Relationships

During field education, the most usual ethical dilemmas faced by students are associated with boundaries and confidentiality. Practising with integrity means being transparent about multiple roles and disclosing any potential conflicts. As Reamer (2013) points out in his ethical decision-making model, consultation is key. If there is any doubt about a boundary issue or potential conflict, consulting with field education faculty and agency supervisors virtually always resolves any concerns quickly and positively.

The CASW *Code of Ethics* (2005a) provides principles for integrity in professional practice. Value 4 is as follows:

> Social workers value openness and transparency in professional practice and avoid relationships where their integrity or impartiality may be compromised, ensuring that should a conflict of interest be unavoidable, the nature of the conflict is fully disclosed. (p. 6)

Prior to being placed in an agency, students should have advised their field coordinator of any potential conflicts. This would include any prior contact the student or a close family member has had as a service user with the agency, any personal relationships with any staff or board members at the agency, or other interactions that may affect learning.

In most situations, these prior relationships do not negate the student from completing their field education in the particular agency. However, it is important for related safety measures to be put into place (e.g., a service user's file may need to be removed from the central filing system) and for the supervisor to be aware of prior relationships that may affect the student's learning or an employee's role.

Sometimes these conflicts do not become apparent until the student has been placed in the agency, in which case the situation should be disclosed to the agency supervisor at the earliest time possible.

## Separating Personal and Work Life

An important boundary issue that all social work students and all social workers must deal with at some point is how to keep work and personal life separate. Determining the boundary between the two spheres is not always easy, and depends on the issue as well as the context of work and personal life. We all have personal issues, such as unresolved trauma and conflict, and day-to-day stressors. While it isn't our intention to take personal matters to work, sometimes they can leave us feeling tired, distracted, or unmotivated.

Similarly, at work we may hear people describe aspects of their lives that are troubling, stress producing, and exhausting. In school, students are often admonished to separate work and home. While this might be an ideal, it is simplistic and impossible to accomplish all of the time.

Separating personal and work life is an area of learning and growth that many students incorporate into their learning plans. It may include incorporating practices pre- or post-work to separate work and home. Parking farther away from your work site, or walking an extra block on a public transportation route can provide some reprieve from family interactions in the morning, and a similar re-energizing in the afternoon to prepare for the evening family routine. Listening to soothing music on the way home can be helpful. Some people use symbolic gestures (e.g., stopping at the end of the driveway and mindfully wrapping up the day's work and placing it at the door to be picked up the following day). Other people, and agencies, provide a debriefing at the end of the day to avoid brooding over the day's issues at night.

Learning to reduce the carry-over stress from work to home and vice versa is an important goal to set during field education to help offset future burnout and cumulative stress. ■

# Reflection, Learning, and More Practice

## Field Education Practicalities

1. Advise the field supervisor and faculty supervisor of any potential conflicts or dual relationships that may exist in your field placement.

2. Review, with your field supervisor, any ethical dilemmas that may arise for you based on your personal values. Discuss with your supervisor the process for working through them in your placement.

3. Review the confidentiality and privacy policies in your field agency. Pay particular attention to confidentiality of record keeping, documentation, file security, and Internet usage. Identify the process for service users to access their records.

4. With your field supervisor, review the boundaries and responsibilities each of you have in this important mentoring relationship.

5. Develop a self-care plan that will help you ensure a work–home balance in your life. Your plan should be incorporated into your learning goals.

## Journal Ideas

1. Identify a situation that has occurred, or could occur, in your field setting, which may be troublesome to you in terms of the core values of social work (e.g., self-determination, confidentiality/privacy, or boundaries and dual relationships). Explain the strategies you will put into place to ensure your work is in the service user's best interests.

2. Review and evaluate the social media policy at your agency. Do you think it is up-to-date and in keeping with today's world?

3. Write a journal entry about a difficult ethical situation that evoked negative emotions in you. Identify alternative responses to thinking about and resolving this dilemma.

## Critical-Thinking Questions

1. Identify a central ethical dilemma in your field placement that reflects a tension between micro practice for individuals and macro practice aimed at addressing social inequities.

2. Codes of ethics represent a set of principles, but provide little guidance, on how to act in a particular situation. What other documents or frameworks may be useful in moving from the principles to decisions and actions?

3. In a legislated context, such as in child welfare, it may be difficult to adhere to the value of self-determination. How can service user self-determination be protected in such settings?

4. Many argue that there is a difference between "boundary bending" and "boundary violations." Discuss the merits of this distinction. How does this distinction fit with the social work code of ethics and standards of practice in your jurisdiction? How does it fit with the organizational policies in your field agency?

5. Racialized social workers (or social workers that may be understood as "other") may experience marginalization in their social work practice. If you can, provide an example of a situation in which a social worker's social location resulted in "othering." Critically assess the contributing factors in this situation. What is your responsibility when you witness a social worker colleague being marginalized?

6. Discuss with a colleague the ethical risks and challenges associated with providing some or all services online, such as through social media, texts, and email.

7. A central idea in the notion of "informed consent" is that of the service user having the "capacity" to make the decision. How does a social worker assess for this in the case of someone who has a severe mental health disorder, has an intellectual or developmental diverse ability, is young or elderly, etc.?

# Chapter Review

Codes of ethics and standards of practice serve to unify a profession and can act as a guide to everyday practice. However, while adhering to social work values and ethics seems simple enough in the classroom, it quickly becomes complex in practice as one is faced with competing interests and tensions.

Many social workers will make ethical transgressions, mostly minor and unintentional, with minimal consequences. But it is not difficult to find examples where such transgressions have had major consequences for service users and social workers. Sometimes, the inappropriate ethical actions are exposed through government inquests, judicial processes, and the media.

Students develop ethical decision-making skills through everyday experience. Erika learned that consulting can provide a range of options for action and limit the risks associated with subsequent action. Some students learn ethical decision-making through systematically journalling a critical incident. Most students quickly understand individual ethics such as respecting self-determination and confidentiality, but struggle with balancing individual rights with structural injustice.

The practice scenarios in this chapter highlight the importance of communication and relationship building. They describe relatively common dilemmas associated with legislative reporting and competing interests between individuals (child and parent, and between siblings).

Ethical dilemmas are challenging and occur throughout practice. At this point in your field education, the inherent tensions should be more visible, and your capacity to identify them and consult with your field supervisor should be developing. Applying the principles within a code of ethics involves taking into consideration the broader context, recognizing issues of diversity and difference, and communicating with service users and colleagues in intelligent and flexible ways.

## Developing Ethical Adherence in Practice

This chapter outlines numerous ways in which students can develop their ethical decision-making skills. Here are some highlights and further suggestions:

- Identify competing tensions between individual services and social justice inequities.
- Recognize how emotions affect sound judgements and ethical decisions.
- Navigate legalistic requirements through relationship building and appropriate use of power.
- Ensure that the service user's right to self-determination is authentic (choices must be provided with no coercion or bias).
- Understand ethics within a cultural context.
- Ensure confidentiality and privacy rights through processes of informed consent.
- Practise privacy rights through all aspects of electronic media and communication.
- Support people who do not have the capacity to give informed consent by enlisting a significant friend or family member to assist in the decision-making.
- Ensure that one's own needs are met through personal social relationships, not through relationships with service users.
- Maintain separation between personal and work social media accounts, email, and other online communications.
- Recognize and support social workers who are recipients of misogynistic, racial, or other marginalizing comments and actions in their work.
- Accept that, regardless of experience, consultation is key to working through ethical dilemmas.

# Respecting Diversity and Difference

4

# Chapter at a Glance

# Spotlight on Social Work Luminaries
## Wanda Thomas Bernard

**Wanda Thomas Bernard**, a Canadian senator since 2016, was formerly a social worker from East Preston, Nova Scotia. In 2005, she was awarded the Order of Canada for her work addressing racism and diversity in the field of social work. A founding member of the Association of Black Social Workers, Bernard was awarded the Order of Nova Scotia in 2014.

In the course of their daily work, social workers become involved with unique individuals who have very complex personal histories. Social workers are required to acknowledge the diverse experiences of people, and the intersections of differing self-identities. In addition, they must take into account that everyone does not have equal access to social power, life opportunities, and material resources.

Personal and social identities have traditionally been constructed around the triad of race, class, and gender. More recently, this list has been expanded to include areas such as sexual orientation and gender identity, age, and ability. Today, an intersectionality approach is needed in order to address the full range of issues that can affect an individual's life chances. It is also important to recognize that all individuals have their own unique experiences.

This chapter examines the many complexities associated with working with and being an ally to people who represent diversity. The areas of diversity considered in this chapter are culture and race, including immigration experiences; sexual and gender identity, including masculinity and caring; ability; and aging. It underlines the importance of listening to service users' experiences of diversity and marginalization, and working with them to ensure equal opportunities, safe and respectful services, and all the benefits of a just society.

## Key Concepts

- Intersectionality
- Cultural safety
- Cultural appropriation
- Gender identity and expression
- Human rights model of diverse ability
- Dementia

## Developing Competence as a Social Worker

Some ways to develop the meta-competency of "**respecting diversity and difference**" are as follows:

- Be self-aware about the beliefs, values, and assumptions you carry with you about people and populations of diversity.

- Identify small daily practices that enhance your role as an ally when working in areas of difference.

- Find opportunities to develop dialogues with service users about everyday experiences that may contribute to social marginalization.

- Adopt inclusive, gender-neutral language that resists normativity.

# Respecting Diversity, Difference, and Intersectionality

**Intersectionality**

Intersectionality refers to the interconnections of various forms of oppression (racism, sexism, homophobia, ableism, etc.).

Underlying this concept is the need to acknowledge the multiple positioning of individuals and to avoid bias and stereotypes.

Respecting diversity and working with difference is a basic tenet of social work practice. The Canadian Human Rights Act explicitly prohibits discrimination based on race, national or ethnic origin, colour, religion, age, sex, sexual orientation, gender identity or expression, marital status, family status, genetic characteristics, and disability.

Social workers also are aware of diversity in relation to power, privilege, class, wealth, and access to resources. Social workers draw on this broad knowledge and conceptual base to understand how exclusion, exploitation, and marginalization affect individuals and entire populations in different ways. Understanding the service user's experiences of diversity and difference is a core competency of social work practice today.

## Intersectionality

Social work programs prepare students to work mindfully with the dynamics of cross-cultural, racial, religious, gender, and cross-class diversity (Berry Edwards, 2016). Nevertheless, it is impossible to be fully "competent" and to know everything about all ethnicities and cultures. Social workers are taught only a limited number of professional responses. However, they are taught to acknowledge difference and to develop competency in recognizing the inter-relationships between societal structures and the oppression and marginalization of individuals and groups.

Social relationships are complex, multiple, and intersected. Social workers are required to acknowledge the multiple positioning and diverse experiences of individuals based on the intersections of differing identities along with differential access to power, privilege, and resources (Robinson, Cross-Denny, Lee, Werkmeister Rozas, & Yamada, 2016).

Davis (2008) defines **intersectionality** as follows:

> the interaction between gender, race, and other categories of difference in individual lives, social practices, institutional arrangements, and cultural ideologies and the outcomes of these interactions in terms of power. (p.68)

Social workers are generally self-aware of the conscious and unconscious beliefs and stereotypes they bring into their work. Social work practice intends to be respectful and attentive to difference, including within-group diversity. Practising with intersectional sensibilities requires attention to differences, identities, and interactions (Berry Edwards, 2016). Nevertheless, practising with competency in respect to diversity and difference can be challenging and somewhat elusive.

By applying an intersectional approach to practice, social workers reduce the likelihood of making erroneous assumptions or unfair generalizations (Robinson et al., 2016).

Social workers work with many populations who have been marginalized, discriminated against, and oppressed. Respecting diversity at a micro level requires respecting the dynamic of difference in cross-cultural, racial, religious, gender, sexual, age, ability, and class relationships.

## CASWE-ACFTS *Standards for Accreditation*

The fourth core learning objective of the CASWE-ACFTS *Standards for Accreditation* (Canadian Association for Social Work Education–Association canadienne pour la formation en travail social [CASWE-ACFTS], 2014) states:

4. Support and enhance diversity by addressing structural sources of inequity

 i) Social work students recognize diversity and difference as a crucial and valuable part of living in a society.

 ii) Social work students have knowledge of how discrimination, oppression, poverty, exclusion, exploitation, and marginalization have a negative impact on particular individuals and groups and strive to end these and other forms of social injustice.

## Professional Regulation and Competency

The Canadian Council of Social Work Regulators (CCSWR, 2012) competency profile incorporates the meta-competency of "**respecting diversity and difference**" throughout. For example:

17. Identify linkages between situation/problem and life conditions, with particular attention to issues of oppression and discrimination.

18. Analyze, formulate, and advocate for policies that advance social justice and well-being.

22. Identify how a culture's structures and values may oppress, marginalize, alienate, or create or enhance privilege and power.

43. Assess the impact of biopsychosocial history, including social isolation and marginalization, on the service user system.

105. Provide services in [a] manner that reflects the needs and sensitivities of vulnerable populations.

## Association of Social Work Boards (ASWB)

Within the 25% of the ASWB BSW exam on "Human Development, Diversity and Behaviour in the Environment" is a focus on diversity, social/economic justice, and oppression.

Questions on the following topics may be included:

- Feminist theory
- The effect of disability on biopsychosocial functioning throughout the lifespan
- The effect of culture, race, and ethnicity on behaviours, attitudes, and identity
- The effects of discrimination and stereotypes on behaviours, attitudes, and identity
- The influence of sexual orientation on behaviours, attitudes, and identity
- The impact of transgender and the transitioning process on behaviours, attitudes, identity, and relationships
- Systemic (institutionalized) discrimination (e.g., racism, sexism, ageism)
- The principles of culturally competent social work practice
- Sexual orientation concepts
- Gender and gender identity concepts
- The impact of social institutions on society
- The effect of poverty on individuals, families, groups, organizations, and communities
- The impact of the environment (e.g., social, physical, cultural, political, economic) on individuals, families, groups, organizations, and communities
- Person-in-environment (PIE) theory
- Social and economic justice
- Criminal justice systems
- The effects of life events, stressors, and crises on individuals, families, groups, organizations, and communities
- The impact of the political environment on policy-making ■

# Cultural Intelligence and Mindfulness

**Cultural safety**

Culturally safe social work practice involves critically evaluating one's own beliefs, values, and assumptions. It also involves respecting and building on the values and cultural beliefs of the communities one interacts with.

The social work profession aims to "create service providers who are culturally competent or cross-culturally sensitive to people who are not like them" (Baskin, 2016, p. 84). Cultural intelligence results when service providers become both aware and mindful of the specific norms, practices, and behaviours of a cultural or ethnic group. Being mindful by paying attention to the present moment is an opportunity to learn about oneself and one's biases. In fact, mindfulness plays an important role in developing cultural humility and safety in one's practice (Yeager & Bauer-Wu, 2013).

## Cultural Competence and Cultural Safety

Some scholars have critiqued cultural competency models, taking the position that they reproduce "simplistic assumptions about various populations that are reminiscent of the imperialism, racism, and paternalism of an earlier social work era" (Baskin, 2016, p. 85). They argue that cultural competence assumes uniformity within a particular culture and does not allow for within-group diversity or intercultural interactions (Berry Edwards, 2016).

Further, some have argued that cultural competency models "reduce the understanding of the difficulties that particular individuals face when accessing social services to cultural differences, rather than attending to the social, economic, and political realities that support systemic inequalities" (Baskin, 2016, p. 85). In short, cultural competency models are limited, as they do not attend to power differences and the ways in which power is maintained through a social hierarchy that marginalizes particular groups of people.

Cultural competency models imply that the practitioner is a member of the dominant population and therefore "culture-free." Yet, everyone has a culture, and everyone in the helping professions needs to examine their own cultural standpoint. Furthermore, the helping professions are largely shaped by the particular understandings of the dominant group. "Even if a social worker is a member of an Indigenous or other minority group, they will inevitably practise social work, at least in some measure, using the cultural understandings of the dominant group" (Baskin, 2016, p. 86).

The concept of **cultural safety** originated in New Zealand in the 1980s and is emerging as a more appropriate model. From this perspective, "culturally unsafe practice involves any action that diminishes, demeans or disempowers the cultural identity and well-being of an individual" (National Aboriginal Health Organization, 2007, slide 7).

Baskin (2016) suggests that cultural safety is a concept that moves beyond cultural awareness, sensitivity, and competence to involve reflections on racism, power relations, and one's own privilege. Although the definition for cultural safety continues to evolve, the concept defines safety in relation to service users who guide the practices according to what they feel is safe for them. Cultural safety, in this sense, can be crucial to the establishment of mutual trust between social workers and service users (National Aboriginal Health Organization, 2007).

## Cultural Intelligence as a Continuum

Ramsden (1992) is one of many health professionals who view cultural competence and safety along a continuum. According to Ramsden, cultural awareness is the beginning step in the learning process, which involves understanding difference. Cultural sensitivity is an intermediate step during which the student's self-exploration begins. Cultural safety is the final outcome of this learning process. A social worker who practises culturally safe care interacts with service users in such a way that those who receive care define that care.

To ensure a culturally safe environment for Indigenous service users, non-Indigenous social workers should do the following:

- Learn about the health and social challenges that Inuit, and First Nations and Métis peoples face.

- Be aware of broad health determinants that may apply to Inuit, and First Nations and Métis peoples (social, economic, historical, and political).

- Learn about the history of colonization and its impact on the current health and social status of Inuit, and First Nations and Métis peoples.

- Be self-aware and evaluate what baggage (e.g., beliefs, values, assumptions) one brings to the relationship (National Aboriginal Health Organization, 2007, slide 11).

- Ensure that the Indigenous service user has the power to incorporate their cultural location, values, and preferences into services (Brascoupé & Water, 2009).

**Figure 4.1** A Model of Cultural Intelligence

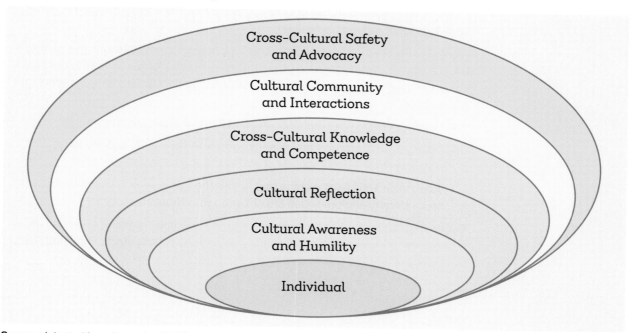

**Source:** Adapted from Ramsden (1992).

# Being an Ally

Social workers are focused on making a positive difference, and generally they do. However, in the past, social workers, in the guise of "helping," have practised in ways that have created harm.

In Canada, harms have been most notable with Indigenous communities where social workers, under the auspices of residential school and child welfare policies, have been instrumental in the removal of children from their families and communities. These policies and programs wreaked havoc on Indigenous individuals, families, and communities, and their legacy continues to be felt to this day.

Being an ally means shifting the context of social work away from being merely a "helper." An ally does not believe that an individual or group requires "help." Instead, an ally recognizes oppressive policies and systems, aids in resistance, and walks beside people who have been marginalized and oppressed as a supporter of and advocate for social justice and basic human rights.

## Being a White Ally

While few would identify as an active or unintentional racist, Wing Sue (2017) contends that there are very low numbers of true white allies who undertake the emotionally and psychologically exhausting journey of attempting to disrupt racism and fight against injustice and unfairness.

Wing Sue (2017) points out that being an ally and participating in anti-racist actions can be uncomfortable and stressful. Individuals are products of their social conditioning and of a worldview that has shaped and influenced their reality. Overthrowing one's cultural conditioning is a monumental task and can present challenges that may be unpleasant.

Being a white ally means understanding the privilege associated with the dominant belief systems. Wing Sue (2017) offers the following guidelines on how to become a valued and authentic collaborator in the struggle against racism and promotion of equal rights:

- Develop trusting and authentic relationships with people of colour.
- Develop an awareness of whiteness and white privilege, and the many obstacles that discourage social advocacy and social justice.
- Take on an anti-racist identity that "walks the talk"—awareness of one's own racial identity and privileges are not enough without social action.

Becoming an ally requires a commitment to social action in small ways and in larger socio-political ways in order to facilitate institutional and societal change that leads to a more socially just and equal society.

## Avoiding Cultural Appropriation

It is also important for social workers, and it is their responsibility, not to imitate cultural practices that are not their own. When learning Indigenous ways of teaching and helping, it is important to neither appropriate nor misappropriate Indigenous knowledge (Baskin, 2016).

While many Indigenous organizations partner with mainstream service agencies to include Indigenous ways of knowing and healing alongside other strategies, social workers should not imitate cultural practices that are not their own.

Lowman and Barker (2015) define **cultural appropriation** this way:

> Appropriation can be understood as the removal of an element of culture, a concept or idea, or a symbol or practice out of its original context, and its redeployment in a new cultural or social context for the gratification or profit of the appropriating person or group. ... Appropriation in colonial contexts is the assertion that one has the right to take something, regardless of what the group being taken from may say, think, or feel. (pp. 39–40)

It may be easier to understand the harm appropriation can cause by considering how tourist centres appropriate Indigenous knowledge and culture through the selling of fake Indigenous artwork. As Shain Jackson, a Coast Salish artist, notes:

> 80% of Aboriginal art and giftware has nothing to do with Aboriginal People, there is no Aboriginal involvement. It's like they've taken a cliché of a design and splashed it on mugs and backpacks. ... [All] the resources have gone to non-Aboriginal companies or persons. In Canada, the most marginalized and impoverished communities are Aboriginal communities and we're hoping that the consumer wants to make sure that that is alleviated by purchase of our own art, which is our gift to you. We want you to have the real thing, there is meaning in our art work. (as cited in Indigenous Corporate Training, 2018)

Just as these knock-offs perpetuate the demoralization of Indigenous peoples and harm Indigenous communities both culturally and economically, so too does the appropriation of Indigenous approaches to healing by non-Indigenous people.

For a healing practice to be authentic and to have cultural meaning to service users, it is necessary for social workers to be transparent and represent their culture and worldview from a place that honours the implicit and nuanced meaning of the practice. It is not acceptable to simply imitate or copy another culture's practice.

Baskin (2016) notes that non-Indigenous practitioners can (and should) understand and respect Indigenous worldviews, but they should not appropriate the cultural or spiritual practices and ceremonies. Social workers are not prevented from learning from Elders or participating in Indigenous cultural practices. However, such experiences do not entitle social workers to lead Indigenous practice.

**Cultural appropriation**

When someone from one culture chooses to emulate members of another culture for entertainment, it is more than culturally disrespectful, it is symptomatic of the history of colonialism.

When social workers admire an aspect of another culture, they learn about it, and don't "borrow" it, to show cultural respect (Indigenous Corporate Training, 2018).

# Social Worker Exemplar

## Learning Cultural Humility

Robin Carr

**Robin is a Euro-Canadian social worker who thought she was open to multiple perspectives, worldviews, and cultures. However, like a lot of social work learning, it was easier to be open in theory than in practice.**

"Lia taught me as much about cultural humility as anyone I know," Robin says. "Working with her, and thinking a lot about the underlying issues, I also began to understand more about the social work values of self-determination and empathy."

Lia was a 28-year-old, second-generation South Asian, Canadian woman who was then living with her family (mother, father, and older brother). She had lived in Canada all of her life. Her Sikh culture and identity were important to her, and she attended the Sikh temple regularly with her parents.

Her parents were arranging a marriage for her.

Lia explains that she had similar freedoms to other Canadian students while attending school, although she was not allowed to date. Her parents informed her in her teens that they would be arranging a marriage for her. However, she was able to negotiate with her parents to postpone the marriage so that she could attend university.

Lia ultimately received a bachelor of arts in psychology and then began working as a support worker at the high school that she herself had attended. She was frequently called upon by other agencies to assist with translation and for cultural learning. She also had an active social life, with both her Sikh friends and others in the community.

### Arranged Marriage

Lia attended counselling because her parents had begun seriously looking for a husband for her. They had introduced her to three men, none of whom she was attracted to. Her parents then started talking about having their family in India identify someone who would be brought to Canada with the express purpose of marriage. At this point, as she had not agreed to any other opportunities, she was given no choice about this marriage. She was told that she would meet her prospective spouse just days before the marriage.

Lia was devastated. She spoke about how she had, for the most part, respected the teachings and expectations of her parents. She had never drunk alcohol nor dated, until recently. Over the previous two years, she had met and become friends with a South Asian male, Inder, who was the same age as her and was also a second-generation Canadian. Although they both knew of the prohibitions, their friendship grew strong. Over the last month or so, they talked about their feelings for each other. Inder was aware of the arrangements being made by Lia's parents.

Lia was in a position similar to many second-generation immigrants. There were intersections between being a Canadian woman and a woman from another culture, and there were also tensions between the generations.

As a Euro-Canadian woman only a few years older than Lia, I was overwhelmed with empathy and concern. However, I realized that it was my job to try and understand the situation and options from Lia's Sikh perspective.

## Learning to Be Culturally Humble

As much as I had talked with others about arranged marriages for South Asian women, and the tensions and challenges that can arise, I had very little understanding of the true dilemma Lia was facing. I needed to learn from her, and ultimately from others in the community.

Lia described the tension as being what she wanted (self-determination) versus what her parents and community expected (cultural context). She described the continuum of norms within the South Asian community. She knew families where women had run away from arranged marriages, and had been shunned from the community and their own families. She even knew of circumstances where a woman had been killed. She was also fearful of what may happen to Inder.

I did know one other woman in her mid-40s in the Sikh community well enough to find out more. To my surprise, this woman said that her own marriage had been arranged, that they had not met prior to the wedding, and today (20 years later) they are in love. She described that, because of the emphasis on shared values and practices, many arranged marriages shifted into love marriages.

I started to recognize that I had constructed this situation from my own cultural perspective. I also realized that I was overidentifying, and perhaps overempathizing. While it was important for me to learn about Lia's world, I had to separate my perceptions from the situation. It was also important to contextualize Lia's decision and recognize that we were distinct individuals with separate personalities and life histories.

I was challenged to put aside my own perceptions and biases. I had to stop evaluating and judging. I realized I had been seeing my culture as privileged and her culture as oppressive—this was not consistent with having cultural humility.

Just like my work with any other service user, my job was to help Lia explore her options so that she could come to a decision that was best for her at that moment in time. ■

## Reflections on Robin's Story

In this situation, Robin recognized that her own social location was influencing her perceptions and her conversations with Lia, who had a very different cultural context. For Robin, the intersection between gender and culture was becoming more complex.

Cultural humility requires a humble and respectful attitude toward individuals from other cultures, and pushes one to challenge one's own biases by exploring one's assumptions, judgements, and prejudices. Mindfulness and reflexivity are both required for cultural humility to occur.

In this exemplar, Robin describes consciously applying and working through those processes.

### From Theory to Practice

As you reflect on Robin's story, give some thought to the following points:

1. Based on your self-awareness and self-knowledge, describe your view of arranged marriages. How does this view compare with your beliefs about love and marriage?

2. In the end, did Robin show cultural competence and cultural humility? How was this done, or not done?

3. How could Robin have increased her cultural knowledge and cultural humility?

4. Do you think Robin acted as an ally in this situation? Is "being an ally" the appropriate role?

5. Describe a situation in which you were challenged to be culturally mindful.

## Gender identity and expression

Gender identity is each person's internal and individual experience of gender. It is their sense of being a woman, a man, both, neither, or anywhere along the gender spectrum. A person's gender identity may be the same as or different from their birth-assigned sex. Gender identity is fundamentally different from a person's sexual orientation.

Gender expression is how a person publicly presents their gender. This can include behaviour and outward appearance such as dress, hair, make-up, body language and voice. A person's chosen name and pronoun are also common ways of expressing gender.

# Gender Identity and Expression

Freedom from discrimination and harassment because of **gender identity and expression** is a core social work value, yet many social workers have little preparation for working with sexual minority populations. As with any other group, there are multiple intersections and within-group differences, but there are also commonalities that constitute a collective cultural identity. People who identify as lesbian, gay, bisexual, transgender, queer, and two-spirited (LGBTQ2S+) are "bounded by the challenges of coping with social oppression in the forms of heterosexism homophobia, and rigid interpretations of gender expression" (Morrow, 2006, p. 7).

Social work ethics and values provide a context for working with LGBTQ2S+ people and communities. For example, respect for inherent dignity ensures that social workers honour the worth and dignity of LGBTQ2S+ people and work affirmatively on their behalf. The LGBTQ2S+ population frequently encounters discrimination. Thus, working from an empowerment perspective means identifying and honouring their strengths in planning intervention strategies (Morrow, 2006).

## Being an Ally with LGBTQ2S+ Individuals

Allies are individuals who are members of a privileged social group who support and advocate for members of an oppressed group (Washington & Evans, 1991, as cited in Rostosky, Black, Riggle, & Rosenkrantz, 2015). Practising social justice so that all people have the same basic rights and protections requires social workers to conduct research that is inclusive of LGBTQ2S+ issues, advocate for policy practice that make visible the existence of sexual minorities, and promote laws to ensure equal rights and decriminalize behaviours that blur the lines of sexual and gender expression.

Heterosexual allies are important to ending stigma and achieving equal rights for LGBTQ2S+ individuals. In addition, allies serve as advocates at multiple levels, from one-on-one interactions to high-profile social activism. Activists work toward having the actions and behaviours associated with sexual minority groups recognized as being natural and normal (Messinger, 2006).

In a recent study, individuals who self-identified as straight/heterosexual allies with LGBTQ2S+ completed an online survey to identify the positives they experienced (Rostosky et al., 2015). The participants reported that being a heterosexual ally fostered their personal knowledge growth, increased awareness and skills, and gave them opportunities to live according to their highest values about social justice and equality:

> The participants perceived that their ally identity provided them with knowledge and awareness, satisfying interpersonal relationships and community belonging, and a sense of meaning and purpose as they actively contributed to social change. (p. 336)

Overall, these research findings suggest that it can be rewarding to be included in the LGBTQ2S+ community as an ally and that heterosexual-identified people might benefit from more focused ally-to-ally mentoring and role modelling.

# The Contributions of Queer Theory
## Disrupting Male/Female Binaries

Since the early 1990s, the term "queer" has been used to signify a wide-ranging resistance to normative models of sexuality. Queer theory rejects the taken-for-granted and binary categories of straight and gay, and invites a critical questioning of all sexuality.

## Queer Theory

Queer theory developed from lesbian and gay studies, which were largely silent on differences associated with class, race, and culture. Following a critical theory tradition, queer theory

> problematizes and destabilizes all sexual identities and practices, and encourages "folks of different strokes" to participate in the conversation, not just those identified as "LGBT." (MacKinnon, 2011, p. 140)

The focus of queer theory is on the language of sexuality. Halperin (1995) argues for a Foucauldian approach, in which sexuality is understood "both as the result of powerful practices of knowledge and as a site for the construction and renewal of continually changing identities" (as cited in Hicks & Jeyasingham, 2016, p. 2359).

A key concept in queer theory is the idea of "heteronormativity," which is described by Berlant and Warner (1998) as "the institutions, structures of understanding, and practical orientations that make heterosexuality seem not only coherent—that is, organized as a sexuality—but also privileged" (p. 548). Heteronormativity is reinforced through the institutions of marriage, taxes, employment, and adoption rights, among others. Heteronormativity is a form of power and control that applies pressure to both straight and gay individuals through institutional arrangements and accepted norms.

Queer theory makes the argument that sexuality categories are contingent on a female/male binary that emerges out of a gendered discourse. Queer theorists contend that there is no set normal. The main challenge identified by queer theorists is to disrupt sexual binaries in order to remove difference and inequality.

## Post-queer Theories

Some queer theorists criticize radical and anti-oppressive theories as reinforcing the fixed hetero/queer binary insofar as they underscore heterosexual practices as normative, with lesbian, gay, bisexual, transgender, queer, and two-spirited (LGBTQ2S+) identities being marginalized and oppressed (MacKinnon, 2011). The argument is that these theories assume that heterosexual practices are dominant, while queer sexual practices and identities require a fuller understanding.

Much of social work theory and research, including radical social work, avoids discussions of queer theory. To address this shortcoming, Hicks and Jeyasingham (2016) have introduced a "post-queer" lens to social work theory, one that includes an analysis of power, class, and race.

For these authors, the positive representations and greater visibility of social structures such as gay marriage and same-sex adoption are presented as solutions to the problem of heterosexist or homophobic attitudes. They argue that norming such practices leads to the concept of "homonormativity," which continues to reproduce a narrow understanding of contemporary family formations and intimate relationships.

Instead, these authors argue for a deeper engagement with the ways in which individuals experience social marginalization through intersections between sexuality, race, gender, and class.

## Queer Safe Spaces

Universities are increasingly providing inclusive queer safe spaces to ensure that everyone is able to feel safe, accepted, and supported in an environment that best suits them. These spaces are important for many students, as university is the time and place to explore their identity. Using positive space posters and stickers on office doors is an increasingly visible sign that people in the space are supportive of LGBTQ2S+ people. ■

# Gender-Sensitive Practice with Men

Much attention in social work is rightly accorded to women who are marginalized and oppressed in multiple ways in Western society. Certainly, the disadvantages women face as women is, and should be, an overriding concern. However, this concern should not obscure the fact that gender disparity for men can occur in the area of family and emotional power.

In general, social work research and practice pay little attention to supporting men as fathers, or providing them with opportunities to express emotions, or to work through their involvement in intimate partner violence beyond the social construction of "perpetrator." Men, like women, are complex individuals with distinct personalities, histories, and needs. Many have roles and identities as fathers, stepfathers, uncles, and grandfathers. However, their needs and relationships are often ignored.

## Fathers and Child Welfare

Despite the increasing recognition of the importance of fathers' involvement in children's lives, fathers are rarely included in child welfare interventions. Moreover, social workers' engagement with fathers is often fraught with negative bias. Baum (2017) notes:

> Scholars have suggested that involving fathers in social work interventions should provide a necessary corrective for the finger pointing at mothers in cases of child maltreatment and make clear fathers' responsibility for their children's care. (p. 1)

Fathers are frequently discounted or not considered at all in child welfare. When present, they may be seen as deviant, dangerous, irresponsible, and irrelevant (Brown, Callahan, Strega, Walmsley, & Dominelli, 2009).

In a Canadian study, Brown et al. (2009) found that even when a father, or man who functioned as a father, was present in the family, he was rarely considered as a placement resource, even when the alternative was permanent guardianship. The authors point out that a kind of gender bias occurs in child welfare work, and this has remained unaltered despite progressive initiatives such as gender-neutral language and substitute terms such as "caretakers" or "parents" instead of "mothers" or "fathers."

Recommendations for social workers working with men/fathers include the following:

- Seek to understand how fathers perceive and experience social services.
- Recognize that fathers are not only fathers, but whole individuals with other identities and roles.
- Acknowledge and deal with personal fears of working with men.
- Recognize the important gender differences in communication.
- Do not assume that mothers necessarily always have a greater impact on children than fathers.

# Indigenous Men and Domestic Violence in Quebec
## The Effects of Assimilation and Colonization Policies

Studies on domestic violence in Indigenous families are few and primarily focus on women as victims and men as perpetrators. That is because in most instances, women are the victims. However, Ellington, Brassard, and Montminy (2015), using Statistics Canada data, report that almost 20% of Indigenous men identify as being victims of intimate partner violence.

### "Inner Suffering"

It is well recognized that domestic violence among Indigenous peoples occurs within a broader historical and cultural context, and is a symptom of a range of assimilation and colonization policies. Further, Indigenous men are a marginalized group (low socio-economic status, high unemployment, and poor living conditions). For these men, there are multiple intersections of privilege and oppression, ultimately leading to higher rates of incarceration.

Ellington et al. (2015), associated with universities in Laval and Montréal, spoke with 39 Indigenous men in Quebec about their experiences of and roles in domestic violence. The research hoped to identify new approaches for intervention, other than the typical socio-judicial responses.

Their findings identified a wide range of socio-cultural, structural, and individual factors in the men's experiences. Domestic violence occurred in a context of negative emotionality that included historical violence in their families and personal lives, poor living conditions, and lack of supports.

The men described their experience of "inner suffering," and violent behaviours as a way of taking back a modicum of control in their lives.

Some of the men in the study were unclear whether they were victims or instigators; however, one-third defined themselves as victims of domestic violence and felt powerless in the face of their partner's violent behaviour. A minority (two) described themselves as the main instigators.

### Conflict Regulation and Family Healing

Ellington et al. (2015) suggest that domestic violence is typically not a one-off incident. For example, most men in the study had experienced domestic violence more than once.

Interactional dynamics between partners was an important aspect of understanding the complexity of intimate partner violence. Roles changed and shifted over time and context. There was frequent verbal, psychological, and/or physical violence in which both partners acted as instigators or victims. In addition, inter-conjugal violence was also a factor—forms of violence in one relationship caused reactive behaviours in subsequent relationships.

A conclusion of the study was that "the perceived roles of instigator and victim are thus not fixed or permanent and may change over time and through life experience" (Ellington et al., 2015, p. 296). Further, the authors stated that experiences of domestic violence stem from interactive and conflict-based dynamics that are context-dependent, interactive, and reciprocal.

Given the heterogeneity of situations and the scale of domestic violence, Ellington et al. (2015) concluded that support was required for Indigenous men to stop engaging in violent behaviour as well as support for when they are victims. The authors recommended joint couple and family therapies, as opposed to one-to-one psychosocial interventions, along with conflict regulation and family healing models that take into account the historical–cultural dimensions and relational dynamics of the couples.

### Waseya Holistic Healing Program

Breaking the cycle of intergenerational domestic violence and repairing the resulting harms require addressing underlying causes such as the impacts of residential schools, and family and community unhealthiness. Waseskun House in Quebec provides pioneering and innovative programs that include therapeutic techniques such as healing circles, drumming ceremonies, sacred fires, cleansing ceremonies, sweat lodges and traditional feasts in addition to standard cognitive-behavioural practices (Aboriginal Healing Foundation, 2019). ■

## Human rights model of diverse ability

The UN Convention on the Rights of Persons with Disabilities manifests the paradigm change from a medical model to a human rights model.

These rights include recognition of equality, the right to independent and community living, and the right to accessibility, reasonable accommodation, and inclusive education (Degener, 2014).

# New Understandings of Diverse Abilities

The experience of people with diverse abilities varies greatly, and the population is not heterogeneous. Almost everyone, at some point in their life, will experience a temporary or permanent impairment in their functioning. The term "diverse abilities" is increasingly being used to focus on all of us being different, but able.

In 2017, about one in five adult Canadians (6.2 million individuals) reported being limited in their daily activities due to a disability (Morris, Fawcett, Brisebois, & Hughes, 2018). Of the adult Canadians with a disability, 37% reported a mild disability, 20% a moderate disability, 21% a severe disability, and 22% a very severe disability. Disability rates among Indigenous people are over twice the national rate.

### The Human Rights Model

Today, the social work profession is moving away from the medical model of disability (also referred to as the "personal tragedy" model) and adopting a "rights-based" perspective. In the medical model, management of a disability is aimed at finding a "cure."

In contrast to the medical model, the "social model of disability" views people as being disabled by societal barriers rather than their bodies. It is inaccessible environments that create barriers to participation and inclusion.

The **human rights model of diverse ability** focuses on a number of human rights, including the right to equal opportunities, the right to health care (physical and psychological), and the right to education and employment. This model is based on empowerment (see Figure 4.2). The person with diverse abilities and the person's family decide on what services and supports they wish to benefit from.

The service provider's role becomes one of offering guidance and help in carrying out the service user's decisions. Community integration is supported by "a broad array of habilitation, rehabilitation, residential and community integration services, including physical health care, sexual health education, school support, employment support, and home-living support" (Caux & Lecomte, 2017, p. 462).

**Figure 4.2** An Empowering Human Rights Model of Diverse Ability

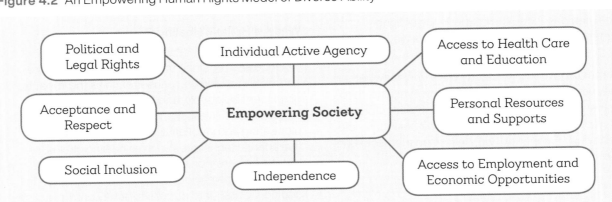

## Acquired Brain Injury: A Human Rights Response

Intellectual disabilities, to take one form of diverse ability, can have a variety of sources. According to Brain Injury Canada (n.d.), Acquired Brain Injury (ABI) affects over 1.5 million Canadians. Traumatic Brain Injury (TBI) is the leading cause of disability and death among Canadians under the age of 40 (Brain Injury Society of Toronto, n.d.). The most common causes of ABI are falls, assaults, road traffic accidents, sports injuries, and domestic violence (Holloway & Fyson, 2016).

The impact of ABI varies. While some people make a good recovery, others are left with significant ongoing difficulties, including "physical difficulties, cognitive difficulties, impairment of executive functioning, changes to a person's behaviour and changes to emotional regulation and 'personality'" (Holloway & Fyson, 2016, p. 1303). Providing supports to a person with ABI is complex, in part because of the heterogeneity of symptoms and in part because of the invisibility of damage to executive functions. Despite a social work imperative to provide autonomy and self-determination, individuals with ABI may have difficulties in communicating their views, wishes, and feelings as a result of their cognitive and executive impairments. The needs of a person with ABI may differ from those of a person with another type of cognitive impairment.

All social workers should be equipped to recognize and refer individuals who might be struggling with a brain injury. Knowing who is at risk and what to look for is an important first step. If a brain injury is suspected, social workers can, during an interview, ask several questions that may shed light on the individual's history of head trauma. These questions include the following:

- Have you ever been hit in the head?
- Have you ever lost consciousness?
- Have you ever had a concussion?
- Do you, or did you ever, play contact sports?
- Have you ever been in a car accident?
- Have you ever been in a physical fight or been a victim of violence?
- Are you a veteran? Were you ever injured in service?

If an event with the potential to have caused head trauma is found, social workers should follow up with questions about the immediate effect of the trauma, including amnesia, disorientation, or confusion, and then with further questions about the impact of the trauma on functioning in the weeks, months, and even years following the trauma.

Although the immediate response to a brain injury is medical in nature, social work has an important role to play in rehabilitative and longer-term support (Holloway & Fyson, 2016). Social work tasks may include assessing need, assessing mental capacity, assessing risk, and providing ongoing support and advocacy for the individual and others with similar injuries. Such a perspective is consistent with a human rights and social justice model of practice.

# Social Worker Exemplar

# Transitioning from "Helper" to "Ally"

## Alysha Piva

**During her field placement, Alysha began to develop a deeper understanding of oppression and the multiple ways she could work to combat oppression and violence and promote social justice.**

Alysha's first field placement was with an agency providing a range of life-skills programs for adults with diverse abilities. Her only relevant prior experience was with an aunt who had diverse abilities. Although this aunt had been in a violent relationship for 25 years, no one in the family knew about the abuse.

Alysha's initial response to a service user experiencing intimate partner violence may have been personally driven, but she used her earlier experiences to think about her role as a social worker in helping to combat intimate partner violence and promote social justice.

My first field placement was with a community agency that provided life-skills programs for adults with diverse abilities. One service user I remember well was Mandy. She was a 28-year-old woman with mild cerebral palsy who told me about the frequent verbal abuse and increasing physical abuse she received from her boyfriend. As she showed me a bruise on her forearm, I realized that I was becoming much angrier than I would have expected, and that I felt powerless to help. I kept asking myself "How could anyone ever harm a woman with diverse abilities?"

I believe that I have the personal characteristics of patience and understanding. I understand the professional value of respect for the inherent dignity and worth of individuals and the skill of unconditional positive regard. I have a good knowledge of person-centred approaches and anti-oppressive practices. In my practice, I strive to learn from service users by respectfully asking questions about their story. For example, when talking with a woman with diverse abilities who has experienced violence, I am mindful of how I may be perceived; being aware of the physical boundaries that she may have; and the importance of centring the conversation on the woman rather than her diverse abilities or the violence that she has experienced.

My only prior experience with the diverse abilities community was a remarkable aunt. My aunt had competed in the Special Olympics in snowshoeing, and had even slowed down at the end of the race so that her friend coming in behind her could win. However, she had lived most of her life in a violent relationship that was kept well away from the rest of the family and her friends.

Undoubtedly, my empathy and concern for Mandy were related to my experiences with my aunt. As I reflected on Mandy's circumstances, I thought about the underlying vulnerability factors for women with diverse abilities, especially physical vulnerability and those associated with low income. I also began to think about my own health and welfare. A few years ago, I was diagnosed with mild Crohn's disease and had to change my eating patterns and diet. However, I have always focused on strengths and didn't perceive myself as a hapless victim—as others sometimes did.

## The Power of Self-Reflection

My social location has sheltered me in certain aspects of my life, and this has led me to become curious and questioning. I also began to reflect on my own privileged situation. Prior to my practicum, I had not realized the reality of surviving on social assistance.

The women I encountered not only had diverse abilities, but also had a variety of other intersecting factors contributing to their oppression. I was born in a position of privilege, and my social location gave me opportunities to make decisions that would further enhance my privilege. Being in university, and now working with women with diverse abilities who are experiencing violence in their lives, had allowed me to assess myself more critically.

I also reflected on my understanding of power. I began to think about my initial sense of helplessness and realized that being an ally requires a commitment to social actions. I continue to ask myself: "What can I do in the agency on a day-to-day basis that might contribute to bring about more equal outcomes for everyone?"

I also realized that I could use my position to educate other service providers about the oppression that women with diverse abilities face and how violence is an added factor in a complex equation. I realized that I can act as an advocate for these women so that they can create their own solutions for dealing with violence. Other strategies could include reaching out to other service providers who advocate on behalf of women to see if the intersection of ability is addressed in their work.

Using a social work practice framework and viewing the situation from a feminist, ecosystems, and anti-oppressive lens, I was able to gain a deeper understanding and see below the proverbial iceberg.

My experiences in practicum changed my entire worldview. They taught me how to use reflexivity to integrate theory and practice, and to recognize intersectionality and multiple oppressions.

Most importantly, these experiences taught me to act not only as a helper but also as an ally. ∎

## Reflections on Alysha's Story

Alysha used her learning journals to document and reflect on her personal reactions to a situation she was already somewhat familiar with—intimate partner violence perpetuated on a woman with diverse abilities.

She used these earlier experiences to deepen her understanding of what social work was about, and what she and others could do to advance the interests of persons who are marginalized and oppressed. Alysha's practicum experience was transformational for her—it deepened her theoretical and practice knowledge, and strengthened her resolve to infuse an anti-oppressive perspective into her future practice as a social worker.

### From Theory to Practice

As you reflect on Alysha's story, give some thought to the following points:

1. What are other steps that Alysha could possibly take to be an active and authentic ally to these women?

2. What are some ways in which Mandy could be involved in activities alongside Alysha?

3. What other organizations and groups could Alysha and Mandy reach out to for additional strength and support?

4. What are some of your personal experiences that may situate you in a position to be an ally?

# Coming to Terms with Aging

There is increasing public concern about the treatment of elderly people in Canada, particularly in long-term care facilities. Moreover, negative images of aging abound. As with other lifespan populations, it is important to gain an understanding of older people's needs. This understanding can come through skillful assessment, education, and training.

Social work practitioners frequently take a routine and administrative approach to working with older adults. Those working in elder care settings end up having contact with some of the most disadvantaged and vulnerable people, and are at increased risk of developing distorted and negative views of old age (Richards, Donovan, Victor & Ross, 2007).

In a survey of social work practitioners, Richards et al. (2007) discovered that the most prominent understanding about old age was the practitioner's own personal experience of working with and knowing older people—usually aging parents or grandparents. Any explicit or implicit evidence of recognizable theoretical understandings of aging or old age, such as life-course development, remained vague. Additionally, the practitioners in the survey were more likely to attach greater weight to evidence from surveillance (community services they were attending) than to information that came directly from the older person or caregivers.

### Dementia: A Strengths-Based Approach to Practice with Older Adults

Dementia is an overall term that describes a group of symptoms associated with a decline in memory and problem-solving skills which reduce a person's ability to perform everyday activities. Dementia is common among older adults and is one of the major causes of dependency later in life.

A recent cross-Canada study revealed several overarching themes for providing dementia-related community care services (Tam-Tham et al., 2016). These include the importance of future planning and related services, educational and social support services, and home care and respite services. However, considerable variability was found across Canada in the provision of and access to these services.

Another Canadian study sought to understand emergency departments' responses to older adults with dementia in rural settings (Hunter, Parke, Babb, Forbes, & Strain, 2017). It found that, while there were limited health-care services, and less access to in-home support and respite care, health-care providers identified a "rural advantage" that was tied to their knowledge of the community. The health-care providers who participated in this study identified that "knowing the person from repeat visits to the emergency department in a small regional hospital and knowledge of who to connect with in local community services and how to do this" was an advantage (p. 9). They were also aware that familiarity could also be a disadvantage if it leads to assumptions about the individual and complacency in looking for changes in functions and health status.

---

## Dementia

Dementia is not a specific disease. Many diseases can cause dementia, including Alzheimer's disease, vascular dementia (due to strokes), Lewy body disease, head trauma, fronto-temporal dementia, Creutzfeldt-Jakob disease, Parkinson's disease, and Huntington's disease. These conditions can have similar and overlapping symptoms.

Dementia is progressive, which means the symptoms will gradually get worse as more brain cells become damaged and eventually die.

Social workers can provide strength-based practices to focus on "what remains" as opposed to what is lost (McGovern, 2015).

## Indigenous Knowledge and Healthy Aging

Although the Indigenous population is younger than the rest of the Canadian population, the population of Indigenous seniors is rising. In 2006, only 4.8% of the Indigenous population was 65 years of age or older. However, by 2016, this proportion rose to 7.3%. It is projected that the senior Indigenous population could more than double by 2036 (Statistics Canada, 2017).

While life expectancy is improving, poor social determinants continue to mean that Indigenous people have shorter lifespans on average than other Canadians. Indigenous seniors are more likely to face issues related to poverty (23% of Indigenous seniors live in poverty compared with 13% of non-Indigenous seniors) and food insecurity (9% of Indigenous seniors experience food insecurity as compared with 2% of non-Indigenous seniors) (O'Donnell, Wendt, & National Association of Friendship Centres, 2017).

The concepts and meaning of health and well-being are different for Indigenous people than non-Indigenous people. In general, Indigenous people focus on positive health, whereas Western medicine focuses on what's wrong. Good health in general and good health in aging are seen as a matter of resilience and as a balance in physical, mental, and emotional well-being (Canadian Institutes of Health Research, 2015).

Elders are often described as the "heart" of First Nations teaching and learning in Indigenous communities. According to the 1996 Royal Commission on Aboriginal Peoples, "the term Elder is used in an Aboriginal context to describe someone who is a cultural and spiritual guide and who has insights, understandings, and communication abilities to transmit the wisdom of previous generations" (as cited in Baskin & Davey, 2014, p. 47).

Elders hold crucial roles in imparting tradition, knowledge, culture, and values (First Nations Pedagogy Online, 2009). As Turcotte and Schellenberg (2007) note:

> Seniors are revered in many Aboriginal cultures for their knowledge and experiences, and the integral role they play in the vitality and well-being of their families, communities and nations." (p. 221)

Collings (2001) points out that Inuit of Holman, Nunavut, view successful old age as the ability of the individual to manage declining health, rather than a state of good health. Moreover, the most important determinant of a "successful" elderhood is ideological, not material. Collings observes that "an individual's attitudes in late life, and particularly their willingness to transmit their accumulated wisdom and knowledge to their juniors, are the critical determinants of whether an Elder is viewed as having a successful old age" (p. 127).

# Critical Theory and Immigration Practices

Canada often prides itself on welcoming immigrants, and many Canadians celebrate the diversity resulting from successive waves of newcomers. The three studies below demonstrate how a critical theory analysis makes visible some of the racialized and intersectional inequalities associated with Canadian immigration and settlement experiences.

## (1) Racist Practices Continue with the "Canadian Experience"

In 2008, the Canadian Experience Class (CEC) was introduced as a program that allows individuals who have worked in Canada for at least one year to gain permanent resident status. The CEC was developed for temporary foreign workers and foreign graduates with qualifying Canadian work experience. This requirement includes "soft skills" (knowledge of Canadian values, behaviours, identities as well as communication skills) and "hard skills" (credentials from recognized institutions). However, the CEC requirement has been identified as a barrier for skilled immigrants and has been identified by the Ontario Human Rights Code as a racist hiring practice (Bhuyan, Jeyapal, Ku, Sakamoto & Chou, 2017).

In a discourse analysis of Canada's immigration policies, Bhuyan et al. (2017) examined government policy documents and three major English-language daily newspapers. These researchers found a persistent discriminatory effect on racialized immigrants gaining employment, related to the introduction of the CEC. Their analysis suggested that the CEC requirement negatively affects racialized minority applicants and contributes to the construction of "other-other." The authors concluded that its effect was to whitewash "racist undertones that have always been fundamental to both immigrant selection policy and the structural barriers that racialized immigrants face in Canada" (p. 60).

## (2) Diverse Ability and Immigration: "Othering of the Other"

In another study using a critical lens, El-Lahib (2017) examined how diverse abilities constitute another form of "othering the other" in the immigration process. Her discussion is contextualized within a Global North–South divide in which the North represents dominant knowledge and the South the colonized other.

El-Lahib (2017) argues that the "medical model of disability masks the marginalization of people with disabilities within immigration" (p. 640). The dominant medical model discourse constructs people with diverse abilities as potentially dependent and therefore inadmissible. She provides an example of a Costa Rican family denied residence in Canada because of a 13-year-old son with Down's syndrome, thus reinforcing ableist ideas of people with diverse abilities as "burdens."

El-Lahib (2017) concludes that the medical model discourse has a "direct bearing on marginalization and exclusion of people with disabilities in immigration, as they construct people with disabilities as a potential 'burden' on health and social service systems should they be granted immigration status" (p. 649).

### (3) A "Double Minority": Young Chinese Immigrant Gay Men

Chinese gay men, frequently defined as a "double minority," have been described as having post-migration experiences characterized as challenging, socially exclusionary, and violent. Huang and Fang's (2019) study of young Chinese immigrant gay men explored their intersectional minority identities and experiences in Toronto.

While most of the participants in this study indicated that they did not experience identity conflicts between their sexual orientation and their Chinese cultural background, some did describe intersectional marginalization—for example, a 20-year-old Taiwanese man stated, "If I were a White gay man, everything would be easier" (Huang & Fang, 2019, p. 32). However, almost all participants described discriminating dating experiences. For example, on online gay dating websites, "Chinese gay men have been repeatedly relegated to an invisible, undesirable, and/or unpopular position, as exemplified by the phrase 'No Asian!'" (p. 32).

A third theme in the study was the contesting and expanding of the oversimplified idea of being a "double minority." Some participants detested the term "minority," with its derogatory meaning, and instead stressed that their unique situation served as a source of social support. The participants also commented that other factors helped to shape their social experiences and sense of self. These included factors such as socio-economic status, physical attractiveness, and religion.

### Implications for Social Work Practice

Although Canada's immigration policies appear to be working well in many respects, there continues to be a widening socio-economic gap between newcomers and the Canadian-born population, with newcomers experiencing higher unemployment and lower income levels. A large majority of newcomers do not take advantage of the availability of education, language classes, and/or employment training. Possible explanations for this include a lack of programs commensurate with education and work experiences, lack of accessible transportation to the programs, and lack of child care. In addition, particularly for women, there may be gender and cultural barriers to economic and social integration (Sethi, 2015).

Understanding a social group through an intersectional lens means gaining a nuanced understanding of personal experiences, as each person's context is unique. Social workers have responsibilities to pay attention to both "individual and structural factors in assisting immigrants settle successfully in their host communities" (Sethi, 2015, p. 156). This can be done by partnering with immigrant and refugee community agencies and by ensuring social work graduates have the knowledge and tools to help newcomers navigate their new terrain.

Finally, while ensuring that services and resources are in place for newcomers, social workers should also consider using asset-based practice models in which racial and intersectional identities are seen as a source of strength and community connection.

# Practice Scenarios

Working in areas of difference and diversity means paying attention to the variations between populations and within a social group. Individuals are not simply victims or perpetrators, oppressed or oppressor. Each individual has nuances of privilege and marginalization.

In all situations, socials workers have responsibilities to facilitate access to services and to challenge barriers to individual resilience. They also have a social justice responsibility to make visible the structures that marginalize and exclude groups of people based on their race, age, ethnicity, religion, sexual orientation and gender identity, and/or abilities.

In these practice scenarios, consider both individual barriers and individual strengths, as well as structural challenges to one or more dimensions of marginalization.

---

## 4.1 Transitioning to an Independent Lifestyle

Logan, now in his early 20s, was a troublesome and challenging adolescent. He had some minor run-ins with the law, was not attending school, and was using substances to the point of blackout and overdose. He was living at home, but not contributing or heeding family rules, when, at 18, he had a serious motorcycle accident that resulted in paraplegia. He also sustained major head injuries. Since the accident, his parents have been meeting all of his care needs.

Now Logan has significant challenges with impulse control, emotional self-regulation, and motivation. He is angry much of the time, which he displays to his mother frequently through swearing and throwing items, including his catheter bags. Although he is able to wash and get dressed, he does not initiate any other activities, including making food or drinks for himself. His family would like him to move out and begin a more independent life, but wants supports in place for the transition.

1. What are some of the barriers and challenges for someone who had a significant accident in their late teens?

2. How does having a diverse ability at 18 intersect with human development theory?

3. What individual services could be offered to the family?

4. What structural challenges may impede Logan and his family's wishes?

## 4.2 Spirituality and Cultural Safety

You are a non-Indigenous mental health worker who has been asked to provide a three-day workshop on grief in a remote Indigenous community. Throughout the workshop, the concepts of holism and connections to nature, the environment, and spirituality have been explored.

The group has requested that the final exercise incorporate a prayer circle and a fire ceremony. This is not part of your cultural belief system—either personally or professionally.

1. How does the intersection of cultural safety and spirituality inform your actions?

2. What are the strengths of these community members as they work through their grief?

3. What are ways to proceed that respect the needs of the group without appropriating cultural beliefs and practices?

4. Describe instances when you have been asked to facilitate a practice that is not consistent with your own cultural belief system.

## 4.3 Family Caregiving across Cultures

You are working at Immigrant and Refugee Services, when Marta, who is part of a church group that sponsored a Syrian family, comes in to report a concern about an infant being neglected. She describes the family, who arrived to Canada from Syria two years ago, as Haya (mom) and Aland (dad), and four children, aged 12, 9, 5, and 18 months. Justina, the youngest, was born in Canada. Both parents attended English-language school, and the father has attained a job in a restaurant kitchen.

Justina has not started walking, and is very tiny. She rarely interacts with Marta when she visits, not making eye contact, playing, or chatting with her. Haya is often in bed when Marta visits, and the 12-year-old daughter seems to be the primary caregiver for Justina. Marta is aware that Haya was a victim of sexual violence and lost a child in the refugee camp. However, now Marta is wondering whether child protection should be involved to investigate Justina's care.

1. How might the norms associated with family caregiving be different between a Syrian family and a Canadian family?

2. How would the experience of being in a refugee camp and being a refugee in Canada affect the family?

3. What are the strengths in this family?

4. How do culture and ethnicity interface with mental wellness?

# Field Education Practicalities
## Supervision and Feedback

Receiving supervision and hearing feedback is an important part of field education and will continue to be important throughout one's career. When working in areas of difference, it is particularly important to seek feedback to ensure that one's practice is inclusive, safe, and respectful.

Practising self-supervision and giving oneself feedback is a very productive form of assessment. Feedback from others is best understood as a strengthening exercise rather than criticism. Further, feedback is simply someone's perspective. How one chooses to receive it, and what one chooses to do with it, after listening openly, is within one's control.

Receiving supervision and feedback from colleagues and supervisors is essential to continuous learning and improvement. As such, the CASWE-ACFTS *Standards for Accreditation* (2014) include the following requirement:

> The field placement/setting assures that the field instructor has sufficient time and resources within the work schedule to develop planned learning opportunities and tasks, to prepare for educational supervision with the student, to attend school-sponsored workshops and to prepare reports and evaluations. (SB/M 3.2.18, p. 15)

Receiving supervision and feedback is a continuous process that will occur post-degree and throughout your career. Learning to participate in a process of self-supervision and learning to accept supervision and feedback are skills worth practising during field education.

### Making the Most of Supervision

The process of self-supervision, supervision, and receiving feedback occur both informally and formally. The informal process begins early in one's field education and is generally supportive and formative (it helps students identify strengths and target areas that need work). The formal processes are summative and evaluative in nature, usually occurring at the midpoint and end of your field education.

Throughout the practicum, and indeed throughout your career, it is helpful to undertake a self-supervision process prior to participating in formal supervision. Self-supervision refers to reflecting on your role and performance in the activities you are involved in (O'Hara, Weber, & Levine, 2016). O'Hara et al. (2016) describe self-supervision as a process of recalling experiences and observations, and then reflecting on feelings, thoughts, and actions.

Supervision is a necessary component of social work, and it is essential in the practicum. It is intended to assist you with the formation of your confidence as a social worker—it is not simply a monitoring function. It is important for you to be proactive as a supervisee in the supervision process.

### A Key Component of Learning

The supervisory relationship in field education is key to integrative learning and transformative experiences. In Ketner, Cooper-Bolinskey, and VanCleave's (2017) study on the perspectives of social work students on supervision in field education, students identified the benefits of receiving feedback from supervisors as being crucial to their learning. Supervision provided students with confidence and assurance, as well as the opportunity to develop critical thinking. Additionally, the ability to ask questions increased the sense of ability to undertake social work practice.

While most students are satisfied with the supervision and support they receive during placement, differences occur between the frequency of supervision, type of learning activities, and who provides the learning opportunities (Cleak, Roulston, Vreugdenhil, 2016). Cleak et al. (2016) suggest "that students are most satisfied across all aspects of the placement where there is a strong on-site social work presence" (p. 2036).

Receiving feedback helps improve one's practice. It is an important component of any interactional model of communication and a key to professional development. However, it is important to remember that feedback is simply one person's perception, based on their knowledge and experience.

### Improving Feedback

The Johari Window model is a psychological tool created by Joseph Luft and Harry Ingham in 1955 to improve self-awareness and mutual understanding within a group (Luft & Ingham, 1955). The model can be adapted to understand feedback situations.

The model works using four quadrants (see Figure 4.3):

- **Open area.** Anything you know about yourself and are willing to share is part of your "open area."

- **Blind area.** Any aspect that you do not know about yourself, but that others have become aware of, is in your "blind area."

- **Hidden area.** There are also aspects about yourself that you are aware of, but might not want others to know about—your "hidden area."

- **Unknown or unconscious area.** The fourth quadrant, the "unknown or unconscious area," is unknown to you or to anyone else.

The balance between the quadrants can change. You might want to tell someone about an aspect of your life that you had previously kept hidden from everyone. It is also possible to increase your open area by asking for feedback.

By working with others, it is possible for you and others to discover aspects of yourself that you had never appreciated before. ■

**Figure 4.3** The Johari Window Model for Improving Self-Awareness and Mutual Understanding

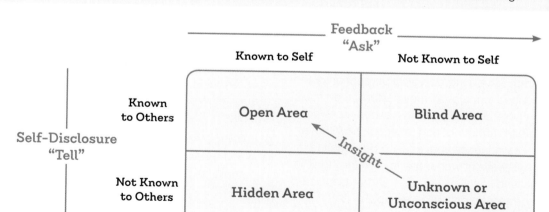

**Source:** Adapted from Luft and Ingham (1955).

# Reflection, Learning, and More Practice

## Field Education Practicalities

1. Discuss with your field colleagues how their, and your, social locations and intersections affect the work of your field agency.

2. Identify the programs and services that are available for people with Acquired Brain Injury in your community or for people with diverse abilities who are from Indigenous communities.

3. Identify queer safe spaces in your university and community.

4. Review written materials in your field agency for the use of inclusive language.

5. Identify examples of cultural appropriation in your agency, community, or region. Describe ways you can ensure you are always acting in culturally appropriate ways, given your social location.

6. Ensure that you have incorporated some formal supervision and feedback time with your field supervisor and/or colleagues.

7. Ensure also that you allow some time for self-supervision in your daily activities.

## Journal Ideas

1. Identify a population you believe you are an ally to. Describe some small ways, in your daily practice, in which you can demonstrate that you are an active ally.

2. Any social worker, regardless of their gender identity, may have a stereotypical perception of the traits ascribed to males as they perform their social role as fathers. Journal your own experiences as they relate to "fathering" and reflect on how those experiences influence your social work practice. Identify two ways of working with men through the emotional and social power differences associated with male interpersonal relationships.

3. Describe your preparation to work in a specific area of difference.

## Critical-Thinking Questions

1. Social work students are tasked with developing competency in "working with difference." How would you assess the program you are in with respect to developing that competency? What could be done to improve your competence in this area?

2. Often, social activism is associated with participating in large public events (e.g., parades, protests). Is it possible to incorporate social activism in small ways in everyday practice? What types of activities could be incorporated into your daily work that may influence broader social change and social justice?

3. In 2017, many Canadians celebrated the 150th anniversary of Confederation. Indigenous groups planned protests to remind Canadians that 150 years of cultural genocide and colonial oppression is nothing to celebrate. Consider the differences between these two views.

4. What are some of the factors associated with successful and healthy aging in Indigenous peoples? If you are not an Indigenous person, how does this compare to your own culture's perspectives on aging?

5. Compare and contrast the medical model of disability with the human rights or social model of diverse ability.

6. Research the relevant legislation in your province or territory in relation to persons with diverse abilities. Which diverse ability ideology does it take?

7. Investigate Human Rights Commission complaints in your province or territory. What issues are the complaints commonly related to?

# Chapter Review

While it is impossible to be fully competent in all the variability and fluidity associated with identity intersections, social workers are required to acknowledge the multiple positions and diverse experiences of individuals and societal structures of oppression and marginalization.

As social workers develop competency in working in areas of diversity, becoming an ally means developing authentic relationships with people with differences and to be a valuable collaborator in the struggle for equal rights.

Working with difference requires having conversations with and creating safe spaces for Indigenous and racialized people, for women's voices, for men's inclusion in family life, for queer identities, for people with diverse abilities (including those who have intellectual or psychiatric differences), and for older adults. Individuals' lived experiences and intersecting identities may serve as both a form of oppression and a form of privilege. Social workers listen for opportunities to learn from unique individuals who have variable experiences with self-identity. Simultaneously, social workers seek opportunities to understand communities as empowering and strengthening, and identify ways to be an ally in social justice endeavours.

Alysha recognized that seeing a person with diverse abilities as a victim was not necessarily consistent with the person's self-identity. She also recognized the importance of individual empowerment and strengthening resilience at an individual level as well as her ability as an ally to make visible the intersection of diverse abilities and gender violence.

In the practice scenarios, it is important to develop an awareness of the challenges of groups of people who are marginalized, while seeing the inherent strengths in individuals.

Ultimately, developing openness to seeking feedback and reflecting on one's use of language will support the development of competent practice in areas of difference.

## Respecting Diversity and Difference in Practice

This chapter outlines numerous ways in which students can develop culturally safe practices as they respect diversity and difference. Here are some highlights and further suggestions:

- Be aware of your own "baggage" and how it may influence your understanding of people and populations who represent diversity.
- Talk with people about their lived experiences as "double minorities," and when multiple differences intersect for them.
- Develop culturally safe practices by learning about and listening to people's experiences.
- Ask people who represent difference from you what "safe care" means to them.
- Become an ally through finding small ways to practise social action.
- Participate in socio-political actions to facilitate societal change aimed at social justice.
- Do not imitate cultural practices that are not your own.
- Include men in conversations about family care and emotional well-being.
- Use inclusive and gender-neutral language.
- Be aware of hetero-normative language.
- Recognize the hidden impairments associated with Acquired Brain Injury.
- Question how societal change can influence respect for ableism.
- Pay attention to the changing and diverse needs of older adults.
- Recognize individual variations and strengths as differences intersect.

# Conducting Assessments 5

> Psychosocial assessments are the foundation of service delivery and underpin targeted and needs-based interventions.
>
> —Australian Association of Social Workers, *Scope of Social Work Practice: Psychosocial Assessments*, 2015, p. 5

# Chapter at a Glance

# Spotlight on Social Work Luminaries
## Andrew Turnell and Steve Edwards

**Andrew Turnell** and **Steve Edwards**, social work scholars from Western Australia, have attracted international attention for their strengths-based and safety-organized approach to child-protection assessment. Their "Signs of Safety" model has attracted international attention and is used in jurisdictions in Canada, the United States, Europe, and Australasia.

Accurate and holistic assessments are the bedrock of social work practice. Assessments are completed in practice areas in which multiple issues intersect and are highly complex (e.g., mental health, substance use, and child welfare). In these contexts, the assessment is essential for bringing together all the elements of the situation in order to develop an intervention plan.

An assessment is both a process and an outcome. Its purpose is to develop a holistic understanding that identifies needs, strengths, and coping capacity as well as available formal and informal resources and support networks.

The assessment process itself is service user-centred and collaborative, and involves the application of "multiple knowledges." This chapter looks at the social work principles that guide conducting assessments in a way that engages the service user and respects the key ethical principles of informed consent, transparency, and appropriate record-keeping.

# Developing Competence as a Social Worker

Some ways to develop the meta-competency of "**conducting assessments**" are as follows:

- Become familiar with the policies and tools associated with screening and assessment in your field agency.

- Ask permission to shadow colleagues as they undertake a complete assessment process. Know that an assessment may occur over multiple sessions.

- After attending an assessment session, complete your own written assessment. (Note: This is for personal learning; your assessment should subsequently be shredded.)

- Take an opportunity to sit with a long-term service user and ask them about their story. Pay close attention to how they perceive their interactions with social workers.

- Commit to conducting interviews that are focused on the service user as someone who has both strengths and resources that can be brought to bear on the situation.

## Key Concepts

- Counselling and interviewing skills
- Unconditional positive regard
- Social history assessment
- Assessment in the moment
- Mental Status Examination (MSE)
- Diagnostic and Statistical Manual of Mental Disorders (DSM)
- CAGE screening tool
- Cultural Formulation Interview (CFI)
- Thunderbird Partnership Foundation

## The Assessment Process

The purpose of assessment is to collect all the relevant information so that the social worker can then go on to recommend a course of action that will effectively address the service user's concerns. Assessments can be conducted for an individual, family, community, or a particular population.

### Case Conceptualization

The assessment phase is the initial step in developing a case conceptualization. The case conceptualization consists of a clear and comprehensive written statement of the problem (or problems) at hand, including the likely causes, the antecedents, and the maintaining influences. The case conceptualization is an ongoing process that can be reviewed and amended, if necessary, as the intervention proceeds.

The pre-conditions for good assessment are the development of a positive relationship with the service user as well as the use of sound **counselling and interviewing skills**. Successful psychosocial assessments depend on the following:

- Establishing an empathic and respectful working relationship with the service user
- Exploring and understanding the service user's difficulties, strengths, and resources
- Gathering information from the service user's family members and others so as to build a comprehensive understanding of the broader context of the service user's life
- Working from a culturally informed and anti-oppressive framework that fully considers the cultural context of the service user's life
- Identifying and assessing relevant risk indicators in order to minimize hazards to the service user or to others
- Applying knowledge and theory in order to develop a comprehensive statement summarizing the service user's individual functioning (strengths and difficulties)
- Reviewing the assessment statement with the service user to ensure a mutual understanding and agreement
- Regularly reviewing the assessment to ensure continuing shared understanding of their difficulties and strengths
- Maintaining accurate records (Australian Association of Social Workers [AASW], 2015)

At the first meeting, both the service user and the social worker are naturally somewhat anxious, nervous, and hopeful. The first task of the social worker is to help the service user feel more comfortable. This can be achieved in part by initiating friendly introductions and an agreement on how to refer to each other.

The first meeting is also the time to provide basic information to the service user about what to expect. Topics covered include confidentiality, informed consent processes, policies about between-meeting contacts (e.g., phone and electronic contact), and any other constraints.

### Counselling and interviewing skills

Positive relationships with service users require sound counselling and interviewing skills.

Merrill (2013) emphasizes that communications should be:

- **Friendly.** Social workers should always be warm, compassionate, concerned, supportive, and service user-centred.

- **Frank.** Social workers should be direct, candid, and unafraid to ask or talk about risks plainly.

- **Firm.** Social workers should ask questions in a confident tone and insist that the discussion is essential, imperative, and necessary.

Conducting an assessment is required to develop a complete picture of the service user's situation in order to provide the most efficacious interventions. The importance for social workers to have assessment skills is entrenched in all the frameworks and standards that inform this text and guide integrative learning in field education.

## CASWE-ACFTS *Standards for Accreditation*

The ninth core learning objective in the the CASWE-ACFTS *Standards for Accreditation* (Canadian Association for Social Work Education–Association canadienne pour la formation en travail social [CASWE-ACFTS], 2014) states:

9. Engage with individuals, families, groups, and communities through professional practice.

   i) Social work students are equipped with knowledge and skills to competently perform various interactive practices such as engagement, assessment, intervention, negotiation, mediation, advocacy, and evaluation.

## Professional Regulation and Competency

The Canadian Council of Social Work Regulators (CCSWR, 2012) identifies "**conducting assessments**" as a meta-competency, which is described as follows:

Assess clients' situation and needs in relation to current professional standards and jurisdictional requirements.

This meta-competency includes the following subcompetencies:

23. Assess service users' eligibility for services.

24. Assess the strengths, needs and resources of individuals, groups, families, and communities.

[. . .]

26. Assess service users' risk of danger to self and others.

The CCSWR (2012) lists a number of other factors that need to be considered in a complete biopsychosocial-spiritual assessment (e.g., substance use, housing, employment, isolation, marginalization, cultural and sexual/gender factors, and readiness for services).

The CCSWR identifies two additional competencies associated with assessment:

- Gather pertinent information by systematic questioning and discussions.

- Inform and involve service user in the intake/assessment process.

For a full list of the CCSWR sub-competencies in relation to assessment, refer to the CCSWR *Entry-Level Competency Profile for the Social Work Profession in Canada* (CCSWR, 2012).

## Association of Social Work Boards (ASWB)

For social workers aiming to write the ASWB BSW exam, knowledge, skills, and abilities associated with assessment comprise 29% of the exam.

The major sections within this area are as follows:

- Biopsychosocial history and collateral data

- Assessment methods and techniques

- Concepts of abuse and neglect

Examples of subsections include:

- The components and function of the mental status examination

- The indicators of mental and emotional illness throughout the lifespan

- Methods to assess motivation, resistance, and readiness to change

- Methods used to assess trauma

For a full list of the ASWB content areas in relation to assessment, refer to the *Content Outlines and KSAs* (Association of Social Work Boards, 2018). ∎

# Developing Professional Relationships

**Unconditional positive regard**

Unconditional positive regard is a concept developed by American psychologist Carl Rogers. Rogers was a founder of the humanistic (or "client-centred") approach to psychology.

According to Rogers (1980), "The central hypothesis of this approach can be briefly stated. It is that the individual has within him or her self vast resources for self-understanding, for altering her or his self-concept, attitudes, and self-directed behavior— and that these resources can be tapped if only a definable climate of facilitative psychological attitudes can be provided" (Rogers, 1980, p. 115).

One of the meta-competencies identified in this book is "**developing professional relationships**." This meta-competency involves being collaborative and empowering, demonstrating genuine concern and empathy, and respecting the self-determination of service users.

Although social workers have multiple roles, at the core of all of these roles is being able to develop professional relationships in intelligent and flexible ways. Many students initially see this as the easy part of social work, but soon begin to appreciate the complexity of this essential skill. They also discover that, despite mastery of relationship-building skills, one can still fail to develop a meaningful connection with a service user on occasion.

A professional relationship is the foundation of effective social work practice, whether that relationship involves providing assessment and interventions to individuals and their families, to groups of people and communities, or to policy-makers in the context of social justice advocacy.

### Engagement in Helping Relationships

In virtually all communication and counselling textbooks, the core conditions of engaging in a helping relationship draw upon the work of American psychologist Carl Rogers (1902–1987). Rogers described **unconditional positive regard** as the quality that creates the best conditions for personal growth (Shebib, 2017).

Through showing unconditional positive regard, regardless of what the person says or does, practitioners can provide the best possible conditions for personal growth to the service user. Key factors in unconditional positive regard are warmth, empathy, genuineness, and non-verbal cues.

### *Warmth*

Warmth communicates comfort and trust, and is particularly important in the early phase of connecting. It suggests that "I'm approachable, you do not need to be afraid of me, I won't take advantage of your vulnerability, I'm a kind person" (Shebib, 2017, p. 67). Of course, social workers need to be flexible in terms of how they express this warmth, as some service users may interpret warmth as manipulative, and others may be uncomfortable or suspicious.

### *Empathy*

Likewise, empathy communicates understanding and acceptance. Empathy is characterized by one's willingness to learn about someone else's world. According to Shebib (2017), empathy has two components. First, one must be able to perceive the service user's feelings and perspectives; second, one must be able to make an empathic response.

Empathy begins with suspending judgement and requires considerable discipline in terms of controlling one's personal biases, assumptions, and reactions that otherwise might contaminate mutual understanding (Shebib, 2017).

### Genuineness

Being genuine is important as well. It means being authentic and real in relationships. Shebib (2017) states that "counsellors who are genuine show high consistency between what they think and do, and between what they feel and express" (p. 69).

To be genuine requires social workers to have a high level of self-awareness with respect to both how they themselves are feeling and how they are transmitting their feelings to service users.

### Non-Verbal Cues

As much as 65% of a message may be conveyed non-verbally. Social workers need to interpret the service user's non-verbal cues with caution. In the development of a professional relationship, social workers also have to be aware of how their own non-verbal behaviour may be interpreted by the service user. Frowning, turning away, or increasing one's physical distance may be interpreted as displeasure. By contrast, smiling, using a pleasant tone of voice, increasing eye contact, and leaning toward the service user may be interpreted by the service user as an expression of interest and warmth (Shebib, 2017).

During interactions with service users, social workers should look for non-verbal cues from the service user. These clues may indicate that they are speaking too much or that the mood of the conversation has shifted one way or the other.

## Fostering Healthy, Professional Relationships

Shebib (2017) suggests that social workers should ask themselves a number of introspective questions to better understand their attitudes and behaviours in helping relationships:

- How can I act so that service users will see me as trustworthy? (This means that social workers do what they say they will do and act in a way that is consistent with how they feel. It requires social workers to communicate without ambiguity and contradiction.)

- Can I permit myself to experience positive attitudes of warmth, caring, liking, interest, and respect toward service users?

- Am I strong enough as a person to maintain a professional distance from service users? This requires a high level of maturity, self-awareness, and courage. Rogers summarizes this challenge:

    Am I strong enough in my own separateness that I will not be downcast by [service users'] depression, frightened by [their] fear, nor engulfed by [their] dependency? Is my inner self hardy enough to realize that . . . I exist separate from [them] with feelings and rights of my own? (Rogers, 1961, p. 52)

- Am I secure enough to permit service users their separateness? (Service users are not under social workers' control, nor are they to be moulded into what social workers feel they should be.)

- Can I let myself fully empathize with the service users' feelings and world perspectives without evaluating or judging?

# The Social History Assessment

The most common assessment is the **social history assessment** (also called a "social assessment"). This type of assessment focuses on the social aspects of the service user's functioning and situation. Typically, it is concerned with how well the service user's needs align with the resources available to meet those needs.

## The Principles Associated with Assessment

There are many formats for the social history assessment, depending on the agency and the type of issues involved. If a social history assessment is to be undertaken, then the service user should be informed that the first session will be different from subsequent ones. For example:

> "Today, I am going to be asking quite a few questions to try and understand your situation better. At the end of this meeting, I can provide some ideas on how we are likely to proceed—and I may give you some ideas for things to try this week—yes, homework! Next week, we will then start working in a different way, and I will not be asking as many questions."

When compiling the background information of a service user, you will likely have to take written notes (ages, dates, medications, etc.). In subsequent sessions, remembering the content and then developing written notes immediately afterwards is a recommended practice (Goldbloom, 2010, p. 2).

In order to develop a comprehensive assessment report, social workers must pay attention to relationship building and cultural safety throughout the session. They must also ensure that the following three areas are covered:

- **Informed consent.** It is important to advise the service user about confidentiality issues, and the limits to confidentiality (e.g., harm to self/others; court subpoena, child abuse). If you are taking notes (or recording sessions) during or after a session, inform the service user about who has access to these notes and any subsequent clinical records, as well as their rights to access them.

- **Transparency in assessment.** At the first meeting, it is necessary to inform the service user of the purpose of the assessment and how it will be used. The service user should be encouraged to ask questions about the assessment itself and the assessment guidelines of the agency. Some practice frameworks require that service users sign off on the assessment and the treatment plan to ensure full transparency.

- **Remembering and recording.** An important aspect in assessment is keeping accurate, comprehensive, and meaningful records (Brew & Kottler, 2017). Taking notes during a session has the advantage of an almost-literal transcript. However, it has multiple disadvantages. When taking notes, it is challenging to maintain eye contact and listen effectively to what the service user is saying. Additionally, taking notes may be distracting to the service user who may wonder why you are writing some things down and not others.

A social history assessment is a professional document that social workers prepare that describes the social aspects of the service user's functioning and situation.

## Assessment in the moment

Assessment may occur over a period of time or it may be an **assessment in the moment**. Thom Garfat at Ryerson University and Grant Charles at the University of British Columbia have extensive experience in the field of child and youth care, particularly in mental health. They have carefully studied and explored what they call the "intervention moment."

As they describe it, the "intervention moment" begins with an initial observation during which the social worker notices the need or opportunity for intervention. Once this moment is identified, the worker attempts to understand how this individual's behaviour connects to the broader context, taking into account the meaning given to the events by that individual. Then a decision about whether to take any action is made (Garfat & Charles, 2012).

Garfat and Charles indicate that this process of meaning-making and conceptualization has four parts:

- **The situation.** Noticing the opportunities to intervene.
- **The framework.** Connecting the situation to the context and larger systems.
- **The interpretation.** Being self-aware and consciously reflecting on the meaning you give to the situation.
- **The intervention.** The decision to intervene, or not, and deciding what type of intervention is best.

Following the intervention, the social worker then needs to reflect on their own experience of the situation. This requires being self-aware and reflective of internal processes, experiences, and responses.

Self-reflective questions might include the following:

- Why did I notice the events when I did, what caused me to become aware, and why was it important enough for me to notice?
- Would another worker have noticed it?
- Is there something I'm not seeing? How would someone else see it?
- Am I thinking about the situation because of my own social location?
- Am I annoyed by it? Why? If not, why not?

The decision to intervene, or not to intervene, is based on the worker's analysis and experience of the moment, checking in with self, and the meaning given to the events by the service user. Ultimately, the decision to intervene has to be made on the basis of what is deemed to be in the best interest of the service user at that particular time.

## Assessment in the moment

Frequently used in residential facilities, assessment in the moment refers to the understanding and meaning-making that is attached to behaviours as they are occurring.

# Social Worker Exemplar

## Assessing for Risk of Violence

Caroline Neale

**Social workers are often called upon to provide independent assessments for risk of violence. All potential risk situations warrant careful and diligent attention and consideration of services that may mediate future escalation or occurrences.**

As a community worker with experience in mental health counselling, Caroline was asked to be available to assess an employee flown in from a remote work camp.

Many men and women work in such environments throughout Canada. They live in proximity to virtual strangers, away from their family and natural support systems.

The supervisors at this particular camp had concerns that an employee was becoming increasingly violent, and perhaps even experiencing mental health decompensation.

I met a slightly built young man in a waiting room. He was dressed appropriately in clean jeans and shirt, and appeared well groomed. He smiled and shook my hand and introduced himself as Devon. His general demeanour was typical for a first-time interview, although he appeared a little nervous. I spoke briefly with Devon and the supervisor, and Devon willingly agreed to meet with me in a private office.

Following an initial exchange, I asked Devon if he knew why he had been brought into the office. He responded that he wasn't sure, although there were two or three incidents at the work camp over the previous week or so that may have led to this visit. He reported a situation in which a co-worker had been cajoling him into working in an unsafe way. He didn't want to do it and felt he was being set up. He later reported the incident to a supervisor. Two days later, some of his co-workers ridiculed him at the dinner table in front of others. Devon felt uncomfortable and unsure of what to do.

Devon was a 22-year-old Indigenous man who had experienced bullying throughout his childhood and early teen years. This was his fourth rotation (three weeks in/one week out) at the work camp. As a teenager, he had learned Karate in order to feel more confident. As a young man, he developed some expertise with nunchuks (a martial arts weapon consisting of two sticks attached by a short chain or rope). When he was feeling especially stressed, he would find a quiet place and practise nunchuk routines, which he did the night of the dinner ridicule.

A couple of days after that dinner incident, the taunting began again. This time, cultural and homophobic slurs were thrown into the mix. Devon said he felt powerless to respond at the time, but that night he decided that he was going to confront the main guy who was bullying him. He went to that person's room and began banging on the door. When the other person didn't open, he began shouting, swearing, and being generally offensive. Security was called. They removed Devon and told him to leave this fellow alone.

The next day, Devon was informed that he was to attend counselling. Devon told Caroline that he had no history of violence, no criminal record, and no mental health history. He used no substances while in the work camp.

## Assessment in the moment

Devon did say that he was beginning to feel like he did not know what to do or whom to trust. I asked for an example: He described that when he arrived at the airport earlier that day, he could see police walking around. He felt that the police were there because he was there—although he wasn't approached by the police. However, the way they were looking at him made him uncomfortable. He eventually asked the supervisor he was with if the police were there because of him. The supervisor said "no."

At this stage in the assessment, my perception was that there was nothing noteworthy about Devon's general behaviour, mood, flow of thought, memory, attention, etc. I could see no evidence of mental health decompensation. If anything, I was feeling a great deal of empathy for him. He had very rapid speech. I asked him directly about this, and he attributed it to nervousness. He also said that he hadn't slept well the night before, as he knew he was in trouble, and he didn't want to lose his job.

I asked permission from Devon to speak with the supervisor alone to get some collateral and contextual information. I asked the supervisor to recount his knowledge of the events leading to Devon's being flown out of the work camp. The supervisor's account supported Devon's account. The supervisor also added that there is often some quasi-hazing of the younger men. Moreover, although the supervisors try to monitor it, they know they are not entirely successful in stopping it. He also said that nunchuks were now going to be banned from the site.

My last question to the supervisor was this: "Were the police at the airport in attendance due to Devon being brought in?" His answer was "yes."

On balance, I assessed no immediate danger to Devon or anyone else at the work camp. He had supports in the community and was staying with them during his time in town. Devon did attend counselling two more times during his brief time in town. Alternative stress-reduction skills and assertiveness skills were discussed. ∎

## Reflections on Caroline's Story

This situation required assessment in the moment. Like many such assessments, virtually no information was available prior to the meeting. The first step was to begin to develop a relationship with Devon. Then it became important to get an understanding of the situation and contextualize it.

Devon seemed authentic and was able to recount the events calmly and with accuracy. His story was supported by the supervisor who also recognized that there may be better ways to respond to workplace hazing/bullying.

In general, though, Caroline had no problem recommending a return to work.

### From Theory to Practice

As you reflect on Caroline's story, give some thought to the following points:

1. How did Caroline go about developing a trusting relationship with Devon?

2. How was the practice of assessment in the moment used in this situation?

3. Are there cultural factors to consider in this situation? If so, what are they?

4. Is the presence of the police at the airport an important factor in the assessment process? Why or why not?

5. Did Caroline include a mental health screening (see p. 124) in her assessment? What were the indicators she looked at?

6. Do you concur with Caroline's assessment that there was minimal risk of further violent outburst by Devon on his return to the work camp? Why or why not?

A formal process
that includes both
objective and subjective
observations to describe
the mental state and
behaviours of the person
being observed. The
focus of the MSE "is on
current signs, symptoms,
affect, behaviour, and
cognition" (Zimmerman,
2013, p. 138).

# Mental Health Screening

Regardless of the agency setting, all social workers should be able to screen for mental health and substance-use concerns that may warrant further assessment with a specialized practitioner. Two of the most frequently encountered screening tools are the Mental Status Examination and the CAGE screening tool for substance use.

### The Mental Status Examination

In many generalist practice settings, social workers are not required to complete a formal **Mental Status Examination (MSE)**. Nevertheless it is helpful to understand the various domains that are covered—especially if the service user is presenting extreme symptoms of disorientation or unusual behaviour.

The MSE provides a framework to examine service user behaviour systematically. "The mental status examination is analogous to the physical examination. The focus is on current signs, symptoms, affect, behaviour, and cognition" (Zimmerman, 2013, p. 138). Although there are various models of the MSE, Zimmerman recommends that the following components be assessed:

- **Appearance.** This includes body build, posture, eye contact, dress, grooming, manners, attentiveness, alertness, and any distinguishing or prominent physical features.

- **Motor skills.** This includes any slowed movements, agitation, unusual movements, and gait.

- **Speech.** This includes rate, rhythm, volume, amount, articulation, and spontaneity.

- **Affect.** This includes stability, range, appropriateness to content, and the service user's report of mood changes.

- **Thought content.** This includes suicidal ideation, homicidal ideation, depressive cognition, obsessions, phobias, ideas of reference, magical ideation, delusions, and overvalued ideas.

- **Thought process.** This includes associations, coherence, logic, stream of consciousness, and perception (hallucinations, depersonalization, etc.).

- **Intellect.** This includes global evaluation (average, above average, or below average).

- **Insight.** This includes the service user's own awareness of illness.

The challenge in psychiatric diagnosis of mental disorders is that there is a heavy reliance on clinical expertise in assessment, as there are no laboratory tests available to establish the presence of mental illness. In Canada, there are two classification systems for use with mental disorders: The International Classification of Diseases (ICD) and the Diagnostic and Statistical Manual of Mental Disorders (DSM). These two systems are regularly refined in an effort to enhance diagnostic accuracy and incorporate new research (Goldner, Jenkins, & Bilsker, 2016).

# Men's Suicide and Mental Health in Quebec
## Implementing Gender-Specific, Reflexive Practices

Suicide is a major cause of premature and preventable death in Canada. According to Statistics Canada (Navaneelan, 2017), almost 3.5 million people aged 15 and over reported that they have seriously contemplated suicide in their life.

There were 3,890 deaths attributed to suicides in Canada in 2009, a rate of 11.5 per 100,000 people, although this rate may be somewhat under-reported (Navaneelan, 2017). The suicide rate for men is three times higher than that for women (17.9 versus 5.3 per 100,000).

Research indicates that mental illness is the most important risk factor for suicide. Working with individuals who have suicidal ideation is emotional and challenging, and a specialized area of practice.

The province of Quebec witnessed a drastic rise in adult male suicide between 1990 and 2000 (Roy, Tremblay, & Duplessis-Brochu, 2017). By the end of the 1990s, male suicide was being constructed as a social issue requiring gender-responsive strategies. The Quebec government mandated a committee to produce a task force report on suicide prevention and help for men.

Rather than view the rise in male suicide from an individual and pathological perspective, the Quebec government viewed it from a social perspective.

### A Strengths-Based Approach

Even though men occupy a privileged position in society, social workers have observed that men have difficulty seeking help. Using a humanistic (seeing the person behind the problem) and strengths-based approach, suicide prevention programs are now beginning to focus on promoting the acceptability of seeking help.

In Saguenay–Lac-Saint-Jean, a suicide prevention action plan for men was developed to do the following:

- Focus on education and sensitization with communication tools to promote a positive and accessible message about men's health and to reduce mental health stigmas around distress

- Train professionals to improve suicide screening and interventions with men

- Create self-help and support groups for men going through adversity

Social workers and other service providers were trained in strategies aimed at breaking men's affective isolation, creating outreach programs, adapting existing services, and implementing gender-specific, reflexive practices.

Since the implementation of these strategies, there has been a continuous decline in male suicide rates in Quebec. In 2005, a men's health agency was introduced in the Ministry of Health and Social Services.

### "Hegemonic Masculinity"

"Hegemonic masculinity" was identified as an important contributing factor adversely affecting men's mental health. This term refers to a prevailing construct of masculinity, in which men are taught to deny manifestations of weakness and to avoid seeking help. Roy et al. (2017) challenge social workers to address the unmet needs of specific subgroups of men, such as men with children, men in the military, immigrant men, Indigenous men, and men living in remote areas. ■

## Diagnostic and Statistical Manual of Mental Disorders (DSM)

The DSM is in its fifth edition (DSM-5), published in 2013. While the DSM is the most popular diagnostic system for mental disorders in the United States and Canada, the International Classification of Diseases (ICD) is used more widely in Europe and other parts of the world, giving it a far larger reach than the DSM.

## CAGE screening tool

Developed in 1968, the CAGE screening tool is a questionnaire created by Dr. John Ewing, founding director of the Bowles Center for Alcohol Studies at the University of North Carolina at Chapel Hill.

The CAGE screening tool is widely used as a starting point to assess potential substance-use problems.

## Screening for Substance Use

The **Diagnostic and Statistical Manual of Mental Disorders (DSM)** is commonly used by clinicians and psychiatrists to diagnose psychiatric illnesses, including substance-use disorders. Published by the American Psychiatric Association, the DSM covers all categories of mental health disorders for both adults and children. The newest version of the manual, known as the DSM-5, was released in 2013.

The most recent DSM-5 has raised controversy because it expands the criteria for diagnoses in such a way that more individuals may now receive psychiatric diagnoses. While the benefits of treatment may extend to a larger proportion of individuals, there is a risk of labelling large numbers of people as suffering from mental illness who would not have been labelled as such previously (Goldner, Jenkins, & Bilsker, 2016).

The DSM is clearly slanted toward a medical model, and psychiatric and psychological responses. The lack of cultural and gender lenses within the DSM requires social workers to take ethnicity and spiritual beliefs into account. As Brew and Kottler (2017) point out:

> What may be auditory hallucinations in one person might very well be a transcendent religious experience in another. Or what might strike you as antisocial behaviour in one adolescent might very well be entirely normative within another person's peer group. (p. 173)

Although assessing substance use is a specialized area in social work, all generalist social workers can support good referrals through the use of questionnaires such as the CAGE screening tool. This tool can provide a starting point in the assessment process and indicate potential substance-use problems (Johnson, 2004, p. 183).

The **CAGE screening tool** consists of four questions. CAGE is an acronym formed from the first letters of the four items being assessed, appearing in bold in the list below. A response of two or more positives correlates with excessive substance use and is an indicator for further assessment (Ewing, 1995). The social worker (in these words, or similar words) asks the service user the following questions:

- "Have you ever felt you should **C**ut down on your drinking?"
- "Have people **A**nnoyed you by criticizing your drinking?"
- "Have you ever felt bad or **G**uilty about your drinking?"
- "Have you ever had a drink first thing in the morning to steady you nerves or get rid of a hangover (**E**ye-opener)?"

A more complete substance-use assessment will incorporate many of the elements of the generalist biopsychosocial assessment, with a particular focus on how substance use is impacting all areas of the service user's life. Special attention will be paid to collecting a comprehensive history of current and past substance use, which includes previous treatments; identification of all the drugs (illicit and legal, including prescriptions and nicotine) that are being used and have ever been used; patterns of use (e.g., time of day, associated social activities, when stressed etc.); consequences of use (overdose and bad reactions); longest periods of abstinence; and what has, or hasn't, worked or been helpful in the past.

# Critical Approaches to Mental Health and Substance Use
## From Individual Illness to Social Equity

Substance use is a multilayered and multifactorial problem. The dominant framework for understanding causes, maintenance, and treatment in the substance-use field has been a biopsychosocial-spiritual approach.

### Integrated Mental Health and Substance-Use Services

Due to the co-occurrence of substance-use disorders and psychiatric disorders, services and systems in these two areas have increasingly been integrated. Research indicates that multiprovider, integrated and coordinated service delivery models and practice guidelines are "consistently superior compared to treatment of individual disorders with separate treatment plans" (Kelly & Daley, 2013, p. 388).

In many jurisdictions, however, the integration of mental health and substance use (MHSU) has resulted in an uncritical embrace of medical models that locate the problem within the individual. Morley (2003) contends that

> removing societal responsibility from the source of the distress by constructing the issues as individual problems operates to maintain inequitable social arrangements. (p. 76)

Morley (2003) argues that the traditional approach to psychiatric disorder "largely neglects social work approaches which utilize critical principles" (p. 61), whereas

> social work, with its holistic and contextualized analysis of social issues, could in fact have a primary role in developing and offering alternatives to mainstream psychiatric approaches in the mental health field. (p. 62)

This can occur through relabelling, recontextualizing, and normalizing experiences and responses that have been medically defined as pathological.

### A Critical Perspective on Mental Health and Substance Use

Ultimately, embracing a critical social work approach to MHSU demands

> that social workers actively engage with their responsibility to deconstruct how medical discourses operate to maintain social order and obscure inequitable power relationships. (Morley, 2003, p. 79)

This is consistent with Ife's (1997) contention that "conservative, traditional casework approaches … function to reconcile people in their lot in an unjust society, rather than seeking to change it" (as cited in Morley, 2003, p. 79).

The Australia Association of Social Workers (AASW) practice standards for mental health are consistent with such a critical framework (AASW, 2015). The AASW identifies the role of the social worker as the interface between the individual and the environment.

The AASW standards describe the domain of social work as having social context and social consequences. The purpose of mental health practice is as follows:

> to promote recovery, restore individual family, and community well-being, to enhance development of each individual's power and control over their lives, and to advance principles of social justice. (p. 8)

This critical perspective links issues of individual personality (vulnerability, resilience, strengths, and stressors) with interpersonal aspects of family functioning and personal relations, and broadens them to include social issues of economic well-being, employment, and housing. ■

# Screening for Harm to Self or Others

In generalist practice, likely the most emotionally charged assessment is screening for harm—to self or to others. It is important for all social workers to be able to screen for the risk factors associated with suicide and dangerousness.

The analysis of the information collected is best done in consultation with colleagues and supervisors, but all generalist social workers should be able to present their concerns in a coherent manner. Merrill (2013) developed a framework of questions to ask service users to screen for risk of harm (see Table 5.1).

**Table 5.1** Therapeutic Common Factors in Social Work Practice

|  | **"Suicidal Risk" Questions** | **"Homicidal Risk" Questions** |
|---|---|---|
| **Ideation** | • When someone feels as upset as you do, they may have thoughts that life isn't worth living. What thoughts had you had like this? | • When someone feels as upset as you do, they may have thoughts about hurting the person who has upset or hurt them. What thoughts have you had like this? |
| **Planning and means** | • If you decided to try to end your life, how would you do it? Tell me about the plans you've made. | • If you decided to try to hurt _____, how would you do it?<br>• Tell me about the plans you've made. |
| **Access to means** | • You mentioned that if you were to hurt yourself, you'd probably do it by [describe method]. How easy would it be for you to do this? | • You mentioned that if you were to hurt _____ you'd probably do it by [describe the method]. How easy would it be for you to do this? |
| **Protective factors** | • People often have very mixed feelings about harming themselves. What are some reasons that would stop you or prevent you from trying to hurt yourself? What is it that most holds you back from actually doing this? | • People often have very mixed feelings about harming other people. What are some reasons that would stop you or prevent you from trying to hurt _____? What is it that most holds you back from actually doing this? |
| **Past experiences** | • What have been your past experiences of making attempts to hurt yourself?<br>• What other people do you know who have tried to or have ended their own life? | • What have been your past experiences related to hurting people who have hurt you? |
| **Future expectations** | • What are some things happening in your life or likely to happen in your life right now that would either make you more or less likely to want to hurt yourself?<br>• How do you think people who know you would react if you killed yourself? What would they say, think, or feel? | • What are some of the things happening in your life or likely to happen in your life right now that would either make you more or less likely to want to hurt _____?<br>• How do you think people who know you would react if you actually did this? What would they say, think, or feel? What would be some of the consequences? |

**Source:** Adapted from Merrill (2013).

## Harm to Children: Reporting Obligations

Generalist social workers have a legislative responsibility in all Canadian jurisdictions to recognize, identify, and report child abuse and neglect. Reporting is a challenging requirement for most social workers, and it should always occur with the involvement of immediate supervisors and be documented clearly.

It is also important to consult with your jurisdiction's child-protection ministry to identify any guidelines that it may have about reporting child maltreatment and the specific legislation that applies.

The Safeguarding Children Board (n.d.) provides the following general guidelines for deciding when to make a referral to the appropriate children's ministry:

- Any situation where there is clear evidence of abuse or neglect;
- Any allegation of sexual abuse;
- Physical injury caused by assault or neglect that may or may not require medical attention;
- Incidents of physical harm that alone are unlikely to constitute significant harm, but that, when taken in consideration with other factors, may do so;
- Children who suffer from persistent neglect;
- Children who live in an environment that is likely to have an adverse impact on their emotional development (e.g., where a child experiences a low level of emotional warmth and a high level of criticism);
- When parents' own emotional impoverishment affects their ability to meet their child's emotional and/or physical needs, regardless of material/financial circumstances and assistance;
- Where parents' circumstances are affecting their capacity to meet the child's needs because of the following:
    - Domestic abuse
    - Drug and/or alcohol misuse
    - Mental health problems
    - Previous convictions for offences against children
- A person has a known criminal history of violence to children and has significant contact with children;
- A child living in a household with, or having significant contact with, a person at risk of sexual offending;
- A child under 13 who is sexually active;
- An abandoned child;
- Bruising to an immobile baby;
- Pregnancy, where previous children have been removed;
- Suspicion of fabricated or induced illnesses;
- Child who persistently runs away from home or school; and/or
- Children who are sexually exploited.

# Presenting Assessment Information

In typical situations, the service user is bursting to talk to the social worker about an issue (and has often rehearsed how to present it). Once the social worker has an understanding of the service user's perception of the issue, it is important to continue to collect as much information as possible in order to understand the possible causes, maintenance, and precipitating factors. There are multiple ways of presenting this information, and most agencies will have a standardized assessment format that can be used for this purpose.

The following categories for assessment can be adapted to and incorporated in an assessment report. Less or more depth of understanding may be required in certain areas, depending on the service user's presenting issues and the agency mandate.

- **Service user identification and presenting problem**
  - Age, marital status, children, racial/cultural background
  - Service user's perspective of presenting issues and symptoms; causes and evolution of problem
  - History of when the symptoms started, how often and where they occur, and their intensity
  - Strategies used to manage the problem and the symptoms
  - Precipitating event leading to seeking help (Why now?) and expectations for treatment
  - The level of motivation for change

- **Psychosocial situation**
  - Family situation—current family composition, family member roles, sibling relationships, power balances, etc. (genogram, if applicable)
  - Financial situation—present sources of income, money management problems; and any related financial stressors
  - Housing situation—current housing arrangements and any related stressors
  - Medical situation—current medical status and any related stressors
  - Legal situation—current legal problems and any related stressors
  - Education and work situation—educational background, work history, and any related stressors

- **Personal history**
  - Family of origin (parents, siblings, and significant others)
  - Description of childhood and adolescence
  - Incidents of attachment problems or trauma

- **Mental health history**
  - Previous psychological, psychiatric, or counselling history and/or hospitalizations
  - Substance-use history, listing each substance used, history of consumption, and related problems
  - History of gambling problems
  - Family history of psychiatric, substance-use or gambling problems, and related treatments
  - Lifetime history of stressful events, emotional responses, and coping mechanisms
- **Social worker assessment observations**
  - Current mental status/behavioural observation
  - Description of the Mental Status Examination (MSE)
  - Risk assessment—suicide; homicide; child abuse; and intimate partner violence

## The Importance of Incorporating Culture in Assessment

Incorporating issues that may be associated with cultural identity and cultural safety is a way of shifting the focus of the assessment from "disease and pathology" to the service user's circumstances and experiences. This component of assessment has become more common over the last four decades (Aggarwal, Desilva, Nicasio, Boiler, & Lewis-Fernández, 2015).

The Outline for Cultural Formulation (OCF) was developed as part of DSM-4. In the DSM-5, it is referred to as the **Cultural Formulation Interview (CFI).** The CFI and its companion, the Informant Version (IV), provide four domains for cultural interviews:

- Cultural identity
- Cultural explanations of the illness
- Cultural factors associated with psychosocial and environmental functioning
- Cultural elements of the relationship between the individual and the practitioner

Understanding the service user's cultural perspective will likely help to improve the service user's satisfaction with the treatment and lead to closer adherence to it. A study in New York found that the use of the OCF improved cross-cultural communication. The most notable conclusion was the enhancement of rapport resulting in better satisfaction with the interview. As well, the OCF interview made it easier for the service user to describe their situation and perspective. The OCF guidelines separate the cultural elements from the context of the psychiatric labelling and provide other dimensions that need to be explored in the assessment process (Aggarwal et al., 2015).

**Cultural Formulation Interview (CFI)**

The CFI facilitates the evocation of the person's own narrative (personal and cultural) of a problem.

Social workers can use the CFI in many interactions with service users, as all individuals have their own cultures, values, and expectations which, in turn, will influence service approaches and outcomes.

# Social Worker Exemplar

# Mental Health Assessments

## Hilary Greelish

**Being a social worker requires an ability to adapt to multiple situations. In Hilary's job as a substance-use counsellor, she was frequently working in smaller communities, in borrowed space, and with little information about the individuals who had booked appointments.**

"In this particular community, I was given a small office that had just enough room for three chairs around a very small table," Hilary recounts. "In the waiting room, I introduced myself to Jeannie who was in her mid-30s and was accompanied her five-year-old son, Jack. As there was no reasonable place for Jack to wait, or an available person to care for the five-year-old, I invited her to bring Jack into the session."

Jeannie immediately apologized for bringing Jack along to the interview, but said that she had been unable to find a babysitter. She also said that as he was part of her concern, it might be helpful for him to see me as well. I had done family work before, but I generally try to get a summary from the adults without the children present.

Nevertheless, Jeannie had made it to the appointment and was doing her best to entertain Jack. She had brought an iPad with her, with headphones, for him to play with. She suggested that he sit on the floor against the wall, which he seemed content to do.

### The Interview

Once Jack was settled, I reviewed with Jeannie the informed consent form, confidentiality issues, and the overall process usually undertaken in the outreach program. I then asked Jeannie what had brought her in on that day, and what she hoped I could help with.

Jeannie stated that she and her husband (Steve) had split up about three months before. Her husband had told her that he was gay and that he could no longer cover it up, that he still loved her, but didn't want to live with her anymore. At this point, she was crying softly. She said she was having trouble sleeping, was filled with self-doubt about whether Steve had ever loved her, was concerned about how Jack was going to manage in the separation, and wanted some ways of coping for herself and looking after Jack. I empathized about her separation and how difficult that can be, and let her know that children are very resilient and, if the parents can work together, co-parent separation doesn't have to be traumatizing for children.

At this point, I had some idea of the precipitating problem. My initial impression was that Jeannie's (and Jack's) appearance, motor skills, speech, affect, and thought content all were within the normal and expected range. I did have some questions about anxiety and depression, but my general pattern was to hold off on those questions until I got a better sense of the psychosocial situation. I was also unsure of how Jeannie was accepting her husband's disclosure of being gay. However, at this point, I noticed that Jack was continuing to look up from his iPad, particularly when he noticed his mom crying.

I knew this was going to be a challenging session for me, too.

## Jack Enters the Conversation

At this point, Jack was clearly getting bored. He had come over to his mom several times and then sat with us at the table. I decided that, as I hadn't touched on any serious risk areas, I would bring Jack into the conversation.

I began by saying to him that I had been asking his mom a bunch of questions, and if it would be alright if I also asked him some. I looked at his mom, and with a non-verbal cue, checked whether it was okay with her. She nodded affirmatively. I asked Jack if he knew who I was and why I was talking with his mom. He said, yes and that I was someone who could help mommies when daddies were no longer living at home.

I decided to change things up a bit. I had seen a whiteboard in the room with several different colour markers. I asked Jack if he wanted to draw a picture of his family for me on the whiteboard. He agreed. However, I said to Jack that how I draw pictures of families may be different from how he usually does it, and asked if he would be willing to try my way. He smiled and agreed. I asked him to draw himself as a square. Then I asked him to draw his mom above him as a circle, and his dad above him as a square (I was writing in the names, or relationships). I then asked him about who else belonged to his family. He told me about the dog, which we drew in, and his sister, Emmy, who was eight years old at the time. I then asked him about anyone else in the family. He told me about his Gramma Ann (his paternal grandma). After prompting, he was able to tell me (accurately) about all of his grandparents and his aunts and uncles.

In the discussions about the genogram, we were able to bring up many conversation areas. He was able to tell me, and his mom could hear, his perception of his dad leaving. He was very sad, but was still hopeful that he would see his dad to go fishing and for their "Friday-night hamburgers." He was worried about his mom crying all the time and hoped she would cuddle him more, like she used to do.

When asked if he thought his dad and mom had new friends in their lives after the separation, he said his mom's friend Pam had been coming around more often to support her and that his dad's friend Mike also seemed to be with his dad more often. When asked if he liked Pam and Mike, he said he did and that both were nice to him. ∎

This was an unusual assessment in some ways, and its course was not entirely predictable. From it, Hilary learned that children can sometimes participate in the assessment process to the benefit of all concerned. The core of the assessment—strengthening the relationship between Jeannie and Jack—was what was most important.

The genogram worked well, too. Through the genogram, Jack was able to tell Hilary about his temper tantrums (Hilary simply asked who in the family was the easiest to get along with, who in the family has a bad temper—Jack included himself, and they were able to explore this further).

Toward the end of the time allotted, Hilary asked Jack to play with his iPad again so that she could speak to his mom. Hilary reiterated to Jeannie that they could have a separate session. Jeannie said that, for her, just hearing what Jack said was helpful and that she thought she had gotten what she wanted. Hilary encouraged Jeannie to come in the next time she was in town, but Hilary never saw her again.

## From Theory to Practice

As you reflect on Hilary's story, give some thought to the following points:

1. What is your perspective on completing family assessments with children in the room?

2. How could Hilary have worked with Jack's mom's tears differently? If Jack hadn't been in the room, what would have been different?

3. Could an assessment be written up from this process? What was missing and could be followed up on in a subsequent session?

4. Are there some circumstances in which it would have been inappropriate to have Jack in the room while his mom presented her situation?

5. Do you think a further risk assessment should have been conducted? Why, or why not?

6. How would you write a clinical impression (or summary) for this assessment?

# Assessment with Indigenous Peoples

**Thunderbird Partnership Foundation**

The Thunderbird Partnership Foundation promotes a holistic approach to healing and wellness that values culture, respect, community, and compassion with its work in building capacity in First Nations and Inuit communities.

The use of Western values and frameworks for understanding, diagnosing, and treating mental illness and substance use is the subject of tremendous debate among practitioners working with Indigenous peoples (Evidence Exchange Network for Mental Health and Addictions, 2014).

Owing to oppressive social policies, particularly related to residential schools and child welfare services, Indigenous people continue to experience transgenerational psychological distress, despair, and trauma. As Adams, Drew, and Walker (2014) note:

> This situation reinforces the need for more culturally sensitive and appropriate assessments and testing of Aboriginal people who are experiencing extreme levels of trauma and grief and [social and emotional well-being] SEWB issues. (p. 271)

Across Canada, there is interest in the development of new assessment tools, or the adaptation of existing ones, in an attempt to bridge Western and Indigenous knowledges. Developing tools that incorporate Indigenous knowledges and learnings is important to ensuring that Indigenous peoples receive the services they need and want.

## Canadian Assessment Tools for Indigenous Peoples

In 2015, the Native Mental Health Association of Canada (NMHAC) joined with the National Native Addictions Partnership Foundation (NNAPF) to form the **Thunderbird Partnership Foundation**. This group promotes Indigenous holistic approaches to healing and wellness with the First Peoples of Canada. From this perspective:

> Mental health is a sign of balance, harmony and connectedness among the interior aspects of the human person (spirit, mind and body) and the world he or she lives in. It is a characteristic of families and communities, as well as individual human beings. (Thunderbird Partnership Foundation, 2019, para. 1)

The Thunderbird Partnership Foundation has developed an instrument to measure the effect of cultural interventions on a person's wellness from a whole person and strengths-based perspective.

For its part, the Centre for Addiction and Mental Health's Health Promotion Resource Centre (CAMH HPRC)—Ontario's source for health promotion regarding mental health and substance use—is also providing leadership in this area. They are working on making their Child and Adolescent Needs and Strengths (CANS) tool reflect culture-based information and recognize culture as a strength in a child's life.

The CANS tool has a focus on serving the needs of the child, rather than fitting the child into the services and programs, and is designed to be adapted to reflect the local cultural context. Following the formation of an Indigenous working group, The Métis Nation of Ontario and Inuit Tapiriit Kanatami have successfully adapted the tool to reflect the unique experiences of the Métis and Inuit communities (Centre for Addiction and Mental Health, 2014).

## Principles of Culturally Safe Assessments

In the Australian context, Westerman and Garvey identified a number of elements of good practices in the initial engagement phase of an Indigenous assessment (as cited in Adams et al., 2014, p. 279). To begin with, practitioners need to consider whether they are the most appropriate people (or agency) to conduct the assessment. The gender, age, and cultural identity of a practitioner could all be relevant in the decision to accept or not accept a referral.

Westerman and Garvey (Adams et al., 2014) offer the following recommendations for practitioners who plan to conduct assessments in an Indigenous community:

- **Use cultural consultants.** Cultural consultants are a valuable resource in facilitating access to and building good relationships in the community.

- **Become familiar with the community.** Taking the time to become known in and familiar with the community is especially important in regional and remote communities.

- **Adhere to community protocols.** This includes notifying and seeking permission from community councils, reporting to the community office on arrival, and seeking permission to move around the community. These are all signs of respect, courtesy, and cultural competence.

- **Contact the community.** Learning more about the local context of service provision ensures that appropriate recommendations can be made.

Assessment tools and procedures—when understood, developed, and implemented appropriately and sensitively—can significantly enhance the capacity of social workers to develop culturally situated assessments and provide quality care.

## Reflective Questions to Assess Cultural Safety

As the cultural formulation of the assessment process is completed, continuing to work with a cultural consultant can ensure that adequate explanations and intervention strategies are negotiated and planned with the individual and family (Adams et al., 2014).

Key questions to reflect on post-assessment include the following:

- Has the team understood the meaning of mental health for the community they are working with?

- Has the assessment presentation been understood in the context of the service user's own culture and history?

- Is the treatment appropriate to the person's cultural belief system?

- Has the impact of trauma, grief, and loss been considered?

# Practice Scenarios

When conducting screenings and assessments, multiple skills and knowledges are used. As a social worker, it is important to pay attention to the social and cultural contexts as well as to the strengths and resources of the individual being assessed.

In these practice scenarios, consider the broader social context and constructs that may be relevant to the situation, as well as how they may be acting on the individual. In each scenario, important decisions need to be made, even though there is limited information.

As always, it is important to pay attention to your own reaction and emotional response to the situation, and then to understand the situation from the service user's perspective. Prior to acting, it is important to be conscious of why you are deciding to act in a particular way rather than another way. This requires conceptualizing, for yourself, how you see the situation and why you may be viewing it this way.

## 5.1 Assessing for Strengths

You are working in an education and training centre for people with diverse abilities. Meagan is a 21-year-old woman who received supports through her K–12 schooling and then entered a skills-development program at her local college. There, she had a placement in a local restaurant, where she provided general kitchen duties. She thoroughly enjoyed this work and received positive feedback. Unfortunately, there was no available job after her placement ended.

Today, you have asked Meagan to interview at a local coffee shop. She is thrilled, as she often goes there herself and is on friendly terms with many of the employees. However, her mother, who is with her, doesn't approve the choice of location and wants an alternative. She is concerned that Meagan will lose this social network and be treated differently if she identifies as "having a disability" because of the referral from this program.

1. In the moment, what is your assessment of the competing needs, strengths, and concerns of Meagan and her mom?

2. How do you decide whose priorities are most important?

3. What are some of the broader socio-political circumstances that influence your decision?

4. How do you proceed and why?

## 5.2 Assessments in Emergency Shelters

You are working in an emergency evacuation shelter. A young 14-year-old girl, who identifies as a Syrian refugee, has been staying in the group lodgings for seven days due to an evacuation from her home town. As required by the Red Cross, the stay has to be re-evaluated.

As you find out a little more about the girl's situation, you discover that she was evacuated with her grandmother who is very elderly and quite sick. The grandmother has not moved out of her cot in the local hockey arena, where she has been for the last five days. The girl's parents were working in a different town at the time of the evacuation and, although they are aware of the situation, will not be able to get to this community for at least another week.

You mention to the young girl that perhaps her grandmother should go to the hospital. Her face quickly shows fear and anger, and her previously friendly demeanour changes to resistance. She clearly states: "No, we are not doing that. I am staying with my Grandma," "We are ok."

1. How do you account for the girl's sudden emotional change when the hospital is raised?
2. What are the cultural elements to be considered?
3. How do you proceed?

## 5.3 Assessing for Harm in Everyday Life

You are on a day off and walking through a local park when you see a young girl (your guess is about six years old) leaning against the outside wall of a public washroom and crying uncontrollably. There is no adult close to her, and you cannot see another adult watching her.

Use an assessment in the moment practice to determine what to do.

1. In assessing the situation, what do you start looking at and observing?
2. What is the context you are observing?
3. What possible interpretations are you giving to your observation? Where do these interpretations come from in your own experiences?
4. What is your conscious awareness of self? What questions do you need to ask yourself about your interpretation?
5. What do you decide to do?

# Field Education Practicalities
## Preparing for Midpoint Assessments

Most social work programs incorporate a midpoint assessment. It is a time for taking stock and setting new goals.

However, for many students, the anticipation is stressful. The anxiety can be reduced significantly if you are prepared and open to feedback.

By this time, the initial phases of field education are coming to an end. Many interactions have evolved into trusting relationships, and new ideas and skills are being developed. The reality of the work in the agency and the challenges the service user population faces are becoming more apparent. The next stage, the middle stage, is usually associated with preparing for the demands of work. This stage is similar to a counselling process that begins with building trust and is followed by a deeper exploration of issues.

At the midpoint, the task is to identify completed tasks and meta-competencies that are strong, and then to develop a further plan to deepen learning and skill application. This is also the point at which many find the challenges hard and difficult to sustain. It is important to be prepared for this process. However, as a student on the pathway to becoming a social worker, this is just one more challenge to work through in the journey to professionalism.

The key to the midpoint assessment is for you to be able to highlight, often with examples, your learning and strengths. In addition, it is important to show that you are open to continuous learning and identifying further goals for the remainder of the field component.

The midpoint assessment likely comes at the same time as other midterm exams and assignments. Sometimes, there is a tendency to want to focus on those aspects of social work education—particularly when everything in field seems to be going well. But be careful to pay attention to the midpoint assessment too, as it is the time when additional tasks may be presented as a way of deepening your skill attainment.

Staying focused on self-care at this stage of field education is important. Many students are balancing multiple roles and responsibilities in addition to the learning associated with field education. In Hemy, Boddy, Chee, and Sauvage's (2016) literature review on social work students' experiences in field placement, they found that conscious attention to active problem-solving, engaging support, and reframing or modifying expectations were key to coping and building capacity.

### Preparing for the Midpoint Assessment

Prepare and have ready all of the paperwork associated with the midpoint assessment. Be sure that you know when this meeting will take place, and what your responsibilities are. In general, you will be asked to identify the competencies you have learned, identify your strengths, and then identify other opportunities you would like to access during the remainder of the time in the field.

Prior to meeting with the agency supervisor and field faculty, it is worthwhile to undertake a self-supervision process. Review the learning plan developed at the beginning of the term. Identify whether you have "met," are "working on," or have "not started" each competency or task. Identify examples of how you have come to that conclusion. For example, what situation indicated that you have met your goals, what projects are you working on that indicate that your are in the processof developing a competncy, and what are the barriers to not starting on developing a competency?

Remember, no one meets all their learning goals and the reasons may, or may not, be within your control. This may also be a time to modify one's expectations of self.

## The Midpoint Assessment

It is likely that an agency supervisor and a field instructor will be present. Both want you to be successful, and will identify your strengths and areas to continue to work on.

Identifying ongoing goals, or raising areas of concern, is a normal and expected element of this midpoint meeting. Managing your anxiety and being open to feedback may also take additional attention at this time.

## Post-midpoint Assessment Reflection

Following the midpoint assessment, there may be a requirement to submit further paperwork. If not, it is always a good time to reflect on the assessment process—what have you learned about yourself? How was it to accept positive regard? How did you feel when asked to challenge yourself further? What is your own action plan for the remainder of the course?

The final step of the midpoint assessment is to be kind to yourself, and to undertake self-care. This should be a rejuvenating moment, a time to congratulate yourself for moving onto the second half of the course. ■

**Figure 5.1** Questions to Consider When Preparing for the Midpoint Assessment

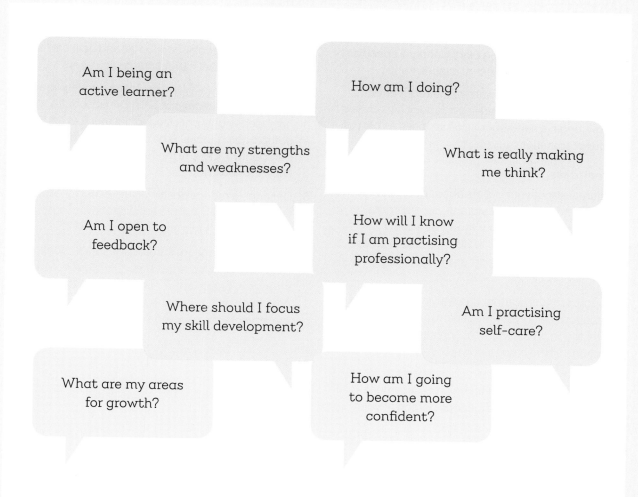

## Field Education Practicalities

1. In your practicum setting, review any complete clinical assessments that are available to you. These assessments may have been completed by social workers at your agency or by a psychologist or psychiatrist acting as part of an interprofessional team. Read the assessments for content as well as to understand the process of decision-making.

2. Imagine that you could ask a new service user only three questions and that, based on the answers, you would then have to construct an intervention plan. What are the three questions you would want to ask?

3. As part of your learning plan, identify a specific goal related to an aspect of assessment.

4. Ensure that you are aware of the requirements and processes involved in a midpoint assessment. Now, begin a self-supervision process as part of your preparation.

## Journal Ideas

1. Journal about your beliefs about people with mental health and substance-use disorders. Then journal about your thoughts about how to recognize a mental health or substance-use disorder, and how to address these issues in practice situations.

2. In your learning journal, if possible using an actual situation during your practicum, describe an interaction "in the moment." Ensure that you work through all the steps involved.

3. List the cultural considerations that might be important when conducting an assessment with a racialized or Indigenous person at your field agency.

4. Review the biopsychosocial screening and assessment processes in the agency. Evaluate the strengths of the processes and identify areas for further improvement.

## Critical-Thinking Questions

1. Describe the overall purpose of an assessment in social work practice.

2. Identify ways to ensure that service users are included in the assessment process. Should there be a way to ensure that service users are able to view their assessment and treatment plan? If so, how can this best be achieved?

3. Consider the framework for assessment that is used in your field education site. Does this framework represent anti-oppressive practice? How could this framework be adapted to move even more away from a medical model of assessment and treatment to include looking at how broader social, economic, and political factors may be negatively affecting service users?

4. The DSM is a classification system widely used in mental health diagnoses in Canada, but it has been widely criticized for its medical and pathologizing focus. From an anti-oppressive perspective, identify the "pros" and "cons" of the DSM framework.

5. Describe a mental health initiative that incorporates critical approaches to mental health services. How successful was this intervention?

6. A "risk-minimization" focus continues to dominate most assessment processes. Consider how a strengths-based approach might also be built into screening and assessment tools. What would be the advantages of doing so?

# Chapter Review

The assessment process, which may take one or several meetings, is completed with a report that synthesizes the key factors that contribute to and maintain the challenges being addressed. This case conceptualization, developed in close collaboration with the service user, forms the foundation for subsequent intervention planning.

Assessment skills may be utilized "in the moment" or over a longer period of time. In the situation with Devon, who was being assessed for dangerousness, the social worker used a combination of interviewing, empathy building, and questioning skills in addition to verifying information through collateral sources in order to assess Devon's safety risk.

Clinical assessments have traditionally focused on individualized pathology; however, this is changing. The inclusion of cultural factors provides meaning to the presenting problems and is integral to understanding the salient issues. This is evidenced by the inclusion of cultural formulation even within the DSM. For social workers, the inclusion of cultural elements is a mainstay in all practice assessments.

A challenging area for social workers in mental health and substance-use practice is examining an individual's situation from the broader social constructs. The practice in Quebec related to men's suicide provides an example of the merits of this approach. Social workers have a responsibility to work with individuals to ameliorate their distress. They also have a responsibility to address the social inequities that lead some individuals and populations to experience heightened vulnerability through multiple societal stressors.

At this point, you are likely close to the midpoint of field education. That means that it is time to assess your competencies and to modify existing goals or develop new goals for the remainder of your field practice.

## Conducting Assessments in Practice

This chapter outlines numerous ways in which students can develop proficiency and competency in conducting social work assessments. Here are some highlights and further suggestions:

- Be familiar with the screening and assessment tools and frameworks in your field setting.
- Observe how colleagues and other professionals conduct their assessments.
- Read assessments that others in your field have written.
- Use a friendly, frank, and firm interviewing style to conduct an assessment.
- Ensure transparency in the purpose and use of the assessment and informed consent procedures.
- Develop capacity in remembering interviews and documenting post-interview.
- Employ evidence-based screening tools for mental status, substance use, child harm, and harm to self and others in all assessments.
- Incorporate culturally safe practices in assessment processes.
- Be self-aware of your own beliefs about substance use, mental health, child protection, and other areas of assessment.
- Develop a strengths-based approach to assessment.

# 6

# Applying Knowledge of Human Development and Behaviour

*A human lifespan is less than a thousand months long. You need to make some time to think how to live it.*

**—Anthony Clifford Grayling,** British philosopher and author

# Chapter at a Glance

# Spotlight on Social Work Luminaries
## Mary Ainsworth

**Mary Ainsworth (1913–1999)** earned a BA, MA, and PhD in developmental psychology from the University of Toronto. She designed the "strange situation" procedure as a way to observe and assess early bonds between children and their primary caregivers. Her research in this area is the basis of attachment theory.

An understanding of human growth and development is a required knowledge area as well as a practice competency in Canadian social work. Applying human development theories to practice situations requires an understanding of the physical, cognitive, and social changes that occur over the lifespan and the life course.

The human lifespan is usually divided into broad age-ranges: the prenatal period (conception to birth), infancy (birth to 2 years), early childhood (2 to 6 years), middle childhood (6 to 12 years), adolescence (12 to 20 years), young adulthood (20 to 40 years), middle adulthood (40 to 65 years), and late adulthood (65 to death). However, it is now recognized that there can be substantial variation within each age category for particular individuals, and that the meaning and understanding of each stage is socially and culturally constructed.

The focus of this chapter is on children's lives, as children and families constitute a major practice area for social workers. Some attention is also given to working with older adults. The theoretical emphasis in this chapter is the application and utilization of attachment theory and trauma theory.

## Developing Competence as a Social Worker

Some ways to develop the meta-competency of "**applying knowledge of human development and behaviour**" are as follows:

- Identify the predominant human development approaches being used in your field agency.

- Observe a child, without taking notes, and subsequently write down the emotions, thoughts, and feelings evoked within you; then, conceptualize your observations from a human development perspective.

- Review a child's plan of care and assess whether the goals are consistent with human development knowledge and trauma-informed practice.

- Consider the resiliency, strengths, and cultural interpretations associated with different lifespan phases.

### Key Concepts

- Human development theory
- Child abuse and neglect
- Attachment theory
- Ethnic identity
- Gender identity
- Trauma-informed care (TIC)
- Resilience
- Tavistock Observation Method (TOM)
- Disorganized attachment
- Deficit model of social work practice

Human development theory

Human development theory focuses on how people grow and change over the course of a lifetime.

Those who specialize in this field are concerned not only with the physical changes people experience as they age, but also the social, emotional, and cognitive development that occurs throughout life.

# Human Development Theory

The term "human development" is often used interchangeably with the terms "lifespan" and "life course." **Human development theory** provides a paradigm to understand the influence of various factors over one's lifespan. For social workers, human development refers to a general orientation to practice rather than a rigid set of developmental tasks that are followed sequentially. The human development approach blends well with interprofessional practice, since psychology and sociology have also made strong contributions to knowledge in this area.

## On the Shoulders of Giants

A large number of theorists have contributed to our current understanding of the human lifespan (see Table 6.1 on p. 148). Modern social work practice builds on these earlier theories and seeks to apply them to real-world experiences. For example:

- Sigmund Freud's ideas about the importance of childhood experiences and unconscious desires shaped early theory about the human personality as well as the subsequent development of Erickson's eight-stage theory of psychosocial development.

- Behaviourists such as John Watson and B.F. Skinner shifted the focus away from psychodynamics and unconscious processes to understanding human development as a reaction to environmental stimuli (reward, punishment, and reinforcement).

- Cognitive theorists such as Jean Piaget focused on how people's thinking and mental patterns inform their responses and behaviours.

- In the mid-twentieth century, humanists such as Abraham Maslow and Carl Rogers, responding to the limitations of earlier theories, began to consider the whole person and the unique, subjective experiences of each individual. (A summary of these four perspectives appears in Table 6.1.)

Building on the ideas of these early thinkers, human development today is understood as being far too complex to be captured in distinct "ages and stages." Nor can it simply be split into dichotomies of "nature versus nurture" or "cognitive versus behavioural." Scholars such as Lerner and Konowitz (2016) have described a relational developmental systems (RDS) perspective that considers the mutual interaction of the individual and their context (biology, culture, and history). The authors emphasize that a holistic approach, a relational analysis, and multiple perspectives are critical in fully understanding human development.

Social workers today are bringing all these strands of knowledge into their daily practice and adapting them to unique circumstances as they see fit. They are paying special attention to such things as resilience (the ability to meet age-salient tasks in the face of serious obstacles); resources and assets (the human, social, or material resources that individuals draw on when confronted with difficult challenges); and protective factors (those broader characteristics that are associated with positive outcomes for individuals facing serious risk or adversity) (Masten & Reed, 2002).

# Accreditation and Regulatory Requirements
## Applying Knowledge of Human Development and Behaviour

Social workers practising a human development approach seek to understand the lived experiences and interpretations of life events from the service user's perspective. Consistent with a strengths-based approach, attention is paid to resilience, resources and assets, and protective factors alongside identifying challenges and risk factors.

### CASWE-ACFTS *Standards for Accreditation*

The Canadian Association for Social Work Education–Association canadienne pour la formation en travail social (CASWE-ACFTS, 2014) *Standards for Accreditation* states:

> **3.1.1** The BSW curriculum equips students with knowledge in the humanities and relevant social sciences, including knowledge related to human development and human behaviour in the social environment.

### Professional Regulation and Competency

The Canadian Council of Social Work Regulators (CCSWR, 2012) does not specifically include knowledge of human growth and development in its competency profile. However, the Association of Social Work Boards (ASWB) examination includes knowledge of human growth and development, and of human behaviour in the social environment as 25% of its BSW exam.

The ASWB has identified the following topics that may be included in the exam:

#### Human Growth and Development

- Theories of human development throughout the lifespan (e.g., physical, social, emotional, cognitive, behavioural)
- The indicators of normal and abnormal physical, cognitive, emotional, and sexual development throughout the lifespan
- Theories of sexual development throughout the lifespan
- Theories of spiritual development throughout the lifespan
- Theories of racial, ethnic, and cultural development throughout the lifespan
- The effects of physical, mental, and cognitive disabilities throughout the lifespan
- The interplay of biological, psychological, social, and spiritual factors
- Basic human needs
- The principles of attachment and bonding
- The effect of aging on biopsychosocial functioning
- The impact of aging parents on adult children
- Gerontology
- Personality theories
- Theories of conflict
- Factors influencing self-image (e.g., culture, race, religion/spirituality, age, disability, trauma)
- Body image and its impact (e.g., identity, self-esteem, relationships, habits)
- Parenting skills and capacities
- The family life cycle
- Systems and ecological perspectives and theories
- Models of family life education in social work practice
- Strengths-based and resilience theories

#### Human Behaviour in the Social Environment

- Family dynamics and functioning and the effects on individuals, families, groups, organizations, and communities
- Theories of couples development
- The impact of physical and mental illness on family dynamics
- Psychological defence mechanisms and their effects on behaviour and relationships
- Addiction theories and concepts
- Role theories
- Theories of group development and functioning
- Theories of social change and community development
- The dynamics of interpersonal relationships ■

**Table 6.1** Four Major Perspectives on Human Development

| Perspective | Description | Representative Theorist |
|---|---|---|
| **Psychodynamic theories** | Psychodynamic theories attempt to explain personality and behaviour in terms of subconscious desires and fears that we may not be consciously aware of or have little or no control over.<br><br>Their main proponent, Sigmund Freud, based his theory on three states of the mind: the "unconscious," the "preconscious," and the "conscious." More commonly, these are known as the "id" (biological urges and desires, such as eating, sleeping, and functioning, as well as aggression and sexual urges); the "ego" (the reality-centred, logical aspect of the mind); and the "superego" (a sense of morality and conscience). Modern-day psychologists generally believe that the mind is more complex than just a repression of urges. | Sigmund Freud (1856–1939), Austrian neurologist and the founder of psychoanalysis |
| **Behavioural theories** | The behaviourists were the first psychologists to begin to see their work as positive science. They introduced the concepts of empirical data collection and reproducibility to their experiments, which were mainly concerned with observing behaviours.<br><br>The behavioural school was less concerned with the thoughts and feelings behind the behaviours, believing that all behaviours were essentially determined by environmental stimuli and by conditioning. | B.F. Skinner (1904–1990), American psychologist, author, and social philosopher |
| **Cognitive theories** | Cognitive psychologists returned to looking into the mind to study the origins of behaviour. Cognitive theories hold that our behaviour starts with an event or stimulus. We interpret that stimulus using our thoughts and then we react to it, first emotionally and then behaviourally.<br><br>Accordingly, changing our thoughts and thought processes consciously, such as by Cognitive Behavioural Therapy (CBT), can lead to changes in feelings and behaviour that can manage psychological disorders. | Jean Piaget (1896–1980), Swiss psychologist known for his work on child development |
| **Humanistic theories** | Humanistic theories involve a "person-centred" notion of human behaviour. Humanistic psychologists adopt a non-judgemental approach, recognizing the importance of human agency. Their approach is to explore the whole person rather than focus solely on behaviour or the mind.<br><br>Humanism centres on a subjective view of what it is really like to be a particular person, which is then used to formulate specific interventions for that person. | Carl Rogers (1902–1987), American psychologist and founder of "client-centred" psychology |

# The Life Stages of Anishinaabe Women
## The "Seven Fires" of the Saulteaux

In her book *Life Stages and Native Women*, Kim Anderson (2011) describes the Anishinaabe life cycle, which stresses (among other things) "that the health and well-being of the individual is dependent on how well she or he fulfills his or her life stage roles and responsibilities" (p. 4). Anderson summarizes two perspectives on the Indigenous life cycle, in which the roles and responsibilities throughout the life cycle shape individuals' identities and their place in Indigenous society.

### 1. The Four Hills of Life among the Anishinaabe

Among the Anishinaabe, life stages are typically described as "the four hills of life" that progress from infancy to youth, to adulthood, and to old age.

Anishinaabe author and ethnologist Basil Johnston describes how "physical life stages have corresponding moral stages of development, which are preparation, quest, vision, and fulfillment of vision" (as cited in Anderson, 2011, p. 7).

Johnston relates that youth must learn to hunt, fish, sew, and cook, while adults must ensure survival through caregiving and providing. While the physical challenges of doing so may be formidable, it is the corresponding moral journey that gives meaning to human life and makes the difference between merely existing and fully living.

From this perspective, infants and children, although portrayed as frail and helpless, represent potential for the future and bring happiness and hope to all. During infancy and childhood, children prepare for the vision associated with being a youth. Although this may start early, or later, and may take as long as necessary, youths cannot proceed to the adult stage until they have received a vision particular to their life's purpose.

Visions are achieved through fasting and isolation, during which the individual has the opportunity to seek communion with their inner self.

### 2. The "Seven Fires" of the Saulteaux

In her book, Anderson (2011) also describes Dr. Danny Musqua's overview of human development according to Saulteaux oral traditions.

In the Saulteaux oral tradition, human growth and development is described as follows:

> a progression through seven fires: conception and life in the womb; birth to walking; walking to seven years of age; little men and little women; young adults; adult development; and old age and death. This model includes three types of Elders: "community Elders, ceremonial Elders and earth Elders," categories which are based on the specific areas of knowledge that have been attained. (p. 8)

Musqua describes the Saulteaux view as a learning journey in which one's spirit strives to learn about the physical state of existence:

- In utero, the spirit is more conscious, but due to the shock of arrival in the physical world, the spirit enters a subconscious state early in its lifetime. From this perspective, ceremonies are an important part of the learning journey, as they acknowledge the spirit and mark important milestones.

- Infancy and early childhood involve being nurtured, depending on others, and developing trust. As children grow older, they learn about discipline and taking up responsibilities.

- Youth is a time when individuals begin to assume adult responsibilities and are charged with caregiving duties for the young and old in the community.

- Adults carry responsibilities of providing for family, and Elders are the teachers and keepers of knowledge, law, and ceremony. ■

# Conception, Infancy, and Early Childhood

Human development approaches generally begin with a focus on the period of conception, pregnancy, childbirth, and the health of the newborn child. In the economically developed world, remarkable medical progress has been made in this area over the past century, although certainly much more remains to be done in the underdeveloped countries in Asia, Africa, and Latin America.

Typically, social work involvement during infancy is with the biological mother and immediate family, although social workers are increasingly involved with issues associated with involuntary childlessness, international adoptions, surrogacy, and a range of Assisted Reproductive Technologies (ARTs).

### Adoption, Surrogacy, and Assisted Reproductive Technologies

Today, a number of ways exist to build a family, including adoption, surrogacy, and fertility treatments. Social workers have a special role in the development of practice and policy frameworks in these areas.

Many children are adopted from the child welfare system into a "forever family," as adoption is a particularly important form of permanency. Social workers practising in the adoption field have a responsibility to prepare, educate, and support parents throughout the adoption process. They are also responsible for providing support in the post-adoption stage, as the child, the parents, siblings, and extended family all adjust to their new family arrangements.

A longitudinal study of children born through ARTs found that some children experienced adjustment difficulties at age seven, and this poses challenges for some parents (Golombok, Blake, Casey, Roman, & Jadva, 2013). This finding suggests that there is a need for post-reproduction support in such cases, for both children and families. As a result of their close involvement with children and families, social workers are especially well placed to cut across the disciplinary silos in this area.

Social workers also have a role in the development of international reproductive policy and practices, especially in relation to mothers. A study conducted by the Centre for Social Research in India on international surrogacy reported insufficient legal safeguards, the flaunting of ethical medical guidelines, and the exploitation of poor women (Centre for Social Research, 2013). The women "risk community disapproval, lose independence for the duration of their pregnancies, enter into contracts they do not understand, risk their health and experience the unknown impacts of relinquishing the children" (Vora, 2009, 2012, as cited in Fronek & Crawshaw, 2015, p. 740).

Social workers can contribute to policies and laws by voicing and advocating for those affected by adoption, donor conception, and surrogacy. They can highlight the social and economic power relations and speak to common human rights violations (Fronek & Crawshaw, 2015).

## The Effects of Childhood Trauma and Adverse Childhood Experiences

The majority of children in Canada are healthy during infancy and early childhood, with the greatest risk coming from accidents (Feldman & Landry, 2017). However, social workers recognize that severe childhood experiences, such as abuse, neglect, and household dysfunction, are still widespread across Canada and are a major contributor to biopsychosocial susceptibilities and overall functioning later in life (Larkin, Felitti, & Anda, 2014).

Research shows that stressful events such as **child abuse and neglect** negatively impact a child's overall development and contribute to challenges in adaptive coping and resilience building. The greater the number of such childhood experiences, the greater the impact on overall health. As a result of accumulated stress and trauma, it becomes more challenging to develop protective resources to mitigate the effects of stressful events on well-being. Stress and trauma are common and pervasive problems that correlate with difficulties across the lifespan (Plumb et al., 2016).

A recent Canadian study identified that almost one-third (32%) of all children have experienced child abuse (Afifi et al., 2014). In the United States, it is estimated that almost half the country's children have experienced childhood trauma (National Survey of Children's Health, 2011). While stress sometimes can have a positive effect in terms of fostering resilience, severe or prolonged stress results in an acute vulnerability and seriously affects brain development. Children who experience high levels of stress are unable to achieve their full potential. The priorities of the brain and body become redirected to the immediate challenge, rather than the normal processes of healthy growth and development. In fact, childhood trauma has been found to have negative consequences across virtually all domains of life.

## The Adverse Childhood Experiences Study

The Adverse Childhood Experiences (ACEs) study, originally published in 1998, involved a sample of 17,000 children. The results showed a high prevalence of adverse experiences in childhood and strong correlations between such experiences, health risk behaviours, and negative health and social outcomes in adult life (Thomas, 2016).

Over time, the child's cognitive functioning and ability to cope with negative emotions is impaired, leading to unhealthy coping mechanisms that may contribute to disease, disability, and social problems (e.g., substance use, suicide attempts, high-risk sexual behaviour, and premature mortality) (Substance Abuse and Mental Health Services Administration, 2018).

It is believed that the chronic stress in childhood stimulates specific neurotransmitters that "turn off" the brain's ability to regulate emotions (Egan, Combs-Orme, & Neely-Barnes, p. 274). Children who experience abuse or neglect are therefore more likely to have difficulty with critical brain functions and experience difficulties in focusing, learning, self-regulation, attention, impulse control, decision-making, and higher order thinking. In effect, the child cannot discriminate between safe and unsafe environments.

### Child abuse and neglect

Child abuse and neglect does not have a universal definition, but is defined through legislation across the country.

"Child abuse" is generally considered an act of commission that results in harm. By contrast, "child neglect" is generally considered an act of omission, which also results in harm. Today, most legislation also includes witnessing intimate partner violence as harmful to children.

The responsibility to assess child abuse and neglect is a specialized practice. Recognizing signs and symptoms of child abuse and neglect and reporting them are a citizen's responsibility. All social workers have the responsibility to report concerns and to work to prevent children experiencing abuse and neglect in all its forms.

## Attachment theory

Attachment theory describes the interpersonal relationship between a child and a primary caregiver. It was developed by John Bowlby, a British psychologist who followed the experience of hundreds of thousands of British children who were separated from their parents during World War II.

## Infancy and Attachment

The most important aspect of social development is the formation of attachment, which is "the positive emotional bond that develops between a child and a particular, special individual" (Feldman & Landry, 2017, p. 130).

**Attachment theory** in developmental psychology originates with the work of John Bowlby in the 1940s. Attachment theory holds that young children acquire mental representations of their own worthiness based on other people's ability and willingness to provide care and protection. The nature and strength of attachment during infancy influences the formation and maintenance of relationships throughout life.

Mary Ainsworth, an influential American developmental psychologist who worked with Bowlby, developed a classification system for different kinds of attachment. Ainsworth initially described secure and insecure attachment as follows:

> Some parents are more sensitive towards the child and so the child learns that the parent is available for them in times of need. Such children would usually be described as having secure attachment relationships. Other parents may be less sensitive or only intermittently sensitive. The children of these parents would usually be described as having insecure attachment relationships. (Wilkins, 2017, p. 71)

A further distinction was made in the classification of insecure attachment in the 1980s. Children with avoidant-insecure attachments "were generally found to have predictably insensitive caregiving environments, whilst for children with ambivalent-insecure attachments, they were generally found to have less predictable caregiving environments, at times insensitive but at other times highly sensitive (sometimes even becoming intrusive)" (Wilkins, 2017, p. 71).

A further expansion to Ainsworth's framework included a category for "disorganized-disoriented" patterns where children show inconsistent, contradictory, and confused behaviour (see Table 6.2).

**Table 6.2** Classification of Infant Attachment (Mary Ainsworth)

| Type of Attachment | Seeking Contact with Caregiver | Maintains Contact with Caregiver | Avoids Contact with Caregiver | Resists Contact with Caregiver |
|---|---|---|---|---|
| 1. **Secure** | High | High (if distressed) | Low | Low |
| 2. **Avoidant** | Low | Low | High | Low |
| 3. **Ambivalent** | High | High (often pre-separation) | Low | High |
| 4. **Disorganized-disoriented*** | Inconsistent | Inconsistent | Inconsistent | Inconsistent |

* The "Disorganized-disoriented" category was added later by Mary Ainsworth and her assistant, Mary Main.
**Source:** Adapted from Feldman and Landry (2017).

## Cultural Differences in Attachment

Despite a widespread adoption of attachment theory, research on the applicability of the model with different cultural groups has been somewhat limited (Neckoway, Brownlee, & Castellan, 2007). Keller (2014) argues that

> contextual variations need to be systematically incorporated into attachment theory to lead to a radical shift from the view of attachment as a universal human need that has the same shape and emerges that same way across cultures to the view of attachment as a universal human need that looks differently and has different developmental trajectories across contexts. (p. 2)

Critics have pointed out that attachment theory represents more of a Western philosophy of child rearing than a proper scientific theory. For example, attachment theory makes assumptions about the ideal dyadic relationship based on a mother–infant bond. However, not all cultures expect mothers to be the sole caregiver; and not all cultures interpret the child's needs in the same way or have the same reactions to emotional expression. For example, an infant's crying may have multiple interpretations (Neckoway et al., 2007). Keller (2014) argues that in order to understand children's development on a global scale, including Indigenous views on attachment, attachment should be seen as a biologically based—but culturally shaped—construct.

In reviews of attachment research, there appears to be agreement and convergence around the conception of secure attachment, but wide variations in cultural beliefs and practices associated with non-adaptive insecure forms of attachment (Feldman & Landry, 2017; Keller, 2014). "Cultural contexts differ widely in their models of autonomy and relatedness, socialization goals, and caregiving strategies" (Keller, 2014, p. 12). For example, the aim in Japanese culture is to promote interdependence, while in Western culture the aim is to promote independence:

> In Western culture the expectation is that a parent will respond sensitively to a child's needs as a reaction to explicit signals from the child. In Japanese culture the expectation is different, a parent is expected to engage in a high level of emotional closeness and to anticipate a child's needs rather than wait for a signal from the child. (Rothbausm, as cited in Neckoway et al., 2007, p. 68)

From a Western perspective, this type of interaction in Japan could easily lead to an assessment of anxious-resistant infants (Neckoway et al., 2007).

Ahnert and colleagues conducted a series of studies with infants from East and West Germany before, during, and after reunification. In their studies, despite East and West Germany having quite different child-rearing practices, they found that the rates of secure attachment were virtually identical. However, West German infants showed higher than average results in the disorganized category before and after reunification. Meanwhile, East German infants showed higher than average results in the avoidant attachment category in all three periods. These findings led the authors to question the reliability of the attachment concept across cultures (as cited in Neckoway et al., 2007).

The lesson here is that any social work assessments or interventions need to incorporate cultural and contextual understanding in their interpretation of child–caregiver attachment.

# Social Worker Exemplar

# Childhood Neglect and Trauma

## Lorry-Ann Austin

**Lorry-Ann had been providing developmental disability mental health services for 10 years when she encountered Lucy, who was caught in a downward spiral out of her control.**

When Lucy met Lorry-Ann, she was a 14-year-old in a grade 8 life-skills program due to her developmental disabilities. She had been referred to the agency due to aggressive rage reactions.

Eventually, Lorry-Ann was able to understand the multiple factors contributing to Lucy's violent outbursts and erratic behaviour. Lucy's ability to respond to perceived threats was compromised as a result of multiple adverse childhood experiences.

Lucy needed an advocate, not incarceration.

Lucy's long-term foster family had broken down after Lucy had smashed windows and destroyed other family property. She was now staying in a staffed residential home in the hope that staff could better manage her outbursts. Following conversations with the residential care staff and a social worker, I met with Lucy to gain her perceptions about the incidences and what might be helpful for her.

Lucy easily engaged and openly related her early history. Her mother abandoned her to her father when she was a toddler. Her father, whom Lucy stated loved her very much, was himself struggling, and physically and emotionally abused her. Lucy was removed from her father's care by child-protective services when she was six years old. She had not seen him, her mother, or her extended family since her removal.

Lucy remembered being placed in a series of foster homes before being placed with her long-term family at age eight. She enjoyed the fact that she was the only child in the home and described a close attachment to her foster parents, whom she called "auntie" and "uncle." She could not explain the recent change in her behaviour or the escalation in property damage and physical aggression that led to her being removed from her foster home.

Over the course of the following few weeks, I gathered more collateral information about Lucy's past. She had been diagnosed with fetal alcohol spectrum disorder and a mild intellectual disability shortly after she was placed into foster care. Her aggressive behaviour was not new, but had been documented since she entered protective care.

I documented all of this in my assessment and queried an attachment disorder complicated by anxiety. I shared my assessment with our team psychiatrist, who in turn diagnosed a reactive attachment disorder as well as a generalized anxiety disorder. She prescribed Lucy an antidepressant and a medication to help with emotional regulation.

Lucy continued to have rage reactions and she began to push, hit, or kick out at staff when they tried to contain her. To protect her when she fled the home, the staff were ordered to follow her. This resulted in Lucy becoming even more agitated. She began throwing rocks and swearing at the staff who followed her.

## A Turn for the Worse

At an interprofessional meeting, the agency staff raised their plan to charge Lucy with assault, should the physical aggression to staff be repeated. This troubled me. I shared my concerns that Lucy lacked the capacity to understand the consequences of her actions. She was emotionally, intellectually, and socially much younger than her physical age. The meeting became heated as the supervisor asserted the need to protect her staff.

After our meeting, I reflected on the suggestion that Lucy be criminalized if her aggressive behaviour continued. Lucy had experienced severe childhood trauma and was in a constant emotional state. How could we hold her accountable when she lacked capacity and had been conditioned to respond to threats in the very way that she was responding?

From a lifespan developmental approach, we can see multiple environmental factors that shaped Lucy's temperament and personality (exposure to alcohol in utero, abandonment as a toddler, traumatization in early childhood, and attachment injuries throughout her early childhood and adolescence). We can understand that Lucy's difficulty in regulating her emotions resulted from past trauma and abandonment. Her lack of trusting care providers in early childhood left her in a perpetual state of fear and mistrust of those around her.

Six months later, Lucy was arrested and charged with assaulting a police officer. She had apparently become enraged when she was told by a new staff member that she could not doodle in her school textbook. She ripped up the book, threw it at staff, and ran from the residence. Eventually, she ran to a nearby car dealership where she began throwing rocks at the cars and damaging them. The police were called, and officers had to subdue her.

She was taken to RCMP cells for the night and sent home the next day after seeing a judge who provided her with her next court date. She was now entering the criminal justice system. ∎

## Reflections on Lorry-Ann's Story

Lucy's fight-or-flight reaction could be viewed as a conditioned response to adverse childhood experiences. Her experiences taught her that the world is an unfriendly place, and this belief contributes to her constant state of heightened arousal, always expecting the worst to occur.

Lucy's abilities to learn and understand are also compromised by her intellectual disability and fetal alcohol spectrum disorder. This, in turn, makes it difficult to reason with her or to reframe her experiences and adjust her responses. Lucy lacked the safe social interactions required for prosocial development.

### From Theory to Practice

As you reflect on Lorry-Ann's story, give some thought to the following points:

1. What approach did Lucy's team generally adopt in working with her? Were they focused on her as an individual or did they focus on her environment? What different outcomes might result from these two approaches?

2. Should learning challenges and diverse developmental abilities change the degree to which we hold individuals accountable for their actions? Why or why not? Do you think the current criminal justice system meets the needs of individuals with diverse developmental abilities?

3. What is your perception of Lucy's participation in the assessment and planning? What could be done differently?

4. How might a perspective that incorporated Lucy's strengths, resiliencies, and protective factors have assisted in working with Lucy?

**Ethnic identity**

Ethnic identity refers to the extent to which a person identifies with a particular ethnic group and the extent to which one's thinking, perceptions, feelings, and behaviour relate to belonging to that ethnic group. An ethnic group is a distinct population that shares a common cultural background.

# Identity Formation in Childhood and Adolescence

Psychosocial development typically occurs during middle childhood and adolescence. It involves the development of an individual's understanding of oneself (i.e., one's self-concept) and one's ethnic and gender identity.

### Ethnic Identity

The terms "race," "culture," and "ethnicity" are frequently used interchangeably, but they are not the same. Traditionally, "race" denoted biological and genetic characteristics. However, this notion has been challenged, and race is increasingly recognized as being socially constructed (Quintana et al., 2006).

**Ethnic identity** is generally understood as a shared sense of identity and history that distinguishes one group from another (Connolly, 2005). This may be related to skin colour, nationality, religion, language, or shared cultural traditions. Ethnicity is not simply about skin colour, as many ethnic groups are not distinguished primarily in these terms. Ethnicity pertains to shared culture. Thus various minority groups can be part of the same ethnic group. Being "white" is also an ethnic identity, although it is rarely questioned and often treated as the "norm."

Children learn about ethnicity and develop their own sense of ethnic identity through their immediate family, their local community, and what is portrayed through media and television. This identity development starts young—even infants are able to distinguish different skin colours, although it is only later that they begin to attribute meaning to ethnicity (Feldman & Landry, 2017). In Northern Ireland, Protestant and Catholic children were found to demonstrate notable differences in terms of which national flags they preferred by the age of three; although those same children showed little knowledge of what those flags actually represented (Connolly, 2005).

In a pluralistic society made up of diverse and coequal cultural groups and that aims to honour and preserve unique cultural features, understanding how children develop their own ethnic identity is important. Forgerson Hindley and Olsen Edwards (2017) argue that it is a common fallacy that children are "colour blind," do not notice racial characteristics, and are untouched by racism and prejudice. They suggest that the human brain is "hardwired" to work at deciphering who is like me and who is different. Unless a child has significant experiences to contradict predominant social attitudes, by age eight racial attitudes are well developed. DeCaroli, Falanga, and Sagone's (2011) study of Italian, Chinese, and African pupils found that ethnic awareness and self-identification are present in children by as early as ages four and five.

Today, the concept of a "bicultural identity" is emerging, in which "an individual lives as a member of two cultures, with two cultural identities without having to choose one over the other" (Feldman & Landry, 2017, p. 212).

## Gender Identity

**Gender identity** refers to a sense of being male, female, or something else, and this identity is well-established for most children by the time they reach the preschool years. Most preschoolers are able to label themselves, and others, as a boy or a girl.

Developmental theorists have varying explanations of how gender identity forms. From a biological perspective, hormones and physical characteristics lead to gender differentiation. However, behavioural characteristics cannot be attributed entirely to biological factors (Feldman & Landry, 2017). From a social learning perspective, children adopt gender-related behaviour and expectations by observing others, including parents, teachers, siblings, and even peers. Books, media, television, and video games all play a role in perpetuating traditional views of gender-related behaviour. Cognitive theorists argue that forming a clear sense of self-identity involves establishing a gender identity or a perception of oneself as male or female (Feldman & Landry, 2017).

It is now well understood that, while most children's gender identity aligns with their biological sex, for some children the association is not so clear. The social construction of what it means to be "male" or "female" continues to evolve. All children exhibit behaviours and traits associated with both genders.

Many children have interests and traits that may align with a different sex than was assigned at birth, and some children do not identify with either gender. Gender non-conforming children may identify more clearly with their assigned sex or the opposite gender later in life; others will grow to become transgender adults.

Although some transgender children and youth are healthy and resilient, many are told that they "do not fit in" and are at a greater risk of depression, anxiety, self-abuse, substance use, suicide, and family violence (Mallon & DeCrescenzo, 2006). Gender variance is often confused with sexual orientation. However, gay boys and lesbian girls do not necessarily express dissatisfaction with their gender, or their sense of maleness or femaleness (Mallon & DeCrescenzo, 2006).

Nowadays many social work programs are beginning to prepare practitioners to work with gender variant children and youth, and their families. New social workers are encouraged to take a "trans-affirming" perspective in support of young people who have transgender feelings and needs. They are encouraged to do the following:

- Educate themselves about transgender children and youth;
- Ensure that treatments for depression and associated conditions focus on a trans-affirming approach;
- Support parents and young people to keep communication open, with parents continuing to show love, acceptance, and compassion; and
- Assist parents in resisting electroshock and aversion-type treatment as they are unethical and dangerous (Mallon & DeCrescenzo, 2006).

**Gender identity**

Gender identity is a person's sense of being male, female, both, neither, or somewhere along the gender spectrum.

A person's gender identity may be the same as or different from the gender typically associated with the sex they were assigned at birth. Some people may feel as though they were born with the "wrong" body parts, or in the "wrong" body because their gender identity does not correspond with their birth-assigned sex.

# Mental Health in Childhood and Adolescence

Through its unique mandate from the Government of Canada, the Mental Health Commission of Canada (MHCC) supports federal, provincial, and territorial governments as well as health-care organizations in the implementation of sound public policy in the area of mental health. The MHCC's 2015 report card on mental health identifies that over three-quarters (77.2%) of Canadian adolescents between the ages of 12 and 19 report their mental health as very good or excellent. Nevertheless, a large percentage of youth report that they have received a diagnosis of an anxiety or a mood disorder. The number reporting anxiety and mood disorders is higher than in previous surveys, although it is unclear whether the increasing rates reflect better detection by health-care professionals.

It is also estimated that one in four kindergarten-aged children (26%) are vulnerable to one or more of the five dimensions reflecting emotional, social, and cognitive development in the Early Development Instrument (EDI). This finding is particularly troubling, as the EDI predicts poor school performance and has implications for mental health and social outcomes (Mental Health Commission of Canada, 2015).

## Suicide Risk

It is estimated that 1.2 million children and youth in Canada are affected by mental illness, with a large proportion, estimated to be over 80%, not receiving appropriate treatment (Mental Health Commission of Canada, 2019). In particular, suicide risk is a serious concern and the second leading cause of death for Canada's youth (Mental Health Commission of Canada, 2015).

The rate of young people aged 15 to 24 who have had serious thoughts about suicide is high, with 6% reporting having had suicidal thoughts in the past year (Findlay, 2017). Among those aged 12 to 16, up to 10% of boys and 20% of girls have considered suicide (MedBroadcast, n.d.). Suicidal thoughts are serious, as they are associated with emotional distress and severe forms of depression, and are much more common in youth than in other age groups.

## College and University Students

Approximately one in five college or university students discloses that, at some time in the past, they have seriously considered suicide or have intentionally injured themselves. Over 6% of college and university students reported intentional self-harm. While deliberate self-harm often occurs in the absence of suicidal intent, it is considered a clear sign of emotional distress that can result in accidental death or serious injury, and is a risk factor for suicide (Mental Health Commission of Canada, 2015).

A majority of college and university students seek out stress-reduction supports during their college or university lives. Risk indicators of serious mental health problems include binge drinking, self-harm, and suicidal thoughts (Mental Health Commission of Canada, 2015). Binge drinking is a leading cause of injury and death among college and university students. While slightly over one-third report that they routinely set limits on the number of alcoholic drinks they will have when partying or socializing, this leaves a large number of students with high risk for harms (Mental Health Commission of Canada, 2015).

## Trauma-Informed Care

Trauma is what happens when the alarm centre of the brain is repeatedly triggered. Trauma theories provide direction both to help the survivor manage their trauma response and to attend to the social and systemic forces that gave rise to the traumatic experience in the first place (Wilkin & Hillock, 2014).

**Trauma-informed care (TIC)** incorporates an understanding of the frequencies and effects of early childhood adversity on psychosocial functioning across the lifespan. The primary goal is not to address past trauma directly, but to view presenting problems in the context of the child's traumatic experiences (Levenson, 2017). According to Levenson (2017):

> Trauma-informed social workers rely on their knowledge about trauma to respond to clients in ways that convey respect and compassion, honour self-determination and enable the rebuilding of healthy interpersonal skills and coping strategies. (p. 105)

Trauma-informed social workers appreciate how widespread childhood trauma is and understand that violence and victimization can negatively affect psychosocial development and lifelong coping strategies. They deliver support services in a manner that recognizes the emotional vulnerability of trauma survivors and avoids inadvertently repeating dynamics of abusive interactions in the helping relationship (Levenson, 2017).

To become effective in trauma-informed practice, social workers must be trained to examine the multiple dimensions of trauma and to think critically about their own experiences and knowledge in this area (Wilkin & Hillock, 2014).

## Resilience

An important area of lifespan research is identifying risk and protective factors to psychosocial adjustment and well-being.

Individual responses to harms, stress, trauma, and abuse can vary immensely. Simply put, **resilience** refers to the positive adaptation following risks or threats to the person. Today, resilience is understood as a more dynamic process and refers to the "capacity for, or pathways and patterns of, positive adaptation during or following significant threats or disturbances" (Masten, 2011).

Among children, resilience refers to how well the child can adapt to adverse childhood events—a child with good resilience has the ability to bounce back more quickly. Rutter offers a more nuanced perspective:

> Children's resistance to stress is relative, rather than absolute; the origins of stress resistance are both environmental and constitutional; and the degree of resistance is not a fixed individual characteristic. Rather resistance varies over time and according to circumstances. (as cited in Daniel & Bowes, 2010, p. 824)

Today, resilience is understood as a journey from being a victim and vulnerable to being a survivor.

# Skills for Working with Children and Families

**Tavistock Observation Method (TOM)**

The unique feature of this method of child observation is that the observer is immersed in the interactions that take place between the infant or child and others present, all the while remaining as non-interventionist and as unobtrusive as possible.

It is common for social work students to be provided with a foundation of generic communication skills, plus basic child-focused proficiencies and child development knowledge (Lefevre, 2015). However, specialized knowledge and skills—including how practitioners should engage and communicate with children and how children's developmental stage might influence the method of communication—is often limited.

## Observing Children

Observing children for purposes of assessment and intervention is an advanced skill. It requires developing a capacity to understand something of the child's inner world based on the minutiae of the moment-by-moment experiences between caregiver and child (Ng, Bampton, Stevens, & Woods, 2017).

The **Tavistock Observation Method (TOM)** for structured child observation is a distinctive experiential approach developed at the Tavistock Clinic in London, England, by child psychoanalyst Esther Bick. The Tavistock method focuses on "being" rather than "doing" in the observations, a process that promotes students' internal reflections on the self as an observer (Lefevre, 2015).

In the Tavistock method, the observer remains non-interventionist and as unobstrusive as possible, with the aim of being present in the moment and open to perceiving as much as possible. The observer takes no notes, photos, or videos, but instead writes a report of the observation as soon as possible following the event. The observation report aims to encapsulate not only what was seen, but also what was felt by the observer—the emotions, thoughts and feelings that were evoked (Brooker, 2017).

Following the writing of the observation report, discussing "theoretical perspectives can enable an abstract conceptualization to be formed about some of the different ways in which children communicate and engage and relate in their social worlds both directly and indirectly" (Lefevre, 2015, p. 220).

This skill can be practised when accompanying a worker to a home visit, in a child-care setting, or by observing a typical child over time. In a study in England (Hingley-Jones, Parkinson, & Allain, 2016), student social workers who participated in baby and child observation gained learning in three ways:

- They encountered and learned about the complexity of child development from the direct experience of observing.
- They found that observing facilitated the development of important skills for practice, including the "use of self."
- They developed the capacity to take up and sustain a professional role.

## Observing and Interpreting Unusual Behaviours in Children

Attachment theory is an important framework in social work and understanding parent–child behaviour. Bear in mind that many maltreated children come to fear an abusive parent while remaining attached to that parent, resulting in an experience of need and fear at the same time. This experience can lead to **disorganized attachment**.

According to Shemmings and Shemmings (2011), disorganized attachment can result in heightened anxiety and displays of unusual behaviour (e.g., the child may freeze, warily approach a parent, or physically attack them) (as cited in Wilkins, 2017). It is relatively rare for a maltreated child not to display disorganized attachment behaviour, at least in early childhood (Wilkins, 2017).

A study of 24 social workers in England looked at how key ideas in attachment theory were applied in practice when working with children who had been abused or neglected (Wilkins, 2017). The social workers had recently completed professional development in the area of disorganized attachment. They described how, by using attachment theory and research associated with disorganized attachment, they were able to:

- Focus on and better understand the child. For example, they could better interpret the meaning of the children's behaviour to understand what was really going on.

- Take clear decisions and intervene purposefully. Understanding that few children exhibit disorganized attachment behaviour without first being abused or neglected helped the social workers more clearly identify the type of intervention required.

- Emphasize the primacy of relationships and partnership. This emphasis improved the quality of the social work assessment of children because the social workers felt more confident about their direct work with children. It also helped the social workers understand relationships between different members of the child's family. As well, it helped social workers avoid blaming parents, and explained why parents may be reticent to speak with social workers or may not want to talk about certain things.

- Offer a general framework for understanding and helping parents. Knowledge of attachment theory allowed the social workers to understand the children's behaviour and help parents understand their own motivations and behaviours. For example, this knowledge helped a mother who was unable to understand her child's feelings of lack of love and neglect connect her interpretation to her own childhood experiences.

When interviewed about their work, the social workers made frequent reference to theory and research related to disorganized attachment. Wilkins (2017) concluded that attachment theory may be a particularly "good fit" with child-protection social work.

## Disorganized attachment

Disorganized attachment is a pattern of behaviour said to result when the parent or person who should be a child's safe haven is also a source of fear or even terror. Children who experience disorganized attachment have no way to receive comfort and protection or deal with anxiety.

Disorganized infant attachment may be more common among maltreated infants, but it is not necessarily an indicator of maltreatment.

# Early, Middle, and Late Adulthood

### Early Adulthood

Early adulthood, the period from approximately ages 20 to 40, is a time of continued psychosocial development. From a physical perspective, young adults are generally as fit and healthy as they will ever be. For some young adults, this period is the first time they have had to deal seriously with the negative consequences of developmental change. One such area of change is diet—weight control is challenging for many young adults, as they must reduce their caloric intake and be active in order to maintain their health (Feldman & Landry, 2017).

This is also a time when stressful events may increase. Entering university or college, starting a first job, forming intimate relationships, marriage, the death of a parent, the birth of children and parenting, buying a house—these are all milestones associated with early adulthood. Stress can be experienced as either negative or positive. In early adulthood, some of the early physical consequences of stress include headaches, backaches, skin rashes, indigestion, and chronic fatigue.

### Middle Adulthood

Middle adulthood is a time of significant transition: people change their views on their careers, evaluate their marriages, and experience an "empty nest" when grown children leave home (Feldman & Landry, 2017). Middle age is also a period of deepening roots, as family and friends ascend in importance and career ambitions begin to take a backseat. Many adults in middle age experience challenges at work. This can result in switching or starting careers—either voluntarily or involuntarily. Physically, middle age is associated with changes in sexuality, including menopause, and increasing concerns related to heart disease and cancer.

Stress continues into later adulthood and can have a significant impact on health. Although the triggers may have changed, the result is similar. Direct physiological effects include symptoms such as elevated blood pressure, decrease in immune-system functioning, increased hormonal activity and psychophysiological conditions. Harmful behaviours, such as the increased use of nicotine, alcohol, and other licit and illicit drugs, poor nutrition, and decreased sleep, are frequently an outcome of stress (Feldman & Landry, 2017).

People in middle age may also experience "boomerang" children (children who return home) and/or be sandwiched between the generations—caring for children boomeranging back while also caring for aging parents. This may occur simultaneously with becoming grandparents.

Interestingly, there appears to be continuity to personality throughout adulthood, with the "big five" basic personality traits—neuroticism, extroversion, openness, agreeableness, and conscientiousness—staying remarkably stable across adulthood (Feldman & Landry, 2017). People who are even-tempered at 20 are still even-tempered at 40 and 75.

## Late Adulthood

The period of late adulthood is generally considered to start around age 65 and is characterized by great changes (Feldman & Landry, 2017). There are many negative stereotypes about persons in this age group. While older adults face profound physical, cognitive, and social changes, most maintain physical and mental strength virtually until the day they die. While experiencing a gradual transition from full strength and health to an increasing concern about illness, pain, and disease, many older adults stay healthy for quite a long time and continue most, if not all, of the activities they enjoyed when they were younger.

Cognitively, older people seem to adjust quite well to the changes that seem designed to impede them. They do so by adopting new strategies for solving problems and compensating for lost abilities (Feldman & Landry, 2017).

## Death and Dying

We associate death with old age, but death occurs across the lifespan. People of every age can experience the death of friends and family members, as well as their own death. Culturally, there are many different understandings and responses to death. Coming to terms with death, one's own or someone else's, is culturally and socially contextualized. Social workers are often involved with individuals and/or family members through this process.

In Western societies, death is viewed as atypical, rather than expected, which makes the grief all the more difficult to bear (Feldman & Landry, 2017). Socio-cultural norms and customs determine the nature of funerals and/or "celebrations of life." Following the death of a loved one, many people are ill-prepared for the grief that follows.

A period of adjustment typically follows the death of a loved one. Grief, the emotional response to a loss, appears differently for different people, based on their age, their individual personality, the nature of the relationship with the deceased, and the opportunity for them to continue their lives after the loss. The stages of grief do not unfold the same way for everyone. As Feldman and Landry (2017) state:

> Ultimately, most people emerge from grieving and live new, independent lives. They form new relationships, and some even find that coping with the death has helped them to grow as individuals. They become more self-reliant and appreciative of life. (p. 440)

Nowadays, many people wish to exercise some control over the place and manner in which they die. This may involve having Do Not Resuscitate (DNR) instructions, living wills, and health-care directives. End-of-life care may involve many such options, including assisted-dying protocols.

Social workers can assist individuals and their family members explore choices in empathetic and understanding ways, while ensuring that autonomy and right to self-determination are maintained.

## Critical Theory and Child Development

**Deficit model of social work practice**

Deficit-based approaches to child and youth development emphasize the "deficiencies" in a family or community—for example, personal failure, a sense of helplessness, and low expectations.

Deficit-based programs focus on what children and youth are doing wrong and what outside resources are needed to fix problems, rather than on the strengths and capacities children and youth have to build resilience and coping mechanisms.

While human development theory has much to offer social work practice, social workers must continue to maintain a critical and reflexive lens in their adoption and application of this theory.

Daniel and Bowes (2010) argue that a "lifespan" approach to understanding childhood harm and abuse can provide a deeper understanding and more effective practice in protection services. Both systems theories and ecological theories, they maintain, tend to focus only on a snapshot in time. A lifespan approach would shift the attention of researchers from the individual to the structural factors across the lifespan, which can elevate risks for particular groups and communities.

### Criticisms of the Deficit Model

Traditional child development and lifespan theory is framed within a **deficit model of social work practice**. With this approach, children's skills and attributes are understood largely as part of a biological process that unfolds naturally in fixed life stages (Graham, 2011). A presenting problem is seen as a result of personal or familial failure, or of helplessness and low expectations.

Critical theorists postulate that children should be seen not as passive subjects but as active participants who interact with and shape their social world. A related criticism is that universalist claims about children and families mistakenly promote "sameness," as if children were the same across time and space.

Another limitation of traditional human development theories that critical theorists point to is the lack of attention paid to the factors that promote resilience (Smith-Osborne, 2007). The argument is that we know more about the causes of pathology than we know about the reasons why some children in adversity become well-functioning adults. Ungar (2003) argues for a postmodern approach that shifts the focus to discovering the factors that help to strengthen resilience among persons who face adversity (as cited in Graham, 2011, p. 1537).

# Indigenous Child-Rearing
## The Circle of Caregivers

The Truth and Reconciliation Commission of Canada's (2015) calls to action recommend increasing the numbers of Indigenous professionals in the health-care field and providing cultural competency training for all health-care professionals.

Call to action #23 states unequivocally:

> 23. We call upon all levels of government to:
>
> i. Increase the number of Aboriginal professionals working in the health-care field.
>
> ii. Ensure the retention of Aboriginal health-care providers in Aboriginal communities.
>
> iii. Provide cultural competency training for all health-care professionals.

### Cultural Competency

It is imperative for health-care and social workers to understand Indigenous child-rearing practices. Similarly, the Aboriginal Working Group that guided the development of Best Start: Ontario's Maternal, Newborn, and Early Child Development Resource Centre encourages all social and health-care workers to recognize how "colonization, the residential school system, as well as ongoing discrimination [have] affected Aboriginal people's ability to trust non-Aboriginal people" (Fearn, 2006, p. 37).

Although non-Indigenous workers may not fully understand an Indigenous person's experiences, it is essential to be gentle in one's approach, to recognize that everyone has a different paradigm of experience, and to allow the family to take ownership of their situation (Fearn, 2006). As one Elder stated:

> "Before you speak, think of how your message will be received. You may say things with the best intention and still offend someone." (Fearn, 2006, p. 38)

For example, Indigenous approaches to child-rearing stress the holistic connections between the child, family, community, and the natural and spiritual worlds.

Indigenous children are recognized as persons and encouraged to make their own decisions and develop independence (Muir & Bohr, 2014, p. 70).

### The Circle of Caregivers

Indeed, the circle of caregivers in Indigenous communities may go well beyond the primary caregivers, and include older siblings, aunts, uncles, extended family, and others. In many Indigenous communities, grandparents have historically played an important role in socializing, providing physical care, and training for grandchildren (Muir & Bohr, 2014). Other adults in the community also act as caregivers to children, even if they are not blood relations (Anderson, 2011).

In a Canadian study, Neckoway et al. (2007) observed the following:

> in a context of multiple caregivers living in the same household, the mother can afford to be less vigilant and can have an expectation that someone will be available to attend to the infant's signals and needs. (p.71)

Discipline may also look different in Indigenous communities. Praise for good behaviour and storytelling as a way of learning life lessons are much more prevalent (Anderson, 2011). In many Indigenous communities, parents do not readily use physical punishment with their children. They are more likely to respond to aggression in their children with goals that teach values, societal rules, or important life lessons that could benefit the child.

Muir and Bohr (2014) caution the following:

> when western assessment tools are used to assess Aboriginal children, these children may appear to be delayed in their skill development because the yardstick used to measure Aboriginal child development is mainstream Western child development and thus, Aboriginal children are deemed to fall short. This in turn may be a contributing factor when children are placed in foster care. (p. 74) ∎

# Social Worker Exemplar

## Reflecting on Personal Biases

Brit Sluis

**Social workers naturally bring a lifetime of personal experience to situations. Using friends and colleagues to help think through any unconscious biases or difficult situations can be a valuable learning opportunity.**

Brit was a mature, single-parent student. It was her dream to be placed in an agency providing holistic services to women and families in the areas of substance use, mental health, pregnancy, and child care.

Being a parent herself, it was not easy to separate out her own view on pregnancy, substance use, and parenting. Doing so was a valuable learning experience for her.

Brit has since graduated with a BSW and continues working in this area.

I was excited to begin my field placement in this particular agency, as I had always wanted to work with women and children. However, I was shocked when I realized that I was being judgemental when working with pregnant women using substances. I suppose this bias came from having my own son (who was three at the time). I could not imagine using drugs or putting my baby at any sort of risk. How could a woman knowingly put her baby in harm's way?

I knew this was a bias, and an especially emotional one for me. I also knew that I had to try and work through it. So, I reached out to an instructor whom I respected and knew had practical experience in substance use and child welfare. I wanted help in order to be more open and useful at my field site. I was anxious that she might see me as a "bad" worker for having these biases, but I was pleased that I had already developed a relationship with her. We had a really good talk.

We talked over a number of things. I remember feeling relieved when she said that my judgementalness in this regard was not unusual, and that it was likely the result of a societal stigma that all of us were exposed to. Although we had learned a lot about stigma in classes, the value of being non-judgemental never really occurred to me. I hadn't been aware of it in my own life.

We then talked about the value of harm-reduction strategies in substance-use programs. I thought I was a supporter of harm reduction, and was in favour of programs such as the needle exchange. However, I hadn't thought of the issues of harm reduction in relation to pregnant women who were still using.

We also talked about feminist theory, and the concept of women controlling their own bodies. I totally agreed with this—except, in my mind, when the baby took precedence over the mother. But I had to realize this was my perspective.

My instructor asked me whether I thought we should imprison women who drank when pregnant to ensure the baby's safety. Of course, I didn't think that was appropriate. She also noted that under the province's child-protection legislation, the fetus is not a child in need of protection. While I thought I disagreed with this, I could see the intention behind the legislation in terms of protecting the rights of women.

## Practising Unconditional Respect

She even integrated child development knowledge into the discussion, asking me what I knew about the effects of drugs on the unborn baby. We talked through the peculiar way drugs can act on the fetus and about the fact that alcohol and drugs used one day may not have the same effect on the baby a month later.

We then talked about the practice basis of service user-centred work and the ethic of self-determination. What did that really mean to me? Did I really believe a woman who was pregnant and who drank was a "bad" person," or did I believe she was a woman who had an addiction? What did I believe about helping? Did I believe that she was deserving or undeserving of help?

By the end of the conversation, my instructor helped me see that the majority of women who have used drugs during pregnancy do not want to harm their baby. They are mired in a lifestyle where they have little supports. I also realized that for many such women, life is chaotic, and so is their menstrual cycle, and they may not even realize they are pregnant until it is too late to make alternative choices. In many ways, their options are limited. If they do stop using drugs, they may experience serious withdrawal symptoms that also could be harmful to their baby.

I learned that anyone—everyone—who is reaching out for help is trying to heal. I also learned that it is important to understand not only women's current situation but also their past. I began to wonder whether women's trauma history and childhood experiences were possible influences on their current behaviour. Surely, having empathy for their experiences could assist them now.

I learned that everyone and every circumstance is different. What I did during my pregnancy may not necessarily work for other women. It is important to go out of my way to not add my own biases to an already difficult situation for these women. ■

## Reflections on Brit's Story

As you read Brit's experiences, consider the situation from a complex practice behaviour model (see p. 35) and from a lifespan development perspective. Also consider the associated ethical issues.

Brit quickly became aware of her own emotions and judgements and was clearly showing a high level of self-regulation. Most importantly, she was dedicated to the reflexive process and was willing to seek out others with whom she could talk through her feelings about what to do. She also wanted to gain a better understanding of a myriad of theories that could be used to assist her in her practice with pregnant women using substances.

### From Theory to Practice

As you reflect on Brit's story, give some thought to the following points:

1. What are some of the structural and societal attitudes that may be affecting mothers-to-be who are, or have been, substance users?

2. What are some of the possible developmental issues that can affect the children of women who use substances when pregnant?

3. How could knowledge about trauma-informed practice or disorganized attachment assist in working with women who are pregnant and using substances?

4. How could Brit ensure a partnership approach to working with women she was encountering in her agency?

5. How do you know when you have a bias that may be affecting your work?

6. What is the best way to work through personal biases, knowing they could negatively affect your relationship with a service user?

# Practice Scenarios

Applying a human development perspective requires knowledge of physical, cognitive, emotional, and sexual development. However, any developmental framework has to be considered flexibly and contextualized within the unique circumstances and culture of the individual or family concerned.

The role of the social worker is to develop a range of possible explanations and hypotheses about the causes and perpetuation of social problems. These ideas can be rejected or further developed as one works with members of the family, and perhaps the community, to enhance understanding. Central to this approach is an understanding of the interplay of biological, psychological, social, and spiritual factors as well as an understanding of the principles of attachment, bonding, and trauma.

---

## 6.1  Assessing Infancy Trauma in Toddlers

Jaymie is three years old. At birth, she had a prolonged stay in the hospital because of her mother's opiate use during pregnancy. At birth, Jaymie's mother, Sarah, began attending a recovery program, and Jaymie stayed with a foster family. At six months, Sarah was reunited with Jaymie. Initially, Jaymie reacted to the change, and was having challenges eating and sleeping. However, Sarah worked through the transition well. Sarah has remained clean and sober, is attending counselling, and has taken parenting classes. She is now concerned that Jaymie has developmental delays. Jaymie shows little emotion when Sarah leaves her, has trouble making friends, is very active, and quickly moves from one play area to another. Sarah is also having trouble toilet training her. Jaymie refuses to dress herself, and she screams when given a bath.

1. From a developmental perspective, how might Jaymie's birth and infancy have had an effect on her current behaviours?

2. Using an attachment theory lens, what are some approaches that could be recommended to Sarah to strengthen her attachment with Jaymie?

3. What are alternative ways of understanding Jaymie's current behaviours? Are they within the bounds of normative development, or is Sarah right to be concerned?

4. From a strengths-based and trauma-informed practice, how could you proceed to continue to develop Sarah's capacity?

## 6.2 Cultural Differences during Childhood

You are a social worker with the family services department of a child-protection ministry. Johnny is a 10-year-old who was recently removed from his home in a remote fly-in Indigenous community due to parental abuse related to substance use. You are working with the parents and the community leaders to ensure a cultural plan, but everyone agrees that Johnny should stay in the new community where he was placed. He sees aunts and uncles once a week.

You have received a call from the school—Johnny is far behind in his work, is aggressive with other boys, does not sit still during class, often leaves without permission, and has been in trouble on the playground for being boisterous and running too much. This week he lost privileges to the playground equipment because he played on it on the wrong day.

1. From a developmental perspective, what is the range of psychosocial and cognitive-behavioural expectations in middle childhood?
2. What are some behaviours one might assess as "normal and expected" when a 10-year-old experiences the trauma of being removed from home and community?
3. How does one consider a cultural lens when responding to the school's concerns?
4. What are some approaches that could be considered to assist Johnny as he transitions into the new community?

## 6.3 Trauma in Adolescence

In a family services agency, you are working with Harry and Jeanette and their daughter Kyra, age 18. Kyra is an only child and was adored by her parents all through elementary school. She was a good student, polite to adults, took dancing and gymnastic lessons, and had plenty of friends.

When Kyra was in grade 9, her father was laid-off from his job in a massive factory shutdown. As a result, they eventually lost their house. They briefly had to rely on welfare subsidies and social housing. After a while, Harry got another job with a much lower salary outside of their community, and he was home for only five days every three weeks. In grade 10, Kyra got caught shoplifting costume jewellery. She also became "obsessed" with her body image and started losing weight. Her parents were sure she had started drinking, and were suspicious that she was experimenting with other drugs. Two weeks ago, while at work, her father was shown a revealing picture of his daughter on a social media site.

1. From a developmental perspective, how might one consider Kyra's behaviour?
2. What are the social and emotional milestones associated with adolescence?
3. What is the importance of the significant social changes that occurred to Kyra, related to her father's lay off?
4. Who is the primary service user here? Kyra? Harry and Jeanette? The family? Why?

# Field Education Practicalities
## Working in Teams

Social workers frequently work on a team. The team may come together to plan for a particular service user or be created to respond to or advocate for a specific issue or task. It may consist of all social workers or, in the case of interprofessional teams, of social workers and other allied health- and social-care professionals. It may or may not be inclusive of community members and service users.

Ultimately, teamwork and team decision-making provide the opportunity to pool information from diverse sources in order to make better decisions and take the most effective actions.

Working effectively as part of a team is central to social work practice, and, consequently, it is a competency to be developed in field education.

Social workers are well placed to be successful in teams, whether as active participants or in leadership roles, due to their understanding of interpersonal communication and their attentiveness to processes.

Fundamentally, teams allow organizations to accomplish tasks that are too big for one individual. By having more than one set of eyes focused on a problem, the collective wisdom of the group can result in greater involvement, more consensus, better problem solving, and a higher quality of service (Johnson, 2017).

## Characteristics of a Team

Just because a group of people are assigned to work together does not mean that they will function well as a team. The basic characteristics of a team include the following:

- Interaction techniques that are respectful and supportive
- A responsible distribution of roles and functions among team members
- Shared leadership, depending on the situation; each member has the right to a leadership and a member role on the team (Vaicekauskienė, n.d.)

Fujishin (2012) describes three characteristics essential to strong teamwork:

- **Openness.** Openness is described as welcoming communication with warmth, cheerfulness, and genuine concern, and seeing the best (or looking for the 80% positives) in the other person.
- **Flexibility.** Flexibility is described as the willingness and ability to bend, accommodate, and even change one's opinions, feelings, and behaviours, and the ability to adapt to new situations and circumstances.
- **Kindness.** Kindness is described as having an attitude of friendliness, warmth, and generosity in supporting and complimenting others.

Of these three essential characteristics, it is kindness, while not always associated with workplace environment, that Fujishin contends has the greatest impact and produces the maximum benefit in the workplace.

## Interprofessional Practice

Various terms ("multidisciplinary," "interdisciplinary," "multiprofessional," and "interprofessional") are used to describe the practice of people with a variety of experiences and backgrounds working together.

When the prefix "multi-" is used, it generally refers to two or more disciplines or professionals providing care independently. When the prefix "inter-" is used, it generally refers to collaboration among members of a team, who build on one another's expertise.

Today, the term "interprofessional" is increasingly used to refer to practice that "occurs when individuals from two or more professions learn about, from, and with each other to enable effective collaboration and improve health outcomes" (Nester, 2016, p. 128).

## Ways of Working Together

Interprofessional practice can be challenging because professional values and theories vary. Team members represent a variety of ideological and epistemological frameworks, and these inform how they view and interpret information (Johnson, 2017).

As a team, considerable attention (and time) is required to find a common framework for interaction. It is the development of this shared framework that ultimately provides a common ground so that the team can effectively communicate and apply collective wisdom to a problem.

Johnson (2017) describes four broad frameworks that characterize team operations. Understanding these frameworks can facilitate collaboration with respect to information seeking and decision-making.

The frameworks are as follows:

- **Formal.** This approach to team operations relies heavily on explicit knowledge and well understood rules. It is typical in bureaucracies in which the actors are governed by the requirement of the positions they occupy in a formal structure. Communication and information gathering in this type of team is frequently related to formulating a question in the desired way and directing it to the right person.

- **Informal.** Interactions in this type of team are more emotional and intuitive. Accessing information and the quality of the response is more often tied to prior experience with a person and that person's trustworthiness. A challenge in this type of team is developing a network of relationships and connections in order to be trusted and to receive good information.

- **Markets.** Market relationships are based on exchange relationships, with trust being of paramount importance. From this perspective, information is sought out from others because people have differing views. This way of working is particularly common in the health and social work fields because the professionals possess distinct knowledge to broaden the overall understanding of the situation.

- **Professional.** This type of teamwork is governed by a team culture that provides a framework for communication and information sharing. Professionals are challenged to maintain their professional autonomy while working as part of a collective.

Although social workers may be trained in approaches that are different from other health- and social-care professionals, individual social workers often find themselves acting with others on problem solving and information sharing. It is through such a process of collective sense-making that the ground can be laid for effective decision-making.

To function productively, team members must be independent, interdependent, and flexible. They must share the team's goals and apply themselves individually and collectively to finding the best ways of achieving these goals (Johnson, 2017). ■

# Reflection, Learning, and More Practice

## Field Education Practicalities

1. Stress and mental health problems are commonplace among university students. Investigate the initiatives and resources available to you at your university or in your community.

2. Identify teams that you are a part of in your field agency. What are your strengths and areas for enhanced growth in terms of being a team player?

3. How do you see interprofessional practice being conducted in your field agency and community?

## Journal Ideas

1. Observe a child–caregiver interaction, and document your interpretation and understandings of the child's and caregiver's behaviours.

2. A human development approach recognizes the uniqueness of individuals and the multiple factors and circumstances that contribute to an individual's life course. Journal about a situation in which considering social and cultural factors may contribute to a different understanding of someone's behaviour.

3. Consider a service user's situation in your field agency and journal how different theories/ perspectives on lifespan development could lead to different understandings of the situation and possibly different interventions.

4. Using an attachment theory lens, consider how an individual's behaviour might be better understood as a form of "disorganized attachment."

5. Describe working with the service user population in your field agency from a trauma-informed practice model.

6. Working with children who have experienced someone's death requires age-appropriate responses. Research the resources available to children in your community, learn about their approaches to supporting children who are grieving, and journal about your learning.

## Critical-Thinking Questions

1. Human development is increasingly looking at neurobiology as an alternative way of understanding human behaviour. How does this bio-anatomy approach align with the social work notion of "person-in-environment"?

2. The CCSWR includes theories of sexual development and spiritual development as competencies. How has your social work education informed your knowledge in these areas? Do you think that these areas should be included in social work competencies?

3. Why do social workers focus on the importance of strengths and resilience? Why do they also focus on understanding so-called problem behaviours as the result of deep-seated factors such as adverse childhood experiences and/or trauma?

4. Think about the influence of cultural factors on your own personal development and how your own personal outcomes may have been different in a different cultural context.

5. Explore how you have developed your own ethnic and gender identity.

6. Explain how you would see a "trans-affirming" perspective being applied in a practice setting. How important is this perspective at your current site?

7. Consider how death and dying are viewed by different cultures, and how your own values inform your thoughts on practices such as assisted dying.

8. Consider an ethnic or racial population in your region. How might its child-rearing practices be different from your own or those of the dominant Western paradigm?

# Chapter Review

Applying a human development approach to social work practice requires an understanding of the physical, social, emotional, cognitive, and behavioural indicators of personal development. These indicators need to be viewed in relation to the unique cultural and lived experiences of the individual.

Many social workers meet individuals who have been affected by adverse childhood experiences within a family environment or from a system designed to protect them. The long-term effects continue through adolescence and into adulthood. As a social worker, Lorry-Ann drew on this information in advocating for services that could be supportive rather than further punishing and traumatizing.

Brit, as a student, struggled with competing priorities as she worked through her own biases related to substance-using pregnant women, and applied a human development approach to consider both the unborn baby and the mother.

In the practice scenarios, a multiplicity of factors were affecting the children. Considering their circumstances from a human development perspective provides opportunities to respect their resilience rather than focus on their misbehaviour. It also provide opportunities to find ways to work with them to reframe and rework some of their neurological "fight" or "flight" responses.

Social workers using a lifespan approach across all ages must resist focusing on deficits and sameness, and instead focus on a service user's resilience and abilities within a cultural context.

Working in the area of human growth and development frequently requires interprofessional collaboration through teamwork. Characteristics essential to teamwork are openness, flexibility, and kindness.

## Applying Knowledge of Human Development and Behaviour

This chapter outlines numerous ways in which students can develop their social work skills using a human development approach. Here are some highlights and further suggestions:

- Contextualize lifespan development indicators within the services user's lived experience.
- Pay attention to indicators of resilience, assets, and protective factors.
- Learn from Indigenous Elders about the local descriptions and meanings associated with life cycles for Indigenous people.
- Recognize that chronic childhood stress may result in brain development that affects long-term functioning.
- Ensure that attachment theory is understood within a cultural lens.
- Take a trans-affirming approach to practice, recognizing that children and youth are developing their gender identity.
- Talk with children and youth about what their ethnic and/or bicultural identity means to them.
- View presenting problems in children and adults within the context of their traumatic experiences.
- Observe children and reflect on your conceptualization of their communication and interactions.
- Know that an understanding of attachment theory assists social workers in helping parents in the child welfare system.
- Be sensitive to cultural understandings and responses to death and grieving.
- Listen to children and youth in care about their experiences and perspectives.

# Planning and Delivering Services and Interventions

## 7

Direct practice social workers today are challenged to address the requirements of the complex array of professional, organizational, institutional, and regulatory demands placed on them in the broader socioeconomic context of fewer resources and diminished public support for social welfare services.

—Mark Cameron and Elizabeth King Keenan, "The Common Factors Model: Implications for Transtheoretical Clinical Social Work Practice," 2010

# Chapter at a Glance

# Spotlight on Social Work Luminaries
## Rosemary Brown

**Rosemary Brown** (1930–2003) studied social work at McGill University and the University of British Columbia, and was the first Black Canadian woman to be elected to a provincial legislature. A determined feminist, Rosemary worked throughout her life to promote equality and human rights. After leaving politics, she became a professor of women's studies at Simon Fraser University.

**F**ollowing the completion of the assessment process, which may involve aspects of human development and other biopsychosocial-spiritual functioning, the social worker pulls together the salient information and produces a summary impression. A treatment or intervention plan is then developed. This process continues to be collaborative, involving both the service user (and/or community) as an active participant and the social worker.

At this point, it is easy to become overwhelmed by the plethora of practice models and the conflicting pressure to balance best practices with agency pressures for briefer interventions and accountability. However, eventually, a thoughtful decision has to be made about the type and modality of any treatment or intervention plan.

In this chapter, the emphasis is on direct micro practice. Specifically, it focuses on the importance of developing service and intervention plans that are rooted in social work values, but also take into account the specific and unique situation of the service user. This "bottom-up" approach is consistent with "generalist-eclectic" (or holistic) social work practice.

## Developing Competence as a Social Worker

Some ways to develop the competency of "**planning and delivering services and interventions**" are as follows:

- Describe the practice paradigm forming the basis of a particular intervention plan, and be able to articulate alternative approaches.

- Explain the importance of service user involvement in decision-making, and review whether this process is apparent in written intervention plans.

- Review all the background facts and develop a full intervention plan for a service user associated with your agency.

- Discuss with your agency supervisor ways of working with service users who may be challenging, including possible ways to diffuse anger and volatility.

**Key Concepts**

- Clinical impression
- Generalist-eclectic direct practice
- Therapeutic common factors
- Shared decision-making (SDM)
- Expectation for change
- Endings and terminations
- Structuration theory

# Completing the Assessment

After completing an assessment, conceptualizing the service user's situation and circumstances can be a challenge. It requires synthesizing all of the relevant issues, including the service user's strengths and resources, into a summary statement often referred to as a **clinical impression**.

The formulation of the situation summarization is informed by the worker's professional and theoretical orientation. Therefore, the issues identified as most pressing and the resulting synthesis may look different from a medical, psychodynamic, developmental, or behavioural perspective.

In the end, the social worker "must come up with at least a working hypothesis and structure for figuring out what is going on" (Brew & Kottler, 2017, p. 187). It is a social worker's task to formulate and share with the service user their overall synthesis and their recommendations for further work. Social workers must be transparent about what they think caused the problems in the first place, what precipitated them in this instance, and what factors are helping to maintain them.

A clinical impression may include the following:

- An opinion on the service user's present condition
- A description of the level of functioning of the service user
- A statement as to the nature, severity, and duration of the problem or problems
- An acknowledgement of the coping mechanisms already being used by the service user
- A statement of the service user's strengths and limitations
- An indication of the service user's motivation for change, capacity for change, and ability to engage in treatment
- An indication of the systemic factors that may contribute either to the maintenance of the problem or to its possible resolution

Drawing on these observations, the final phase of an assessment is to develop a detailed intervention plan. This takes discipline and critical reflection on the part of the social worker. Intervention plans generally include the following:

- **Short-term goals.** These are the things to be worked on before the next session, including tasks for the service user and social worker.
- **Long-term objectives.** These are goals that are to be worked on over a period of time, and they may evolve over time.
- **The nature of the agreement.** This includes the frequency and estimated duration of the intervention.

There are multiple ways and frameworks for writing up a treatment or intervention plan. A service user-centred approach requires collaboration and transparency, always ensuring that the service user is an active participant and is in broad agreement with the focus of future sessions.

Following an assessment, the social worker is required to synthesize the information and then develop an intervention plan that outlines what needs to be done and how to accomplish it.

Providing services and interventions requires an openness to using a myriad of theories and techniques that are most relevant to the unique situation the social worker is presented with.

## CASWE-ACFTS *Standards for Accreditation*

The ninth core learning objective in the Canadian Association for Social Work Education–Association canadienne pour la formation en travail social (CASWE-ACFTS, 2014) *Standards for Accreditation* states:

9. Engage with individuals, families, groups, and communities through professional practice

   i) Social work students are equipped with knowledge and skills to competently perform various interactive practices, such as engagement, assessment, intervention, negotiation, mediation, advocacy, and evaluation.

   ii) Social work students have relevant knowledge and skills to actively promote empowering and anti-oppressive practice.

   iii) Social work students acquire skills to practise at individual, family, group, organization, community and population levels including advocacy and activism.

   iv) Social work students are prepared for interprofessional practice, community collaboration and team work.

   v) MSW students develop knowledge and skills in advanced practice, and/or in specialized practice with individuals, families, groups, and/or communities.

## Professional Regulation and Competency

The Canadian Council of Social Work Regulators (CCSWR, 2012) competency profile identifies "planning interventions" as a meta-competency, with the following subcategories:

- State clearly the nature of the service users' problems or needs being addressed

- Identify potential interventions appropriate to service users' problems

- Elicit the service users' point of view, suggestions and consent, about the proposed interventions

- Select, from a universe of potential interventions, the intervention that will most likely alleviate service users' problems/needs

The CCSWR (2012) meta-competency of "delivering services" includes the following subcategories:

- Explain the intervention plan to relevant stakeholders involved in the intervention delivery

- Document various steps in the intervention plan

- Implement the intervention according to the established plan

- Promote self-determination of service users

- Assess and adjust process of intervention

## Association of Social Work Boards (ASWB)

For those writing the ASWB entry-to-practice examination, 26% of questions are related to direct and indirect practices, with questions on the following:

- Intervention processes and techniques

- Matching intervention with service user system needs

- Documentation

- Use of collaborative relationship ▪

# Generalist-Eclectic Direct Practice

**Generalist-eclectic direct practice**

This approach to social work involves using a variety of models, theories, and techniques to initiate a treatment plan that is most likely to meet the desired outcome for a particular service user.

**Therapeutic common factors**

Therapeutic common factors are factors that are common to multiple intervention theories and have been associated with positive outcomes for service users. These factors offer a relatively coherent and accessible way to conceptualize social work practice and to assess the appropriateness and effectiveness of interventions (Cameron & Keenan, 2010).

A plethora of practice models are available to social workers—psychodynamic, cognitive behavioural, humanistic, critical, and postmodern. At the beginning of their careers, however, most social workers favour **generalist-eclectic direct practice**. Even for social workers involved in specialization areas, the principles and holistic perspective associated with a generalist-eclectic approach continue to be a necessary foundation for their speciality practice (Coady & Lehmann, 2016).

Some degree of eclecticism is necessary because no single practice model can adequately address the broad array of problems that human beings present in their daily lives. Generalist-eclectic direct practice allows for a flexible response to the service user's preferred cognitive and communication styles and enhances an ability to tailor treatment (Pearson, 2012).

Cameron (2014) has concluded that eclecticism, which is idiosyncratically shaped by the unique needs of service users as well as the attributes of the practitioner, is the most effective practice modality.

## Therapeutic Common Factors

Determining which theory or model to base one's practice on can be bewildering. Early on, case work and psychodynamic theories provided a foundation for social work practice. In the 1960s and 1970s, functionalist and task-centred models emerged, with ecological and general systems theory gaining some traction. More recently, practice models have focused on the social, cultural, and political aspects of human functioning, such as empowerment, service user strengths, multiculturalism, and social justice (Cameron & Keenan, 2010).

A number of factors have been found to be common across a range of practice models. For example, the service user–social worker relationship (or alliance) has been accepted as the "quintessential integrative variable" and incontrovertible pillar of good practice (Watkins, 2014). Ultimately, direct practice is more than simply applying scientific theory, since it requires empathic listening, inductive reasoning, and intuition in order to find durable solutions. Research suggests that service users tend to place more value on factors such as a strong working relationship, facilitated by an empathic and experienced clinician, than on how efficacious any particular treatment plan is "in theory" (Swift & Callahan, 2010).

Cameron and Keenan (2010) have identified a number of **therapeutic common factors** associated with positive service-user outcomes. They describe these common factors as "the non-technical aspects of therapeutic work" that have been shown to be associated with successful outcomes. The common factors include attributes of the practitioner and service user, the support systems available to the service user, and the strategies employed by the practitioner, service user, and all those involved in work that promotes change (Cameron, 2014). (See Table 7.1.)

**Table 7.1** Therapeutic Common Factors in Social Work Practice

| Social network factors | <ul><li>Supportive values</li><li>Supportive knowledge</li><li>Supportive funding, policies, procedures, and practice guidelines</li><li>Service user social support</li><li>Service user social support views social work as credible</li></ul> |
|---|---|
| **Social worker factors** | <ul><li>Well-being</li><li>Acceptance</li><li>Genuineness</li><li>Empathy</li></ul> |
| **Service user factors** | <ul><li>Distress</li><li>Hope or expectation for change</li><li>Active help seeking</li><li>Views social worker as credible</li></ul> |
| **Relationship factors** | <ul><li>Engagement in relationship</li><li>Engagement in change work</li><li>Productive direct and indirect communication</li><li>Mutual agreement on problems, roles, tasks, and goals</li><li>Collaboration</li></ul> |
| **Practice strategies** | <ul><li>Rationale for change</li><li>Modelling</li><li>Feedback</li><li>Ventilation</li><li>Exploration</li><li>Awareness and insight</li><li>Emotional learning</li><li>Interpersonal learning</li><li>Knowledge</li><li>Information</li><li>Development and practice of new behaviours</li><li>Success and mastery</li><li>Reinforcement</li><li>Desensitization</li><li>Suggestion</li><li>Advocacy</li></ul> |

**Source:** Adapted from Drisko (2004); Grencavage and Norcross (1990).

# Social Worker Exemplar

## Interprofessional Practice

Rebecca Sanford, PhD, RCSW

**Interprofessional practice calls upon unique skills. One is understanding the lens that social workers use in their practice; a second is being able to communicate this lens clearly to professionals outside the field.**

In the mid-2000s, Rebecca was a social worker doing community-based mental health work with children, youth, and their families in a large metropolitan city.

She worked with families that had multisystem involvement, including with juvenile justice and child welfare. Her role consisted of clinical counselling and case management with youth and their families, and participating as a member of the care team.

Her work with Alan, age 14, helped her see the importance of social work theory and values in the context of an interprofessional team.

Alan was on probation for drug-related offences and was referred for counselling along with his family. He was 14 years of age. During the assessment process, we learned that Alan had experienced extensive trauma in his short life, including exposure to his mother's drinking, lack of involvement with his biological father, and witnessing a family member sexually assaulting his older sister.

Alan's mother struggled to enforce strict rules in the home, and she acknowledged that she often let Alan have his own way as a way of alleviating the guilt she felt. Alan frequently didn't come home at night and spent most of his time with older youth at the basketball court. He also engaged with the older youth in property destruction, drinking, and other similar behaviours. Alan's first contact with the juvenile justice system was following a fight on the basketball court. The police charged him with simple possession of marijuana, for which he received probation.

In addition to his involvement with the juvenile court system, his family had an open case with child protection. Alan was also on an IEP (Individualized Education Plan) and attended an alternative educational program in the community. I had been working with Alan and his family for six months when I received a call informing me that Alan was in a juvenile detention facility and awaiting a court hearing as a result of being arrested for breaking into an abandoned building.

The team assigned to Alan and his family had met regularly and, for the most part, had worked well together. The team came together to review recommendations to be made to the court.

Anne, the probation officer, and I had quite different perspectives. Anne recommended that Alan be held in detention for two weeks. The severity of the offence and his past contact with the system led her to believe that detention was a necessary consequence for his behaviour.

For my part, I thought that detention would be disruptive to the progress he was making in school and in his therapeutic group.

## Communication Skills Are Essential

In a conversation with Alan prior to the team meeting, I learned about the precipitating events that day. He told me that he had received a failing grade on a test that he thought he had aced. He went home to tell his mother, who reprimanded him for the poor grade. Alan said, "I just lost it. I hate it when mom drinks because she gets so mean and yells a lot. It's hard to be around her like that, so I just left. I know I shouldn't have gone to that building, but I had nowhere else to go. My friends were happy to see me and made me forget about my bad grade."

Through a trauma-informed lens, and looking at the entire family dynamics, it seemed to me that the best outcome was to find a way to help Alan reconcile with his mother and work through the experience without recourse to the youth justice system.

Ultimately, the probation officer prevailed. Alan was remanded to detention for 10 days. I left the hearing feeling frustrated and disappointed.

As I reflected on the meeting and court hearing afterwards, it occurred to me that the probation officer was viewing the situation from a completely different lens than I had been. While the probation officer was focused on the behaviour (breaking into the abandoned building), I was focused on everything that preceded it, the motivation driving the behaviour, and how to turn it around for Alan and his family without making it worse in the short term.

Theories inform what we pay attention to or focus on, what we see, and how we understand it or make sense of things. The probation officer and I had a different understanding of the issue and the types of services and interventions required to address Alan's needs.

This experience brought home to me why and how social work theories are so essential and why communication skills are so important in interprofessional practice. ■

## Reflections on Rebecca's Story

Being fully aware of the theoretical lens used in practice is important, but it's just as critical to be able to articulate this perspective to service users and other professionals.

For Rebecca, advocating for service users meant that she needed to have greater awareness about the varied perspectives of the team members. She also needed to know how to communicate a perspective rooted in social work theory.

Beyond simply talking about how she felt or her personal point of view, she had to make a conscious effort to communicate the rationale for her dissenting views. The final outcome might not have been different, but the starting point is skills in interprofessional communication.

### From Theory to Practice

As you reflect on Rebecca's story, give some thought to the following points:

1. How does this situation exemplify the challenges and strengths of interprofessional team work?

2. How does Rebecca conceptualize Alan's situation? How does her interpretation differ from that of the probation officer?

3. What therapeutic common factors does Rebecca appear to be using?

4. Does Alan have any agency in this situation? How could an advocate support his involvement in the recommendations to the court?

# Shared Decision-Making

Certainly, the importance of having a collaborative relationship with service users in all decisions related to them is a core social work value. Regardless of the dire circumstances or vulnerabilities (age, mental health status, ability), service users are knowledgeable actors in their own lives. They are not simply vulnerable people "at risk" or "in need of protection."

### Service Users as Active Participants

In the traditional medical practice model, practitioners decide on the type of treatment and treatment format; they are considered the experts, based on their previous experiences and their knowledge of the research literature. However, clinical errors in decision-making are associated with this model for a number of reasons:

- It fails to account for service user characteristics, values, expectations, and preferences.
- It deprives service users of valuable learning experiences.
- It does not provide service users with opportunities for empowering processes to build their self-confidence (Park, Goode, Tompkins, & Swift, 2016).

At the other end of the continuum is the "independent-choice" practice model in which all decision-making is given to the service user. This model, according to Park et al. (2016), provides opportunities for the service user to be involved, but clinical errors occur because the service user does not always know the possible treatment options and lacks the skills to critically evaluate the "pros and cons" of different options.

The **shared decision-making (SDM)** practice model, the middle position in the continuum, involves close collaboration between the social worker and service user. Park et al. (2016) describe the SDM practice model as requiring both parties to do the following:

- Be actively involved in the decision-making process;
- Share information with each other (social worker shares knowledge and clinical experience with treatment options, and service user shares experiences, values, preferences, and other factors that may have an impact on the efficacy of a particular intervention approach);
- Discuss the benefits and drawbacks of each option; and,
- Develop a collaborative agreement about which option to implement.

The benefits of this model include service users having a say in their care, which is consistent with a human rights perspective on decision-making. Additionally, service-user collaboration is associated with more positive outcomes. It means a higher personal investment in the treatment process, which in turn leads to increased service-user satisfaction, increased completion rates, and higher success rates for service users (Park et al., 2016).

## Service User Preferences

Including a service user's preferences in all aspects of decision-making is central to social work values and evidence-based practice. The importance of this level of collaboration is supported by empirical research conducted in this area.

Swift, Callahan, and Vollmer (2011) conducted a meta-analysis of 35 studies to understand the influence of preferences on treatment outcomes. They considered three types of service user preferences:

- Role preferences (e.g., therapist offering advice or the service user doing most of the talking during the session)
- Therapist preferences (e.g., empathic, belonging to a specific population, or high level of experience)
- Treatment preferences (e.g., medication, religious counselling, behavioural, psychodynamic)

The results of the meta-analysis indicated that when service users were matched with their preferred therapy conditions, they were less likely to drop out and more likely to show improvement over the course of their treatment.

From this meta-analysis, the authors concluded that it is important for practitioners to elicit service user preferences before the start of treatment and to continue to address these preferences throughout the treatment process (since service users may change their preferences or feel like their preferences are not being incorporated). Moreover, when practitioners believe that a service user's preferences are not in that person's best interests, they should raise their concern to ensure collaborative decision-making.

## Expectation for Change

Having hope, or an **expectation for change**, is a particularly important therapeutic "common factor" that affects both the service user and the social worker. Research in the field of psychotherapy has found that service user expectations predict treatment initiation, dropout and duration, and treatment outcomes (Swift, Derthick, & Tompkins, 2018).

A US study by Swift et al. (2018) examined whether service users and therapists-in-training differ in their expectations for treatment length and outcome. The study found that "when therapists-in-training were thinking about service users in general, they expected them to attend significantly fewer sessions and expected them to have significantly worse treatment outcomes compared to predictions for a specific client" (p. 90). It also found that student therapists' duration and outcome expectations for a particular service user seemed to match that service user's expectations.

Swift et al. (2018) concluded that it is "important that service users are hopeful that treatment might be able to help alleviate their problems, but it is also important that therapists believe that treatment will be of some benefit" (p. 92). The results of their study also suggest that a practitioner's expectation that therapy can benefit the service user may be a variable that contributes to positive treatment outcomes.

### Expectation for change

As social workers gain experience, they also develop confidence in their ability to facilitate positive change with service users.

Through this process, social workers gain more optimism and hopefulness about the change process. This, in turn, can be shared with the service user as an expectation that positive change will occur. This hopefulness has been shown to be a factor in the desired change actually occurring.

# Intervention Principles in Practice

Ultimately, social work practice aims to ensure positive change and outcomes for individuals, communities, and society. The examples below of real-life practice initiatives highlight the importance of the common factors in social work service provision.

### Therapeutic Alliance and Youth in Group Care

Youth in out-of-home group care face a great number of challenging and pervasive problems. Although the overall efficacy of this type of care can be questioned, studies indicate that having a positive staff–youth relationship is associated with decreased symptom severity, decreased substance-use relapse, and improved family relationships. A study of 400 girls and boys in 70 family-style group homes in a large US Midwestern city found a high correlation between youth ratings of therapeutic alliance and positive outcomes. When staff adhered to a higher ratio of positive to negative interactions with youth, there was an improvement in youth emotional and behavioural functioning (Duppong Hurley, Lambert, Gross, Thompson, & Farmer, 2017).

The authors concluded that improving therapeutic alliance may be a promising avenue to enhance the quality of care for youth in residential care.

### Program Adaptation for Indigenous Youth and Substance-Use Prevention

Providing interventions that are both culturally safe and evidence-based often seems incompatible because so many programs are not designed for a given cultural group. When interventions are culturally adapted, studies indicate that there is increased service user engagement, increased retention, and improved treatment outcomes (Marsiglia & Booth, 2015). Program adaptation requires paying attention to both the content (inclusion of culturally specific factors) and the process (co-creation of lived experiences).

Building on a long-standing partnership with the Ojibwe community, McGill University researchers used a community-based, participatory approach in order to adapt the substance-use prevention program "Strengthening Families Program for Parents and Youth (10–14)." The program is a seven-week intervention aimed at reducing substance use among 10- to 14-year-olds and improving the parent–child relationship by teaching communication and problem-solving skills to parents and adolescents (Ivanich, Mousseau, Walls, Whitbeck, & Whitesell, 2018).

Positive changes were identified at the two-year evaluation point in the areas of family communication, child anger management, children's perception of parental monitoring, and teaching children and family members the appropriate way to approach Elders for help and advice. The substance-use prevention aspects of the program were also positive. The adaptation of this program to the Ojibwe community focused on community enfranchisement. This process of cultural and contextual adaptation can now be considered by other communities.

# Integrated Health-Care Solutions in Quebec
## Shared, Non-hierarchical Decision-Making

The Quebec Ministry of Health and Social Services is enhancing intervention services through integrated care. Here, we describe the findings of two studies examining the fidelity and effectiveness of these approaches.

### Implementing Substance-Use Services in Primary Health-Care Clinics

Maynard et al. (2015) examined the implementation of screening, brief interventions, and referral (SBIR) in substance-use services in Quebec's primary health clinics between 2007 and 2012. They found a wide variation in the fidelity of the implementation process.

While a majority of the centres used standard tools to screen service users, not all of the centres followed up using the recommended procedures when the service user was screened as positive for substance use. Inversely, some centres did not systematically screen all service users, although they may have followed recommended procedures when service users were screened as positive.

Half of the centres had formal procedures for internal referrals, and two-thirds had formal procedures for external referrals. In terms of brief interventions, close to two-thirds of the centres had a trained worker who could offer one or more forms of brief intervention.

The key elements conducive to high fidelity in the implementation of SBIR were (1) developing formal action plans and (2) putting into place organizational measures to support and adapt the SBIR to the local context.

Maynard et al. (2015) stressed that an important factor in the successful implementation was the adoptions of a shared, non-hierarchical decision-making process in which the addictions workers and management worked collaboratively, and the addictions workers had the freedom to take initiative toward new ventures.

### Older Adult Care

As a result of organizational reforms to the Quebec health system in 2004, local health networks were formed, including one for older people.

In their qualitative study on the perspectives of health-care providers on integrated care for older adults, Wankah, Couturier, Belzile, Gagnon, and Breton (2018) noted:

> Regarding provider–patient interactions, all providers reported sharing decision-making with patients and their caregivers. This facilitated patients' participation in the elaboration and implementation of care plans, transmission of information to the patient, prioritisation of the needs patients felt most strongly about, and self-management support. (p. 5)

The researchers also noted that providers "were generally enthusiastic about, and felt empowered by, working together in multidisciplinary teams" (p. 12).

There were some challenges, however. The providers identified difficulties balancing service user needs with the services offered. The ministerial policy documents promoted a needs-oriented system, and the providers viewed the system as still being more service oriented.

Nevertheless, research (as cited in Wankah et al., 2018) has shown that integrating care for older people offers a number of benefits:

- Better service user satisfaction
- Better continuity of services
- Better care coordination
- Better quality of services
- Less fragmentation of services
- Better interdisciplinary collaborations ■

## Advocacy and Social Activism

Advocacy on behalf of individuals and communities is a core intervention strategy for social workers seeking justice for individuals and wanting to bring about broader social change. What follows is a summary of "advocacy in practice" for low-income residents who have experienced relationship violence, sexual assault, and child abuse in the small community (population, 10,000) of Nelson, British Columbia. The story was reported by Amy Taylor (2018) in *Perspectives*, the newsletter of the BC Association of Social Workers.

Advocacy in the small community of Nelson is difficult because government decision-makers are increasingly located far away from the town. Amy Taylor notes that "old fashioned advocacy, which relied on a high level of personal credibility, is no longer realistic and systems change is virtually impossible as they require complex processes and legalistic challenges that are inaccessible locally." Nevertheless, the community found that an effective advocacy strategy was to partner with larger public interest groups based in bigger urban centres of the lower mainland, who were willing to represent cases of social injustice at the local level.

Taylor discusses an example concerning the financial abuse experienced by a separated partner in a shared-living situation. The woman lost her disability allowance, and an appeal to her tribunal was unsuccessful. However, the lower mainland legal assistance society submitted the case for judicial review, with the outcome that social assistance was reinstated. Further, this case led the Ministry of Social Development and Social Innovation (now the Ministry of Social Development and Poverty Reduction) to change its definition of "spouse." Working for a specific change on a "doable concrete thing" and having an interdisciplinary approach can make a difference, Taylor maintains.

Systemic (or cause) advocacy in British Columbia was significantly curtailed with the adoption of the province's Lobbyists Registration Act in 2001. The act defined "lobbyists" as persons who, on behalf of their employers or service users, communicate with public office holders in an attempt to influence their decision. Nevertheless, as a work-around, Nelson community groups have found that working closely with a sympathetic MLA can be effective in bringing about change. For example, local MLA Michelle Mungall "was able to stop the 'claw back' of social assistance for single moms who received support for their children. She was able to do this by gathering and publishing many individual stories. A grassroots swell made it impossible for government to ignore this injustice" (p. 23).

In a different context, the Nelson Advocacy Centre and other community groups collected data on the community impact of a reduction of workers and hours in the local Income Assistance Office. By working with other local community organizations, and by making presentations to the Select Standing Committee on Finance and Government Services, more office hours were made available locally to serve the needs of social assistance applicants.

These examples show how citizens working together can mobilize and engage in advocacy initiatives that bring about real and lasting change in their communities.

# Jordan's Principle
## Ensuring First Nations Children's Access to Services

Using common practice principles in the development of service interventions occurs at all system levels. A good example is the advocacy and research undertaken by the Jordan's Principle Working Group. This collaboration of First Nations organizations, children's rights and pediatric organizations, and university researchers advocated for equitable access to services for First Nations children.

Excerpts from the working group's 2015 report, *Without Denial, Delay, or Disruption: Ensuring First Nations Children's Access to Equitable Services through Jordan's Principle*, appear below.

### What Is Jordan's Principle?

Jordan's Principle is a child-first principle intended to ensure that First Nations children do not experience denials, delays, or disruptions of services ordinarily available to other children due to jurisdictional disputes. It is named in honour of Jordan River Anderson, a young boy from Norway House Cree Nation in Manitoba. Jordan encountered tragic delays in services due to governmental jurisdictional disputes that denied him an opportunity to live outside of a hospital setting before his death in 2005. (p. 4)

Jordan's Principle states that in cases involving jurisdictional disputes the government or government department first approached should pay for services that would ordinarily be available to other children in Canada; the dispute over payment for services can be settled afterwards. (p. 4)

A motion endorsing Jordan's Principle was unanimously adopted by the House of Commons in 2007.... [However], there is growing recognition that the governmental response to Jordan's Principle does not reflect the vision advanced by First Nations and endorsed by the House of Commons. Reviews by the Canadian Paediatric Society and UNICEF Canada have highlighted shortcomings in the governmental response. (p. 4)

### "Without Denial, Delay, or Disruption"

[The] report presents the results of two studies conducted by the research team [of the working group]. (p. 5)

The first reviewed over 300 Jordan's Principle related documents to describe ... the ways in which the current governmental response has limited the population and range of jurisdictional disputes ...; instituted barriers to the timely application of Jordan's Principle; and severely restricted accountability, transparency, and stakeholder participation. Finally, it identifies major features of the response that must be amended to better ensure that First Nations children receive equitable services without denials, delays, or disruptions. (pp. 5–6)

The second study involved 25 interviews with professionals in health and child welfare services from across Canada, [and a] review of the existing literature on health and child welfare services for First Nations children. This research describes the widespread jurisdictional ambiguities and underfunding that can give rise to Jordan's Principle cases ... and describes the systemic issues that must be addressed to ensure equitable services for First Nations children. (p. 6)

Based on review of the evidence presented by these studies, the Assembly of First Nations, the Canadian Paediatric Society, and UNICEF Canada call on federal, provincial, and territorial governments to work with First Nations, without delay, in order to:

1. Develop and implement a governmental response that is consistent with the vision of Jordan's Principle advanced by First Nations and endorsed by the House of Commons.

2. Systematically identify and address the jurisdictional ambiguities and underfunding that give rise to each Jordan's Principle case. (p. 6) ∎

When goals are reached,
a specific time frame has
ended, or the service
user no longer wants to
continue, a systematic
process for disengaging
the working relationship
occurs.

# Successful Endings and Terminations

Just as shared decision-making is important in treatment decisions, collaboration is also critical in ensuring successful **endings and terminations**. Goode, Park, Parkin, Tompkins, and Swift (2017) observe the following:

> Taking a collaborative approach when working toward a successful psychotherapy termination involves actions that the therapist can take from the initial treatment session to the last. These actions include strategies for facilitating a two-way discussion about termination expectations, regularly checking in on the goals and planned timing for termination, and equalizing the therapeutic relationship. (p. 10)

These authors make a number of recommendations about collaborative approaches to termination in a therapeutic environment:

- At the initial session, discuss how long it might take to meet goals.
- At the initial session, discuss how to end treatment goals once they have been achieved.
- Inquire about the service user's previous experiences with termination and whether treatment ended in a mutual or unilateral decision.
- Periodically discuss termination throughout the treatment process (e.g., ask the service user to identify goals they would like to achieve prior to ending treatment).
- If a specific termination date is known (due to insurance, service user move, social worker transfer), remind the service user of that date on a regular basis and ask them to think about how they might best use their time leading up to that date.
- As the time for termination approaches, work collaboratively to develop an agreed upon plan (e.g., spacing out the treatment sessions, any ethical issues about gift giving).
- In the final session, help the service user recognize that there was a joint process, with both parties making vital contributions (it is essential for the service user to be able to take ownership for gains they have made).
- Help the service user recognize the active role they have played in the change process.
- Share what both the social worker and service user have observed to be helpful in treatment.
- Work collaboratively to develop a future plan for the service user's continued growth.

While many service users will share their gratitude, it is also important in a collaborative model for social workers to express their own appreciation for being a part of the process and to acknowledge that the relationship was meaningful for them as well.

## Making Referrals

In situations where additional or alternate services are needed, referrals to other professional service providers do not necessarily mean that work with the service user has ceased. More often than not, a referral just means that a team approach best meets that person's needs at that time.

The following list, developed by the New South Wales Department of Education (n.d.), identifies some of the factors associated with making good referrals:

1. Make sure you know what policies and procedures your agency has for making referrals.

2. Always know the agency or person to whom you make the referral. Don't send a service user off to someone or some organization you know nothing about.

3. Contact the agency or worker you are thinking about referring the service user to and discuss the possibility of a referral. Ask who their target group is, what services they provide, and what their criteria for access is (i.e., who they will accept and what information they need). Don't give out any identifying details about the service user at this stage.

4. Explore the readiness of the service user to be referred. Open and honest discussion about referral and the reason for it will enable the service user to feel more in control of the situation. If there is a choice of services available, make sure the service user has information about each service and can make an informed choice.

5. Be very aware of confidentiality issues. Get the service user's consent for you to contact the agency or worker, and give the service user's details to the new worker. Remember that the service user must give informed consent (the service user must know what is being consented to and the consequences of giving such consent).

6. Let the service user make the appointment, rather than making it for them. Again, this is more empowering.

7. Help prepare the service user for the first appointment. Talk through with them what information they will have to provide, how to get to the appointment, and what they will have to take (if appropriate). Some service users may want you to go with them as an advocate or as support.

8. Maintain your relationship with the service user until the referral process is complete. It's no use, for example, referring a service user to an organization for an appointment in six weeks time and then leaving the service user without support in the interim. Sometimes, it is useful to continue support work with a service user, even though the service user is receiving other services. This type of collaborative work is often useful in community services work, as each worker has different areas of expertise that they can offer a service user.

# Structuration Theory and Human Agency

**Structuration theory**

The idea behind structuration theory is that "structure" is not something that exists outside of individuals. Instead, it is a set of recurring patterns of practice by individuals.

Individuals always have some form of agency (or ability) to transform a situation. As practices change, so can structure, and vice versa.

In traditional, or foundational, social work theory, the "micro" and "macro" are typically dichotomized as "either/or." Critical theory sets out to remove this bifurcation by recognizing individuals as active actors in their own lives and as co-constructors in their social environment.

Kondrat (2002) re-visioned the relationship between person and social environment (or person-in-environment) through a critical theory lens, drawing on Anthony Giddens's "structuration theory." Giddens (1990) describes his work as "radicalized modern," and his focus is on the role of human agency in political engagement and social change (as cited in Kondrat, 2002, p. 436).

## Structuration Theory

Structuration theory was first proposed by sociologist Anthony Giddens in his 1986 book *The Constitution of Society*. **Structuration theory** holds that human agency and social structures are integrated and recursive, not separate entities. Instead of viewing people's actions as constrained by powerful societal structures or as functions of individual will (i.e., agency), structuration theory acknowledges the interaction of both. Kondrat (2002) notes:

> In structuration theory, recursiveness refers to the way certain processes in society repeat and reproduce themselves in an ongoing cycle. Specifically, the theory refers to the processes through which society and its structures shape the activity of individuals, although those structures, in turn, are constituted by the very actions they shape and condition. (p. 437)

In other words, "social structures and institutions are maintained because of the structured and patterned way people act and interact over time; people learn to act and interact the way they do because of their immersion in a society which is supported by certain structures and institutions" (Kondrat, 2002, p. 437).

In structuration theory, human actors have "knowledge" and "agency." That is, they are social actors who know a great deal about the society of which they are members, they routinely and reflexively monitor their own social performances, and they are knowledgeable co-constructors of the larger social environment.

The concepts of power and empowerment are also central to structuration theory. Power (being able to get things done) is associated with resources and rules. Resources may be allocative (e.g., property and money) or authoritative (e.g., belonging to a family with status, holding a degree, having an effective support network). Rules define how resources are allocated and how relationships are arranged. Access to power and empowerment depends heavily on how one's social location aligns with the dominant resources and rules of allocation.

Traditional social work theory has typically emphasized the influence of the environment on individual behaviour. Structuration theory emphasizes a recursive and interactive process in which the links between the person and the environment are mutually maintained and reproduced.

## Applying Structuration Theory in a Mental Health Emergency Setting

Kondrat (2002) provides an example of how structuration theory can be used in practice at the micro and mezzo level.

Independent consultants were called in to address concerns in a community mental health centre in the United States, in which African American service users of the agency's emergency unit had proportionally higher rates of hospitalization and higher rates of non-voluntary commitments than did white service users. Although the agency had a reputation for being concerned about cultural competence, these disproportional rates suggested some form of systemic racism.

The consultants observed the everyday interactions in the delivery of services, with the central question being: How were these unequal outcomes being structured in the day-to-day routine world of crisis management?

The social workers began to examine how what they had perceived as threatening behaviour on the part of service users might be better interpreted as resistance to further marginalization, disempowerment, and disrespect. They began to examine how their clinical choices and interactions might change if they were to begin viewing some of the emergency room "presenting behaviour" as a potential strength—an opposition or challenge to further disempowerment—instead of viewing it as threatening acting-out behaviour. As a result of these reflections,

> social workers began to understand how some of their decisions to recommend hospitalization or to involve security personnel in particular cases may have been based on misconstruing of the relations of power and marginalization in that setting. (Kondrat, 2002, p. 445)

By focusing on recurring interactions between practitioners and service users, it became clear how group-based inequality of outcomes was constructed in the ordinary and taken-for-granted world of routine interactions.

In this example, the social workers had not given much thought to the power they possess or the consequences of their decisions. There was little thought given to how members of the dominant group (in this case, the professionals) may have showed disrespect to members of a racialized group. The professionals had also not taken into account that individuals will act back, resist, and challenge authority, especially when they believe they are being threatened (Kondrat, 2002, p. 445).

Understanding how unequal group outcomes can be constructed during routine interactions provided insights about what may need to change in order to improve services for this minority service user group.

# Social Worker Exemplar

## Indigenous Worldviews

**Dionne Mohammed**

**As a daughter of a residential school survivor, Dionne holds a deep understanding of intergenerational trauma. She believes that healing begins with one's sense of identity—knowing one's land of origin, language, and traditional ways.**

Dionne is of St'át'imc Nation, Mauritian, and English ancestry. Prior to enrolling in the social work program, she worked for 15 years in the education system supporting Indigenous students, and served a three-year term as an elected band councillor.

Instead of continuing to bear witness to the ongoing marginalization of her people, she decided to contribute to change through advocating and practising decolonized social work.

Dionne currently manages an Indigenous Family Support Program at an Indigenous health agency. These are excerpts from her journal as a student.

My practicum is at a supportive housing and outreach program. While I appreciate much of what the program does, I am noticing a gap in Indigenous understanding, despite the fact that there are a large number of residents in the complex who are Indigenous.

For example, today I overheard a manager ask one of the male Indigenous residents when he was going to cut his hair because it needed a good cutting. This man, who usually uses humour in conversation, completely changed his voice tone and facial expression—clearly it bothered him. The manager persisted, and the man finally walked away, head down, and returned to his room.

The manager didn't seem to think anything of this, but I did. The act of hair cutting is a mourning ritual and is not taken lightly. Furthermore, when an Indigenous man wears his hair long, he is owning his identity as an Indigenous man, which means he feels empowered by it. Social workers should support this kind of self-identity as much as possible so as not to diminish the person's cultural pride—it would have taken much for the person to arrive there.

I spoke to my field instructor about the incident, and she said she felt it was important for staff to know this. I was afraid, but she supported me a few days later in speaking with staff about it. They said they had no idea about the significance of long hair for Indigenous men. The next time I saw that man, I made a point of saying to him that his hair was great and not to listen to anybody who says he should get it cut. He smiled, and I saw pride in his face.

That afternoon was spent with an Indigenous participant who described his experience of being in foster care since the age of four. He said he had never understood why his mother had abandoned him and that, because of this, he denied his ties to his Indigenous background. He spoke of being called a "wagon burner" and being treated abusively by his foster parents.

He said he finally Googled his place of birth and found out that he came from the Ojibwe people. He said he never knew anything about his culture and would tell people to "fuck off" if they ever asked him if he was "native." He said he got mad when people assumed that he takes part in sweats, smudging, and "all that stuff."

## Understanding Indigenous History

I was able to share some historical knowledge around residential schools with the participant and talk about how this has had a negative effect on generations of Indigenous people and their ability to thrive as parents. I explained that schoolchildren were taken from their parents and were never shown the skills of how to be mothers and fathers. I explained that because they were forced to believe in Catholicism, they were told that using birth control was a sin. I also explained that most also experienced physical, sexual, and verbal abuse.

I let him know that I too had a mother who was unprepared to care for my brother and me when we were children due to what residential school assimilation practices had done to her and her parents. He asked how it was that I was able to do something positive with my life. At this moment, another participant came into the office, and our conversation ended.

Providing skills and education by means of group get-togethers is very common in this agency. Today, the subject was a healthy balance pie chart. The next time I meet with my supervisor, I want to mention that the chairs were in two rows facing each other with a coffee table in between, and that there was no acknowledgement that the balancing circle model originated with Indigenous people.

Today, I finally worked up enough courage to tell a manager that the wellness plans developed with the program participants do not include Indigenous culture, Indigenous identity, connection to community, or anything to do with intergenerational trauma and holistic wellness. The lack of Indigenous connection negatively affects every aspect of their lives.

The manager asked me, "Why do you think that an Indigenous person should have a different wellness plan than a non-Indigenous person?" By her tone, I could tell that she was likely not in support of what I was trying to say. I responded, "because Indigenous people cannot heal in isolation from their culture and Indigenous identity."

Her face softened, and I exhaled. ∎

## Reflections on Dionne's Story

Dionne was working in a residential-care setting where managers and social workers would have had training in cultural sensitivity, and yet were unable to see how the structures and processes in place were not culturally safe for a group they were providing services to. By not adapting programs to be inclusive, they were—at the very least—underserving Indigenous people. At the worst, they were further oppressing and colonizing these participants.

Dionne's courage to speak up highlighted the difference a social worker can make. Fortunately, in this case, there was receptiveness to making positive change.

### From Theory to Practice

As you reflect on Dionne's story, give some thought to the following points:

1. Can you identify instances from your own practice where a Western worldview was inadvertently imposed on someone of another culture?

2. Can you identify instances in your current field education site where an interaction reflects a culturally unsafe practice?

3. Can you suggest a group process or another component in your field education site that could be adapted to be more inclusive of Indigenous worldviews and histories?

4. Can you identify any practices in your field education site that are being appropriated from Indigenous (or other) cultures without being acknowledged?

5. Can you identify a courageous moment in your own practice where you pointed out disempowering and oppressive practices that only serve to further colonize and oppress Indigenous or other marginalized people?

# Practice Scenarios

Social workers must choose from among a plethora of practice models as the basis for the services and interventions they provide. At the outset of their careers, most social workers choose to follow a generalist-eclectic direct practice approach. This includes the involvement and collaboration of the service user in both identifying the key issues to address and developing a service plan.

Central to effective interventions is the therapeutic relationship and shared decision-making in which the service user is an active participant, and hopeful, optimistic expectations from the social worker about the potential outcomes.

In these practice scenarios, consider the approach you would typically take, the approach predominant in your field site, and a critical approach that considers an analysis of dominant power.

---

## 7.1 Engaging with Non-communicative Youth

Your placement (as a female student) is in a youth group shelter with five young people. All of the youth have multiple traumas and unique histories, often resulting in poor self-regulation. Throughout your placement, you are thoroughly enjoying getting to know them and believe you have a good relationship with them.

Recently, a young 14-year-old boy was admitted. You have attempted to get to know him better, but he has remained sullen with you and seems unwilling to open up. You notice that, overall, he seems to have more communication with the male staff than the female staff, but that the communication is pretty informal, of short duration, and superficial in nature.

You wonder how to connect with him.

1. What common factors would you want to pay attention to?

2. If this young man has been constructed as a "difficult" service user, what can be done to modify the social worker's approach to him?

3. How are the practices of the youth group shelter influencing the young man's behaviour? On the flip side, how is the young man's behaviour reinforcing the structures in the shelter? How could the issues be framed differently?

---

## 7.2 Successfully Ending Complex Relationships

In your field placement at a substance-use agency, you have been assigned a number of service users. Although you believe your relationship-building skills are good, you are having trouble connecting with one woman. You have met with her five times. After the last meeting, you met with your field supervisor and explored a number of strategies that may be helpful for you to engage with this service user.

The service user is much older than you (she is closer to the age of your parents), has a lot of experience receiving services, and has complained to you about the ineffectiveness of previous counsellors. Today, she says directly to you: "You don't like me very much, do you?"

1. What is your initial emotional reaction to this direct question?

2. What are some of the practice strategies that you would want to implement as you respond to her question?

3. Would a referral be appropriate here? What would need to be done to implement a referral in order for it to be successful?

4. Given this woman's multiple service experiences, and your rapidly approaching exit from the agency, what is the best approach to having a successful ending to this relationship?

## 7.3 Culturally Adapting a Parenting Program

You have been co-facilitating a group on parenting skills for parents of three- to five-year-olds. The initiative has been highly successful.

Your supervisor has asked you to help adapt the procedures and materials that you have developed for this group in a way that may be more culturally relevant to a particular ethnic group in your community.

1. How do you go about this task?

2. Which social work values and principles would you incorporate when addressing this request?

3. How will you involve community partners?

4. What are some culturally specific factors you would want to include in the adaptation?

5. How will you ensure that culture is incorporated in a way that is meaningful to the group's lived experience?

# Field Education Practicalities
## Working through Difficulties

Sometimes, the relationship between a social worker and a service user becomes strained. As with any other interaction, one has to do some self-reflection to identify ways to work through such difficulties.

Three common challenges when faced with so-called difficult service users are (1) the need of the helper to be liked, (2) being able to work through resistance, and (3) working one-on-one with angry and hostile individuals.

Another challenge or difficulty faced by social workers is deciding on a course of action when they perceive a colleague's actions to be unethical. Fortunately, the Canadian Association of Social Workers (CASW) *Guidelines for Ethical Practice* provide some direction.

Most social workers want to be liked by service users and their co-workers, which is not altogether a bad thing (Alle-Corliss & Alle-Corliss, 1998, p. 189). Certainly one doesn't want to alienate anyone. However, at times social workers must encourage service users to talk about difficult or painful feelings, identify service user behaviours that may be impeding treatment progress, or confront service users about their inappropriate behaviour.

Neglecting to raise issues because of one's own need to be liked is a disservice to the service user. For example, if a service user is aggressive in their communication style, explaining this to them may be helpful. If a service user is moving toward flirtation, it is appropriate to identify this behaviour in order to maintain boundaries and mutual safety. If an adolescent's misbehaviour in a group home is likely to have negative consequences for them and others in the home, then it is appropriate to provide that feedback to the young person.

### De-pathologizing Resistance

An advanced skill in counselling communication is to be able to work through service user behaviour that indicates a reluctance to participate or overt opposition. This behaviour is sometimes constructed as resistance. However, it can also be understood as a result of a negative interpersonal dynamic or an interactional style. From this perspective, resistance is created when the needs of the service user are mismatched with the perspectives or the interventions of the social worker.

Mitchell (2007) suggests that if one views resistance as an interactional mismatch between the service user and the social worker, the social worker is empowered to change the interaction. This change can occur if the social worker spends more time to understand the service user's worldview or changes communication style with the service user.

Working through resistance requires patience. Social workers may need to explore how family and friends treat the service user, and how the service user perceives the presenting issue and the counselling process. Expressing empathy is an important way of acknowledging the service user's situation.

## Working with Angry and Hostile Service Users

Although it is unpleasant to consider, some service users may show resistance through anger and hostility. Service users may be verbally abusive, curse and shout, or even threaten a social worker with harm or assault. This behaviour may be related to poor impulse control, lack of anger-management skills, substance-use impairment, or resentment about being forced into social work interventions (Royse, Dhooper, & Lewis Rompf, 2012).

While ensuring your personal safety at all times, it is important to stay calm and composed. Remember that the service user's anger may be understandable, given the situation. The service user may have strong feelings of social injustice and experience the system as too impersonal, bureaucratic, and inflexible (Royse et al., 2012).

Expressing empathy often diffuses hostile situations. Speaking gently and calmly encourages the service user to address their anger and complaints. If the service user doesn't want to sit down, you may offer a glass of water or coffee (which provides some space for them to calm down naturally), or suggest that the service user go for a walk (letting them know that you are willing to address all of their complaints when they return). Always ensure your own safety, and do not position yourself in a corner or behind furniture, where it is difficult for you to escape if necessary.

Always ensure that you do not reflect back any anger you may feel. More than likely, the service user is watching how you react. Your actions can further agitate or diffuse the service user's volatility.

As Royse et al. (2012) state:

> Above all else, do not take risks that will jeopardize your personal safety. If your intuition tells you that a situation is dangerous, do not plow headstrong into it because you don't want to be embarrassed that you couldn't handle it. Always seek help when you sense that your safety or that of others is in danger. Discuss with your field instructor and other staff members your apprehensions and ways to handle difficult situations. (p. 78)

## Addressing Unethical Practices by Colleagues

At times, students and social workers may be challenged by a colleague's conduct that they perceive as unethical or even illegal. It can be difficult to know how to act in such situations.

In some cases, a colleague may be suffering from compassion fatigue or even burnout, and inappropriate ethical behaviour or misconduct may require some supportive intervention. In very few cases, there are egregious acts of unethical conduct that warrant disciplinary behaviour.

The CASW *Guidelines for Ethical Practice* (2005b) states:

> **7.2** Address Unethical Practices of Colleagues
>
> **7.2.1** Social workers take appropriate action where a breach of professional practice and professional ethics occur, conducting themselves in a manner that is consistent with the *Code of Ethics* and *Guidelines for Ethical Practice*, and standards of their regulatory body.
>
> **7.2.2** Social workers who have direct knowledge of a social work colleague's incompetence or impairment in professional practice consult with colleagues about their concerns and when feasible assist colleagues in taking remedial action. Impairment may emanate, for example, from personal problems, psychosocial distress, substance abuse or mental health difficulties.
>
> **7.2.3** Social workers who believe that a colleague has not taken adequate steps to address their impairment to professional practice take action through appropriate channels established by employers, regulatory bodies, or other professional organizations.
>
> **7.2.4** Social workers do not intervene in the professional relationship of other social workers and clients unless requested to do so by a client and unless convinced that the best interests and well-being of clients requires such intervention. (pp. 22–23)

Reporting misconduct should not be taken lightly. It is never an easy process and should always be supported by good evidence. ■

# Reflection, Learning, and More Practice

## Field Education Practicalities

1. Following the midpoint assessment, identify one or two competency areas that will require more attention in the last stages of your field education.

2. As part of your overall learning plan, identify a new goal for yourself that involves practising a new approach to service provision.

3. Review the policy in the agency for reporting illegal or unethical behaviour by colleagues. Explain why you agree or disagree with this policy.

4. In addition to showing service users "respect," "empathy" and "acceptance," challenge yourself to find ways to demonstrate "authenticity" and "optimism."

## Journal Ideas

1. Describe the relevance of understanding service users as active agents in knowledge production for the purposes of social work interventions.

2. In your field education setting, interview colleagues and service providers to find out about their predominant theoretical approach to intervention and treatment.

3. Consider how you use the therapeutic common factors of social work practice in your practice setting.

4. Are the preferences of service users fully incorporated into service planning in your field education site? If not, how could they be?

5. Write a clinical impression and treatment plan that provides evidence, or not, of service user involvement and shared decision-making.

6. Take an issue or clinical problem frequently seen in your field education site, and compare and contrast the understanding of the issue or clinical problem from the perspective of multiple theoretical models.

## Critical-Thinking Questions

1. What are the benefits and drawbacks of adopting a generalist-eclectic approach to practice compared with adopting a specialized approach?

2. Imagine that you are being interviewed by your local media and are asked the following question: "What is the basic approach that you take to working with service users?" How would you answer this question?

3. Shared decision-making is consistent with a human rights perspective, but it may be challenging to carry out in highly bureaucratic or legislated situations. Describe strategies and practices that social workers can use to encourage shared decision-making as a regular part of practice.

4. Working with Indigenous service users requires focusing on community holism and spirituality. If your field site typically follows Western practice models, consider ways in which the agency might introduce alternative practice models that are more inclusive and anti-oppressive.

5. Critique the benefits and challenges of integrated health care in your region. Evaluate the role of health and social work in integrated care situations and think of how social work values can be incorporated into existing practice models.

6. Evaluate how critical and postmodern theory is used in your field education site, if at all, and what contributions such ideas make or potentially could make to populations served by the agency.

# Chapter Review

The meta-competency "**planning and delivering services and interventions**" is developed through the skillful use of common factors (relationship building, collaborative practices, and exuding optimism and hope) in combination with knowledge of multiple approaches to practice that can be applied in flexible and unique ways.

Planning for interventions always begins with summarizing the key issues to be addressed. This requires attention to the factors that cause, precipitate, and maintain the issues of concern. Most social workers then utilize some form of generalist-eclectic practice as they proceed with providing services.

Service planning occurs not only at the micro level but also at the mezzo and macro levels, with activities such as the co-creation of culturally adapted programs and with advocacy and social justice initiatives. A core principle with all service planning and implementation is shared decision-making. This involves incorporating service user preferences throughout the entire process, including the ending and referral processes.

Working interprofessionally can be challenging, but, as Rebecca learned, it is made easier when one is clear about how to assess a situation from a social work perspective. While an outcome may be different from what they desired, social workers learn to respect the diversity of professional responses and continue to listen to and advocate for service users.

In Dionne's situation, her courage to raise awareness of practices that were culturally oppressive or culturally appropriated led to new conversations and, potentially, program changes within the organization.

For critical social workers, it is important to provide evidence-based services while at the same time take into account structural issues. This means looking at how service users' behaviour is influenced by social structures and how social workers' conduct and agency are influenced by service users' behaviour. Power and empowerment are also important in ensuring positive change.

## Planning and Delivering Services and Interventions in Practice

This chapter outlines numerous ways in which students can develop proficiency and competency in planning and delivering services and interventions. Here are some highlights and further suggestions:

- Align service users with their preferred service conditions, since doing so will encourage them to stay with the service and show greater improvements.

- Develop a clear case conceptualization, or clinical impression, in order to provide a foundation for service interventions.

- Know that therapeutic common factors (in particular, a strong service user–social worker relationship) are associated with positive outcomes, regardless of the type of intervention.

- Recognize that social issues and individual problems can be understood from multiple theoretical paradigms.

- Understand that practice validity is enhanced when social workers listen to how service users understand their own experiences.

- Know that youth in group homes improve their emotional and behavioural functioning when there are positive staff interactions.

- Understand that social justice advocacy is enhanced when initiatives are undertaken collaboratively.

- Develop a shared, non-hierarchal decision-making process when implementing new programs.

- Understand that community connections and addressing community wellness is central to Indigenous health.

- Apply a structural approach to address disproportional oppression in service delivery in order to empower service users.

# Promoting Community Sustainability

## 8

*There is immense power when a group of people with similar interests gets together to work toward the same goals.*

—Idowu Koyenikan, *Wealth for All: Living a Life of Success at the Edge of Your Ability,* 2016

# Chapter at a Glance

# Spotlight on Social Work Luminaries
## Alexa McDonough

**Alexa McDonough** worked as a social worker after graduating from Dalhousie in 1965. In 1980, she became the first woman to lead a major political party (the Nova Scotia NDP). Subsequently, from 1995 to 2003, she was the federal NDP leader. McDonough retired from politics in 2008. In 2009, she was made an Officer of the Order of Canada.

Even when an agency's main focus is on micro-level interventions with individuals and families, collective action and social activism are critical practice skills. Indeed, it is this level of focus that distinguishes social work from other professions. The next three chapters look at macro-level social work—community development, human rights and social justice, and social policy and research practice.

Community social work, the focus of this chapter, has a long and distinguished history in Canada. It involves a grassroots approach, one that seeks to help communities define and then reach goals set within their own locality. It also involves identifying gaps in service (or the impacts of cuts in service) and then collaboratively finding solutions.

In general, community social work adopts a "strengths-based" approach—building on existing community assets and developing solutions from within rather than imposing them from the outside. Community work is based on the idea that community participation can lead to solutions that are not only inclusive and just, but also meaningful to the individuals involved.

## Developing Competence as a Social Worker

Some ways to develop the meta-competency of "**promoting community sustainability**" are as follows:

- Identify a problem or issue in your community that is using, has been using, or possibly could use a community approach to achieve its goals.

- Describe possible ways to expand the scope of an ongoing community initiative in order to encourage more service user participation.

- Identify individuals and organizations within your community, who might be willing to join a particular community initiative, and suggest arguments that could be used to solicit their active participation.

### Key Concepts

- Settlement House Movement

- Community empowerment

- Conscientization

- Rothman's models of community development

- Strengths-based community development

# Community Responses to Social Problems

Community development—sometimes referred to as "community organizing" or "community building"—has deep roots in social work, starting with the Settlement House Movement in the late nineteenth and early twentieth century. The settlement houses marked a radical break in the way social problems were conceptualized and addressed. From that point onward, the focus for those seeking social change was the community, not the individual.

## The Community as a Focus for Social Change

The **Settlement House Movement** was a collaborative response to the rapid urbanization and poverty associated with the Industrial Revolution. Community cohesion was seen as "vital to the long-term stability and vigour of the modern democratic society" (James, 2001, p. 64). Mainly middle-class volunteers lived (or "settled") alongside people living in crowded poverty and disease-ridden areas. They provided services such as daycare, education, and health care. These settlements began in the 1880s in England and spread to the United States and Canada at the turn of the twentieth century.

The goal of those involved in the Settlement House Movement was to practise active participation in the life of the community in order to increase social equality and democracy. This response to social problems was in sharp contrast to existing solutions based on providing individual charity, an idea rooted in an artificial distinction between the "deserving" and "undeserving" poor.

The 1960s and 1970s saw a renewed interest in community development practice. The emphasis on locally developed models of intervention was part of a wholesale rejection of traditional models of social work that focused more on individual case work. Community-based interventions were widely adopted by human rights movements—such as the US civil rights movement, the women's movement, the gay rights movement, the disability rights movement, and the labour movement—to effect social change. In Latin America, prominent activist and educator Paulo Freire was effective in bringing about lasting political change by organizing the poor, encouraging community participation, and raising the consciousness of oppressed populations (Holland & Scourfield, 2015).

More recently, community-based approaches have been used successfully in relation to health reform (e.g., the AIDS crisis), sexual harassment (e.g., the #MeToo movement), gun violence in the United States (e.g., "March for Our Lives" following the school shooting in Parkland, Florida), and Indigenous land rights (e.g., the anti-pipeline protests at Kinder Morgan).

Community organizing methods have also figured prominently in large-scale environmental efforts, such as promoting environmental sustainability, combatting climate change, and protecting endangered species. Social workers and community activists have played an indispensable role helping to build and lead such efforts (Schmitz, Stinson, & James, 2010).

Community social work is a collaborative and anti-oppressive practice that recognizes the importance of community strengths, resources, and skills.

## Meta-Competencies in Macro Practice

Regehr, Bogo, Donovan, Lim, and Anstice (2012) identified meta-competencies for social work students working in the community organization and social policy context. These meta-competencies include self-awareness, compassion, motivation, and a commitment to social justice. The procedural competencies associated with community development work include project management, presentation skills, and an ability to articulate and implement steps to attain goals.

Gruidl and Hustedde (2015) undertook a research project to identify the specific competencies associated with community development. The community development competencies they found to be key were (1) listening, (2) emotional awareness, (3) cultural awareness and humility, (4) public deliberation, (5) facilitation, (6) appreciative inquiry, and (7) empowerment.

## CASWE-ACFTS *Standards for Accreditation*

The ninth core learning objective in the CASWE-ACFTS *Standards for Accreditation* (Canadian Association for Social Work Education–Association canadienne pour la formation en travail social [CASWE-ACFTS], 2014) includes the importance of "community" as a site of intervention:

> 9. Engage with individuals, families, groups, and communities through professional practice
>
> [...]
>
> iii) Social work students acquire skills to practise at individual, family, group, organization, community and population levels including advocacy and activism.
>
> iv) Social work students are prepared for interprofessional practice, community collaboration and team work.

## Professional Regulation and Competency

The Canadian Association of Social Workers (CASW) *Code of Ethics* (2005a) refers to social justice and social action for the overall benefit of society, the environment, and global communities. In addition, the CASW *Guidelines for Ethical Practice* (2005b) states the following under section 8, "Ethical Responsibilities to Society":

> **8.1.1** Social workers identify and interpret ... community ... and ... social problems with the intention of bringing about greater understanding and insight ...
>
> **8.2.2** Social workers endeavour to engage in social and/or political action that seeks to ensure that all people have fair access to resources, services and opportunities to meet their basic needs and to develop fully.

The Canadian Council of Social Work Regulators (CCSWR, 2012) competency profile also notes that macro change is a key competency for social workers. Social workers should be able to:

- Assess adequacy of existing policies and practices in light of professional standards
- Determine the change necessary for improving practices and policies
- Advocate for system change
- Work with existing and emerging community organizations

## Association of Social Work Boards (ASWB)

In the ASWB BSW exam, knowledge and skills on community approaches are included in a number of content areas, including the following:

- Methods to assess the client's/client system's strengths, resources, and challenges
- Community organization and social planning
- Techniques for community participation
- Methods to assess community resources
- Methods to establish service networks
- Theories of social change and community development ∎

# Practice Principles in Community Development

The concept of community is normally associated with a geographical area: a town, city, village, or neighbourhood, but a community may also simply be people who share an interest, status, or faith. A community may be based on culture, ethnicity, diverse abilities, sexual orientation, or gender. For example, a multiple sclerosis or Alcoholics Anonymous community may be spread over a large geographical area but share common goals and experiences. Similarly, nowadays virtual communities connect people online with similar interests from a global geographical area.

Thus, the meaning of "community" is fluid, and one person's definition of a community may not match another's. However, central to defining a community is understanding which individuals are included and not included as members. Sociologically speaking, one could say that the "notion of community refers to a group of people united by at least one common characteristic" (McCloskey, McDonald, & Cook, 2013, p. 2).

## Collective and Holistic Community Development

The United Nations defines "community development" as "a process where community members come together to take collective action and generate solutions to common problems" (UNTERM, 2010). A community development approach seeks to empower individuals and groups with skills needed to effect change within the community.

Community building, which is part of community development, can best be thought of as a form of community education, a process during which community members themselves are active learners and co-participants. Social workers focus on facilitating knowledge development, rather than transferring knowledge, through identifying and developing the knowledge that exists among community members to assist them in achieving their goals (O'Hara, Weber, & Levine, 2016).

Community development has a "holistic" focus—the community as a whole cannot be separated from individual community members and their life context. Community social workers co-create learning through participating in dialogue and respecting the lived experience of community members. Ultimately, community development should be transformative for the community as a whole.

Community development is sometimes thought of as "cause advocacy." This is "where an individual or group advocates on the need to bring about changes to a structure, system, policy or legislation" (O'Hara et al. 2016, p. 342). Cause advocacy parallels the micro concept of "case advocacy," which relates to interventions focused on a particular individual or family. In addition, cause advocacy is a form of social action on behalf of the rights and interests of a group of people whose members share similar concerns and issues. Case advocacy can become cause advocacy when individual service user experiences reveal a need for system-wide or broader policy change.

## Community Empowerment

Empowerment is a central idea in social work generally and in community development in particular. This idea situates human problems in a person-in-environment framework that takes into account the influences of historical oppression and structural inequities (East, 2016). Empowerment is a social action process through which individuals, communities, and organizations gain mastery over their lives in the context of changing their social and political environment to improve equity and quality of life (Rappaport, 1987).

East (2016) describes the key principles of empowerment as follows:

- Intrapersonal, interpersonal, and political
- Ongoing and developmental—not linear but rather circular and interactive
- Service user-driven—based on strengths and competency (not power given but power experienced and exercised)
- Contextual and varying by group, situation, and context—race, ethnicity, class, and gender can influence or inform the empowerment experience

**Community empowerment** encourages community members to begin to reflect critically on the socio-political context and the prevailing distribution of power and resources. It is achieved through campaigning, lobbying, social planning, and policy development. Community empowerment results in increased awareness, and this in turn can lead to a new set of values, assumptions, and expectations that are ultimately embodied in a new set of structures as well as new personal and social relationships.

## Critical Consciousness ("Conscientization")

Related to the idea of empowerment is Paulo Freire's notion of **conscientization** (or, roughly, "critical consciousness"). Freire, a Brazilian educator and community activist, described conscientization as the consciousness that comes from the social analysis of conditions, and the awareness that enables community groups to analyze moments and open spaces to enact change (Minkler & Wallerstein, 2012).

Conscientization is an ongoing process (a "praxis") of both reflection and action. It focuses on achieving a deeper understanding of the world, and allows for the exposure of social and political contradictions. Also, it involves actively seeking to counter oppressive elements, in one's surroundings, that are illuminated through the consciousness-raising part of the process.

Through a process of structured dialogue and continuous reflection and action, community participants "discuss common problems, look for root causes and the connections among the 'problems behind the problem-as-symptom,' and devise strategies to help transform their reality" (Minkler & Wallerstein, 2012, p. 36).

### Community empowerment

Community empowerment is linked to the social work value of self-determination.

Social workers practise community empowerment by ensuring community members have control (power) over decision-making as it affects their community.

### Conscientization

Critical consciousness ("or conscientization") is a process of continuous reflection and action that focuses on achieving an in-depth understanding of the world, which in turn allows for the exposure of social and political contradictions and social oppression.

Critical consciousness also includes taking action against the oppressive elements, in one's life and in society, that are illuminated through that deeper understanding.

# Social Worker Exemplar

## Youth Homelessness

### Katherine McParland

**Katherine is a young social worker who previously was a permanent ward of the foster-care system and went through a multitude of moves that gave her lived experience of being housing insecure.**

After aging out of foster care, Katherine was homeless and living on the streets until she found a sense of purpose.

Katherine's persuasiveness and networking abilities have influenced youth homeless policy within her community and across the country.

Katherine now has a BSW and is currently completing a master's degree at the University of Calgary.

The "A Way Home Kamloops" journey begins with "Youth First Voices," a young people's network for those who have lived experience of homelessness. When working in the network's adult housing-first program, I noticed an increasing number of youth hanging around the building. As I talked with them, I learned that many were fleeing the foster-care system or had "aged out." Something shifted inside of me as I realized that what I had experienced was not an individual fault, but a system failure.

In 2012, I decided to act and gathered together a group of similarly concerned professionals. I knew it was crucial to collaborate with others who had an understanding of youth homelessness and a vested interest in creating change.

At the same time, Kamloops was developing a community plan to end youth homelessness. The initial grassroots committee evolved to include youth and multiple community sectors (e.g., businesses, landlords, non-profits, government, religious organizations, and Indigenous organizations) to form a steering committee to implement the A Way Home plan to end youth homelessness.

The power of collaboration was quickly made evident by the gains we were able to achieve in coordinating services in the community and reducing gaps in access. A shining example was the development of the "Kamloops Youth Housing First Wrapforce." This program resulted in a grassroots housing and supports intake system for youth at risk of, or experiencing homelessness. Sixteen organizations partnered and offered in-kind services and units of housing to create a coordinated response for these youth. Organizations expanded their mandate to support youth aged from 19 to 24 or went from an in-house service to providing outreach supports. The strong support of each organization made a coordinated response to youth experiencing homelessness possible.

Our community developed a scattered site housing program that included business sector–sponsored units of housing for youth (e.g., "Honda Homes" and "Subway Homes") with a year-long rental subsidy. Within three months, the Wrapforce created 14 new program units for youth experiencing homelessness. We started with housing because the need was urgent. Youth were suffering and needed help right away.

## Communities of Practice

Four youth were immediately placed into housing—but with no supports. As the housing units got populated, domestic violence, suicide attempts, sexual exploitation, and drug overdoses occurred. The pilot project was paused until funding for 24/7 support staffing could be secured.

Through advocacy and a partnership with Thompson Rivers University, an employment and education team was developed. Bursaries were offered to youth in the Wrapforce program, a faculty mentorship program was developed to support educational success, and the community provided mentors to create pathways into employment.

"Youth Against Youth Homelessness" was formed with a group of 12 youth with lived expertise. Today it is the centre of A Way Home. Two youth advisers are employed to provide peer support and chair A Way Home committee meetings. This team puts on community events and educational seminars to raise awareness, is currently working on a book to share their lived experiences of homelessness, and provides the ConNext table to connect youth to housing and supports before they "age out" of foster care.

A Way Home Kamloops was the first community in Canada to conduct a youth-specific homeless count. Through this count, we learned that lived experience is a powerful tool for gaining media attention and a direct line to all levels of government.

I now understand that youth homelessness is a complex issue that must be addressed at all levels of government. At the local level, the changes created by implementing Safe Suites would never have been achieved without provincial investment and support. At the federal level, I have been appointed to the federal government's Advisory Committee on Homelessness to help inform the redesign of the Homelessness Partnering Strategy.

In 2017, as a co-founder and chair of the BC Coalition, I began a provincial initiative on homelessness. This community of practice is represented by 35 members from across the province with the goal of ending youth homelessness. ■

## Reflections on Katherine's Story

Katherine's lived experience of homelessness as a youth was a powerful tool to create change at the community level. Recognizing that she was not alone in her experience, she looked for community solutions. She raised awareness about youth homelessness in multiple ways, especially through social media. Sectors of the community that may not have been aligned with social justice initiatives, such as the business sector, started working collaboratively with her. Through this collaboration, community discourse on, and stereotypes of youth homelessness began to change, reducing the associated stigma.

Katherine matched her personal experience with evidence-based practice and was able to create social change. She practised at the micro level (providing individual and youth housing), the mezzo level (developing a non-profit society), and the macro level (participating in provincial and federal government initiatives on youth homelessness).

While it is challenging to navigate at all of these levels, Katherine is optimistic that youth homelessness can be eliminated through such community development approaches.

### From Theory to Practice

As you reflect on Katherine's journey and advocacy, give some thought to the following points:

1. Which model or framework of community development (see p. 212) would you most associate with Katherine's work?

2. What are some examples of empowerment, conscientization, and cause advocacy that were undertaken?

3. What lessons are there to be learned when the first young people who were placed in housing continued to struggle with social issues?

4. What social work meta-competencies did Katherine use in her work?

Rothman's models
of community
development

Social workers have many
models and strategies
to choose from when
working to change a
community system.

Rothman's models are
not discrete, but generally
"mixed and phased" in
real-life macro practice as
a situation's needs shift
and change.

# Models of Community Development

A number of attempts have been made to conceptualize the scope of community development and the core skills and strategies involved. Below, we look at the primary models of community development used in practice.

## Rothman's Models of Community Development

Perhaps the best-known description of the community development field is associated with Jack Rothman who, in the 1960s, described three distinct models. **Rothman's models of community development** set out to define the macro skills and roles required by a community worker in practice:

> Macro intervention involves methods of professional changing that target systems above the level of the individual, group, and family, i.e., organizations, communities, and regional and national entities. Macro practice deals with aspects of human service activity that are non-clinical in nature, but rather focus on broader social approaches to human betterment, emphasizing the effective delivery of services, strengthening community life, and preventing social ills. Macro practice thus includes the areas of community organization, social policy and administration. (Rothman & Tropman, 1987, p. 3)

Rothman's three models of community organizing are as follows:

- **Locality development.** This approach is usually associated with a particular neighbourhood or geographical area. It is focused on building a sense of community, increasing community resources, increasing member involvement and local leadership, and enhancing community functioning (Lundy, 2011).

- **Social planning.** This is an expert-driven approach to community work, often found in city planning departments. This approach is heavily task oriented and involves information gathering, analysis, and the identification of solutions to solve problems and meet immediate needs, rather than achieve broader social change.

- **Social action.** This is an activist approach to community development that is aimed at increasing the community's problem-solving ability and creating social change through the redistribution of power and resources. Social workers act as advocates and activists, making demands for resources and alternative services as well as program and policy changes.

"Locality development" most closely aligns with what is typically referred to as "community development." In practice, however, social workers employ a range of skills and roles drawn from all three models.

Rothman's typology was the dominant framework for some time. More recently, it has come under criticism for being too problem based and organizer centred (rather than strengths-based and community centred). Rothman's models have also been criticized for their lack of attention to culture as a central issue in many community settings (Laing, 2009).

# Co-constructing Home Care Services in Quebec
## Popular Participation and Community Action

In the early 1970s, Quebec health-care systems underwent reform, and local community service centres (Centres locaux de services communautaires [CLSCs]) were set up to offer a range of basic services. This period stood out for its climate of popular participation "in the form of citizens' committees and the creation of community organizations in poor urban neighbourhoods" (Gaumer & Fleury, 2007, p. 90).

Included within the mandate of CLSCs was a commitment to developing community action which was "defined as the art and method of getting the population to take part in identifying and solving health and social problems" (Gaumer & Fleury, 2007, p. 89).

### Community Action

CLSCs were designed to be the point of entry for service users of the health and social services system. They were developed locally, often at the initiative of individuals or groups involved in the community. The first CLSCs were created by highly committed community activists.

According to Gaumer and Fleury (2007), the 160 CLSCs that existed during that time were

> veritable laboratories for community organizations and a remarkable creative force behind the development of a policy of home support services and mental health in the community. (p. 89)

Since the early 1980s, the Community Economic Development Corporations (CEDCs)—created by community groups involved in health, housing, welfare, and other issues—have become important non-profit organizations in community development in Quebec. CEDCs receive funding support from all three levels of government. "They also have been agents of social cohesion through their involvement in development processes to reconcile diverse concerns and interests and improve the quality of life in their communities" (RELIESS, 2012, p. 1). In 2019, there were 13 CEDCs in Quebec's cities, covering a total population of 1.6 million.

### Home Care Services in Quebec

In Quebec, home care services have been funded through non-profit organizations since the early 1970s. In 1996, 100 or so Domestic Help Social Economy Enterprises (DHSEEs) were developed to complement the province's social services (Jetté & Vaillancourt, 2011). The DHSEEs were social enterprises that received government subsidies (redistribution), user contributions (market), and volunteer involvement (reciprocity).

DHSEEs were positioned to co-produce government-funded and community services. In other words, various private and public sectors could partner to produce collective services. Sometimes, this arrangement is referred to as a public–private partnership. However, the aim of DHSEEs was also to provide government with input to enhance the development of public policies. DHSEEs would influence the co-construction of services by influencing and participating in the development of the policies and programs that determine how services are delivered or produced (Jetté & Vaillancourt, 2011). In this way, DHSEEs would provide upstream input.

In their review of DHSEEs, Jetté and Vaillancourt (2011) conclude that DHSEEs have faced financial, organizational, and political difficulties in the delivery of home care services. They attribute these difficulties to the authoritarian and hierarchical relations that DHSEEs have with certain components of the Quebec state. The authors add that these relations have undermined the ability for true collaboration and partnerships.

- According to Jetté and Vaillancourt (2011), the current administration and organization of home care services "relates more closely to the dynamics of co-production than the dynamics of co-construction. This means DHSEEs are more subcontracting suppliers than true partner suppliers of a service of public interest" (p. 67). ■

**Strengths-based community development**

Social workers practising from a strengths-based community approach see the internal strengths and resources of the community, and build on what is already working in the community.

## Strengths-Based Community Development

Kretzmann and McKnight (1993) developed a strengths-based model of community development in which the internal human and institutional aspects of disadvantaged communities are identified. Instead of asking the question "What is the problem?" the model asks, "How can our community assemble its strengths into new combinations, new structures of opportunity, new sources of income and control, and new possibilities?" These authors developed techniques for mapping a community's assets, capacities, and abilities, with a view to identifying the human and material resources that can be used to bring about lasting change.

Hoefer and Chigbu (2015) have proposed a newer strengths-based model of community development that they call the Motivation and Persuasion Process (MAP). The MAP model includes a place for community members who have mastered the skills of empowerment and evidence-guided decisions. By empowering leadership within the community, the involvement of a third party, or "outsider," may not be necessary—making this practice very consistent with the idea of self-determination.

Healy and Levine (2016) have identified the main features of **strengths-based community development** as follows:

- Change must begin from inside the community.
- Change must build on the capacities and assets that already exist within communities.
- Change is relationship driven.
- Change should be oriented toward sustainable community growth.

Community development recognizes the strengths, talents, and assets of individuals in achieving positive change. Kretzmann and McKnight (1993) proposed a number of steps that can be used by communities to mobilize around a common plan. Mathie and Cunningham (2002) modified them slightly to underscore the importance of storytelling and egalitarianism in the process:

- Collecting stories about community successes and identifying the capacities of communities that contributed to success
- Organizing a core group to carry the process forward
- Mapping completely the capacities and assets of individuals, associations, and local institutions
- Building relationships among local assets for mutually beneficial problem-solving within the community
- Mobilizing the community's assets fully for economic development and information sharing purposes
- Convening as broadly representative a group as possible for the purposes of building a community vision and plan
- Leveraging activities, investments and resources from outside the community to support asset-based, locally defined development

# Indigenous Approaches to Community Development
## Engaging in Traditional Processes

Community is the place where connections take place. From an Indigenous perspective, it is impossible to have individual wellness if the community is unhealthy. The overall well-being of everyone must be considered, rather than the well-being of only a few (Baskin, 2016).

### It Takes a Village

Community development approaches are central to Indigenous social work insofar as the health of the individual is tied to the well-being of the community (Holland & Scourfield, 2015). This may be one reason why studies indicate that Indigenous communities with a strong sense of cultural continuity have lower rates of youth suicide (Chandler & Lalonde, 1998).

Imposing Western models of community work on Indigenous communities has been largely unsuccessful. Durst (2016) emphasizes the importance of the linkage between individual and community well-being, and he underlines the importance of the interdependence of the individuals, families, friends, and extended family that constitute the community.

Holland and Scourfield (2015) remark that community development in Indigenous communities requires sustained relationships with local residents and a deeper understanding of their needs in order to develop local solutions in line with the worldview of those in the community. Community workers in Indigenous communities must ensure that these wider relationships, which are the foundation of Indigenous community, are accommodated and strengthened (Durst, 2016).

### Strengthening Leadership and Social Organization

Wesley-Esquimaux and Calliou (2010) reviewed 13 case studies to identify the key factors of success in Indigenous community development. They concluded that

> a community-centred, strength-based approach, deeply rooted in traditional practice works as it aims to strengthen leadership and social organization among community members who interact regularly and share institutions of social life. (p. 18)

Further, these authors, suggested that

> strengthened social organization is, in turn, a means to enhance the ability of community members to engage in collective problem solving, to improve self-sufficiency and efficacy, bolster internal control, and to make the community a desirable place to live. (p. 18)

Indigenous communities have the knowledge, strength, and resilience needed to live safe, secure, and healthy lives.

For Indigenous people to reclaim and invigorate community practices and promote wellness, Wesley-Esquimaux and Calliou (2010) recommend a return to "wise practices" and to engaging community members (from youth to Elders) in a reassertion of fundamental belief structures, values, and ceremonial practices. ■

### The Spiral Model of Community Action

The Spiral Model of Community Action developed by community activists in Toronto is an example of an action–reflection approach to community development (Arnold, Burke, James, Martin, & Thomas, 1991).

Colleen Lundy (2011) describes the "spiral" as follows:

> The beginning point is the concrete experiences and past actions of the concerned community members; from these, a problem, need, or identified injustice may emerge. The members begin to reflect on their experiences, to identify patterns in what they have reported, and to discern commonalities and differences. New information and theory builds on the experiences and helps to explain them, leading to further debate and discussion. The members apply what they have learned in order to develop a strategy, a plan of action based on their knowledge and experience. Finally, the plan is implemented, and a process of praxis—reflection, action, and reflection—takes place. (p. 264)

The final reflexive stage leads to a circular movement back through the spiral and may result in revised community development strategies (see Figure 8.1).

### Culture-Based Models of Community Development

A critique of many community development approaches, including action–reflection models, is that they often give insufficient attention to the influence of culture (Laing, 2009). Rothman's models, for example, do not fully address the broad range of cultural variations in communities, nor do they fully explore the impact of culture on development (Laing, 2009). Likewise, Kretzmann and McKnight's assets-based model has been criticized for not explicitly exploring how culture might be used as a positive asset that can help facilitate community development (Laing, 2009).

Just as it is important to acknowledge the importance of cultural differences at the micro level, cultural understanding is essential in community development initiatives. Culture-based approaches to community development stress the independent role of culture as a factor that "outsiders" need to consider when entering communities. Along these lines, Rivera and Erlich (1998) recommend the inclusion of two critical factors when organizing in communities:

- The racial, ethnic, and cultural uniqueness of the target community; and,
- The impact of cultural factors on social relationships at the micro, mezzo, and macro levels of community functioning.

Practising community development also requires understanding the impact of one's own social location and one's own cultural perspective. Gutierrez, Alvarez, Nemon, and Lewis (1996) have proposed a model for intercultural community organizing that includes understanding one's social location and one's cultural perspectives in order to develop cultural safety. They also emphasize the importance of the social worker assuming the dual role of facilitator and learner in order to minimize power differentials.

**Figure 8.1** The Spiral Model of Community Action

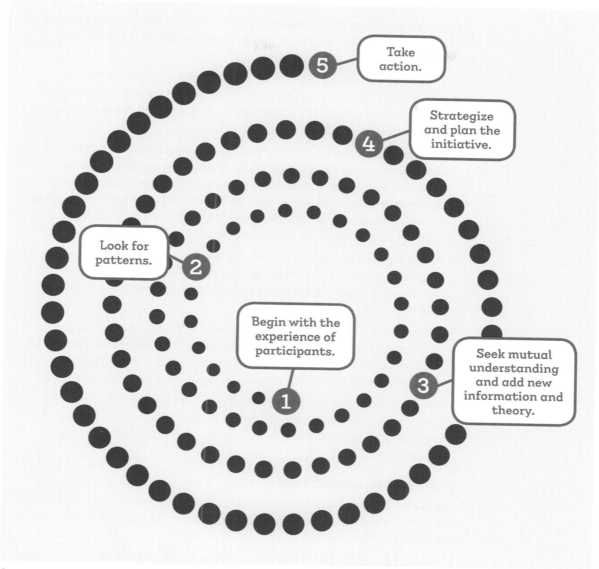

**Source:** Adapted from Arnold et al. (1991).

# The Community Development Process

Community development is complex. McKenzie, Neiger, and Thackery (2009) have identified some key elements of a generalist framework for community development:

- The process starts when someone recognizes a problem exists. The recognition can occur from inside or outside of the community itself. If the issue is identified by an insider, entry into the community is already established.

- As an outsider, entering the community is a critical step. The importance of tactfully negotiating entry into a community—by working closely with those individuals (the "gatekeepers") who control the political climate of the community—cannot be underestimated. Once entry has been gained, then working (organizing) with the people who are affected by the problem and want to see change occur becomes possible.

- Assessing the community takes time and is likely to include both a needs assessment and asset and strength mapping. This research allows organizers to identify the concerns of the community and their capacity to deal with them.

- Following the community assessment, the community group identifies its priorities and what the group wants to accomplish. The priorities should be determined through a consensus. During goal setting, organizers will need to identify the advantages and disadvantages of various courses of action.

- The final steps include implementing the plan, evaluating outcomes, and maintaining or sustaining the outcomes in the community. This part of the process often necessitates a looping back in order to modify steps and restructure the plan.

## Community Development Skills

To be effective, community workers must be competent in a wide range of skills and abilities. In addition to the ability of building rapport, Durst (2016) has identified four essential skills:

- **Organizational skills.** The goal is to enable communities to solve problems and take action on their own. To accomplish this goal, the social worker must be able to assist community members in identifying their assets and strengths, and possess problem-solving skills that will help them find lasting solutions.

- **Communication skills.** Community development workers need to possess skills in several modes of communication, including written, electronic (including social media), verbal, and non-verbal.

- **Strategic/political skills.** The successful social worker needs to be "adept at recognizing the various and often conflicting concerns of community residents, and in working to accommodate these concerns without compromising the community's collective goals" (p. 100).

- **Analytical skills.** Community workers are required to synthesize information, offer new perspectives, and generate options. This requires "a variety of analytical skills, including observation and interpretation, assessment, development of an action plan, and evaluation of outcomes" (p. 103).

**Table 8.1** The Steps in Community Organizing and Community Building

| Initial engagement | • Identify a community issue suitable for cause advocacy.<br>• Learn about the community's demographics, history, and culture.<br>• Understand the formal and informal social and power systems within the community.<br>• Gain entry to the community.<br>• Gather community stories and understandings of the issue(s).<br>• Facilitate or participate in a community meeting to reflect critically on the issue(s). | **Skills:** rapport building; active listening; observing; self-reflection; group work processes; gathering data; listening for strengths<br><br>**Knowledge and values:** culturally safe practice; honesty and authenticity; respect; trustworthiness, co-operation, compassion, patience, specific knowledge about the topic; social systems knowledge; anti-oppressive theory; strenghts-based theories |
|---|---|---|
| Preparation and collaboration | • Assess the community's resources and strengths.<br>• Build informal and formal networks inside and outside the community.<br>• Empower community members to set priorities and goals.<br>• Select an intervention strategy. | **Skills:** helping community members tell stories; communication skills; relationship building; probing for key issues; summarizing; brainstorming; identifying possibilities; developing and shaping goals; managing your own commitment, research skills; assessment skills; critical analysis; collaboration skills; organizational skills; conflict resolution skills; engaging allies; advocacy<br><br>**Knowledge and values:** value of dignity; respect for individual differences; respect for lived experiences; confidentiality; ethical and legal knowledge; empowerment theory; social inclusion theories; participatory action research; social justice commitment |
| Action | • Implement the plan of action. | **Skills:** linking storytelling to action; educational skills; social media networking skills; activism<br><br>**Knowledge and values:** social change theory, holistic theories; transformational theories |
| Continuous praxis: evaluation and action | • Evaluate the outcomes of the plan of action.<br>• Ensure sustainability of positive change.<br>• Loop back to community members and processes, as required. | **Skills:** evaluation skills; accountability<br>**Knowledge and values:** critical reflexivity; sustainability processes |

**Source:** Adapted from McKenzie et al. (2009).

# Critical Theory and Community Development

Community social work is typically locally based, collective, and empowering. It challenges the root causes of exclusion and injustice through a process of exposing the existing power structures and encouraging the participation of community members in the decisions that affect them. Community social work involves an organic, "bottom-up" engagement with community members (Forde & Lynch, 2014). For this reason, community work is a major area of critical social work practice.

Critical social work focuses on identifying and addressing harmful divisions and unequal power relations that create and perpetuate exclusion and disadvantage. It is committed to the pursuit of social justice and practice approaches that make substantive differences in the lives of communities and community members. Postmodern approaches view the community as both a source of oppression and a potential source of power for community members (Lathouras, 2016).

While social workers endeavour to incorporate community work approaches in their practice, how that is done varies from setting to setting. The following three case studies—in Ireland, Australia, and Canada—demonstrate the contributions of critical social work to community development.

## Social Workers Practising Community Development: Ireland

Forde and Lynch (2014) conducted a study in the Republic of Ireland to explore how community development is expressed in contemporary social work practice. The primary themes to emerge from this study included the importance of engaging with communities, the need for collaboration and networking, and the importance of collective action.

Social workers in the study underlined the challenge of practising from a community development approach within more traditional practice settings. Resisting managerialism in favour of democratic and collaborative processes required adopting new models of empowerment and giving voice to the community's own experiences.

The social workers in this study saw community activism as requiring both a responsiveness to diverse and shifting situations and an ability to adapt. They described having to adopt a mix of "insider" and "outsider" roles to influence their own and other agencies. For them, community change was seen as transformational.

At times, protest actions such as picketing were necessary in order to get further meetings with decision-makers and to make things happen. Other initiatives included informing decision-makers in their agency on the impact of policies and decisions on communities and service users. Some social workers were on the front lines, others were active behind the scenes, while still others worked within the system to promote institutional change.

## Social Workers Practising Community Development: Australia

In Australia, government cutbacks and neo-liberal reforms have led to an overall reduction in activity at the community level. The inevitable effect is that vulnerable citizens have been left without support, wealth inequality and poverty have increased, and local community initiatives have experienced a lack of funding (Lathouras, 2016).

In this context, the Coalition of Community Boards (CoCB) emerged in order to create a "bottom-up," collective, and shared community analysis and action plan. The CoCB focused on "building and strengthening the relationships between members to provide peer support around their roles as board members and to develop a collective analysis of trends and issues for them and others in their network" (Lathouras, 2016, p. 33).

The CoCB undertook a power analysis to deconstruct and reconstruct relationships. They explored new ideas related to developing stronger links across systems and launching creative initiatives that would shape local issues and local realities. In other words, the CoCB began to engage citizens in "social transformation."

The CoCB increased its community and political influence by developing meta-networks—networks that "band together to regularly share analysis and to look for patterns, synergies and divergences in their context" (Lathouras, 2016, p. 35). The result was a broader sense of the issues faced by small community organizations, a broader understanding of the causes of the disadvantages local communities were facing, and the kinds of collective initiatives that were necessary.

## Social Workers Practising Community Development: Canada

In Hudson, Alberta, a group of committed citizens in this rural community of 8,600 began to meet informally to talk about improvements in hospice care in their community. Whitfield (2018) describes how a community development approach was taken and how the group came together "one person at a time and in a short time became a group highly committed to addressing a major gap in their community" (p. 6).

While the initial focus had been on establishing a hospice building, the group quickly realized that, by looking to the assets of their community members, it was possible to offer a wider range of supports. The group believed that with so many talented people, there were opportunities to build an even more empowered community.

The factors that facilitated the group's ability to plan for good hospice care were hearing people's personal stories related to end-of-life care and learning about the value of relationships and networks in end-of-life care. However, the group was hindered by "the lack of direction for rural-focused, community-based planning for hospice care by government, and the obscurity associated with hospice in general" (p. 8). This case exemplifies how citizen planning and active community engagement can make a positive difference in the health of a community.

# Social Worker Exemplar

# Community Engagement

**Jackie Stokes**

**Jackie was the executive director of a non-profit society that provided child and youth support programs, a parenting program, as well as mental health and substance-use counselling. This was with a staff of 2.5 FTE. The only children's service in the community was a child and youth support program for children referred by child protection.**

I was working in a small, rural community, two hours from a larger urban centre. Although the core services of child protection, public health, probation, and substance-use counselling were all available, there were few specialized services.

Building on existing strengths and wider community supports (and a great deal of work on everyone's part), we were able to establish a specialized daycare facility that the entire community could benefit from over time.

Sylvia, an articulate woman in her early 40s, came to see me to advocate for more services for children with developmental needs. Her son, Jason, then aged four, had cerebral palsy as the result of a birthing injury. She had been attending monthly meetings in the larger urban centre for most of the previous four years to provide services to Jason. The amount of travelling and appointments seemed to be increasing, and she was wondering what services could be provided in our small town.

Sylvia was compelling in her advocacy and, as a mother myself of two small children, I had empathy for her situation. Although my initial response was that there was no way we could get those kinds of specialized services to our small community, I held that thought to find out more information.

## Community Outreach

At the end of our initial meeting, I asked Sylvia to do some work with her contacts so that we could find out more about what was needed and what resources we might have. I told her about my reservations, but also stated that if we could work together, we might be able to do something to at least minimally assist her—although it would take time and energy. She was very open to that. I asked her to talk to other parents she knew with children with developmental needs, and to ask them if they would be willing to come together as a group and meet with me. I also asked her to talk with the centres and specialists in the urban centre to see if they had any interest in doing some outreach. My role would be to work with the social service professionals in the community to assess their interest and participation. We arranged to meet again the following month.

When we met again, we had much more information about the children's and families' needs and available resources. Sylvia was able to identify six other mothers who had children (from infants to 10-year-olds) who were struggling with transportation and access to specialized services for a variety of developmental needs. These six women were willing to participate in some advocacy. Sylvia had also identified a non-profit society in the larger centre that had an Infant Development Program (IDP); the society was willing to consider sending a specialist to our community once a month for appointments.

## Community Support Mounts

I had met with the existing service providers in the community and received more interest than I had expected. Some of the key players who were interested in being involved included the speech pathologist, the public health nurse, and the child-protection agency. The latter could perhaps even be able to augment the existing child and youth support contract.

After a few more individual conversations, a core group of about eight people were willing to form a working group to look at possible strategies. After a couple of meetings, the idea of developing a daycare centre emerged. The advantages of this were that it focused on preschool children, it was an early intervention program, it would be inclusive of all children, it provided an additional service to the community, and it would provide a location for visiting professionals. In addition, it was possible to offset some of the costs by charging daycare fees.

Thus, I found myself learning about how to operate a daycare centre—not something I had learned about in social work training.

After developing a bit of a strategic plan, and budget, my job was to find some funding and expertise. A location was identified, and the working group was willing to take on some community fundraising for the daycare. The initial contact Sylvia had provided from the IDP in the urban centre was a wonderful resource. It found the daycare funding and the resources to have a specialist visit the community once a month. More importantly, it guided us in the design of the space and the purchase of toys, books, and equipment.

The next challenge was to find the funding for the staff. Interestingly, fundraising in a community is much easier for material, tangible items than for operational costs (such as rent, hydro, and staffing). However, the child-protection ministry was on board and understood the challenges of providing services in a small community. Eventually, this translated into a formal contract. With that core funding, we were able to work out how much we would need to receive from fee-paying children. ∎

## Reflections on Jackie's Story

Jackie's story indicates that a high level of collaboration and openness are required for community development. Although, in this case, some of the timing was particularly lucky, a key to success was being open to a variety of possible options, being inclusive of professionals and those with lived experiences, staying positive, and being flexible.

Approximately two years later, a specialized daycare centre opened. Initially, there was one daycare provider, some parent volunteers, and a monthly visiting IDP worker. Over the following two years, the centre expanded to have two daycare providers, more visiting professionals, an after-school program, and increased one-to-one support for families.

### From Theory to Practice

As you reflect on Jackie's story, give some thought to the following points:

1. How were principles of community empowerment used in this situation?

2. Which model of community development does this process follow? If Jackie had taken another route, what model could she have used?

3. Do you think Jackie used a strengths-based or needs-based model of community development?

4. Describe this community development example, using the spiral model of community action.

5. Describe this community development example, using the steps in community organizing on page 219.

6. In this approach, the group decided on an inclusive daycare. Is this response consistent with an anti-oppressive and critical practice?

7. Operating a daycare centre is not necessarily a high-profile social work role. In this case, do you think undertaking this practice was consistent with social work values and skills? Why or why not?

# Practice Scenarios

Practising community development requires a range of skills that can bring people together to find collective solutions to their problems. At times, social workers may be "insiders" within the community, but more frequently, they are "outsiders." In certain instances, social workers may have been tasked with imposing "top-down" solutions, but are considering alternative, collaborative responses.

In these practice scenarios, the social workers are seeking to find assets within the community that may help address a service need. They are considering opportunities to embrace an approach that engages all community members in finding solutions.

In all of these scenarios, a community development approach means starting with people's experiences, paying attention to patterns, and staying focused on existing strengths within the community.

---

## 8.1 Building Communities on Shared Interests

You are working in a non-profit agency providing support services to people with Acquired Brain Injury. You notice that there has been an increase in the number of service users who have substance-use problems, and they are experiencing additional challenges in the community due to their substance use. You have offered some referrals to a counselling agency, but to date there has been no follow-through. You have also brought in speakers from the local substance-use agency to speak at your weekly information sessions, but again this doesn't seem to have resulted in any change. You have also spoken with the local police detachment after two individuals were arrested (on different occasions) and held overnight in the local cells.

1. How could this pattern (an increasing number of people with Acquired Brain Injury who are experiencing social problems associated with substance use) be framed from a community development perspective?

2. Who would be included in the identification of "community," and who are the stakeholders involved?

3. What are some of the strengths and assets within this community?

4. How could you proceed using a community development approach?

## 8.2 Identifying Community Strengths and Assets

You are a school outreach worker for a middle school located near a community neighbourhood house that provides services and programs for older adults. The school is in a low-income neighbourhood in which the young people are exposed to multiple social problems, including substance use and gang violence. Many of the students come to school hungry and tired, and often struggle with school work.

You have noticed that many of the young people hang around the school after it finishes. Although they state they don't much like school, they continue to stay at the school. You talk with them and find out that most are going to empty homes and prefer to be with their friends. You wonder if there is any capacity for the seniors community centre to provide some programming for the youth.

1. From a community development approach, is it worthwhile approaching the seniors community centre? Why or why not?

2. What important stakeholders would need to be involved?

3. What may be some of the benefits to developing a collaborative response to the young people's after-school needs?

4. What are some of the barriers to collaboration, and how could they be overcome?

## 8.3 Working Collaboratively with a Community around Service Cuts

You are a manager who has been tasked with implementing a 10% cut to family services within your community. There are eight agencies funded directly through your organization and three centres that provide similar services but are not funded by your organization. There have been cutbacks in recent years, and you are aware that simply cutting each program by a further 10% is not going to benefit the service users and may destroy some of the non-profits. In private consultations, you hear that there are duplications of service, and gaps.

You consider taking a community development approach and bring the "community" of family service agencies together to develop an overall service plan from which collaborative decisions can be made about the funding (and funding cuts).

1. Is this an appropriate plan? Or, should a major decision such as service cuts be made in a "top-down" fashion? Why or why not?

2. If you proceed with a community meeting to discuss the possibility of creating a network of services for families, is it important to be transparent about the impending cuts? Why or why not?

3. As a manager, and community developer, how would you proceed?

# Field Education Practicalities
## Staying Healthy in Social Work Agencies

There are times when you will feel overwhelmed either by the nature of issues faced by the service users or by the feeling that change is not occurring as fast as you would like.

All of these feelings are normal.

As one progresses into a social work career, it becomes important to develop strategies to ensure that you protect your own wellness and life balance. Above all, this will require setting more realistic goals for yourself and focusing on what you are doing well.

As the complexity of individual and community issues becomes more apparent, and as the challenges of providing service user-centred, evidence-based, and bureaucratically driven interventions become greater than expected, stress levels can rise.

The profession of social work encourages introspection. Social workers are encouraged to look inward as they work through difficult situations, both professional and personal (Alle-Corliss & Alle-Corliss, 1998). The healthier and more in balanced we are, the more effective we are in supporting service users. That's why it is important to consider some of the personal challenges that social workers have had to work through at some point in their careers.

### Coping with Overwhelming Feelings

Most social work students are empathetic, sensitive, and caring—indeed, these are characteristics that drew them to the social work profession in the first place. However, the flipside of these characteristics may result in students, and social workers, feeling impatient, having "rescue tendencies," and feeling completely overwhelmed.

In field agencies, one is likely to encounter intense human emotions. Certain human troubles may be encountered for the first time, or they may trigger past experiences. Regardless, it is important to recognize that "having such feelings is quite normal and appropriate. If you were so out of touch with your own feelings that you were not affected by service users' suffering, you would most likely not be an effective helper" (Alle-Corliss & Alle-Corliss, 1998, p. 236).

If you are faced with overwhelming feelings, Alle-Corliss and Alle-Corliss (1998) recommend the following:

1. Learn to recognize when you are becoming too emotionally involved;

2. Talk openly about your feelings with your supervisor, colleagues, field instructors, and fellow students; and,

3. Seek counselling help to work through the deeper emotions, if you discover that the feelings are still overwhelming to you.

### Too Much to Do

Most social work students naturally want to take on as many tasks and responsibilities as they can in order to learn as much as possible. However, having too much work and too many responsibilities can be overwhelming (Royse, Dhooper & Lewis Rompf, 2012).

In social work, workloads increase cumulatively and can quickly overload the time available, and some tasks simply take longer than expected. For example, even documenting a file takes students much longer than it does experienced social workers who have become used to the format and know how to quickly conceptualize the most salient information.

At times, most students will feel that they are not as effective as they could be. This too is very typical. Change is small and incremental, and concern about effectiveness is an indicator of good professional commitment.

However, if the stressors are causing more serious symptoms (e.g., trouble sleeping, eating, or concentrating; overwhelming feelings of anxiety or panic; depressive symptoms; or increased substance use), then proactively managing those stressors is important.

Stress management may involve talking with colleagues about your concerns and hearing their experiences, talking to your agency supervisors and other agency staff to be able to reframe or adjust expectations, and talking with your faculty adviser.

Seeking formal helping services for yourself is a strength and is encouraged for all social workers as they develop resilience and strengthen their professional capacities.

Feeling overwhelmed may lead one to questioning their competence and capacity to be an effective social worker. All social workers have had moments when a service user seems to be faring worse than they were before they met you. But it is impossible to help every service user, and it is important to not label yourself as a failure, or become depressed, as a result of a service user or community making choices that are not always in their best interests (Royse, et al., 2012).

## Having Down Days

In many social work practice domains, it is to be expected that service user progress will not be linear. This is particularly true in areas such as substance use and mental health, where relapse almost invariably occurs along the journey toward good health.

During these times, it is helpful to think about the value of self-determination and the principle of service user-centred work. It is also beneficial to adopt a strengths-based approach and consider the individual service user's strengths (apart from the example that is getting you down), your strengths working with other service users, and to reframe your personal perspectives and sense of self within a broader context.

Shifting from "I didn't do 'x' well" to "I believe that the service user will have the strengths to overcome this not unexpected adversity" will help reframe your thoughts about and emotional response to the situation. In addition, being able to share your sense of responsibility and receive feedback from your colleagues and supervisors is essential to rebalancing yourself.

Of course, if feeling down or depressed about the work you are doing is persistent, it is wise to seek additional support and even therapy to ensure your own wellness. ■

# Reflection, Learning, and More Practice

## Field Education Practicalities

1. Talk with your colleagues at the field agency and your agency field instructor about their engagement with their communities and any community initiatives they have undertaken or are currently involved in.

2. Reflect, discuss, analyze, and elicit feedback among colleagues and other students on the importance of seeking out collective solutions to social problems.

3. Develop some summary notes about how your field agency incorporates, or could possibly incorporate, more of a community development perspective into its work.

## Journal Ideas

1. Identify a pressing social issue in your local community and outline a way to move it from "case advocacy" to "cause advocacy," and thereby involve a wider community of interested persons in finding solutions.

2. Non-profit agencies frequently emerge from grassroots community initiatives. Trace back the history and origins of a non-profit agency in your community to its community development roots.

3. Consider a community development initiative in which you would be an "insider," and then one in which you would be an "outsider." Describe the different ways you would approach the community in each instance.

4. Identify an environmental initiative for your community, and the kind of contribution you could make to that initiative.

## Critical-Thinking Questions

1. The CASW *Code of Ethics* does not explicitly highlight community development as a distinct approach to social work practice. Develop a reasoned argument for including community development as a distinct form of social work practice to be included in the code.

2. Critique one of the models of community development discussed in this chapter for how well it incorporates strategies for combatting social oppression and marginalization.

3. Lathouras (2016) posits that community is both the site of power and a source of oppression. Critique this perspective and provide examples.

4. Being a community activist can be achieved in small and large ways. Identify some limited, small-scale actions that would likely result in social change and help to redress inequality over time.

5. When non-profit agencies access government funding, there is normally a requirement for financial, activity, and outcome accountability. What are some strategies that non-profit community organizations can consider in order not to be totally overburdened by having to report endlessly to government funding agencies?

# Chapter Review

At the core of community development work is a strengths-based and collective approach to social change. The initial phases of community development initiatives require time and patience as "outsiders" begin to develop trust with "insiders." Through this process, a mutual understanding of the strengths and assets within the community is established.

Community development approaches are well suited to geographical and cultural communities, as well as special-interest communities. It may be challenging for social workers to use these approaches in organizations that predominantly use individualized approaches. However, social workers have skills in communication, organization, collaboration, and advocacy that can work as a bridge between the community of interest and the managerial systems.

Katherine began her journey of creating social change and empowerment for youth who are homeless by drawing on her own lived experience and that of other youth. From there, she took the risk of inviting some of the youth and interested service providers into the conversation about resolutions. Small solutions started emerging. Not all worked, but the conversations continued and broadened. Today, her work is changing the lives of youth in her community, transforming the business community's understanding of homelessness, and being noticed nationally. Always working from a collaborative and listening perspective, and staying in touch with the affected youth, she is empowering youth to identify ongoing initiatives and have a voice within the same structures that had previously marginalized and disempowered them.

Community development, like many other roles in social work practice, can be challenging and emotionally draining. Talking with colleagues, being patient, and reframing expectations of oneself and others are strategies that can contribute to effective practice in this area.

## Promoting Community Sustainability in Practice

This chapter outlines numerous ways in which students can provide competent services using a community development approach. Here are some highlights and further suggestions:

- Become involved as an activist, such as in the environmental or the #MeToo movement.
- Work with homeless youth and collaborate with the business community to develop housing options.
- Work with Indigenous Elders to reassert Indigenous beliefs, values, and ceremonial practices.
- Reorganize services to co-construct/co-produce and integrate community services associated with health, housing, and welfare.
- Develop opportunities within micro practice to engage with community and develop collaborative and networking endeavours.
- Pursue community development approaches in small ways as an "insider" in your own organization to change practice and to do things differently.
- Advocate continually with decision-makers about the impact of policy and practice decisions on community members.
- Listen to and empower local community boards to increase opportunities for meaningful collaboration.
- Be flexible during the collaboration process to see alternate outcomes than those initially identified.
- Identify community projects of interest to you, and where you may be an "insider" to develop community development skills.
- Ensure that participatory approaches are continued through all phases to ensure you are working "with" the community not "on" the community.

# Advocating for Human Rights and Social Justice

## 9

*Get up, stand up—stand up for your rights.*
*Get up, stand up—don't give up the fight.*

—**Bob Marley** (1945–1981), Jamaican singer, songwriter,
and international cultural icon

# Chapter at a Glance

# Spotlight on Social Work Luminaries
# Cindy Blackstock

**Cindy Blackstock** is the executive director of the First Nations Child and Family Caring Society of Canada and a professor of the School of Social Work at McGill University. A member of the Gitxsan First Nation, Cindy has 25 years of experience in the area of child protection and Indigenous children's rights. Read more about Cindy on page 246.

F ew social workers would dispute that access to income, food, and housing are fundamental human rights, and few would dispute the need for advocacy with governments to provide minimum income levels and affordable food and housing to all citizens. However, in everyday social work practice, it is a challenge to achieve these lofty human rights goals for everyone.

Human rights and social justice are two principles that are central to social work practice. Indeed, these are critical values that differentiate social work from other helping professions. Social work "is the only helping profession imbued with social justice as its fundamental value and concern" (Lundy & van Wormer, 2007).

Advocacy for human rights and social justice in social work occurs at the micro, mezzo, and macro levels. At the micro level, enabling service user rights is a foremost concern. At the mezzo level, participatory democracy is a means through which human rights can be advanced. At the macro level, resource mobilization, consciousness raising, and lobbying are essential components of human rights advocacy (Staub-Bernasconi, 2012).

This chapter focuses on the importance of human rights advocacy in social work at all three levels of practice.

## Developing Competence as a Social Worker

Some ways to develop the meta-competency of "**advocating for human rights and social justice**" are as follows:

- Reframe individual, family, and community issues within a human rights framework.

- Develop an advocacy plan for addressing an issue of social injustice in your community.

- Identify a way of using social media to raise awareness, develop a sense of "community," and address a social injustice.

- Reflect on the use of moral courage in social work practice and in social activism.

## Key Concepts

- Human rights

- International Federation of Social Workers (IFSW)

- Human rights practice

- *Canadian Charter of Rights and Freedoms*

- *United Nations Declaration on the Rights of Indigenous Peoples*

- Truth and Reconciliation Commission of Canada

# Social Problems through a Human Rights Lens

**Human rights**

The *Universal Declaration of Human Rights* (UDHR) sets out 30 human rights—including the right to equality and dignity, and to live free from discrimination and torture—that everyone in the world is entitled to.

Social workers have a professional obligation to advocate for adherence to these rights globally.

Many social work agencies are focused on providing services and programs to people who are not receiving adequate food, clothing, and shelter. The response to meeting those needs is often at an individual (micro) level; for example, providing food and clothing or advocating for social housing on a need-by-need basis. Social work at this micro level can be daunting. Many social workers feel like the proverbial Dutch boy plugging a leaking dike with his finger. In the children's story, the adults in the village find the boy the next day and make the necessary repairs. In reality, waiting for policy changes that ensure all Canadians have a minimal level of social security can seem never-ending.

## Human Rights and Social Work Practice

Social work practice is ultimately about advancing human rights and advocating for social and economic justice. Lundy (2011) describes social workers as "human rights workers, advocating for individual and collective rights every day" (p. 41).

**Human rights** are embedded internationally in the *Universal Declaration of Human Rights* (UDHR). Wronka (2008) notes that these rights are based on five fundamental ideas: (1) dignity; (2) non-discrimination; (3) civil and political rights; (4) economic, social, and cultural rights; and (5) solidarity rights.

Often, the struggle for human rights is divided into three categories, referred to as "generations." First-generation human rights consist of civil and political rights. Second-generation human rights include economic, social, and cultural rights. Finally, third-generation human rights belong to and require the cooperation of people across the globe and include the right to peace, a clean environment, and a system of fair trade (Healy, 2008, p. 736).

Social issues, such as poverty, homelessness, and discrimination, are largely outside of the personal control of individuals. However, when framed as human rights issues, individual personal problems become "rights denied," with governments having a duty to live up to human rights obligations.

The Canadian Association of Social Workers (CASW) *Code of Ethics* (2005a) describes human rights in value 2 ("Pursuit of Social Justice") this way:

> Social workers believe in the obligation of people, individually and collectively, to provide resources, services and opportunities for the overall benefit of humanity and to afford them protection from harm. (p. 5)

Wronka (2008) describes the practice of social work as "creating a 'human rights culture' respecting human dignity, practising non-discrimination, using a non-hierarchal approach, considering and respecting the service user's cultural context, integrating community and service user-driven interventions, using a systems-oriented approach and respecting self-determination" (as cited in Steen, Mann, Restivo, Mazany, & Chaple, 2016, p. 11).

Social work itself was declared a human rights profession in 1988 by the International Federation of Social Workers (IFSW).

Social work is a human rights profession with responsibilities to advocate for individual and collective rights and social justice globally. From a human rights perspective, individual problems such as poverty and homelessness are understood as a denial of human rights and a social responsibility, not an individual problem. Global human rights for peace, a clean environment, and a system of fair trade are contemporary issues.

The IFSW (2018b) advocates strongly for the promotion of equitable social structures. According to the IFSW (2018b):

> Social work today has the responsibility to advocate that human rights are respected all over the world, particularly where new global realities mean that basic elemental human rights are no longer valued and people are often treated as if they don't matter. (para. 1)

## CASWE-ACFTS *Standards for Accreditation*

The third core learning objective in the the CASWE-ACFTS *Standards for Accreditation* (Canadian Association for Social Work Education–Association canadienne pour la formation en travail social [CASWE-ACFTS], 2014) states:

**3.** Promote human rights and social justice

i) Social work students understand their professional role in advancing human rights and responsibilities and social justice in the context of the Canadian society and internationally.

ii) Social work students have knowledge of the role social structures can play in limiting human and civil rights and employ professional practices to ensure the fulfillment of human and civil rights and advance social justice for individuals, families, groups and communities.

## Professional Regulation and Competency

The CASW *Code of Ethics* (2005a) describes human rights as follows:

> The rights of an individual that are considered the basis for freedom and justice, and serve to protect people from discrimination and harassment. (p. 10)

Moreover, value 1 of the CASW *Code of Ethics* (2005a) ("Respect for the Inherent Dignity and Worth of Persons") states:

> Social work is founded on a long-standing commitment to respect the inherent dignity and individual worth of all persons. When required by law to override a client's wishes, social workers take care to use the minimum coercion required. Social workers recognize and respect the diversity of Canadian society, taking into account the breadth of differences that exist among individuals, families, groups and communities. Social workers uphold the human rights of individuals and groups as expressed in the *Canadian Charter of Rights and Freedoms* (1982) and the United Nations *Universal Declaration of Human Rights* (1948).

## Association of Social Work Boards (ASWB)

The Canadian Council of Social Work Regulators (CCSWR) and ASWB, with their focus on protection of the public (primarily at the micro level) allude to the importance of human rights and social justice, but they do not specify competency in these areas. ∎

## International Federation of Social Workers (IFSW)

The International Federation of Social Workers (IFSW) is the global organization for the social work profession.

The IFSW and its national members strive for social justice, human rights, and inclusive and sustainable social development through the promotion of social work best practice and engagement in international cooperation.

The IFSW's *Global Social Work Statement of Ethical Principles* appears in Appendix 1 on pages 284–285.

# Reframing Human Needs as Human Rights

Human rights advocacy has a long history in social work, dating back to Jane Addams (1860–1935), the pioneer American settlement activist and reformer known as the "mother" of social work. In her time, Addams was at the forefront of the struggles for women's suffrage, immigrant education, health care, children's rights, housing, peace, and progressive education.

The worth and dignity of all people is entrenched in social work codes of ethics and human rights principles. Today, social workers are active in supporting human rights for a number of populations, including Indigenous peoples; women; children; families; the poor; and lesbian, gay, bisexual, transgender, queer, and two-spirited (LGBTQ2S+) individuals. Internationally, social workers have been leaders in movements such as the Anti-Apartheid Movement, African American civil rights, women's rights in Afghanistan, and the elimination of torture.

At a collective level, the **International Federation of Social Workers (IFSW)**—the global organization for professional social workers—regularly issues statements to highlight human rights abuses. For example, the IFSW released statements calling for the release of Munther Amira, a Palestinian social worker arrested for peacefully protesting in support of the rights of children who had been detained by Israeli authorities (IFSW, 2018a); supporting the refugee crisis in Europe as a humanitarian obligation (IFSW, 2015); and supporting the affirmation of gender perspectives and equity (IFSW, 2017).

### Human Rights and Social Justice

While social workers believe that everyone has a basic human right to an adequate standard of living, health care, education, and safety, the application of a human rights practice in real-world settings is difficult. Individual problems are not usually framed as human rights concerns.

Social work is typically thought of as a human "needs" profession; for example, social work involves performing "needs" assessments, meeting unmet "needs," and determining resource "needs." However, Ife (2008) and others assert that social work is about more than assessing and meeting human needs. It is also about the "defining, realizing and guaranteeing of human rights" (p. 89). In other words, the immediate needs are not ends in themselves, but rather a means to achieve the broader end of supporting human rights.

A human rights and social justice perspective can be a useful tool in a social worker's arsenal. When a child needs a child-care centre, it is about the rights of parents to be able to participate in the workplace and the rights of the children to receive adequate care. When a child needs special education, it is based on the right of the child to achieve maximum educational potential.

As Ife (2008) suggests, statements of individual needs within social work are also "statements about rights . . . [although] the rights nearly always remain implicit and unstated" (p. 93). An important part of developing the professional identity needed for social work is grasping the interconnections between well-being and human rights (Sherr & Jones, 2014).

## Implementing a Human Rights Perspective in Practice

**Human rights practice** requires both a deductive approach (applying human rights conventions to social work practice) and an inductive approach (identifying issues, needs, or problems), and then seeing what human rights issues lie behind them (Ife, 2008).

The essential task is to reframe personal troubles and individual needs as infringements of human rights. As Lundy and van Wormer (2007) point out, "viewing shelter and food as human rights rather than simply as human needs draws our attention to the political nature of poverty and the necessity of addressing structural inequalities and injustices while providing available resources" (p. 735).

Ife (2008), provides the following example:

> If a person seeks social work assistance because she/he is unemployed, this needs to be framed in human rights terms, most obviously the right to meaningful and rewarding work. But there may be other rights involved as well: for an unemployed person from a racial or ethnic minority there may be issues of the right to be free from discrimination; if the person has a disability there may be another set of discrimination rights; or it may be that the person's right to education has been denied and that this is a contributory factor to his/her unemployment. (p. 157)

A recent study explored how social work students and supervisors apply a human rights perspective in practice (Steen et al., 2017). Participants were asked how they conceptualized human rights and human rights practice. They described a number of human rights issues that they had encountered in their field settings (e.g., poverty, discrimination, violence, dignity/respect). As well, they identified combatting poverty as the most common human rights practice, since poverty interferes with service users' abilities to meet physical and psychological needs. They also saw human rights practice as encompassing the following:

- **Service provision.** This practice area included outreach efforts to underserved communities and working with service users to access services in areas of disability, mental health, homelessness, family violence, and health care.

- **Assessment.** The identification of service users' needs and wishes was seen as a form of human rights practice because assessment is a necessary step before needs and wishes can be met.

- **Strengthening the worker–service user relationship.** Consent forms and the protection of confidentiality were identified as key aspects of human rights practice.

- **Awareness of threats to service users' human rights.** General awareness was also an important human rights practice; for example, "being aware of signs of elderly abuse," "understanding mental health laws and policy," and noticing "any discrimination that marginalized service users face." (Steen et al., 2017, p. 14).

- **Advocacy.** General advocacy, case advocacy, and cause advocacy were all identified as a form of human rights practice.

**Human rights practice**

Human rights practice is interprofessional practice and involves advocacy with organizations, social movements, and community groups.

Social workers are key actors in human rights practice, as they are able to identify and analyze social issues through a human rights lens.

# Social Worker Exemplar

## Public Policy and Human Rights

Bob MacDonald

**Social workers often play an advisory role to policy-makers, whether at the local, provincial, or national level. They are chosen for their expertise in the area. This advisory role is an essential service to the community, and it is one not to be taken lightly.**

Bob was a substance-use counsellor with many years of direct experience both in the field and in advising local and provincial governments.

On this occasion, he was called upon to provide briefing notes to the minister of social services on a disputed youth substance-use treatment centre. In his recommendations, Bob was able to broaden the issue to one involving basic human rights.

A summary of Bob's briefing notes follows.

The challenge of writing briefing notes is to distill complex information into a very short summary as well as to make recommendations that can be acted upon. The following are briefing notes that were prepared in relation to a controversial youth substance-use treatment centre.

### The Context

A decision was made to develop a youth substance-use treatment centre in a family home in a small community in a non-urban region of the province. The decision was made in collaboration with community providers. A local non-profit agency was identified and the executive director took responsibility for identifying a home, working with the neighbours, and developing a treatment model. This work was going well, and the home was purchased and renovations had begun.

However, as the work progressed, all of a sudden, a neighbour organized a group of people with placards that showed up outside the home with various "not in my backyard" (NIMBY) messages. The executive director talked through some of their concerns, but over the following few days, this group attracted regional and provincial media attention.

### Background Considerations

- Substance use affects citizens of all ages. Youths living with substance-use disorders have diverse life experiences, needs, and concerns, and require a variety of culturally appropriate programs.

- Significant work had been done to develop a supportive youth residential home in a community neighbourhood. The provider is a local non-profit that distributed leaflets prior to the purchase of the home to all houses within a two-block radius, explaining the plan.

- Services to youth are guided by the *United Nations Convention on the Rights of the Child* (UNCRC). Access to health services, including the right to necessary social services, is also covered in Article 25 of the *Universal Declaration of Human Rights* (UDHR). Treatment to substance-use services is an essential element of this human right.

- Services to youth must focus on the whole person, which includes maintaining connection to school and other education programs, and relationship building with family, friends, and significant others.
- The majority of youth can receive appropriate services in non-residential community-based services. However, some require the more structured and intense supports offered by residential services.
- For all youth who require specialized substance-use services, access to other sectors of the health-care system must be available.
- This program will be identified as supportive recovery, and the youth will receive counselling, access to education, life-skills training, and family programming, with the aim of reintegrating the youth back into their own community.
- Staffing will be 24-hour/7-days a week awake care and will include cultural Elders and counsellors as well as life-skills workers.
- Youth will be assessed for their willingness to participate in the program to ensure that the services and supports can be delivered in this environment.

### Conclusion and Recommendations

- People with substance-use disorders are frequently marginalized in the mainstream health system.
- There is a gap in service in this region that can be met through a youth supportive residential home operated through a non-profit society.
- This service model has been used successfully in other jurisdictions.
- The executive director has been in touch with the neighbours. She is available to facilitate a community meeting to address concerns. This includes a plan for ongoing communication with them.
- As a long-time local provider of substance-use services in her community and region, it is recommended that she continue with the community meeting. She can then identify any further sensitive items for consultation. ■

## Reflections on Bob's Story

These briefing notes to the minister of social services attempted to summarize the underlying issues and make recommendations that certain actions be taken.

In the end, the community meeting did take place without outside political involvement. Most of the concerns were related to neighbourhood safety and house prices dropping. The former was addressed through a thorough explanation of the number of youth that would be in the home at any one time and the staffing levels.

The house opened in the fall. At Christmas time, the executive director (with the youth's consent) invited the neighbours in for an open house to meet everyone, enjoy some holiday treats, and continue the conversation. Following that open house, no further concerns were raised.

### From Theory to Practice

As you reflect on Bob's briefing notes, give some thought to the following points:

1. What is the role of politicians in the development of services to marginalized service groups? What is the role of bureaucrats? What is the role of local service providers?

2. How did Bob link the individual problem of substance use to a human rights perspective? Could this have been done differently?

3. How were community interests balanced with political interests in this situation? What are other ways this balance could have been achieved?

4. Do you think that the neighbours were sufficiently listened to and consulted, or were there other ways to get their participation?

5. What are ways of minimizing a "NIMBY" response?

6. How should a social worker respond to media requests about social protests?

### Canadian Charter of Rights and Freedoms

The *Canadian Charter of Rights and Freedoms* is a bill of rights entrenched in the Constitution of Canada. It forms the first part of the *Constitution Act*, 1982.

The Charter guarantees certain political and civil rights to everyone in Canada. It is designed to unify Canadians around a set of principles that embody those rights.

# Human Rights and Fundamental Freedoms

Challenging oppression wherever it exists is a key aspect of human rights practice. This includes treating individuals with respect and dignity and promoting practices that treat service users as individuals who are self-determining and have the ability to participate in decision-making that effects their lives.

Three important areas for social work practice in human rights are (1) freedom from discrimination, (2) freedom of gender identity and expression, and (3) freedom from violence and poverty.

### Freedom from Discrimination

The *Canadian Charter of Rights and Freedoms* is part of Canada's *Constitution Act*, 1982. The Charter protects every Canadian's right to be treated equally under the law. It guarantees broad equality rights and other fundamental rights, such as freedom of expression, freedom of assembly, and freedom from discrimination. The Charter's equality rights provisions prohibit government discrimination against populations such as the LGBTQ2S+ community and persons with disabilities. They also prohibit government discrimination in service provision (e.g., housing discrimination, employment discrimination).

Freedom from discrimination includes respecting cultural differences. For example, Ife (2008) argues that to understand "why an elderly person may resist the idea of moving into a nursing home, one needs to understand the cultural values around home, old age, family and institutional care in the particular experience of the elderly person her/himself" (p. 69). Similarly, to understand why a child may be missing school, why a woman is isolated and depressed in the family home, or why a young person becomes dependent on drugs, one must take into account cultural factors.

### Freedom of Gender Identity and Expression

In May 2016, Bill C-16 was introduced in the House of Commons to amend the *Canadian Human Rights Act* and the *Criminal Code* to protect individuals from being the targets of hate propaganda as a consequence of their gender identity or gender expression. In June 2017, the Senate passed this legislation, which applies to federal subjects (airports, banks, and the military) and regulated industries.

In most provinces and territories, "gender identity" is a prohibited ground for discrimination. In some provinces and territories, "gender expression" is also a prohibited ground for discrimination. For example, the Ontario Human Rights Commission (n.d.) has stated that "refusing to refer to a trans person by their chosen name and a personal pronoun that matches their gender identity ... will likely be discrimination when it takes place in a social area covered by the Code, including employment, housing and services like education" (para. 7).

The CASW (2017) applauded the passing of Bill C-16 and saw it as a starting point for the continuing advocacy for equity for trans, gender non-conforming, intersex and two-spirited persons with respect to safety and access to care and service. Indeed, Canada's laws in this area are now the most advanced in the world.

# Critical Theory and Human Rights
## A Participatory Approach

Ife and Tascón (2016) argue that human rights practice is an attractive idea to critical social workers because it implies a progressive approach. However, the authors suggest that while human rights can be a part of progressive social work, they can also be used to maintain traditional needs-based perspectives.

### Public and Private Domains

The rise of human rights occurred during modernity, meaning that our knowledge of human rights is associated with Western patriarchal epistemology and was developed in a top-down process defined by politicians, diplomats, bureaucrats, and academics (Ife & Tascón, 2016).

From a critical perspective, a narrow human rights approach adopts concepts of universality, favours civil and political rights over economic, social, and cultural rights, and focuses mainly on rights in the public domain. By contrast, freedom from violence, gender harassment, and other violations of women's rights tend to occur in private domains.

Ife and Tascón (2016) suggest that social workers have tended to adopt a human rights framework in a matter-of-fact way. Critical social work, on the other hand, uses a more developmental and participatory human rights perspective.

A critical perspective on human rights, Ife and Tascón (2016) argue, requires a broader view. This would begin with a dialogue of what constitutes "humanity," or the "human" who has rights. Conventional assumptions of human rights begin with the universality of humanity grounded in the European Enlightenment (individual, autonomous, young, able-bodied, male, secular, and disconnected from the natural world). Based on this understanding, critical social workers should explore with service users their alternative assumptions about humanity. In this approach, human rights would begin with an examination of service users' culture, life experience, and community norms and values.

### Critical Human Rights Practices

From this perspective, social work shouldn't simply apply human rights conventions. Instead, it should view human rights practice as

> dialogical and transformational, allowing people to articulate their dreams and aspirations located in a set of relationships that can be deemed as "local" and yet to also be imagined as recognizing their relationships to those outside their local space. (p. 29)

In short, human rights "can be seen as requiring people to be bound together in a community of rights and responsibilities" that take into account the immediate locality (Ife & Tascón, 2016, p. 29).

Ife and Tascón (2016) argue that human rights need to adopt and embody a diverse set of epistemologies and to recognize the different ways of understanding humanity.

Critical social workers can play a part in achieving a more dialogical (and inclusive) human rights approach by rejecting the top-down (deductive) approach to human rights practice and instead help to explore and validate other worldviews. ∎

## Freedom from Violence

Freedom from violence is an important human rights protection. Violence can take multiple forms, such as hate crimes, elder abuse, intimate partner violence, child abuse, and sexual assault. Gender-based violence occurs due to a normative understanding of what it means to be a girl or woman.

An area of particular concern is the appalling number of Indigenous women who are victims of racialized and sexualized violence (Brant, 2017). Several Canadian and international reports have highlighted the role of racism and misogyny in perpetuating violence against Indigenous women and the sharp disparities in the fulfillment of Indigenous women's economic, social, political, and cultural rights. In 2016, the "National Inquiry into Missing and Murdered Indigenous Women and Girls" was launched, with a $53 million budget.

Likewise, the #MeToo movement has elevated global awareness about sexual assault and harassment. Sexual harassment and assault are widespread. One of the goals of the movement is to expand the conversation to a broad spectrum of survivors, including young people; people who are LGBTQ2S+; people with disabilities; and women and girls of all communities of colour.

## Freedom from Poverty

Freedom from poverty means freedom from more than just economic deprivation. Poverty is a violation of human rights, as it "erodes or nullifies economic and social rights such as the right to health, adequate housing, food and safe water, and the right to education" (Office of the High Commissioner for Human Rights, 2018, para. 3).

In 2015, the Dignity for All campaign, an initiative by Citizens for Public Justice and Canada Without Poverty, released a model anti-poverty plan. This framework was developed following several years of intensive national consultation with activists and people with lived experiences from all sectors across the country. The plan is based on the principle of human rights and a sense of urgency. O'Leary and Majic (2018) summarized the four pillars of the plan as follows:

- **Comprehensive.** An anti-poverty strategy must involve policy in a minimum of six areas, including income security, housing and homelessness, health care, food security, employment, and early childhood education and care.

- **Rights-based.** An anti-poverty plan must address the most urgent needs immediately, particularly for those who are highly marginalized, including Indigenous communities, new immigrants and refugees, single-parent families, children, people with diverse abilities, and older adults. It must also set strong targets and timelines with a goal of ending poverty in Canada.

- **Legislated.** An anti-poverty strategy requires federal anti-poverty legislation that includes accountability mechanisms for review and evaluation, based in human rights.

- **Fully funded.** Adequate funding commitments must be made to support a robust and responsive anti-poverty strategy.

# Quebec's Anti-Poverty Strategy
## An Action Plan of Solidarity and Social Inclusion

Combatting poverty and social exclusion through the development of an anti-poverty plan is both a federal and provincial responsibility. However, it wasn't until July 2018 that the federal government released *Opportunity for All—Canada's First Poverty Reduction Strategy*. As of 2019, all provinces and territories have poverty-reduction strategies.

### Collective Action

Quebec has politicized anti-poverty for well over two decades. Following a long-term mobilization of social partners since the mid-1990s, Bill 112 was unanimously adopted into law in December 2002. According to Dufour (2011):

> Bill 112 instituted a "national strategy" to address poverty and social exclusion, including a consultative committee and a fund to finance new social initiatives. (p. 46)

Dufour (2011) has highlighted the favourable political context and opportunity for collective action unique to Quebec (among Canadian provinces) that led to the adoption of Bill 112.

In Quebec, state–society relationships are organized around dialogue between certain collective actors or "social partners," such as unions, business organizations, and community groups. These groups are recognized and supported within the provincial policy-making process, which allowed for the claims of community groups to be heard.

The adoption of Bill 112 was followed by a government action plan in 2004 and a second plan in 2010—*Quebec's Combat against Poverty: Government Action Plan for Solidarity and Social Inclusion, 2010–2015*. In December 2017, the Quebec government unveiled its *2017–2023 Action Plan to Foster Economic Inclusion and Social Participation* with the aim of having the fewest poor people among the industrialized nations by 2023. This goal is supported by a $3 billion investment (Government of Quebec, 2017).

### Group Advocacy

Poverty in Quebec is a complex, multidimensional social problem with high costs for society and negative repercussions in early childhood.

Dufour (2011) argues that collective group advocacy, and emphasis on the idea that poor people are the experts of their own situation, created a context for political change and the adoption of Bill 112.

Dufour (2011) notes that in Quebec,

> the public discourse on poverty has changed: poverty is not only a question of work or the will to work, it is a question of access to full citizenship and it is a responsibility shared by the individual and the collective. (p. 55)

Since the implementation of Bill 112 and the 2004 government action plan, there has been some notable reductions in poverty. On the other hand, the initiatives have not changed the lives of all poor people, particularly vulnerable lone adults, single mothers, and immigrant women (Dufour, 2011).

In the 2010–2015 plan, the Quebec government states the following:

> combatting poverty is a long-term endeavour that involves more than countering a lack of income or insufficient income. It also has to promote the social integration of all individuals, ensure their health and education, and exert pressure on many other determinants of poverty. (p. 9)

In the 2017–2023 plan, the Quebec government aims to have a fairer and more egalitarian society by fighting poverty and social exclusion. This plan includes the gradual implementation of a basic income for people with severe employment limitations. The plan seeks to improve the living conditions of many to help them truly take a place in Quebec society (Government of Quebec, 2017). ∎

# Social Justice and the Rights of Indigenous Peoples

Indigenous peoples in Canada have historically not been protected through human rights legislation. That changed in 2017, when section 67 of the *Canadian Human Rights Act* (CHRA) was repealed:

> First Nations individuals who are registered Indians and members of Bands, or individuals residing or working on reserves, can now make complaints of discrimination to the Canadian Human Rights Commission (CHRC) relating to decisions or actions arising from, or pursuant to the *Indian Act*. (Government of Canada, 2017, para. 3)

Increasingly, many issues that directly affect Indigenous peoples are being treated as human rights issues. Examples include land treaty rights (ownership rights over mineral deposits on First Nations land), environmental rights (rights to protect traditional land against oil spills and clear-cutting), and health-care rights (the right to safe drinking water on First Nations reserves).

Two further examples—where battles were fought and recently won (or at least partially won) on issues of human rights—are described below.

### The Human Rights Tribunal Rules on First Nations Child Welfare

In 2007, Cindy Blackstock, executive director of the First Nations Child and Family Caring Society, along with the Assembly of First Nations, filed a human rights complaint against Ottawa.

They argued that the support the federal government provides for child welfare on-reserve is much lower than the support provincial governments provide for child welfare off-reserve. This discrepancy exists even though the needs of children living on-reserve are much greater. Moreover, the result of less funding for family support services on-reserve is that more children end up in care. They also argued that the federal government's interpretation of Jordan's Principle was unlawful and discriminatory.

In January 2016, the Human Rights Tribunal ruled in favour of the Assembly of First Nations and the First Nations Child and Family Caring Society. The ruling was considered a major victory in the fight against inequities in child welfare across Canada (CASW, 2016).

The tribunal's decision stated that the federal government's funding model and management of its First Nations child and family services "resulted in denials of services and created various adverse impacts for many First Nations children and families living on reserves" (CBC, 2016).

The decision further stated that the government must "cease the discriminatory practice and take measures to redress and prevent it" (CBC, 2016). It also called for the redesign of the child welfare system and its funding model, urging the use of experts to ensure First Nations are given culturally appropriate services.

Cindy Blackstock told reporters that the decision was a "complete victory," not only for First Nations children, but "for children everywhere."

## Canada Finally Adopts the *United Nations Declaration on the Rights of Indigenous Peoples*

In 2007, the United Nations General Assembly adopted the *United Nations Declaration on the Rights of Indigenous Peoples* (UNDRIP). The UN declaration guarantees Indigenous peoples individual and collective rights, the right to enjoy and practice their cultures, customs, and languages, the right to live free of discrimination, and the right to self-determination under international law. The United Nations Secretary-General at the time described it as follows:

> a historic moment when UN member states and Indigenous Peoples have reconciled with their painful histories and are resolved to move forward together on the path of human rights, justice and development for all. (UN News, 2007, para. 9)

UNDRIP was 25 years in the making and saw 144 countries vote in its favour. Only four countries voted against it—the United States, New Zealand, Australia, and Canada.

In other words, Canada was slow off the mark. It was not until May 2016 that Canada finally dropped its "objector status" and formally stated its intention to implement UNDRIP in accordance with the Canadian Constitution. Minister of Crown-Indigenous Relations and Northern Affairs Carolyn Bennett told the United Nations that implementing the declaration wasn't something to be afraid of: "We have developed new, more flexible paths to the recognition of rights and jurisdiction and self-determination as well as new fiscal relationships" (Morin, 2017, para. 8).

Although just a formal statement, the final adoption of UNDRIP has far-reaching implications. For example, Chief Wilton Littlechild, who was a commissioner with the **Truth and Reconciliation Commission of Canada**, regards UNDRIP as a fundamental pillar to the commission's 94 calls to action.

> Sixteen of the 94 calls to action are about the UN declaration. The major call to various sectors of Canadian society is to adopt the UN declaration as a framework for reconciliation. It is about the survival, dignity and well-being of Indigenous Peoples; so implementing the UN declaration has the possibility of healing our peoples, strengthening relationships and promoting peaceful co-existence. (Morin, 2017, para. 27)

The Canadian government's eventual adoption of UNDRIP was a landmark moment for Indigenous rights in Canada. Nevertheless, many are dissatisfied with the progress to date in implementing the declaration. For example, Mi'kmaq lawyer, professor, and activist Pam Palmater said that there has been no tangible evidence so far that Canada is moving forward to implement the declaration.

> There can be no reconciliation unless the core articles of UNDRIP related to Indigenous self-determination, land ownership, implementation of treaty rights, and respect for Indigenous laws, governments and jurisdictions are part of the legal foundation of what is now Canada. (Morin, 2017, para. 29)

Palmater and other Indigenous leaders believe that full reconciliation with Indigenous peoples is impossible unless the federal government fully incorporates the declaration into law.

**United Nations Declaration on the Rights of Indigenous Peoples (UNDRIP)**

The United Nations describes UNDRIP as setting "an important standard for the treatment of Indigenous peoples that will undoubtedly be a significant tool towards eliminating human rights violations against the over 370 million Indigenous people worldwide and assisting them in combating discrimination and marginalization" (United Nations, 2007, para. 7).

**Truth and Reconciliation Commission of Canada**

The Truth and Reconciliation Commission of Canada was initially formed as part of the Residential Schools Settlement Agreement. Its purpose was to create a historical account of the residential schools to help people heal and to encourage reconciliation between Indigenous and non-Indigenous people in Canada (CBC, 2008). The commission concluded in 2015 with the release of 94 calls to action.

# Standing Up to Injustice
## Cindy Blackstock, Moral Courage, and the Importance of Self-Care

Cindy Blackstock is a passionate and tireless advocate for First Nations children's rights. She is the executive director of the First Nations Child and Family Caring Society of Canada and a professor in the School of Social Work at McGill University. She has received more than 50 awards and 10 honorary doctorates in addition to having two master's degrees (Management and Jurisprudence in Children's Law and Policy) and a PhD in social work (University of Toronto).

In 2018, Cindy was named one of the Women of the Year by *Chatelaine* magazine. She was featured for her tireless advocacy for First Nations children's rights (Chen, Grief, Philps, Pupo, & Rumack, 2018).

A member of the Gitxsan First Nation, Cindy Blackstock became a well-known activist in 2007 after filing a Canadian Human Rights Tribunal complaint against the federal government for the systemic discrimination of First Nations children in Canada.

Eventually, the Tribunal issued five orders requiring the federal government to properly fund First Nations agencies and family support programs, paying due account to the unique cultures and contexts of First Nations children. Despite this favourable ruling, Cindy's battle for social justice and equality for First Nations children continues.

In her frequent writings and interviews, Cindy provides insight into how she practises advocacy and self-care in the fight for justice for First Nations children.

### Standing Up for the Right Thing

Cindy Blackstock draws on Rushworth Kidder's (2003) work *Moral Courage* to explain the importance of social workers using moral courage to uplift children's lives rather than using moral cowardice, which diminishes children (Blackstock, 2011).

Kidder (2003) describes moral courage as consisting of five universal values: honesty, respect, responsibility, fairness, and compassion. The application of moral courage is consistent with the CASW *Code of Ethics*, First Nations traditional values and worldviews, and anti-oppressive social work practice.

Moral courage means standing up for principles, values, and higher-order beliefs. The morally courageous person stands up for the "right thing," even when it goes against the grain, and negative repercussions can be anticipated. Moral courage takes values from the theoretical realm to the practical, from thought to action. According to Kidder (2003), without moral courage, officials will not act on their own values.

Cindy underscores the importance of standing up against the bureaucracy for the right thing, even if it means risking one's job. She argues that the risks of conforming are generally borne by service users rather than social workers or bureaucrats.

### Moral Courage and Social Work Practice

Cindy describes "moral courage" as a person's ability to do the right thing in the face of negative consequences for themselves. She notes:

> [The moral right] is measured by whether social work does the right thing for people beyond close circles of self-interest and relationships when it knows better and can do better. It is one thing to stand up for yourself or for those you love, but it takes an uncommon level of courage to stand up for people you do not know and that is exactly the type of moral courage that child welfare needs in abundance. (Blackstock, 2011, p. 36)

In an interview with Kharoll-Ann Souffrant (2019), an Arts student ambassador at McGill University, Cindy explains that she was born with a sense of responsibility, passed down through her family, to stand up to injustice. She describes relying on role models, both Indigenous and non-Indigenous, who were generous in telling her when she was going down the wrong path. While she says there is no clear plan for how to address injustice, saying something is better than being silent and still: "We know how that turns out—injustices of all scales are enabled by silence."

In a 2017 interview with *The Globe and Mail,* Cindy said, "I don't give power to negative forces. I've never been someone who dwells on barriers … I only keep focused on what we need, which is these children having a positive childhood" (Wattie, 2017).

In a subsequent op-ed in *The Globe and Mail,* Cindy wrote the following:

> after more than 30 years of seeing the over-representation of First Nations children and youth in child welfare, I know one thing for sure: Unless the public puts pressure on provincial, territorial, and federal government, the good solutions on the books will not be implemented. We must tell our politicians: literally thousands of children need our help. (Blackstock, 2019)

Cindy describes the importance of building social activism and social justice movements on love. "I think too many people base their movements off of anger or sadness" (Souffrant, 2019). She adds that the only way to defeat the darkness is with love and light, and in peaceful ways.

## The Importance of Self-Care

Cindy is fearless in her moral courage. Despite being spied on by the federal government, and the federal government spending millions of dollars fighting against her in front of the Canadian Human Rights Commission, Cindy has remained remarkably humble and down to earth.

Cindy admits that there have been tough times—times when the work bleeds into home, when dark days take over the light, and when injustice is a hard pill to swallow. Through all of these tough times, she describes taking care of her self every single day and knowing when it's time to book off and be on her own. She says:

> "I just need days by myself; I call them 'days of infinite possibilities.' … Long walks and chats with friends and family, shopping and home repairs take [me] away from an intense schedule. Even in difficult times, I just try to put it all in perspective, you know? I am a big believer in Cheezies and bath bombs, … It's my release." (Wattie, 2017) ∎

Photo courtesy of Cindy Blackstock

# Social Worker Exemplar

# Activism for Health Justice

R.J. Fisher

**Social activism is about finding ways to help opposing groups find some common ground so that they can unite and fight together. It takes patience and relationship-building skills.**

R.J. was graduating from a BSW program when he experienced deteriorating personal health. His life went into a downward spiral until he discovered the likely cause of his illness.

In this story, R.J. shares how he and others were able to come together and use social media to fight back against the unfair treatment of people with health conditions such as his own.

R.J. completed his BSW and is now working as a community social worker.

In the fourth year of my social work program, I was living in a mouldy home and began to experience severe health issues (extreme fatigue, migraines, swelling of the hands and feet, full and itchy body rash, and nerve pain). I was losing my vision, and my ears rang so loud that I would cry myself to sleep. Because of the mould, I was forced to abandon all of my belongings and the home I was living in. This resulted in me sleeping outside for 27 days straight and being homeless in my final year of university.

At the same time, coincidentally, my fourth-year practicum involved teaching life skills to adults in the community who are at risk for homelessness. I can honestly say that this was the most humbling experience I've ever had.

As my illness progressed, I became more and more disabled. As a result, I began accessing medical services (walk-in clinics, hospitals, specialists, etc.) on a regular basis, but was constantly told that the symptoms were "all in my head." After being transported by ambulance from my practicum after an episode of fainting and vomiting, my white blood count was identified as 10 times higher than normal. Again, I was told that it was nothing and to go home and rest. I was losing hope and felt like giving up on my health, my schooling, and my life.

I eventually made my way to a naturopath in Vancouver, and she started connecting all of my symptoms and my medical history. After out-of-country testing showed a distinct set of multisystemic symptoms, a clinical diagnosis of Lyme disease and co-infections was established.

Little did I know that Lyme disease was controversial. Doctors are taught that chronic Lyme doesn't exist, and psychiatric diagnoses are frequently used to undermine those suffering from this disabling disease. For so many years, I had thought I was some sort of anomaly. I had faced ongoing abuse and marginalization by health professionals and suffered through multiple mental health diagnoses.

I spent the next year studying the science of Lyme spirochetes. The scientific language was a little foreign to me (I come from a social work background), so I had to seek out help in order to understand the body of evidence around Lyme disease.

## Building Relationships and Empowering People

I have come to see how political and medical structures have made the formal diagnosis of Lyme disease costly and difficult, and how this resulted in a paucity of treatment options. I found multiple examples of flawed, contradictory, and repudiated research on the disease, some of which was associated with the highly political Centers for Disease Control and Prevention (CDC) in the United States. In short, I now see Lyme disease as a social justice issue that marginalizes people in favour of the powerful medical and political establishment.

Through Facebook and Twitter, I joined up with an army of thousands of activists in the fight against Lyme disease and co-infections. Both Facebook and Twitter are empowering tools for disabled activists, as they help us contribute to the cause in a meaningful way in the comfort of our own homes. Together, we have produced blogs and made posters that have been shared more than 100,000 times. We have begun collaborating on contacting government officials, educating the public, and working tirelessly to unite the many groups that are determined to win this war on their own.

After spending a year in what I call "Lymeland," I started to understand that what I learned in school about activism is much different from my experience. Many classes on activism showed people coming together easily to fight a cause. However, bringing people together is not easy. It takes not only patience, but also hours of work to build relationships with multiple opposing groups. Respecting diversity is essential, of course. However, it too can be challenging. At times, factors such as religion and personal choice can become roadblocks to uniting.

Although activism gives me hope and purpose, it does not come without a cost. Each day, we Lyme activists are victims of verbal and emotional abuse. Activism also takes a toll. I am forced now and then to step back and take breaks in order to support my own well-being. ■

## Reflections on R.J.'s Story

In this story, R.J. shares his experiences with the health-care system. He describes the importance of building relationships and empowering people who have shared experiences in order to effect social change.

R.J. points to the new power of social media in helping to bring people together. He notes that it is important to be diplomatic, yet firm and persistent, when attempting to create any kind of change in the system. For him, it is not a race, it is a drawn-out marathon.

### From Theory to Practice

As you reflect on R.J.'s story, give some thought to the following points:

1. In this situation, social justice is equated with health justice. How would you describe health justice?

2. R.J.'s activism has centred on social media. What are the advantages and disadvantages of using social media for activism?

3. R.J.'s remarks suggest that being an activist is challenging, with many ups and downs. What traits do you have that would make you a good activist?

4. How could you be an ally in the fight against Lyme disease and co-infections?

5. R.J.'s research indicated that political and medical structures were influencing individual care and attention to those with Lyme disease. Identify another example in which political and economic factors negatively influence the quality and delivery of health or social care.

# Practice Scenarios

Adopting a human rights and social justice lens to practice requires reframing individual issues as a social issue. It requires understanding the structures, policies, and processes that deny an individual (or a group of individuals) access to fair and equitable opportunities, services, and freedoms. Based on this perspective, a person's needs and problems are viewed not as individual issues but as an infringement of human rights and a social justice issue.

In these practice situations, consider your initial micro response to needs, and then rework the situation based on a human rights and social justice lens. Which rights are being denied? How are freedoms being mitigated? What can be done?

---

## 9.1 Social Justice & Violence against Sex Workers

You are working as an outreach worker with sex workers. Over the last three months, two different women have told you about a prominent local lawyer who has been picking them up and demanding that they perform degrading and violent acts. These acts went far beyond "rough sex." When the women told the man that they were not willing to perform the acts he requested, he told them that they had better comply, and not report it, or he would talk with his "friends" and have them arrested. He then told them there would be no lenience for them in his courtroom.

1. What are the human rights and social justice issues here? Are they being infringed upon?

2. Is freedom from sexual violence a human rights issue for sex workers? Why or why not?

3. For the individual women who came forward, how do you implement an approach that respects their experience as a violation of human rights?

4. Your organization has a micro-level role with sex workers. However, is there a role for broader social justice advocacy? How could that be initiated?

## 9.2 Access to Health Care for the Homeless

You are working in a shelter for homeless people. Kara, a 45-year-old woman who has been living there for a year, recently met with you to talk about her health concerns.

Kara has been diagnosed with breast cancer. She had a previous experience with cancer seven years before, which was successfully treated. Her doctor has told Kara that she was unwilling to begin chemotherapy, even though that is the preferred treatment, because Kara's living situation at the homeless shelter wasn't sufficiently stable as a recovery environment.

1.  What human rights are being denied to Kara? What social justice issues does this scenario raise?

2.  If you were a social worker at the hospital this doctor works at, how would you advocate for Kara and people like Kara?

3.  Precarious housing is correlated with poor health outcomes. As a social work advocate, how could this issue be highlighted? What would be your recommendations for housing and health policies nationally and provincially?

## 9.3 Accessing Complaints Processes

You are working in a community counselling office. A young man with diagnosed post-traumatic stress disorder has been denied income-assistance benefits. He was given a pamphlet on the process for disputing the decision. However, he has no trust that he has any hope of overcoming the bureaucratic government system. In addition, he feels emotionally overwhelmed and unable to complete the paperwork and advocate for himself.

1.  Is having a complaints mechanism consistent or inconsistent with a human rights and social justice perspective?

2.  In your role as a social worker, you will frequently be asked to assist with a complaints process against a person or an organization who forms a part of your professional network. How would you balance the rights of service users to complain about decisions and your professional collegial relationships?

3.  As a registered social worker, you are susceptible to being the subject of a complaint by a service user. What do you think of complaints processes that may require you to be accountable for a complaint against you?

# Field Education Practicalities
## Ending Relationships Successfully

Endings are important, and they can be as anxiety provoking as the beginning and middle stages of a professional relationship.

Students in field education are encouraged to be professional in all their relationships with service users and other members in the agency.

This professionalism must continue in the ending phase of the experience as well.

During the last two or three weeks in an agency, it is important to remind service users that you are there as a student and will be leaving soon. This is a time to remain service user-centred and reflect on the strengths and growth that you have seen in those individuals you have been working with. It is also an important time to talk about transitions. Who will be continuing the work that you have been doing?

### Ending Relationships with Service Users

Some service users may be sad or fearful to learn that you are leaving, while others may re-experience a feeling of loss or trauma in their lives. It is important to be sensitive to service users' concerns and to highlight the strengths you have identified with them. The communication skills of summarization are important in this phase.

Many service users will want to wish you well in your studies and your career. In this final phase, students will again be challenged to make ethical decisions. A service user may want to give you a small gift. Anticipate this, and ensure that you are aware of the agency policy around receiving gifts.

In general, small tokens of appreciation (e.g., cookies, a handmade gift, a card) can be graciously accepted. However, agency policies may differ, and all students should inform their agency supervisor of any gifts and the value of that gift, regardless of its monetary value.

Occasionally, a service user will want to give a gift after the student has left the agency. In general, it is recommended that the service user leave any messages or gifts at the agency or with another worker in order to avoid ongoing entanglements (Royse, Dhooper, & Lewis Rompf, 2012, p. 110).

Of course, it is also common for students and social workers to experience some feelings of sadness or loss at the end of their time at an agency or when a service user no longer attends sessions. These feelings are normal and suggest that positive relationships have been developed. However, despite those feelings, it is unethical to engage in a personal relationship with a service user when the initial involvement was professional.

### Ending the Relationship with an Agency

In most cases, by the end of the field education experience, students have developed a strong and meaningful relationship with the agency's staff and supervisors. Many agency supervisors will talk about their learning and growth as a result of having a student with them.

Throughout the experience, students have been encouraged to be professional in their interactions with others in the agency. The ending phase also requires professionalism. This agency may provide future employment, a job reference, or become part of your networking team as you continue in your professional career. Ending on a positive note is important.

In some agencies, there may be a small celebration over lunch, or you may want to ask one or two key people to have coffee or lunch with you in order to thank them privately. The ending is a time to thank your supervisor and agency's staff, to let them know a little about what you have learned and how it will support your career goals, and to ask for permission for a reference. Also clarify how a reference could be provided (for example, do they need to be informed each time, would they prefer to provide something in writing, or would it be acceptable for you to use them as a reference freely?).

It is important, as you share your debriefing with your agency supervisor (either informally or formally), that you identify areas that you have grown in, and experiences that you have found meaningful. The university is very likely to use this agency again, and the agency is an important and integral part of the field education team. Although you are continuing on to new adventures, this agency will likely welcome another student and be a central part of that student's social work development.

Your ethical obligations to the agency continue after you leave. The need to maintain service user confidentiality is obvious. However, you are also responsible for maintaining agency confidentiality on any agency issues/strategies/or practices that are not common knowledge. For example, occasionally, students learn of practices that may be under investigation by the police or regulatory boards. It is irresponsible to spread gossip throughout the community (Royse, et al., 2012, p. 118).

### Final Evaluation of the Student in Placement

In general, social work programs have a process in place for the final evaluation with students. The final evaluation tends to follow a similar format to the midpoint assessment. Usually, the final evaluation is attended by the student, the field supervisor, and the faculty liaison. In order to prepare for the final evaluation, students should ensure that they have all the appropriate materials prepared. Materials will likely include a written overview of learning and a tabulation of completed hours. However, students should check their program's requirements.

During the final evaluation, there should be no surprises. It is a time to review the student's strengths and the skills the student learned during placement. It may also include a discussion of future career or educational goals.

### Final Evaluation of the Agency

Students are usually asked to provide an evaluation of the agency, which will be used by the program for future decision-making. These evaluations should be written professionally; that is, comments should be specific and clear. Even if there have been some negative experiences, it is helpful to identify clearly what could have been done differently and acknowledge any contextual factors (e.g., staff turnover, internal challenges, external funding pressures).

Even though some of these evaluations may be anonymous, and sometimes the agency supervisors do not see them, any professional documentation should always be written with transparency in mind. The question to ask yourself is whether you are willing to be accountable for your evaluation of the agency— that is, whether you are prepared to stand behind and defend what you have said, even if there were to be an investigation? ■

# Reflection, Learning, and More Practice

## Field Education Practicalities

1. Begin the preparation for ending your field education by preparing service users you have been working with.

2. Identify the field agency policy on receiving parting gifts from services users.

3. Prepare for the final evaluation by reviewing any revised documents from the midpoint assessment.

4. Prepare examples in areas of competency that you have developed during the last stage of the field education.

## Journal Ideas

1. Identify how some issues faced by service users in your field site could just as easily be constructed as human rights concerns. What would this "reframing" look like?

2. Identify a social justice concern in your community and explain how you would approach it from a human rights perspective.

3. Describe how a human rights perspective could be used in a situation from practicum. This may include identifying challenges and making recommendations for policy or practice change.

4. Identify how some of the practices you are using in your field agency could be constructed as human rights practices. In other words, how are they consistent with the UDHR principles?

## Critical-Thinking Questions

1. Describe the association between human rights to minimal security entitlements and the population served by your field agency.

2. Identify one way your agency is implementing a human rights perspective, and describe one improvement that could be made in this area.

3. Describe some of the social structures that represent barriers to human and civil rights in your local community or region. How could these barriers be circumvented or overcome?

4. The CASW and the IFSW regularly release statements that highlight human rights abuses. Do you think that this an appropriate role for these organizations? As a member of these organizations, what is your role in supporting such initiatives to raise awareness of and combat such abuses?

5. Human rights practice in social work programs is traditionally taught using a deductive approach. How could the discourse change to use an inductive approach towards identifying the denial of human rights underlying individual needs and problems?

6. Review an area of human rights and investigate the policies that promote or protect these rights in your province or territory.

7. Examine the poverty-reduction strategy in your province or territory. What are the strengths of the strategy, and what is missing?

8. How well is your province or territory addressing the underfunding of First Nations child welfare on reserves? Identify areas of strength and weakness.

# Chapter Review

Advocating for human rights and social justice requires social workers to not only consider unmet "needs" but to also find ways to pressure governments to take responsibility for denying human rights. Every day, social workers see the effects of food, housing, and income insecurity on individual well-being. As key participants in the promotion and protection of human rights, social workers can become more consciously active in identifying and advocating for ways to build on individual case solutions to influence policy change.

A human rights perspective can be implemented by ensuring equitable service for underserved communities, assessing social needs from the perspective of social injustice, ensuring service users understand their rights to participation in decision-making, including access to complaint mechanisms, and being alert to discriminatory or abusive practices in society.

Human rights and social justice are about respect and dignity, and combatting all forms of discrimination and violence. Taking on this work as an individual is daunting. However, there is power in the collective, particularly when those most affected are empowered to have a public voice. Today, social media are changing social justice advocacy, as R.J. discovered in his fight to improve the formal diagnosis and treatment options of Lyme disease and co-infections.

As your term in field education is ending, it is a good time to consider your commitment to human rights and social justice advocacy. The nature of your social activism will likely be related to experiences you have had in a particular practicum, or other causes that you are familiar with, or have experience of.

## Advocating for Human Rights and Social Justice in Practice

This chapter outlines numerous ways in which students can provide competent services using a human rights and social justice framework. Here are some highlights and further suggestions:

- Reframe individual issues of need into a social justice framework that recognizes denied rights.

- Practise using a non-hierarchal and non-discriminatory approach to considering service users' experiences.

- Become involved in national rights movements such as women's rights, anti-poverty strategies, rights for people with diverse abilities, and gender fluid rights.

- Incorporate cultural rights and understandings into all social work practices.

- Participate in local political policy initiatives that address human rights and social justice issues.

- Build relationships with multiple stakeholders, both in favour of, and opposed to, a particular initiative.

- Develop capacity in using social media and responding to perspectives and comments using a social work perspective.

- Speak out against the racial discrimination of Indigenous peoples in Canada.

- Commit to courageous practice and press for better services, even when doing so may be considered "rocking the boat."

# Engaging in Research, Policy Analysis, and System Change

## 10

> *A world of peace is one that is human-centred and genuinely democratic; that builds and protects sustainable development, equity, and justice.*
>
> —**Douglas Roche,** *The Politics of Hope,* Address to the dinner given by Her Honour, Lois Hole, Lieutenant-Governor of Alberta, in 2004

# Chapter at a Glance

# Spotlight on Social Work Luminaries
## Mary Two-Axe Earley

**Mary Two-Axe Earley** (1911–1996) championed equal rights for First Nations women. Born on a Mohawk reserve in Kahnawake, Quebec, Two-Axe Earley lost her "Indian" status after marrying a non-Indigenous man. In 1966, she began lobbying to amend the *Indian Act*. In 1985, Parliament enacted Bill C-31, which removed discrimination against First Nations women from the *Indian Act*.

Social work practice is informed by social policy and scholarly research, and the profession itself also contributes to new knowledge and research. Social work students are required to develop competence in research and policy analysis, and participate in system change. Front-line workers have multiple opportunities to develop these competencies in everyday practice.

Engaging in research, conducting policy analysis, and participating in organizational and system change are practice competencies that lay a foundation for future leadership in the profession and society at large. Field education provides an excellent opportunity for students to begin to develop such skills. This chapter outlines strategies to incorporate these skills as a standard part of competency development.

## Developing Competence as a Social Worker

Some ways to develop the meta-competencies of "**engaging in research and research-based practice**," "**conducting policy analysis and development**," and "**participating and leading organizational and societal system change**" are as follows:

- Review the policy associated with a large system such as health care, child welfare, or criminal justice in your jurisdiction. Look at one specific area of service delivery and link it to policy and research.

- Examine the knowledge-utilization activities and strategies in a large health-care, child welfare, or criminal justice system.

- Identify a research project or policy practice initiative that could be undertaken in an area of practice that is of special interest to you.

- Examine and evaluate the decision-making processes for organizational and system change that have been developed in your field agency.

**Key Concepts**

- Knowledge utilization
- Practice researcher
- Policy practice
- Social policy research
- Canadian Association of Social Workers advocacy
- Policy advocacy
- Health justice
- Human service organizations (HSOs)

# A Role for Research in Social Work

Social work research generally aims to create new knowledge in order to address pressing social problems. It might include evaluating the effectiveness of social work services and programs, demonstrating the relative costs and benefits of social work services, or analyzing the impact of legislation and social policy.

As consumers of research, social workers are increasingly being asked to be accountable through the use of evidence-based (or evidence-informed or evidence-guided) practice. However, despite the emphasis on the integration of research and practice, sound research evidence seldom informs social work decision-making (Heinsch, Gray, & Sharland, 2016; Hewson, Walsh, & Bradshaw, 2010). There are multiple reasons for this disconnect. They include negative stereotypes about research among social work students and practitioners, arguments that evidence-based practice is too linear and non-reflective, a lack of agreement about what constitutes "evidence," and insufficient time in daily practice to integrate research and practice (Hewson et al., 2010; Wells, Maschi, & Slater, 2012).

### Knowledge Utilization

Increasingly, the term "**knowledge utilization**" is being used in social work to describe the relationship between research and practice (Heinsch et al., 2016). Knowledge utilization emphasizes the need for collaboration between researchers and practitioners. The idea is that cooperative research is likely to lead to more relevant and usable knowledge. In this sense, knowledge is a co-creation process, and knowledge utilization is not a simple "transfer" or application of scientifically and systemically produced research findings.

Social work research has many purposes. Shaw (2012) describes the main ones as follows:

- Generating or enhancing theory and knowledge about social work and social care
- Providing impartial evidence about and for decision-making
- Instrumentally improving practice and organizational learning
- Highlighting the quality of lived experience and advancing practice wisdom
- Promoting justice, social change, and social inclusion

Traditionally, knowledge dissemination has been about communicating evidence gained from research findings. This has been a one-way process. The close collaboration between researchers and practitioners involved in knowledge utilization improves practice and also advances overall knowledge and understanding in the field.

# Accreditation and Regulatory Requirements
## Engaging in Research, Policy Analysis and Development, and System Change

Social workers use research to inform practice, make social policy, and reorganize administrative systems to make them more effective. The core principles of participation, inclusion, and combatting social oppression underscore these initiatives.

### CASWE-ACFTS *Standards for Accreditation*

The sixth, seventh, and eighth core learning objectives in the the CASWE-ACFTS *Standards for Accreditation* (Canadian Association for Social Work Education–Association canadienne pour la formation en travail social [CASWE-ACFTS], 2014) state:

6. Engage in research

i) Social work students acquire knowledge and skills to critique, apply, or participate in social work research.

ii) Social work students at both levels of university education are prepared to apply social work knowledge, as well as knowledge from other disciplines, to advance professional practice, policy development, research, and service provision.

iii) MSW students acquire knowledge and skills in conducting social work research and competence in evaluating professional practices.

7. Participate in policy analysis and development

i) Social work students have knowledge of social policies in relation to the well-being of individuals, families, groups, and communities in Canadian and global contexts.

ii) Social work students have knowledge and skills to identify negative or inequitable policies and their implications and outcomes, especially for disadvantaged and oppressed groups, and to participate in efforts to change these.

iii) MSW students have knowledge and skills to contribute to the development and implementation of new and more equitable social policies.

8. Engage in organizational and societal systems' change through professional practice

i) Social work students acquire knowledge of organizational and societal systems and acquire skills to identify social inequalities, injustices, and barriers, and work towards changing oppressive social conditions.

ii) Social work students develop ability to critically assess the social, historical, economic, legal, political, institutional, and cultural contexts of social work practice at local, regional, provincial, national, and international levels.

iii) MSW students are prepared to take leadership roles in organizational and societal systems, and to work towards changing oppressive social conditions.

### Professional Regulation and Competency

The Canadian Council of Social Work Regulators (CCSWR, 2012) competency profile includes a competency block advocating for the improvement of policies and services to better meet service users' needs. It includes assessing the adequacy of existing policies, advocating for system change, and working with existing and emerging community organizations.

### Association of Social Work Boards (ASWB)

The ASWB entry-to-practice examination includes questions in the following areas related to research, policy-making, and program evaluation:

- Research ethics (e.g., institutional review boards, use of human subjects, informed consent)
- Concepts of social policy development and analysis
- The impact of the political environment on policy-making
- The impact of the environment (e.g., social, physical, cultural, political, economic) on individuals, families, groups, and communities
- Methods to create, implement, and evaluate policies and procedures that minimize risk for individuals, families, groups, organizations, and communities. ■

# Becoming a Practice Researcher

As a part of their program, social work students are typically required to complete research courses to ensure that they graduate with an understanding of how to evaluate the rigour of research studies and undertake research in their own practice. However, due to the many demands on their time, few students expand their research skills during field education.

### Engaging in Social Work Research

Little research has been undertaken to identify ways for social work students to enhance their research capacities in order to become effective **practice researchers**. The following studies from three countries shed some light on students' views on the utility and benefits of research in field education.

- **New Zealand.** In a study by Gibbs and Stirling (2013), student social workers in New Zealand thought research should be an integral part of everyday practice "in an ideal world." However, they also felt that time demands and financial constraints might mean that such research would need to be completed by those outside the agency. They also expressed the view that social work research was more than just collecting and analyzing information—it was about providing the best possible services and about linking social problems to social change. In terms of their own practice, "student social workers believed in collaborative, practice-oriented social work research with a strong values-based framework aimed at improving social work practice and client outcomes" (p. 325).

- **Canada.** Hewson et al. (2010) studied a research-based practicum program at the University of Calgary for both BSW and MSW students. The students in this study wanted to strengthen their research skills and develop a better understanding of research, deepen their knowledge of the field, enhance their curriculum vitae, and improve their chances of being accepted into a master's program. At the end of their field education, the students stated that practicum had helped in "providing exposure and building skills that would be useful to them in future projects and positions; allowing experiences that were new and completely different from previous practice; making them more comfortable with research and evaluation; encouraging the integration of theory learned in the classroom into practice situations" (p. 11). The students also stressed the relevance of the practicum in terms of applying for an MSW program, securing students grants, and applying for a research-based position in a non-profit agency.

- **United States.** Finally, Lyman et al. (2015) undertook a qualitative study of a BSW program that integrated research and practice in field education at Shippensburg University in Pennsylvania. The students in the study "produced qualitative and quantitative research whose results were germane and helpful to their field agencies. The research effort gave them satisfaction, and enabled them to finish their undergraduate program with success and move on to positive career paths" (p. 6).

## Practice-Based Research Methods

Social workers in practice may engage in research in different ways. In some cases, the research is characterized as "academic-partnership" (or traditional) research, and in other cases it is more "practitioner-led" (Shaw & Lunt, 2018). Uggerhøj (2011) describes these two approaches, with a third approach, "practice research," occuring in a middle space.

- **Traditional research.** This research method involves a close collaboration between the practitioner and the researcher, with the final responsibility for defining the research questions resting with the researcher and a research institution. This type of research is practice-based, but theory-driven.

- **Practitioner research.** This research method involves practitioners carrying out research alongside other practice responsibilities. The practitioners are active researchers, and the practice setting itself becomes, in effect, the research institution (Uggerhøj, 2011).

- **Practice research.** Practice research is a more iterative process, located in the middle ground between traditional research and practitioner research. Practice research is directly connected to increasing the performance of everyday practice. As Uggerhøj (2011) notes, in this type of research, "the research question cannot be generated without connecting it to actual problems in practice [. . .] and new questions cannot be generated without connecting and involving explanations, reflections, actions, improvement and new problems from practice" (p. 52). Uggerhøj goes on to state that practice research "is both part of traditional research processes and part of processes in practice and can easily include practitioner research or research light—but it has its own position between research in social work and practice" (p. 53).

**Figure 10.1** Practice-Based Research Methods

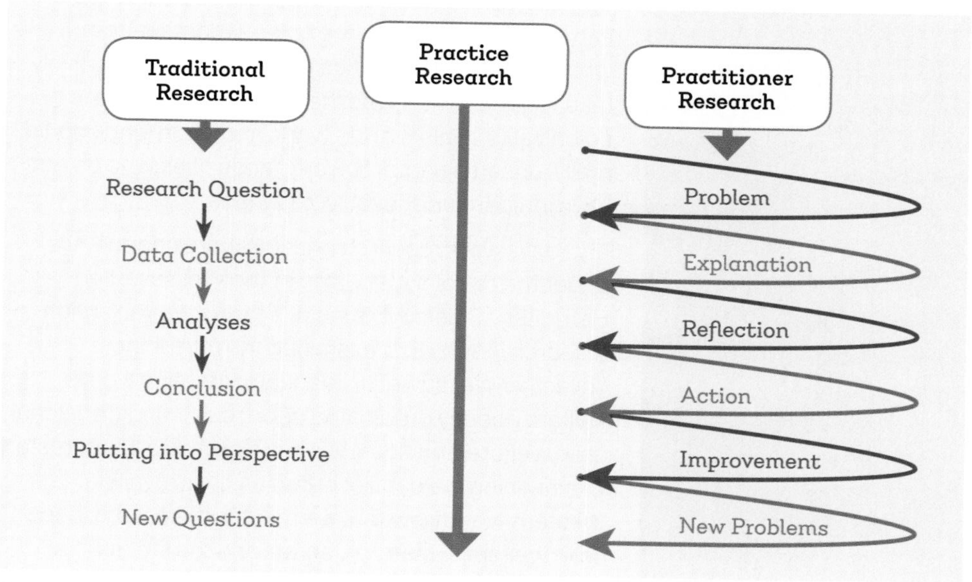

**Source:** Adapted from Uggerhøj (2011).

# Social Worker Exemplar

## Being a Practice Researcher

### Gretchen Woodman

**Good social research can be highly political. Policy practitioners who blend scholarly research with knowledge gained from real-life experience can be agents of effective, innovative, and much-needed social change.**

Gretchen Woodman spent 12 years working in provincial child welfare before accepting an invitation in 2012 from the Wet'suwet'en Hereditary Chiefs to join their expanding child and family wellness initiative.

Her first major project with the Wet'suwet'en was completed within the context of her master's degree. Her subsequent research has built upon that foundation and has focused on expanding the community's wellness initiative. More recently, she has participated with the Wet'suwet'en people in their negotiations with British Columbia and Canada to transfer jurisdiction of child welfare back to the Wet'suwet'en.

The scholar–practitioner professors at graduate school caught my attention and inspired my thinking about what it could mean to be both a practitioner and a researcher in the field of social work. A lively iterative cycle between theory and real-world practice is what interests me most. How can conceptual models and theory inform practice, and how can practice inform conceptual models and theory development?

In my experience, most social work researchers are so busy researching that they don't have time to practise what they are writing about. As a result, sometimes there can be a disconnect between theory and real-world practice. Similarly, most practitioners are so immersed in practice that they don't have time to reflectively write about what they are doing. As a result, sometimes practice can become stuck in habitual patterns (the "how" and "what") where bigger structural questions (the "why"), can go unasked. For me, good social work requires that we constantly ask "why?"

Blending scholarly knowledge with experiential knowledge can create urgently needed social change. This approach is particularly relevant in First Nations contexts, given the privileging of Western epistemologies in theory and practice. In the context of Indigenous child welfare to Canada, a critical examination of social justice involves confronting both the colonial past and the present. Good research can both acknowledge the colonial context from which social work practice has emerged and actively take steps to ameliorate the negative impacts of colonization. This is gritty work, and it can (and should, really) unsettle us, particularly those of us who do not have Indigenous ancestry to Canada.

My social work research projects were conducted under the direct supervision of the Wet'suwet'en Hereditary Chiefs. My master's thesis was an action research inquiry that examined the role of the collective Wet'suwet'en identity in creating a child welfare agency predicated upon reclaiming traditional child welfare practices. We were particularly interested in examining the conflict between the prevailing Western worldview that permeates the established child welfare system in Canada and the Indigenous worldview of the Wet'suwet'en.

### Reclaiming Indigenous Control over Child Welfare

The second major research project I was involved with was a participatory action research study involving over 200 Wet'suwet'en members. The aim was to articulate a distinctly Wet'suwet'en holistic conceptual wellness framework.

The Hereditary Chiefs oversaw this research project, and it took over a year to complete. I was the head researcher, and my job was to collect data in the form of one-on-one interviews with Elders and Chiefs, and numerous focus groups including youth, front-line workers, and local and urban Wet'suwet'en members. The raw data were brought back to the Chiefs to make meaning of it, which involved clustering ideas into themes until the framework emerged.

As a result, the Wet'suwet'en Wellness Conceptual Framework has now replaced the Delegated Aboriginal Agency model previously imposed by Canada (and up until recently the only vehicle by which First Nations in Canada could exert any control over child welfare practices for their people).

This is a significant step forward for the Wet'suwet'en in terms of transferring the jurisdiction of child welfare back to the Wet'suwet'en community. ■

### The Office of the Wet'suwet'en

Governed by the Wet'suwet'en Hereditary Chiefs, the Office of the Wet'suwet'en provides a range of services throughout the First Nation's 22,000 square kilometres of traditional territories in northwest British Columbia, spanning responsibility for human and social services, lands and resources, fisheries and wildlife, and governance.

The Wet'suwet'en have been negotiating with the Government of Canada and the Province of British Columbia to reclaim the right to provide child welfare services to their vulnerable children, youth, and families since 1989. In October 2018, a tripartite agreement was signed recognizing the Wet'suwet'en authority and jurisdiction for child and family services.

## Reflections on Gretchen's Story

Gretchen adopted a practice research model to effect social change. Her collaborative approach honoured and respected Indigenous worldviews. Moreover, her research occurred alongside community Elders and members. She has described herself primarily as a facilitator and "scribe" in the research process, rather than an "expert."

The outcome of her research has been daily practice changes that involve a holistic approach to wellness, and policy change that may have national implications.

### From Theory to Practice

As you reflect on Gretchen's story, give some thought to the following points:

1. Gretchen had a background in the provincial child-protection system. What adaptations to her practice would likely have occurred as she began working with the Wet'suwet'en people?

2. Although her master's research was governed by a traditional research institution, she was working as an "insider" with the Elders. What may be some of the tensions she experienced as a practice researcher governed by requirements such as a traditional ethics approval process?

3. How can some of the principles Gretchen used here be adapted and incorporated into your practice and context?

4. Gretchen says, "This is gritty work, and it can (and should, really) unsettle us." What do you think she means by that?

5. Gretchen outlines her experiences as a practice researcher. Identify a place or problem in your practice that would be amenable to this approach.

# Shaping Policy Outcomes for Canadians

**Social policy research** provides the knowledge that informs and influences the policy-making process. It is the cornerstone of social work's advocacy for social justice.

Social workers may engage in policy research and **policy practice** at the local, regional, or national level. Their efforts may include lobbying for professional interest groups, working with others to resolve government policy problems, participating in a demonstration protesting a government policy, or participating in a hearing or inquiry on a policy matter (Weiss-Gal & Peled, 2009).

### Research for Policy Change: Four Examples

Weiss-Gal (2016) reviewed the literature on policy practice and found a "growing consensus that policy practice is a form of practice that should be adopted by all social workers and not only by a limited group of policy specialists, and consequently should be infused into all social work programmes" (p. 299). Weiss-Gal suggests that policy practice education should focus on experiential learning and hands-on assignments. As well, it should include opportunities to engage in policy processes. Policy practice should be viewed by students as an integral component of practice (Weiss-Gal, 2016).

In Pritzker and Lane's (2014) study of social work field placement practices in the United States, over 50% of the field directors surveyed stated that one or more students had engaged in **policy advocacy** or lobbying, or interacted with professional policy advocates (p. 732). Some of the strategies to incorporate policy practice competency development in field education included ensuring that policy practice was embedded in field learning contracts, and having students participate with their field instructors in community-wide policy coalitions or the preparation of legislative testimony.

The goal of increasing policy practice competency in field education ensures that "students can be better prepared to engage with social problems and injustice at multiple levels and to participate in policy and political decisions that affect our service users, our communities, and our profession" (p. 738). When social workers are not involved in the political process, then people who are not social workers will govern social work practice.

What follows are four Canadian examples where policy research by social workers and their associations has helped to shape policy outcomes for Canadians.

1. Research on child welfare practice
2. Research on federal funding for social programs
3. Research on Indigenous health justice
4. Research on organizational change in human service organizations

---

## Social policy research

Social workers who conduct social policy research develop research tools, analyze data, and compile and interpret statistics on social issues and social policy areas.

## Policy practice

Social workers are engaged in all areas of the development and implementation of social policy. Policy practice involves using social work skills to advocate for and participate in policy change in order to achieve social justice.

## Policy advocacy

Policy advocacy involves mobilizing evidence to hold governments accountable. For example, the Canadian Association of Social Workers (CASW, 2012) proactively explored the roles, policies, and practices related to the Canada Social Transfer, and made recommendations for improvements (see page 270).

# Health-Care Reforms Since the Early 2000s
## Changes in Ontario, Alberta, British Columbia, and Quebec

Health care in Canada is publicly funded but privately delivered, with physicians placed at the heart of the decision-making system at all levels. Since the early 2000s, health-care reform has been far-reaching in Ontario, Alberta, British Columbia, and Quebec.

Themes underlying provincial health-care reforms include improved access to primary care; better coordination and integration; the expansion of team approaches; improved quality of care; a focus on prevention and the management of chronic illness; an emphasis on service user engagements/self-management and self-care; and the implementation of information management systems (Hutchison, Levesque, Strumpf, & Coyle, 2011).

Initiatives that have been implemented through this transformation include the following:

- Interprofessional primary health-care teams
- Group practices and networks
- Patient enrolment with a primary care provider
- Financial incentives and blended-payment schemes
- Primary health-care governance
- Expansion of the primary health-care provider pool
- Implementation of electronic medical records
- Quality improvement training and support (Hutchison et al., 2011, p. 264)

Hutchison et al. (2011) concluded that "a culture change in primary health care is gathering force in several Canadian provinces" (p. 282). They note that some jurisdictions have implemented the following key initiatives: interprofessional team-based care, multicomponent funding and payment arrangements, enrolment of patients with a primary care provider, ongoing performance measurements, and quality improvement training and support.

The full implications of such reforms for social work and other health-care professions are yet to be determined.

## Recent Health-Care Reforms in Quebec

Quebec's health and social services network was dramatically reorganized in early 2015 through Bill 10. According to Trocmé (2016):

> The reform has led to the abolishment of the regional health and social service boards and 184 agency boards. These organizations have been replaced with 13 Centres intégrés de santé et de services sociaux (CISSS), with a further seven establishments remaining independent.... These "mega" organizations ... provide the full range of health and social services for all age groups in each of the 16 new socio-health regions. (p. 144)

While the full effect of these changes is difficult to gauge at this time, Trocmé (2016) notes that the following are concerning signs:

- Supervisory positions in one of the former larger child protection agencies have been significantly cut back to a ratio of one supervisor for 25 to 30 social workers.
- The organizational structures of these mega-health and social service agencies do not include profession-specific units or departments, further limiting social workers' abilities to maintain their professional identities.
- Child welfare agencies, where social workers had played a leading role, have been reintegrated into service delivery departments where social workers are less likely to be able to shape the scope and nature of their work.

Trocmé (2016) points out that an objective of the reorganization is to facilitate access to services by removing interagency and cross-professional barriers. These changes might well end up expanding the demand for social workers.

The impact of these changes needs to be closely monitored to ensure that social workers are in a position to advance a broad vision for their professional mandates. ∎

# Research on Child Welfare Practice

Child welfare practice may be the most complex area of the social work profession. Child welfare workers have a legal mandate to protect children, and to make decisions that can change the trajectory of children's lives. These decisions are based on an assessment of interpersonal issues such as substance use, adult mental illness, intergenerational trauma, and structural issues of inadequate housing, dangerous neighbourhoods, and impoverished communities. With little power to change the broader social context, social workers provide the best available services to meet the individualized needs of families and children.

Research in child welfare often focuses on the case characteristics and social contexts of the situations social workers make decisions on. From a Decision-Making Ecology framework (see Chapter 2), organizational factors and decision-maker characteristics are also critical to decision-making outcomes.

## Canadian Association of Social Workers Advocacy

**Canadian Association of Social Workers advocacy**

One of the roles of the Canadian Association of Social Workers (CASW) is to influence social policy and advance social justice. In that role, they conduct research and publish many policy and position statements. In 2018, the findings of a research study was published, titled *Understanding Social Work and Child Welfare: Canadian Survey and Interview with Child Welfare Experts*.

Throughout Canada, child welfare is decentralized, with each provincial and territorial government establishing child welfare legislation and funding for services. While there are commonalities among jurisdictions, each has a specific definition of "child maltreatment or harm," different time frames for investigation, different procedures, and different assessment tools. These organizational rules and instruments are built on social work knowledge and can support social needs, but the work itself is imprecise. Many situations do not fit neatly into organizational requirements.

Recent criticisms have suggested that the technical and bureaucratic approach to child protection is at tension with holistic approaches. Further, the overreliance on power to achieve change de-emphasizes critical thinking, self-reflection, and autonomy, and results in a de-professionalization of child welfare work (CASW, 2018).

Often, the profession is criticized for either being unsympathetic or too intrusive, especially when a child is removed from a family. Yet, social workers who practice in child welfare develop an identity as a professional that permeates their sense of self. Moreover, their "personal and professional identities merge to form one identity, one that is intimately connected to the society within which (social workers) live and the institution within which (they) work" (Leigh, 2014, as cited in CASW, 2018, p. 22). Child welfare workers who tend to stay in the profession are those who are connected to the work through their own life histories and personal identities.

The CASW (2018), as part of an advocacy initiative on behalf of its members, undertook an extensive survey of social workers in child welfare, past and present, to examine the challenges faced by child welfare practitioners. In particular, the CASW looked for evidence of de-professionalization and actions to address the action plan of the Truth and Reconciliation Commission of Canada. The survey research had three parts: part 1: demographic questions for all respondents ($n = 3,258$); part 2: questions for former child welfare workers ($n = 1,389$); and part 3: questions for those currently working in child welfare ($n = 1,438$).

## Job Satisfaction and Job Challenges in the Field of Child Welfare

Respondents who were no longer working in child welfare were asked about the factors that contributed to their decision to leave. Reasons included heavy work demands, emotional toll, and the complexities of child protection practice. Almost half of the respondents cited that stress, compassion fatigue, or vicarious trauma influenced their decision to leave. Areas of job satisfaction included the belief that they made a difference by providing support and helping relationships to children, youth, and families.

For respondents who were still practising in child welfare, the challenges included the difficulties of providing services to service users with complex needs, unmanageable workloads, increased expectations and procedures, unrealistic expectations by the organization, and work demands that interfered with personal and family life. Burnout, compassion fatigue, and post-traumatic stress were also reported as significant challenges. Sources of support included peers and team members, supervisors, and strong working relationships with community partners.

Almost two-thirds of the respondents reported that they believed there was a trend toward de-professionalism that was compounded by an increase in documentation and administrative tasks. Nearly three-quarters identified the negative impact of system-wide changes. All practising respondents were also asked to report whether, to their knowledge, their child welfare organizations had acted on the action plan of the Truth and Reconciliation Commission of Canada. Almost half (47%) reported that their organizations had acted, while slightly more than half (53%) reported that, to their knowledge, no action had been taken.

In addition to the surveys, semi-structured interviews were conducted with 20 child welfare experts. These experts identified the following organizational issues as critical: staff recruitment; staff turnover; staff training; excessive workload and caseloads; inadequate resources to respond to the emotional impact of child protection work; the tendency for child welfare organizations to respond to critical incidents and public criticism with policies and organizational change; and inadequate funding. They also underlined community issues such as poverty, poor housing, and lack of community treatment services.

Based on the survey and interviews, the CASW's (2018) recommendations for policy-makers included the following:

- Address the disproportionality of Indigenous children and families involved with the child welfare system.

- Improve working conditions for social workers by addressing workload.

- Support the development of national strategies to improve staff retention and reduce turnover for child welfare/service organizations.

- Develop strategies to promote mental health and wellness, and address post-traumatic stress experienced by social workers in this area.

- Raise the value placed on social work knowledge and methods, and ensure that social workers have adequate time to spend with service users.

# Research on Federal Funding for Social Programs

Central to social policy initiatives is funding, particularly federal funding, for provincial programs. The Canada Social Transfer (CST) is the primary source of federal funding for provincial and territorial social programs in the areas of post-secondary education, social assistance, social services, and programs for children. Therefore, the CST has considerable implications for the well-being of Canadians.

Despite evidence that social programs can contribute as much (and sometimes more) to health outcomes as the "illness" system, little attention has been paid to the CST. A research report from the CASW (2012) entitled *Canada Social Transfer Project—Accountability Matters* is an example of how research is being used pro-actively to influence policy-making at the federal level.

### Strengthening Federal Funding for Social Programs

The Constitution Act of 1867 gives the provinces, not the federal government, the responsibility for making and implementing social policy in most areas. This distribution of powers reflects the nineteenth-century view that welfare is largely a local and private matter. In practice, however, the federal government influences social policy in many ways, owing to its powers over individual and corporate taxation.

The exercise of federal spending powers takes the form of fiscal transfers to provincial and territorial governments, the creation of shared-cost programs, and direct spending in areas of provincial/territorial jurisdiction. Canada's fiscal transfers are intended to address economic disparities among Canadian provinces and territories. There are four main ways of transferring funds: (1) unconditional grants (such as equalization payments); (2) conditional grants (CHT and CST); (3) shared costs programs; and (4) direct spending.

With health care being prominant on the political agenda across the country, the amount of federal funds dedicated to the CST has dropped significantly. Moreover, federal contributions are estimated to cover no more than 10% of the costs that provinces and territories incur on post-secondary education, social assistance, and social services (Wood, 2013).

Unlike the CHT, the CST is not backed by federal legislation. This oversight has resulted in uneven standards of social services from coast to coast. Whereas the CHT requires provinces to adhere to the strict provisions of the Canada Health Act, no such conditions exist on the social services side with the CST. Because it lacks these enforceable guidelines, the CST is generally viewed by policy-makers and social welfare advocates as an extremely flawed policy instrument.

Mounting evidence indicates that the social determinants of health—income, housing, education, etc.—are powerful influences on physical illness. A strong case could be made for strengthening the social transfer to promote better health outcomes and minimize the direct health costs of an aging population.

## Social Policy Funding Recommendations

Adopting a proactive approach, the CASW (2012) called for a review of the CST at the federal level. As a contribution to this review, it launched a comprehensive literature search and environmental policy scan related to social program funding and delivery in Canada. A total of 43 relevant articles were reviewed.

The literature review and policy scan were supplemented with semi-structured key informant interviews with representatives of academia, social policy think tanks, past and present government officials, and human rights activists. The key informants were identified through reviewing the authors of CST papers found during the literature review, through recommendations by key informants (snowball sampling), and through CASW contacts.

A sample of nine key informants participated in semi-structured interviews over the phone, ranging from 10 to 50 minutes in length. Most key informants had over 25 years of experience exploring social policy in Canada, with varying degrees of focus on the CST.

Here are the key issues raised in the CASW (2012) report:

- **Accountability and transparency.** By far, the biggest issue with the CST is a lack of accountability and transparency. This is present in three different accountability relationships: from the legislators to citizens for fulfilling social rights, from the executive branch at the federal level to the House of Commons for spending federal money on approved purposes, and between the executive branches at the federal and provincial levels for the obligations they have to each other under the transfer arrangement.

- **Role and relationship issues.** The report also noted that federal–provincial roles have shifted over time, but those changes have not been mutually agreed upon. As a result, a situation now exists where no particular level of government has clear responsibility for delivering key social programs. The outcome has been a lack of consistency in services and service delivery, and both levels of government blaming each other when something goes wrong.

- **Financing issues.** The current fiscal arrangement has created "distorted incentives": (1) provinces have no incentive to control spending, because then their funds would be cut; (2) federal tax negotiations amount to a competition to exploit taxpayers in other provinces; and (3) fiscal transfers, which were once constructive tools for realizing societal rights, are less effective because the federal government unilaterally reduced the funds transferred to provinces and then eliminated the conditions attached to those funds.

The CASW report concluded that the ways to address these accountability issues include creating a shared vision for social programs (informed by principles); developing conditions for receiving the CST; agreeing on an accountability framework; and revitalizing a council for social policy renewal.

# Research on Indigenous Health Justice

## Health justice

Health inequities are associated with the social determinants of health, including poverty, institutional discrimination and marginalization, adverse childhood experiences, and housing/ food insecurity. As well, health inequities are related to social injustice. Health justice advocates for the achievement and delivery of health equity and social justice through collaborative approaches for all population groups (Benfer, 2015).

An issue of deep concern for Canadians is Indigenous **health justice**. The impetus to address this issue has been given additional weight through the Truth and Reconciliation Commission of Canada's 94 calls to action, a number of which (#18 to #24) emphasize the need to identify and close the gaps in health outcomes between Indigenous and non-Indigenous communities. Strategies to achieve more equitable outcomes include recognizing, respecting, and addressing the distinct health needs of Indigenous peoples; addressing the physical, mental, emotional, and spiritual harms caused by residential schools; and valuing Indigenous healing practices.

Much research and many programs are being developed to identify and close the gaps in health outcomes for Indigenous peoples. For example, Richmond and Cook (2016) advocate for public policies that address Indigenous health inequities. They argue that this would require an integrated effort across many sectors of public life and the active participation of the local community in providing, coordinating, and delivering health care and services. Any "healthy public policy should recognize the unique culture of Indigenous peoples, including acknowledging their inherent right to be self-determining and the Indigenous knowledges they hold as a fundamental means through which to create the conditions for equal access to health and health care" (p. 8).

### Initiatives to Address Indigenous Health

A number of actions have been taken across Canada to address Indigenous health. In Ontario in 2015, the Chiefs of Ontario and the provincial government signed a historic political accord to guide the government-to-government relationship between First Nations and the province. This accord was followed by the launch of Ontario's First Nations Health Action Plan, in 2016, to address Indigenous health inequities and improve access to services, including life promotion and crisis support. In 2018, Ontario established the Indigenous Mentorship Network of Ontario at Western University; it brings together 13 research institutions and 70 researchers to conduct community-led research and create "meaningful opportunities where Indigenous communities can participate and lead research on matters they consider important" (Lamberink, 2018).

In Manitoba, the Indigenous Institute of Health and Healing was established in 2017 at the University of Manitoba to "provide leadership and advance excellence in research, education and health services in collaboration with First Nations, Métis and Inuit communities. Its work is guided by Knowledge Keepers and Elders and helps to achieve health and wellness of Indigenous peoples" (University of Manitoba, 2018, para. 3).

In British Columbia, the First Nations Health Authority (FNHA) was established in 2011 to reform the way health care is delivered to BC First Nations (Richmond & Cook, 2016). In a tripartite governance framework that includes BC First Nations, the province, and Indigenous Services Canada's First Nations and Inuit Health Branch, the FNHA seeks to address service gaps through partnerships and systems innovation. Community engagement is central in this effort.

## British Columbia's Aboriginal Infant Development Program

Equitable access for Indigenous families to early childhood programs can be complicated and constrained by intersecting personal, social, and structural factors. Experiences of systemic racism, heightened surveillance from child-protection ministries, and non-Indigenous perspectives on parenting and child rearing contribute to deterring Indigenous caregivers from engaging in programs (Gerlach, Browne, & Greenwood, 2017).

Launched in 1992, British Columbia's Aboriginal Infant Development Program (AIDP) typically provides a combination of home visiting, outreach, and group programming for Indigenous families with children up to six years old. AIDP workers typically have an early childhood education and come from a tacit relational perspective of family well-being. Gerlach et al. (2017) undertook research to examine how intersecting micro- and macro-level social, historical, and political relations and factors shaped families' everyday lives, well-being, and experiences with AIDPs. The study's sample included primary caregivers, Elders, and AIDP workers, and it represented seven urban-based, off-reserve communities.

Three themes emerged from Gerlach et al.'s (2017) research:

- **Overcoming mistrust.** Many caregivers were mistrustful of social workers' concerns, due to the disproportionate number of Indigenous children being removed by the child welfare system. To overcome this mistrust, AIDP workers worked hard to gain trust through "understanding the continuities between families' intergenerational experiences of state intervention, their ongoing involvement with child welfare authorities, and parental concerns and suspicions about engaging in their programs" (p. 1767).

- **Being willing to move a step forward.** Some of the families have been perceived as "hard to reach" or "noncompliant," which tends to focus on individual deficits rather than program shortcomings. AIDP workers worked with Elders to strengthen family engagement, and Elders played a central role in teaching Indigenous knowledge and practices. This involvement fostered "a sense of parental belonging and safety in ways that prescriptive and imported parenting programs may fail to do" (p. 1768).

- **Resisting what is taken for granted.** The research found that AIDP workers had to set aside taken-for-granted policies and assumptions. For example, developmental screening—an early intervention practice—was often postponed until a trusting relationship had been built, at which point the screening could be perceived as strengthening and helpful rather than a pass/fail test.

According to Gerlach et al.'s (2017) research, practising in culturally safe ways requires identifying specific family engagement strategies and approaches that are safe from the caregiver's perspective. Addressing policies to increase accessibility where inequities exist requires "being responsive to the socio-historical realities of Indigenous families' lives and enduring power relations that can constrain Indigenous children's access to beneficial programs" (p. 1770).

# Research on Organizational Change in Human Service Organizations

Ultimately, research and policy practice, and indeed social work, are about social change, and the site of social change is frequently **human service organizations (HSOs)**, whether the HSO is a a non-profit society, a government service, or a private organization.

Social workers require knowledge, values, and skills to be able to work effectively in HSOs. As well, they must have an understanding of the organizational context within which they provide services (O'Hara, Weber, & Levine, 2016). Internally, social workers need a sense of the way in which the organization is structured and of their unique role in the provision of direct services. Externally, social workers need a sense of the political context (including funding priorities), the policies and legislation that govern social work organizations, and service provision demands.

In many ways, a social worker acts as a "policy implementation agent" (O'Hara et al., 2016, p. 305) who develops interdisciplinary and interorganizational skills capacity as a deeper understanding is gained about the interaction between the external and internal environments.

### Participating in Organizational Change

Organizational change is ever present in HSOs, whether it occurs because of external factors, such as funding and policy changes, or internal pressures to adapt and modify the organizations core activities, goals, or services. HSOs struggle with change, even though the espoused need for the change is better outcomes for the populations they serve. Frequently, change is framed as an organizational participatory process, in which service providers and service users can have a voice (Devine, 2010).

In Devine's (2010) study of organizational change from a direct government service model to a community health-governed model of service delivery, front-line social workers felt they had only "minimal to moderate ability to have input and that the input provided was not valued" (p. 124). Despite the rhetoric in the guiding documents on the importance of input, social workers felt that they did not have a say in the process, leaving them feeling disempowered, devalued, and demoralized. Although 12% of the social workers reported being given many opportunities for input, the vast majority (94%) felt that their participation was not received genuinely. Devine suggests that when one does not feel valued, one's sense of "belonging" to the organization is lessened, resulting in a loss of trust and a reduction in commitment to the organization.

This line of reasoning is consistent with other research on organizational change that has found change to be more readily accepted when it is conducted in a participatory and transparent manner. For example, Packard (2017) concluded that having opportunities to express concerns and provide input on implementation details was a necessary factor in staff acceptance of change.

# Critical Perspectives on Service Delivery Systems
## The Need for Equity, Caring, and Social Justice in Human Service Organizations

" Critical theories draw attention to human services as systems of domination or emancipation" (Garrow & Hasenfeld, 2009, p. 51). From a critical theory perspective, the distribution of power in HSOs is an important point of consideration. Ideally, HSOs should be free from domination, and all members should have an equal opportunity to contribute to systems that meet human needs and lead to the progressive development of all.

### Embedded Power Relations

From a critical theory perspective, organizational structures and practices are "understood as social constructions that give preference to certain culturally defined discourses over others" (Garrow & Hasenfeld, 2009, p. 48). Certain versions of reality are promoted through the use of language. For example, moral discourse that is made objective through technical language and rational discourse masks the moral choices being made.

A feminist perspective on HSOs considers the gendered nature of work and power hierarchies. While women constitute the majority of human service workers, men are more likely to assume key administrative positions. Moreover, a feminist perspective

> maintains that organizations are inherently gendered and subordinate women via hierarchical structural arrangements and power relations. (Garrow & Hasenfeld, 2009, p. 47)

An alternative organizational form that imbues feminist values would include participatory decision-making, flexible and interactive job designs, an equitable distribution of income, and interpersonal and political accountability. In organizations with more women in leadership, or enhanced minority group representation, the marginalized populations do better (see Kondrat's [2002] example on social worker decision-making for African American service users in Chapter 7).

### Critical Approaches to Organizational Change

HSOs deliver services within a context of competing principles, limited resources, and increasing demands. As a result, HSO decision-makers frequently find themselves conflicted between management practices that emphasize efficiency and accountability and practice values such as caring and social justice (Clarke, 2012).

For example, Rønningstad (2018) examined organizational change in the Norwegian public welfare organizations. The managers who were change leaders experienced "change fatigue," particularly as they encountered front-line resistance to instructions from "above." The managers frequently felt "caught between two worlds," as they were required to interpret corporate rhetoric that conflicted with their own experience or professional values.

At times, the managers expressed the challenges they faced in implementing change, given limited time, power, or discretion to adapt the changes to local needs.

Ultimately, Rønningstad (2018) suggests that organizational change comes with considerable costs to employees and managers. In order to manage HSO change, Rønningstad recommends adopting more discursive and interpretive approaches. ∎

# Social Worker Exemplar

## Acquiring Research Skills

Theresa Thoms

**Research underpins social work practice, but it is not typically a strong focus in field education. Obtaining such research skills builds confidence and can open new opportunities for work and practice.**

Theresa was in her second year of university when she took a position as a research assistant. As an aspiring social worker, the position gave her a real-life opportunity to build valuable research skills. These skills continued to be developed over the research projects that followed.

In the course of her research work, her understanding of social work values also deepened. She began to grasp the importance of collaboration and engagement and learning from those with lived experience.

In the second year of my bachelor of social work degree at Thompson Rivers University in Kamloops, British Columbia, one of my professors asked me if I would be interested in being a research assistant for a project he was about to start. Before this, I had not considered involving myself in research. The project sounded very appealing to me, particularly as he alluded to a research experience being beneficial for my future career. Little did I know that accepting this offer would lead to me doing four research projects by the time I graduated.

Not only did I assist this professor in his own research twice, but my experience working with him also inspired me to start my own original research project with a social work colleague, and then one more on my own. Without this professor's positive influence and guidance, I do not think that I would have acquired an interest in research. At the start of my degree, I definitely did not imagine myself enjoying participating in and conducting research projects—not to mention four of them!

Engaging in research as a social work student gave me the opportunity to work with and/or advocate for populations of interest to me, such as adults and youth living in homelessness, people with diverse abilities, and Indigenous people. It also gave me an appreciation for the benefits of evidence-based research in informing practice. I gained an especially deeper interest in participatory action research (PAR). PAR is an inclusive approach that aims to benefit research participants themselves—researchers work *with* participants instead of working *on* or *for* them (Csiernik, Birnbaum, & Pierce, 2010).

I am particularly proud to say that all of the research projects that I have been involved in were designed to benefit the community. Three of the projects were created from an expressed community need. In each case, one or more local non-profit organizations partnered with the research team. The fourth project derived from an expressed need from two community members, one of which had lived experience and was a member of the population that the research intended to serve. My experience underlines the importance of doing research that is meaningful to the community.

## Integrating Research, Education, and Action

One of the purposes of PAR is to create new skills and change within the community.

For example, my fourth research project involved a survey on how the Truth and Reconciliation Commission of Canada's calls to action were being implemented by the business sector in my community. Because this research project was focused on Indigenous people, and because I am not Indigenous, I partnered with Indigenous people to create the questionnaire and decide upon the research methodology, methods, and data analysis. The survey was designed to educate the community about reconciliation and the commission's calls to action. This was important as the business sector had limited familiarity with both concepts.

There were many advantages associated with being a social work student heavily involved in community-based research. Working with community agencies and populations in my field meant that I was networking, acquiring knowledge about different population groups, and gaining hands-on social work experience. My research involvement has landed me invaluable references and job opportunities.

During a research meeting with a non-profit organization to provide wraparound services for homeless youth, I was introduced to a foster parent for Indigenous youth in care. This person later contacted the organization to offer me a full-time job over the summer with the option of part-time work during the school year.

The following summer, that same organization was so impressed by my work ethic that they created a job for me! ■

## Reflections on Theresa's Story

Theresa was able to infuse social work professional values into multiple research projects. Choosing PAR as her method of choice underlines her commitment to researching "*with* people," rather than "*on* or *for* people."

Theresa's decision to collaborate with Indigenous groups to educate the business sector on the Truth and Reconciliation Commission of Canada's calls to action demonstrates her understanding of the holistic nature of research and social policy.

These learning experiences led to new job opportunities in social work research that Theresa couldn't have imagined.

### From Theory to Practice

As you reflect on Theresa's story, give some thought to the following points:

1. Theresa has adopted a PAR approach to her research. How does this approach "fit" with research projects that may be occurring in your field site?

2. Theresa is a non-Indigenous person but identifies as an ally. What are some of the ways she resists imposing Western worldviews on her research? Are there other strategies that could be used to augment those she has identified?

3. Knowledge dissemination is an important final component of the research process. What are some ways Theresa could enhance knowledge utilization?

# Practice Scenarios

These practice scenarios provide opportunities to think about situations in which front-line social workers can participate, and influence research, policy-making, and organizational change.

Reflexive practice is required in each scenario. This practice always starts with becoming aware of your initial thoughts and feelings about the situation. As you work through your self-awareness, keep in mind that social work knowledge, values, and principles are incorporated in and affect these initial thoughts.

In each scenario, it is important to consider the social work skills and experiences that can be used not only to resolve the issue, but also to improve social work practice for service users and the broader community

## 10.1 Developing a Research Question from Daily Practice

You are working in a family preservation program for mothers and their children referred by the local children's ministry. You notice that very few Indigenous families attend the agency's program. You are aware that the local ministry office responds disproportionately to Indigenous families. You are also aware of research that indicates that across Canada, investigations are more likely to occur for Indigenous families, but so are substantiations and subsequent removals.

You wonder whether this disproportionate response to Indigenous families is occurring in your community, and how best to address it. When you raise the matter in a team meeting, your supervisor asks you to research this question further and, if possible, to make some recommendations for the agency.

1. In this situation, the social worker has already begun to link social work knowledge to her practice context. What might be a suitable research question?

2. Being a research practitioner means developing projects that can be conducted as a component of regular practice. In this agency, how could a research project be developed that does not require major modifications to other workload responsibilities?

3. Most social workers prefer a participatory and collaborative approach to research. Who could some of the potential partners in this project be?

## 10.2 Developing Service-Oriented Policies

Your community has been working on incorporating more harm-reduction approaches to offset the high number of opioid deaths. This initiative has included setting up safe injection mobile sites and training first responders and outreach workers in the use of naloxone. Over the past year, there has been a small but steady decline in overdose deaths.

The next step in this initiative is to focus on early intervention. You are meeting with a group of health-care providers and social workers in the region to develop strategies and programs for an early intervention policy.

1. What are some of the social work principles and values that you would want to present in your discussion at the first interprofessional meeting?

2. How would you go about researching existing knowledge on evidence-based early intervention substance-use initiatives?

3. What kind of role could service users play in this policy initiative? What service user population characteristics would you want to ensure are represented?

4. Keeping in mind that any policy change affects HSO resources and requires organizational change, what HSO change strategies could you initiate to support the inevitable service changes?

## 10.3 Participation in Organizational Change

You are a well-liked and influential member of the child-protection team at your agency. Your managers have told you that there is a need for better-integrated social services in a local multiracial and impoverished community. They are forming a team to develop a proposal on how to address this matter. The team will include a ministry representative, a child-protection social worker (you), an early childhood educator, a part-time health-care nurse, a family support worker, and a youth outreach worker.

1. As an informal leader, there are opportunities to create a positive culture or develop resistance to change. What are your own perspectives on change?

2. As a member of the interprofessional team, how would you respond to colleagues who are resistant to or skeptical of change, or in a state of change fatigue?

3. The team proposes to develop an interprofessional service delivery model in the community. As a social worker, what principles or values would you want to incorporate into service delivery?

4. What kind of evaluation process should be included as part of the new initiative?

# Field Education Practicalities
## Am I Cut Out for a Career in Social Work?

The field education phase is coming to an end. This may mean that you will move into a paid social work position, continue in social work (or other) education, or adapt your social work knowledge to a related profession.

Regardless of your next steps, the hope is that field education has resulted in an enhanced knowledge and understanding of the complexities of social work practice and a better appreciation as to what it takes to be a part of this great profession.

Your formal program is coming to an end, and you are one big step farther into your journey of becoming a professional social worker. The field component will have clarified many aspects of practice and solidified this journey for you.

For some students, experience in the field results in a time of questioning. Some may ask, "Is this the profession for me?" This is perfectly understandable.

If you are at this juncture, it is important to take the time to clarify your thoughts on the matter. Were you uncertain going into the social work program? Was this particular field experience not a good one for you? If so, what was missing? How can this shortcoming be made up?

### What Now?

A wonderful aspect of generalist social work is that there are many practice options. Ask yourself whether this field experience helped to clarify the type of agency and type of population you want to work with. For example, some people enjoy working with substance-use service users. Although this work is often slow and full of steps forward and back, they find it rewarding. Others prefer working with service users in more stable situations, such as long-term care facilities.

The purpose of field education is hands-on learning. For some students, hearing feedback about changes to be made or areas to improve on can be humbling. However, unless the mistakes were serious, or made repeatedly, it is important to keep in mind that feedback is an essential aspect of learning (Royse, Dhooper, & Lewis Rompf, 2012). Students are not expected to know all the answers, nor perform as expert and competent social workers. However, sometimes feedback can be, or seems to be, overly harsh. Knowing this, it is important to be self-reflective and clear about your hopes and goals, and about the direction you want to take in your career.

On the other hand, if the field education experience clarified for you that you do not want to continue in social work, that is also acceptable. The hope is that you will continue to use some of the core skills—self-knowledge, empathy, and a commitment to social justice—as you pursue another career path.

### Social Work Opportunities

The opportunities for social work graduates continue to be abundant in Canada. From 2017 to 2026 in Canada, new job openings for social workers and related occupations are expected to total 28,000, while new job seekers over this period are expected to total 29,600 (Government of Canada, 2018). This projection indicates that 95% of new job seekers in this field will find employment.

The Labour Force Survey explains the strong employment growth in social work this way:

> Employment growth in this occupation will continue to be fuelled by the public's greater awareness to social issues such as aging population, mental health, violence, etc. However, this strong growth is expected to slow down over the projection period because demand for social workers also depends on the level of public spending, and then be limited by the budget constraints faced by some governments. Positions left vacant because of retirement are expected to account for nearly 45% of available jobs, though the retirement rate is anticipated to be similar to the average for all occupations. With regard to labour supply, school leavers are projected to account for the vast majority of job seekers. However, an appreciable number of workers are expected to seek opportunities in other occupations, notably in management occupations in the social and community services sector. (Government of Canada, 2018, para. 6)

For social workers considering advancement, Canadian Occupational Projection System (COPS) data indicate that of the top five occupations in which job applicants will be insufficient to meet demand (projected to 2020), managers in health care, education, and social and community services come second (Tucker, 2014). Due to an aging workforce and earlier retirements, the projected number (to 2020) of job openings for managers in health care, education, social and community services, and correctional services is expected to be greater than the projected number of job seekers in those fields.

## Pathway to Social Work Positions

The field agency you were working with can provide opportunities for future work and your career. Many students will be looking for part-time or summer paid work that will further help them develop their social work competencies. The agency may also have volunteer or summer positions for which you may be eligible. As well, they may know of other agencies that are looking for people with your newly acquired skills.

At the end of your field education, it is worthwhile revisiting your resumé. Write two or three sentences about the skills and capacities that you have developed as a result of being in the field placement. Remember that these skills and capacities don't have to be at the expert level. They should simply reflect that you have some beginning professional experience in certain areas and with certain populations. Over time, your list of skills and experience will grow incrementally.

For those social workers who are interested in seeking out new experiences and new adventures, there are multiple opportunities in northern and remote Canadian practice. Very adventurous new social work graduates may also want to explore international opportunities. ■

# Reflection, Learning, and More Practice

## Field Education Practicalities

1. Prepare for your final field education evaluation by going through your initial learning plan and articulating how you have developed competency in various areas.

2. Take an opportunity to sit with a colleague and review any career plans you may have, or career support/suggestions they may be able to offer.

3. As you prepare to complete your field education, confirm the process for eliciting a reference for further employment.

4. Identify ways to say appropriate thank yous and goodbyes to supervisors and colleagues who added mentoring to their work responsibilities.

5. Review your resumé and update it to reflect your additional experiences.

## Journal Ideas

1. Identify a practice or procedure that you have observed in the field agency and journal about a research question and approach that could be undertaken in this agency.

2. Journal reflexively about how you would like to integrate being a practice researcher or policy practitioner in a future job.

3. Talk to a social worker who has participated in organizational change, or whose role has changed due to organizational change. Ask them about their coping strategies, and any recommendations they have for managing changes in delivery systems.

4. Attend a policy discussion associated with your field agency (either internal to agency or at the community, regional, or national level). Analyze the principles inherent in the discussions. What approaches are being taken on the social issue? How are social work values expressed?

5. Write a "letter to the editor" or "blog" lobbying for a change in provincial or national policy.

## Critical-Thinking Questions

1. Identify a recent social policy reform that has occurred at the provincial level. Assess the impact of this reform on populations that have been traditionally marginalized.

2. Identify the directions of health-care policy in your province/territory and evaluate the effectiveness of at least one health initiative for a population of interest to social workers at your field site.

3. Explain how child protection and child welfare are managed in your province/territory and evaluate the overall effectiveness of the organizational system.

4. Jordan's Principle is a national initiative that may have been adopted and implemented in various ways across the country. Talk with local and regional child-protection social workers to evaluate how this principle, which is intended to ensure that First Nations children receive seamless services, regardless of jurisdictional issues, is being experienced by the children and families.

5. The CST and CHT were created in 2004 as two separate block transfer payments. One of the reason for this split was to provide greater accountability for federal health funding. What are the strengths and weaknesses of the current CST and CHT, and how have they affected provincial funding?

6. Identify program opportunities in your community or region that could be strengthened, adapted, or modified to provide culturally safe and welcoming services to ensure that Indigenous people have the same opportunities for positive health outcomes as non-Indigenous people in Canada.

7. Evaluate how well interprofessional health teams are providing services to the traditionally underserved and marginalized populations in your province or territory (e.g., transient people, homeless people, or rural populations).

# Chapter Review

It can be challenging for a social worker to develop a practice approach and professional identity that link the individual service user to broader social structures. In many cases, social workers engage in front-line practice, research, or policy implementation, and it is the purview of senior managers to lead organizational change.

This chapter suggests that social workers are well placed not only to connect practice with the broader policy and organizational mandates, but also to inform the development of policy and organizational change. This is because social workers have competency and capacity to utilize evidence-based knowledge, provide participatory and inclusive practice, and communicate in a strengthening and respectful way.

Gretchen showed her perseverance and participatory action focus as she worked with a First Nations community to build trust and a culturally safe and meaningful holistic conceptual wellness framework. This work ultimately led to the attainment of a master's degree and, perhaps more importantly, a new framework for child welfare in her community, with possible national implications. Her practice is truly a grassroots research approach to policy and organizational change.

Theresa began her research career through an opportunity to work with a professor on his own research. While there are many such opportunities at universities and colleges, Theresa took the risk of participating in something she hadn't thought a lot about and found a new interest area and a way of pivoting this experience into meaningful work for her and her community.

The practice scenarios in this chapter are all taken from actual experiences of front-line social workers. They provide an opportunity to think about how your skills, knowledge, and values can be developed further to gain competency and confidence in research practice, policy development, and organizational change.

## Engaging in Research, Policy Analysis and Development, and System Change in Practice

This chapter outlines numerous ways in which students can develop proficiency and competency in research and knowledge utilization, policy analysis and development, and organizational change. Here are some highlights and further suggestions:

- Develop a disciplined and ongoing process to integrate research knowledge into practice as a continuing professional development responsibility.
- Identify and participate in knowledge-utilization strategies within your organization.
- Work with colleagues or other professionals in the community to co-create research processes.
- Commit to a practice research approach to social work, so that research is conducted alongside other practice responsibilities.
- Pay attention to how Western epistemologies are privileged in theory and practice, and adopt decolonizing perspectives.
- Develop relationships with voices and communities that may traditionally have been marginalized within the broader social structures to ensure multiple worldviews are honoured and reflected in policy and service delivery.
- Identify practices and advocate for practice change to reflect the Truth and Reconciliation Commission of Canada's calls to action.
- Become involved with policy and political processes at the local and national level.
- Practise in culturally safe ways to ameliorate and address health and social inequities in service accessibility.
- Participate in surveys and focus groups within your organization that are associated with system change.
- Adopt a self-care approach to change to foster resiliency while maintaining ongoing participation.

# Appendices

# Global Social Work Statement of Ethical Principles (2018)
## International Federation of Social Workers (IFSW)

This Statement of Ethical Principles (hereafter referred to as the Statement) serves as an overarching framework for social workers to work towards the highest possible standards of professional integrity.

Implicit in our acceptance of this Statement as social work practitioners, educators, students, and researchers is our commitment to uphold the core values and principles of the social work profession as set out in this Statement.

An array of values and ethical principles inform us as social workers; this reality was recognized in 2014 by the International Federation of Social Workers and The International Association of Schools of Social Work in the global definition of social work, which is layered and encourages regional and national amplifications.

All IFSW policies including the definition of social work stem from these ethical principles.

*Social work is a practice-based profession and an academic discipline that facilitates social change and development, social cohesion, and the empowerment and liberation of people. Principles of social justice, human rights, collective responsibility and respect for diversities are central to social work. Underpinned by theories of social work, social sciences, humanities and Indigenous knowledge, social work engages people and structures to address life challenges and enhance wellbeing.*

**http://ifsw.org/get-involved/global-definition-of-social-work/**

## Principles

### 1. Recognition of the Inherent Dignity of Humanity

Social workers recognize and respect the inherent dignity and worth of all human beings in attitude, word, and deed. We respect all persons, but we challenge beliefs and actions of those persons who devalue or stigmatize themselves or other persons.

### 2. Promoting Human Rights

Social workers embrace and promote the fundamental and inalienable rights of all human beings. Social work is based on respect for the inherent worth, dignity of all people and the individual and social /civil rights that follow from this. Social workers often work with people to find an appropriate balance between competing human rights.

### 3. Promoting Social Justice

Social workers have a responsibility to engage people in achieving social justice, in relation to society generally, and in relation to the people with whom they work. This means:

**3.1** *Challenging Discrimination and Institutional Oppression*

Social workers promote social justice in relation to society generally and to the people with whom they work.

Social workers challenge discrimination, which includes but is not limited to age, capacity, civil status, class, culture, ethnicity, gender, gender identity, language, nationality (or lack thereof), opinions, other physical characteristics, physical or mental abilities, political beliefs, poverty, race, relationship status, religion, sex, sexual orientation, socioeconomic status, spiritual beliefs, or family structure.

### 3.2 Respect for Diversity

Social workers work toward strengthening inclusive communities that respect the ethnic and cultural diversity of societies, taking account of individual, family, group, and community differences.

### 3.3 Access to Equitable Resources

Social workers advocate and work toward access and the equitable distribution of resources and wealth.

### 3.4 Challenging Unjust Policies and Practices

Social workers work to bring to the attention of their employers, policymakers, politicians, and the public situations in which policies and resources are inadequate or in which policies and practices are oppressive, unfair, or harmful. In doing so, social workers must not be penalized.

Social workers must be aware of situations that might threaten their own safety and security, and they must make judicious choices in such circumstances. Social workers are not compelled to act when it would put themselves at risk.

### 3.5 Building Solidarity

Social workers actively work in communities and with their colleagues, within and outside of the profession, to build networks of solidarity to work toward transformational change and inclusive and responsible societies.

## 4. Promoting the Right to Self-Determination

Social workers respect and promote people's rights to make their own choices and decisions, provided this does not threaten the rights and legitimate interests of others.

## 5. Promoting the Right to Participation

Social workers work toward building the self-esteem and capabilities of people, promoting their full involvement and participation in all aspects of decisions and actions that affect their lives.

## 6. Respect for Confidentiality and Privacy

**6.1** Social workers respect and work in accordance with people's rights to confidentiality and privacy unless there is risk of harm to the self or to others or other statutory restrictions.

**6.2** Social workers inform the people with whom they engage about such limits to confidentiality and privacy.

## 7. Treating People as Whole Persons

Social workers recognize the biological, psychological, social, and spiritual dimensions of people's lives and understand and treat all people as whole persons. Such recognition is used to formulate holistic assessments and interventions with the full participation of people, organizations, and communities with whom social workers engage.

## 8. Ethical Use of Technology and Social Media

**8.1** The ethical principles in this Statement apply to all contexts of social work practice, education, and research, whether it involves direct face-to-face contact or through use of digital technology and social media.

**8.2** Social workers must recognize that the use of digital technology and social media may pose threats to the practice of many ethical standards including but not limited to privacy and confidentiality, conflicts of interest, competence, and documentation and must obtain the necessary knowledge and skills to guard against unethical practice when using technology.

## 9. Professional Integrity

**9.1** It is the responsibility of national associations and organizations to develop and regularly update their own codes of ethics or ethical guidelines, to be consistent with this Statement, considering local situations. It is also the responsibility of national organizations to inform social workers and schools of social work about this Statement of Ethical Principles and their own ethical guidelines. Social workers should act in accordance with the current ethical code or guidelines in their country.

**9.2** Social workers must hold the required qualifications and develop and maintain the required skills and competencies to do their job.

**9.3** Social workers support peace and nonviolence. Social workers may work alongside military personnel for humanitarian purposes and work toward peacebuilding and reconstruction. Social workers operating within a military or peacekeeping context must always support the dignity and agency of people as their primary focus. Social workers must not allow their knowledge and skills to be used for inhumane purposes, such as torture, military surveillance, terrorism, or conversion therapy, and they should not use weapons in their professional or personal capacities against people.

**9.4** Social workers must act with integrity. This includes not abusing their positions of power and relationships of trust with people that they engage with; they recognize the boundaries between personal and professional life and do not abuse their positions for personal material benefit or gain.

**9.5** Social workers recognize that the giving and receiving of small gifts is a part of the social work and cultural experience in some cultures and countries. In such situations, this should be referenced in the country's code of ethics.

**9.6** Social workers have a duty to take the necessary steps to care for themselves professionally and personally in the workplace, in their private lives and in society.

**9.7** Social workers acknowledge that they are accountable for their actions to the people they work with; their colleagues; their employers; their professional associations; and local, national, and international laws and conventions and that these accountabilities may conflict, which must be negotiated to minimize harm to all persons. Decisions should always be informed by empirical evidence; practice wisdom; and ethical, legal, and cultural considerations. Social workers must be prepared to be transparent about the reasons for their decisions.

**9.8** Social workers and their employing bodies work to create conditions in their workplace environments and in their countries, where the principles of this Statement and those of their own national codes are discussed, evaluated, and upheld. Social workers and their employing bodies foster and engage in debate to facilitate ethically informed decisions. ■

*Reprinted with kind permission from the International Federation of Social Workers (IFSW), **www.ifsw.org**.*

# Appendix 2

# Accredited Social Work Programs in Canada

**BSW** = Bachelor of Social Work;  **MSW** = Master of Social Work;
**BTS** = Baccalauréat en travail social;  **MTS** = Maîtrise en travail social

List current as of September 2019

| | | | |
|---|---|---|---|
| Algoma University | BSW | Université de Sherbrooke | BTS MTS |
| Carleton University | BSW MSW | Université du Québec à Chicoutimi | BTS MTS |
| Dalhousie University | BSW MSW | Université du Québec à Montréal | BTS MTS |
| First Nations University of Canada | BISW MISW | Université du Québec à Rimouski | BTS |
| King's University College | BSW MSW | Université du Québec en Abitibi-Témiscamingue | BTS |
| Lakehead University | BSW MSW | Université du Québec en Outaouais | BTS MTS |
| Laurentian University | BSW/BSS MSW/MSS | Université Laval | BSS MSS |
| Laurentian University— School of Indigenous Relations | BISW | University of British Columbia— Okanagan Campus | MSW |
| MacEwan University | BSW | University of British Columbia— Vancouver Campus | BSW MSW |
| McGill University | BSW MSW | University of Calgary | BSW MSW |
| McMaster University | BSW MSW | University of Manitoba | BSW MSW |
| Memorial University of Newfoundland | BSW MSW | University of Northern British Columbia | BSW MSW |
| Nicola Valley Institute of Technology | BSW | University of Regina | BSW MSW |
| Nipissing University | BSW | University of the Fraser Valley | BSW MSW |
| Renison University College | BSW MSW | University of Toronto | MSW |
| Ryerson University | BSW MSW | University of Victoria | BSW MSW |
| St. Thomas University | BSW | University of Windsor | BSW MSW |
| Thompson Rivers University | BSW | Vancouver Island University | BSW |
| Trent University | BSW | Wilfrid Laurier University | BSW MSW |
| Université d'Ottawa | BSS MSS | York University | BSW MSW |
| Université de Moncton | BTS MTS | | |
| Université de Montréal | BSS MSS | | |
| Université de Saint Boniface | BSS | | |

# Appendix 3

# Provincial/Territorial Regulatory Bodies

In Canada, legislation that regulates social work practice is a provincial/territorial responsibility. Each province has enacted legislation and established social work regulatory bodies to govern the profession in accordance with the legislation.

Each province and territory decides on the organization of the regulatory body, and the policy and processes to ensure public accountability. Social workers become registered by becoming individual members of a provincial or territorial regulatory body.

**British Columbia**

British Columbia College of
Social Workers
1430-1200 West 73 Avenue
Vancouver, BC  V6P 6G5
Tel: 604.737.4916 / Fax: 604.737.6809
info@bccsw.ca
**www.bccollegeofsocialworkers.ca**

**Alberta**

Alberta College of Social Workers
#550, 10707 100 Avenue NW
Edmonton, AB  T5J 3M1
Tel: 780.421.1167 / Fax: 780.421.1168
acsw@acsw.ab.ca
**www.acsw.ab.ca**

**Saskatchewan**

Saskatchewan Association of
Social Workers
2110 Lorne Street
Regina, SK  S4P 2M5
Tel: 306.545.1922 / Fax: 306.545.1895
sasw@accesscomm.ca
**www.sasw.ca**

**Manitoba**

Manitoba College of Social Workers
101-2033 Portage Avenue
Winnipeg, MB  R3J 0K6
Tel: 204.888.9477 / Fax: 204.831.6359
info@mcsw.ca
**www.mcsw.ca**

**Ontario**

Ontario College of Social Workers and
Social Service Workers
250 Bloor Street East, Suite 1000
Toronto ON  M4W 1E6
Tel: 1.877.828.9380 / Fax: 416.972.1512
info@ocswssw.org
**www.ocswssw.org**

**Quebec**

Ordre des travailleurs sociaux et des
thérapeutes conjugaux et familiaux
du Québec
255, boulevard Crémazie Est,
bureau 800
Montreal, QC  H2M 1L5
Tel: 514.731.3925 / Fax: 514.731.6785
info@otstcfq.org
**https://otstcfq.org**

**New Brunswick**

New Brunswick Association of
Social Workers
P.O. Box 1533, Postal Station A
Fredericton, NB  E3B 5G2
Tel: 506.459.5595 / Fax: 506.457.1421
nbasw@nbasw-atsnb.ca
**www.nbasw-atsnb.ca**

**Nova Scotia**

Nova Scotia College of Social Workers
1888 Brunswick Street, Suite 700
Halifax, NS  B3J 3J8
Tel: 902.429.7799 / Fax: 902.429.7650
**www.nscsw.org**

**Newfoundland and Labrador**

Newfoundland and Labrador
Association of Social Workers
P.O. Box 39039
St. John's, NL  A1E 5Y7
Tel: 709.753.0200 / Fax: 709.753.0120
registration@nlasw.ca
**www.nlasw.ca**

**Prince Edward Island**

Prince Edward Island Social Work
Registration Board
81 Prince Street
Charlottetown, PE  C1A 4R3
Tel: 902.368.7337 / Fax: 902.368.7180
registrar@socialworkpei.ca
**http://socialworkpei.ca**

**Northern Canada (Northwest
Territories)**

Registrar, Professional Licensing
Health and Social Services
5015-49th Street (7th Floor)
Yellowknife, NT  X1A 2L9
Tel: 867.767.9067 / Fax: 867.873.0484
professional_licensing@gov.nt.ca
**www.hss.gov.nt.ca/professional-
licensing/social-workers**

# References

Adams, Y., Drew, N., & Walker, R. (2014). Principles of practice in mental health assessment with Aboriginal Australians. In P. Dudgeon, H. Milory, & R. Walker (eds.), *Working together: Aboriginal and Torres Strait Islander mental health and wellbeing principles and practice* (pp. 271–288). Barton, Australia: Commonwealth Copyright Administration. Retrieved from https://www.telethonkids.org.au/globalassets/media/documents/aboriginal-health/working-together-second-edition/working-together-aboriginal-and-wellbeing-2014.pdf

Afifi, T., MacMillan, H. Boyle, M., Taillieu, T., Cheung, K., & Sareen, J. (2014). Child abuse and mental disorders in Canada. *Canadian Medical Association Journal, 186*(9), E324–E332. https://doi.org/10.1503/cmaj.131792

Aggarwal, N., Desilva, R., Nicasio, A., Boiler, M., & Lewis-Fernández, L. (2015). Does the Cultural Formation Interview for the fifth revision of the Diagnostic and Statistical Manual of Mental Disorders (DSM-5) affect medical communication? A qualitative exploratory study from the New York site. *Ethnicity & Health, 20*(1), 1–28. https://doi.org/10.1080/13557858.2013.857762

Al-Krenawi, A., Graham, J., & Habibov, N. (2016). Introduction: Social work and diversity. In A. Al-Krenawi, J. Graham, & N. Habibov (eds.), *Diversity and social work in Canada* (pp. 2–12). Don Mills, ON: Oxford UP.

Alle-Corliss, L., & Alle-Corliss, R. (1998). *Human service agencies: An orientation to fieldwork*. Pacific Grove, CA: Brooks Cole.

Anderson, K. (2011). *Life stages and Native women: Memory, teachings, and story medicine*. Winnipeg, MB: University of Manitoba Press.

Androff, D. (2010). Truth and Reconciliation Commissions (TRCs): An international human rights intervention and its connection to social work. *British Journal of Social Work, 40,* 1960–1977. https://doi.org/10.1093/bjsw/bcp139

Antle, B. (2005). *Components of ethical practice*. Paper presented at Canadian Association of Social Workers' Code of Ethics Internal Training, Ottawa, ON.

Aotearoa New Zealand Association of Social Workers. (2015). Code of ethics. Retrieved from https://anzasw.nz/summary-of-the-code-of-ethics/#1455661759310-739c7231-9145

Arnold, R., Burke, B., James, C., Martin, D., & Thomas, B. (1991). *Educating for change*. Toronto, ON: Between the Lines.

Association of Social Work Boards. (2013). *ASWB examination candidate handbook*. Culpepper, VA: Author.

Association of Social Work Boards. (2018). *Content outlines and KSAs*. Culpepper, VA: Author.

Australian Association of Social Workers. (2015). *Scope of social work practice: Psychosocial assessments*. Melbourne, Australia: Author.

Badwall, H. (2014). Colonial encounters: Racialized social workers negotiating professional scripts of whiteness. *Intersectionalities: A Global Journal of Social Work Analysis, Research, Policy, and Practice, 3*, 1–23.

Banks, S. (2008). Critical commentary: Social work ethics. *British Journal of Social Work, 38,* 1238–1249. https://doi.org/10.1093/bjsw/bcn099

Baskin, C. (2016). *Strong helpers' teachings: The Value of Indigenous knowledges in the helping professions* (2nd ed.). Toronto, ON: Canadian Scholars' Press.

Baskin, C., & Davey, C. (2014). Grannies, Elders, and friends: Aging Aboriginal women in Toronto. *Journal of Gerontological Social Work, 58*(1), 46–65. https://doi.org/10.1080/01634372.2014.912997

Baum, N. (2017). Gender-sensitive intervention to improve work with fathers in child welfare services. *Child & Family Social Work, 22*(1), 419–427. https://doi.org/10.1111/cfs.12259

Baumann, D., Kern, H., & Fluke, J. (1997). Foundations of the decision-making ecology and overview. In H. Kern, D.J. Baumann, & J. Fluke (eds.), *Worker Improvements to the Decision and Outcome Model (WISDOM): The child welfare decision enhancement project* (pp. 1–12). Washington, DC: The Children's Bureau.

Beauchamp, S., Drapeau, M., & Dionne, C. (2015). The development of practice guidelines in the social and human services. *Canadian Psychology, 56*(4), 357–367.

Benfer, E. (2015). Health justice: A framework (and call to action) for the elimination of health inequity and social injustice. *American University Law Review*, 65(2), 275–351.

Berlant, L., & Warner, M. (1998). Sex in public. *Critical Inquiry, 24*(2), 547–566.

Berry Edwards, J. (2016). Cultural intelligence for clinical social work practice. *Clinical Social Work Journal, 44*(3), 211–220. https://doi.org/10.1007/s10615-015-0543-4

Bhuyan, R., Jeyapal, D., Ku, J., Sakamoto, I., & Chou, E. (2017). Branding "Canadian experience" in immigration policy: Nation building in a neoliberal era. *Journal of International Migration & Integration, 18*(1), 47–62. https://doi.org/10.1007/s12134-015-0467-4

Blackstock, C. (2011). Wanted: Moral courage in Canadian child welfare. *First Peoples Child & Family Review, 6*(2), 35–46.

Blackstock, C. (2019, January 16). For Indigenous kids' welfare, our government knows better it just needs to do better. *The Globe and Mail.* Retrieved from https://www.theglobeandmail.com/opinion/article-for-indigenous-kids-welfare-our-government-knows-better-they-just/

Bogo, M. (2006). *Social work practice: Concepts, processes, and interviewing.* New York, NY: Columbia UP.

Bogo, M. (2010). *Achieving competence in social work through field education.* Toronto, ON. University of Toronto Press.

Bogo, M., Rawlings, M., Katz, E., & Logie, C. (2014). *Using simulation in assessment and teaching: OSCE adapted for social work (Objective Structured Clinical Examination).* Alexandria, VA: CSWE.

Bogo, M., & Vayda, E. (1998). *The practice of field instruction in social work: Theory and process* (2nd ed.). Co-publication of University of Toronto Press and Columbia UP.

Brain Injury Canada. (n.d.). Acquired Brain Injury (ABI)—The basics. Retrieved from https://www.braininjurycanada.ca/acquired-brain-injury/

Brain Injury Society of Toronto. (n.d.). Acquired Brain Injury. Retrieved from https://bist.ca/facts-about-abi/

Brant, J. (2017). *Missing and murdered Indigenous women and girls in Canada.* Retrieved from https://www.thecanadianencyclopedia.ca/en/article/missing-and-murdered-indigenous-women-and-girls-in-canada

Brascoupe, S., & Water, C. (2009). Cultural safety: Exploring the applicability of the concept of cultural safety to Aboriginal health and community wellness. *Journal of Aboriginal Health, 5,* 6–41.

Brew, L., & Kottler, J. (2017). *Applied helping skills: Transforming lives.* Thousand Oaks, CA: Sage.

Bridgeman, A., & Johns, A. (2015). Critical reflection on risk tolerance in social work practice. *Perspectives, 37*(3), 14–15.

Briskman, L. (2001). A moral crisis for social work: Critical practice and codes of ethics. *Critical Social Work, 2*(1). Retrieved from http://www1.uwindsor.ca/criticalsocialwork/a-moral-crisis-for-social-work-critical-practice-codes-of-ethics

Brooker, K. (2017). Barnet Early Years Alliance. Retrieved from https://www.bera.ac.uk/blog/observing-to-understand-using-the-tavistock-method-of-observation-to-support-reflective-practice

Brown, L., Callahan, M., Strega, S., Walmsley, C., & Dominelli, L. (2009). Manufacturing ghost fathers: The paradox of father presence and absence in child welfare. *Child & Family Social Work, 14,* 25–34. https://doi.org/10.1111/j.1365-2206.2008.00578.x

Burr, V., Blyth, E., Sutcliffe, J., & King, N. (2016). Encouraging self-reflection in social work students: Using personal construct methods. *British Journal of Social Work, 46,* 1997–2015.

Cameron, M. (2014). This is common factors. *Clinical Social Work Journal, 42*(2), 151–160.

Cameron, M., & Keenan, E. (2010). The common factors model: Implications for transtheoretical clinical social work practice. *Social Work, 55*(1), 63–73. Retrieved from https://www.ncbi.nlm.nih.gov/pubmed/20069942

Canadian Association for Social Work Education—Association Canadienne pour la formation en travail social (CASWE-ACFTS). (2014). *Standards for accreditation.* Ottawa, ON: Author.

Canadian Association of Social Workers. (2005a). *Code of ethics.* Ottawa, ON: Author.

Canadian Association of Social Workers. (2005b). *Guidelines for ethical practice.* Ottawa, ON: Author.

Canadian Association of Social Workers. (2012). *Canada Social Transfer project: Accountability matters.* Ottawa, ON: Author.

Canadian Association of Social Workers. (2014). *Social media use and social work practice.* Ottawa, ON: Author.

Canadian Association of Social Workers. (2016, January 26). *CASW applauds Human Rights Tribunal ruling acknowledging discrimination of First Nations children and communities* [Press release]. Retrieved from https://www.casw-acts.ca/en/casw-applauds-human-rights-tribunal-ruling-acknowledging-discrimination-first-nations-children-and

Canadian Association of Social Workers. (2017, June 16). *CASW applauds decision to protect and respect all identities in Canada* [Press release]. Retrieved from https://www.casw-acts.ca/en/june-16-2017-casw-applauds-decision-protect-and-respect-all-identities-canada

Canadian Association of Social Workers. (2018). *Understanding social work and child welfare: Canadian Survey and interviews with child welfare experts.* Ottawa, ON: Author.

Canadian Council of Social Work Regulators. (2012). *Entry-level competency profile for the social work profession in Canada: Executive summary.* n.p.: Author. Retrieved from http://www.ccswr-ccorts.ca/wp-content/uploads/2017/03/Competency-Profile-Executive-Summary-ENG.pdf

Canadian Institutes of Health Research. (2015). Aging well from a First Nations perspective: Working with First Nations communities to focus on wellness. Retrieved from http://www.cihr-irsc.gc.ca/e/49566.html

Caux, C., & Lecomte, J. (2017). Consent to care of persons with intellectual disability in Quebec: From vulnerability to capability. *Salud pública de México, 59*(4), 462–467.

CBC. (2008, May 16). FAQs: Truth and Reconcilitation Commission. *CBC News.* Retrieved from https://www.cbc.ca/news/canada/faqs-truth-and-reconciliation-commission-1.699883

CBC. (2016, January 26). Canada discriminates against children on reserves, tribunal rules. *CBC News.* Retrieved from https://www.cbc.ca/news/indigenous/canada-discriminates-against-children-on-reserves-tribunal-rules-1.3419480

Centre for Addiction and Mental Health. (2014). *New tools for screening and assessment for First Nations, Inuit and Métis populations.* Paper presented at Provincial System Support Program, August 7, 2014. Toronto, ON.

Centre for Social Research. (2013). Surrogate motherhood: Ethical or commercial? Retrieved from http://www.womenleadership.in/Csr/SurrogacyReport.pdf

Chandler, M., & Lalonde, C. (1998). Cultural continuity as a hedge against suicide in Canada's First Nations. *Transcultural Psychiatry, 35*(2), 191–219. https://doi.org/10.1177%2F136346159803500202

Chen, R., Grief, A., Philps, R., Pupo, M., & Rumack, L. (2018, December 29). Meet our women of the year: 32 Canadians who absolutely rocked 2018. *Chatelaine.* Retrieved from https://www.chatelaine.com/news/women-of-the-year-2018/#

Clarke, J. (2012). Managing and delivering welfare. In P. Alcock, M. May, & S. Wright (eds.), *The student's companion to social policy* (4th ed., pp. 265–271). West Sussex, UK: Wiley-Blackwell.

Cleak, H., Roulston, A., & Vreugdenhil, A. (2016). The inside story: A survey of social work students' supervision and learning opportunities on placement. *British Journal of Social Work, 46*(7), 2033–2050. https://doi.org/10.1093/bjsw/bcv117

Coady, N., & Lehmann, P. (2016). An overview of and rationale for a generalist-eclectic approach to direct social work practice. In N. Coady & P. Lehmann (eds.), *Theoretical perspectives for direct social work practice: A generalist-eclectic approach* (pp. 3–37). New York, NY: Springer.

Coates. J., Gray, M., & Hetherington, T. (2005). An "ecospiritual" perspective: Finally, a place for Indigenous approaches. *British Journal of Social Work, 36*(3), 381–399.

Collings, P. (2001). "If you got everything, it's good enough": Perspectives on successful aging in a Canadian Inuit community. *Journal of Cross-Cultural Gerontology, 16,* 127–155.

Committee on Sexual Offences against Children and Youth. (1984). Sexual offences against children: Report of the Committee on Sexual Offences against Children and Youth (the Badgley Report). Ottawa, ON: Department of Supply and Services.

Compton-Osmond, A. (2017). Aboriginal community social work: Committing to anti-oppressive practice. Retrieved from https://casw-acts.ca/sites/casw-acts.ca/files/attachements/angel_compton-osmond_sep_26.pdf

Connolly, P. (2005). *Children and ethnicity.* Retrieved from https://www.open.edu/openlearn/body-mind/childhood-youth/childhood-and-youth-studies/childhood/children-and-ethnicity

Constable, G. (2013). Reflection as a catalyst in the development of personal and professional effectiveness. In C. Knott & T. Scragg (eds.), *Reflective practice in social work* (3rd ed.). London, UK: Sage.

Csiernik R., Birnbaum, R., & Pierce, B. (2010). *Practising social work research: Case studies for learning.* Toronto, ON: University of Toronto Press. https://doi.org/10.1080/08841233.2011.563705

Daniel, B., & Bowes, A. (2010). Re-thinking harm and abuse: Insights from a lifespan perspective. *British Journal of Social Work, 41,* 820–836. https://doi.org/10.1093/bjsw/bcq116

Darrell, L., & Rich, T. (2017). Faith and field: The ethical inclusion of spirituality within the pedagogy of social work. *Field Educator, 7*(1).

Davis, K. (2008). Intersectionality as buzzword: A sociology of science perspective on what makes a feminist theory successful. *Feminist Theory, 9*(1), 67–85.

DeCaroli, M. Falanga, R., & Sagone, E. (2011). *Ethnic awareness, self-identifications, and attitudes toward ingroup and outgroup in Italian, Chinese and African pupils.* 3rd World Conference on Learning, Teaching, and Educational Leadership: Procedia Social and Behavioural Sciences, 00. Retrieved from http://www.fmag.unict.it/Public/Uploads/links/Ethnic%20awareness.pdf

Degener, T. (2014). *A human rights model of disability. Routledge handbook of disability law and human rights.* Retrieved from https://www.researchgate.net/publication/283713863_A_human_rights_model_of_disability

Devine, M. (2010). Participation in organizational change processes in human services organizations: The experiences of one group of frontline social workers. *Administration in Social Work, 34*(2), 114–134. https://doi.org/10.1080/03643101003608679

Dolgoff, R., Harrington, D., & Loewenberg, F. (2012). *Ethical decisions for social work practice* (9th ed.). Belmont, CA: Brooks/Cole.

Drisko, J. (2004). Common factors in psychotherapy outcome: Meta-analytic findings and their implications for practice and research. *Families in Society: The Journal of Contemporary Social Sciences, 85*(1), 81–90. https://doi.org/10.1606%2F1044-3894.239

Drolet, J., Clark, N., & Allen, H. (eds.) (2012). *Shifting sites of practice: Field education in Canada.* Toronto, ON: Pearson Canada.

Dufour, P. (2011). Anti-poverty policies and the adoption of Bill 112 in Quebec: A change of path? *Canadian Review of Social Policy-Revue Canadienne de Politique Sociale, 65–66,* 45–57.

Dunlap, J. (2006). Using guided reflective journaling activities to capture students' changing perceptions. *TechTrends, 50*(6), 20–26.

Duppong Hurley, K., Lambert, M., Gross, T., Thompson, R., & Farmer, E. (2017). The role of therapeutic alliance and fidelity in predicting youth outcomes during therapeutic residential care. *Journal of Emotional and Behavioral Disorders, 25*(1), 37–45. https://doi.org/10.1177%2F1063426616686756

Durst, D. (2016). Macro practice with diverse communities: New challenges for social workers. In A. Al-Krenawi, J. Graham, & N. Habibov (eds.), *Diversity and social work in Canada* (pp. 88–112). Don Mills, ON: Oxford.

Dybicz, P (2015). From person-in-environment to strengths: the promise of postmodern practice. *Journal of Social Work Education, 51,* 237–249.

East, J. (2016). Empowerment theory. In N. Coady & P. Lehmann (eds.), *Theoretical perspectives for direct social work practice: A generalist-eclectic approach* (3rd ed., pp. 373–390). New York, NY: Springer.

Edmond, T., Megivern, D., Williams, C., Rochman, E., & Howard M. (2006). Integrating evidence-based practice and social work field education. *Journal of Social Work Education, 42*(2), 377–396.

Egan, M., Combs-Orme, T., & Neely-Barnes, S. (2011). Integrating neuroscience knowledge into social work education: A case based approach. *Journal of Social Work Education, 47*(2), 269–282.

El-Lahib, Y. (2017). Theoretical dimensions for interrogating the intersection of disability, immigration and social work. *International Social Work, 3,* 640.

Ellington, L., Brassard, R., & Montminy, L. (2015). Diversity of roles played by Aboriginal men in domestic violence in Quebec. *International Journal of Men's Health, 14*(3), 287–300. http://doi.org/10.3149/jmh.1403.287

Evidence Exchange network for Mental Health and Addictions. (2014). *New tools for screening and assessment for First Nations, Inuit and Métis populations.* Retrieved from http://eenet.ca/resource/new-tools-screening-and-assessment-first-nations-inuit-and-métis-populations

Ewing JA. (1995). Detecting alcoholism: The CAGE questionnaire. *JAMA 252,* 1905–1907.

Fearn, T. (2006). *A sense of belonging: Supporting healthy child development in Aboriginal families.* Best Start: Ontario's Maternal, Newborn and Early Child Development Resource Centre. Retrieved from https://www.beststart.org/resources/hlthy_chld_dev/pdf/aboriginal_manual.pdf

Feldman, R., & Landry, O. (2017). *Discovering the lifespan* (2nd Can. ed.). Toronto, ON: Pearson Canada.

Findlay, L. (2017). Depression and suicidal ideation among Canadians aged 15 to 24. *Health Reports, 28*(1), 3–11.

Fine, M., & Teram, E. (2009). Believers and skeptics: Where social worker situate themselves regarding the code of ethics. *Ethics & Behaviour, 19*(1), 60–78.

First Nations Pedagogy Online. (2009). Elders. Retrieved from https://firstnationspedagogy.ca/elders.html

Fook, J. (2016). *Social work: A critical approach to practice* (3rd ed.). Thousand Oaks, CA: Sage.

Forde, C., & Lynch, D. (2014). Critical practice for challenging times: Social workers' engagement with community work. *British Journal of Social Work, 44,* 2078–2094.

Forgerson Hindley, A., & Olsen Edwards, J. (2017). Early childhood racial identity – The potential powerful role for museum programing, *Journal of Museum Education, 42*(1), 13–21.

Fronek, P., & Crawshaw, M. (2015). The "new family" as an emerging norm: A commentary on the position of social work in assisted reproduction. *British Journal of Social Work, 45*, 737–746.

Fujishin, R. (2012). *Natural bridges: A guide to interpersonal communication.* New York, NY: Routledge.

Garfat, T., & Charles, G. (2012). *A guide to developing effective child and youth care practice with families* (2nd ed.). Cape Town, South Africa: Pre-text.

Garrow, E., & Hasenfeld, Y. (2009). Theoretical approaches to human service organizations. In Y. Hasenfeld (ed.), *Human services as complex organization* (2nd ed., pp. 33–58). Thousand Oaks, CA: Sage.

Gaumer, B., & Fleury, M. (2007). CLSCs in Quebec: Thirty years of community action. *Social work in Public Health, 23*(4), 89–106.

Gerlach, A., Browne, A., & Greenwood, M. (2017). Engaging Indigenous families in a community-based Indigenous early childhood programme in British Columbia, Canada: A cultural safety perspective. *Health Social Care Community, 25*(6), 1763–1773.

Gibbs, A., & Stirling, B. (2013). It's about people and their environment: Student social workers' definitions of social work research. *Social Work Education, 32*(3), 317–330. Retrieved from https://ourarchive.otago.ac.nz/handle/10523/6564

Goldbloom, D. (2010). *Psychiatric clinical skills* (Rev. 1st ed.). Toronto, ON: CAMH.

Goldner, E., Jenkins, E., & Bilsker, D. (2016). *A concise introduction to mental health in Canada* (2nd ed.). Toronto, ON: Canadian Scholars' Press.

Golombok, S., Blake, L., Casey, P., Roman, G., & Jadva, V. (2013). Children born through reproductive donation: A longitudinal study of psychological adjustment. *Journal Child Psychology Psychiatry, 54*(6), 653–660.

Goode, J., Park, J., Parkin, S., Tompkins, K., & Swift, J. (2017). A collaborative approach to psychotherapy termination. *Psychotherapy, 54*(1), 10–14.

Government of Canada. (2017). *Indigenous peoples and human rights.* Retrieved from https://www.canada.ca/en/canadian-heritage/services/rights-indigenous-peoples.html

Government of Canada. (2018). *Social worker in Canada.* Retrieved from https://www.jobbank.gc.ca/marketreport/jobs/23025/ca

Government of Quebec. (2017, December 10). *Lifting over 100,000 people out of poverty by 2023* [Press release]. Retrieved from https://plq.org/en/press-release/government-action-plan-economic-inclusion-social-participation-poverty/

Graham, M. (2011). Changing paradigms and conditions of childhood: Implications for the social professions and social work. *British Journal of Social Work, 41*, 1532–1547.

Gray, M., & Coates, J. (2010). "Indigenization" and knowledge development: Extending the debate. *International Social Work, 53*(5), 613–627.

Grencavage, L., & Norcross, J. (1990). Where are the commonalities among the therapeutic common factors? *Professional Psychology Research and Practice, 21*(5), 372–378.

Gruidl, J., & Hustedde, R. (2015). Towards a robust democracy: The core competencies critical to community developers. *Journal of Community Development, 46*(3), 279–293. https://doi.org/10.1080/15575330.2015.1028082

Gutierrez, L., Alvarez, A., Nemon, H., & Lewis E. (1996). Multicultural community organizing: A strategy for change. *Social Work, 41*(5), 501–508.

Healy, K. (2005). *Social work theories in context: Creating frameworks for practice.* New York, NY: Palgrave Macmillan.

Healy, K., & Levine, K. (2016). Asset-based community development: Recognizing and building on community strengths. In A. O'Hara, Z. Weber, & K. Levine (eds.), *Skills for human service practice: Working with individuals, groups, and communities* (pp. 378–399). Don Mills, ON: Oxford UP.

Healy, L. (2008). Exploring the history of social work as a human rights profession. *International Social Work, 51*(6), 735–748. https://doi.org/10.1177/0020872808095247

Heinsch, M., Gray, M., & Sharland, E. (2016). Re-conceptualising the link between research and practice in social work: A literature review on knowledge utilisation. *International Journal of Social Welfare, 25*, 98–104. https://doi.org/10.1111/ijsw.12164

Hemy, M., Boddy, J., Chee, P. & Sauvage, D. (2016). Social work students 'juggling' field placement. *Social Work Education, 35*(2), 215–228.

Hewson, J., Walsh, C., & Bradshaw, C. (2010). Enhancing social work research education through research field placements. *Contemporary Issue in Education Research, 3*(9), 7–16.

Hicks, S., & Jeyasingham, D. (2016). Social work, queer theory and after: A genealogy of sexuality theory in neo-liberal times. *British Journal of Social work, 46,* 2357–2373.

Hickson, H. (2012). Reflective practice online—Exploring the ways social workers used an online blog for reflection. *Journal of Technology in Human Services, 30,* 32–48.

Hingley-Jones, H., Parkinson, C., & Allain, L. (2016). Back to our roots? Re-visiting psychoanalytically-informed baby and young child observation in the education of student social workers. *Journal of Social Work Practice, 30*(3), 249–265.

Hoefer, R., & Chigbu, K. (2015). The motivation and persuasion process (MAP): Proposing a practice model for community intervention. *Journal of Community Practice, 23,* 51–75.

Holland, S., & Scourfield, J. (2015). *Social work: A very short introduction.* Oxford, UK: Oxford UP.

Holloway, M., & Fyson, R. (2016). Acquired brain injury, social work and the challenges of personalisation. *British Journal of Social Work, 46,* 1301–1317.

Huang, Y., & Fang, L. (2019). "Fewer but not weaker": Understanding the intersectional identities among Chinese immigrant young gay men in Toronto. *American Journal of Orthopsychiatry, 89*(1): 27–39.

Humphries, B. (2003). What else counts as evidence in evidence-based social work? *Social Work Education, 22*(1), 81– 91.

Hunter, K., Parke, B., Babb, M., Forbes, D., & Strain, L. (2017). Balancing safety and harm for older adults with dementia in rural emergency departments: Healthcare professionals' perspectives. *Rural and Remote Health, 17*(1), 4055.

Hutchison, B., Levesque, J., Strumpf, E., & Coyle, N. (2011). Primary health care in Canada: Systems in motion. *The Milbank Quarterly, 89*(2), 256–288.

Ife, J. (2008). *Human rights and social work: Towards rights-based practice.* New York, NY: Cambridge UP.

Ife, J., & Tascón, S. (2016). Human rights and critical social work: Competing epistemologies for practice. *Social Alternatives, 35*(4), 27–31.

Immordino-Yang, M.H., & Damasio, A. (2007). We feel, therefore we learn: The relevance of affective and social neuroscience to education. *Mind, Brain and Education, 1*(1), 3–10.

Indigenous Corporate Training. (2018). Why buying authentic Indigenous art is important. Retrieved from https://www.ictinc.ca/blog/why-buying-authentic-indigenous-art-is-important

International Federation of Social Workers. (2015). Statement on the refugee crisis. Retrieved from https://www.ifsw.org/statement-on-the-refugee-crisis

International Federation of Social Workers. (2017). Statement in favour of gender perspective. Retrieved from https://www.ifsw.org/statement-in-favour-of-gender-perspective

International Federation of Social Workers. (2018a). Release social worker Munther Amira immediately! Statement by IFSW Human Rights Commission. Retrieved from https://www.ifsw.org/release-social-worker-munther-amira-immediately-statement-by-ifsw-human-rights-commission

International Federation of Social Workers. (2018b). Statement on World Human Rights Day by IFSW Human Rights Commission. Retrieved from https://www.ifsw.org/statement-on-world-human-rights-day-by-ifsw-human-rights-commission

Isle of Man Safeguarding Children Board. (n.d.). Deciding when to refer to social services. Retrieved from http://www.isleofmanscb.im/files/what_to_do_if_you_are_worried_a_child_is_being_abused_or_at_risk_of_abuse.pdf

Ivanich, J., Mousseau, A., Walls, M., Whitbeck, L., & Whitesell, N. (2018). Pathways of adaptation: Two case studies with one evidence-based substance use prevention program tailored for Indigenous youth. *Prevention Science*, June 6. https://doi.org/10.1007/s11121–018-0914-5

James, C. (2001). Reforming reform: Toronto's Settlement House Movement, 1900–20. *Canadian Historical Review, 82*(1), 55–90.

Jetté, C., & Vaillancourt, Y. (2011). Social economy and home care services in Quebec: Co-production or co-construction? *International Journal of Voluntary and non-profit organizations, 22*(1), 48–69.

Johnson, J. (2004). *Fundamentals of substance abuse practice.* Belmont, CA: Thomson-Brooks/Cole.

Johnson, J. (2017). Framing interprofessional team collaborative information seeking in health care settings. *Information Services & Use, 37,* 33–47.

Jordan's Principle Working Group. (2015). *Without denial, delay, or disruption: Ensuring First Nations children's access to equitable services through Jordan's Principle.* Ottawa, ON: Assembly of First Nations.

Kahneman, D. (2011). *Thinking, fast and slow.* New York, NY: Farrar, Straus and Giroux.

Keinemans, S. (2015). Be sensible: Emotions in social work ethics and education. *British Journal of Social Work, 45,* 2176–2191.

Keller, H. (2014). Introduction: Understanding relationships—What we would need to know to conceptualize attachment as the cultural solution of a universal developmental task. In H. Otto & H. Keller (eds.), *Different faces of attachment: Cultural variations on a universal human need* (pp. 1–26). Cambridge, UK: Cambridge UP.

Kelly, T., & Daley D. (2013). Integrated treatment of substance use and psychiatric disorders. *Social Work Public Health, 28*(0), 388–406.

Ketner, M., Cooper-Bolinskey, D., & VanCleave, D. (2017). The meaning and value of supervision in social work field education. *Field Educator, 7*(2), 1-18

Kidder, R. (2003). *Moral courage*. New York, NY: HarperCollins.

Kondrat, M. (2002). Actor-centered social work: Re-visioning "person-in-environment" through a critical theory lens. *Social Work, 47*(4), 435–448. Retrieved from https://www.jstor.org/stable/23718752

Kreisberg, N., & Marsh, J. (2016). Social work knowledge production and utilisation: An international comparison. *British Journal of Social Work, 46,* 599–618.

Kretzmann, J., & McKnight, J. (1993). *Building communities from the inside out: A path toward finding and mobilizing a community's assets.* Chicago, IL: ACTA.

Ladyshewsky, R., & Gardner, P. (2008). Peer assisted learning and blogging: A strategy to promote reflective practice during clinical fieldwork. *Australasian Journal of Educational Technology, 24*(3), 241–257.

Laing, B. (2009). A critique of Rothman's and other standard community organizing models: Toward developing a culturally proficient community organizing framework, *Community Development, 40*(1), 20–36.

Lam, C.M., Wong, H., & Leung, T.T.F., (2007). An unfinished reflexive journey: Social work students' reflection on their placement experiences. *British Journal of Social Work, 37,* 91–105.

Lamberink, L. (2018, January 11). New Ontario-wide health network supports research by Indigenous people for Indigenous people. Global News. Retrieved from https://globalnews.ca/news/3959803/new-ontario-wide-health-network-supports-research-by-indigenous-people-for-indigenous-people

Larkin, H., Felitti, V., & Anda, R. (2014). Social work and adverse childhood experiences research: Implications for practice and health policy. *Social work in Public Health, 29*(1), 1–16.

Larsen, G. (2012). Theories and values in action. In J. Drolet, N. Clark, & H. Allen, H. (eds.), *Shifting sites of practice: Field education in Canada* (pp. 59–78). Toronto, ON: Pearson Canada.

Lathouras, A. (2016). A critical approach to citizen-led social work: Putting the political back into community development practice. *Social Alternatives, 35*(4), 32–36.

Lefevre, M. (2015). Integrating the teaching, learning and assessment of communication with children within the qualifying social work curriculum. *Child and Family Social Work, 20,* 211–222.

Lerner, R., & Konowitz, L. (2016). Commentary: Theoretical and methodological dimensions of convergence and divergence of adolescent and parent reports about youth development and family structure and function—A relational developmental systems perspective. *Journal of Youth & Adolescence, 45*(10), 2178–2184.

Levenson, J. (2017). Trauma-informed social work practice. *Social Work, 62*(2), 105–113.

Lévesque, S. (2017). History as a "GPS": On the uses of historical narrative for French Canadian students' life orientation and identity. *London Review of Education, 15*(2), 227–242.

Lowman, E.B., & Barker, A.J. (2015). *Settler: Identity and colonialism in the 21st century.* Halifax, NS: Fernwood.

Luft, J., & Ingham, H. (1955). *The Johari Window: A graphic model for interpersonal relations.* Los Angeles, CA: University of California Western Training Lab.

Lundy, C. (2011). *Social work, social justice & human rights: A structural approach to practice* (2nd ed.). North York, ON: University of Toronto Press.

Lundy, C., & van Wormer, K. (2007). Social and economic justice, human rights and peace: The challenge for social work in Canada and the USA. *International Social Work, 50*(6), 727–739. https://doi.org/10.1177/0020872807081899

Lyman, M., Meisenhelter Strayer, S., Koser, V., Stoeffler, S., & Kephart, E. (2015). Integrating research and practice in baccalaureate field education through collaborative student/faculty research. *Field Educator, 5*(20), 1–8.

MacKinnon, K. (2011). Thinking about queer theory in social work education: A pedagogical (in)query. *Canadian Social Work Review, 28*(1), 139–144.

Maclure, J. (2003). *Quebec identity: The challenge of pluralism.* Montreal, QC: McGill-Queens UP.

Mallon, G., & DeCrescenzo, T. (2006). Transgender children and youth: A child welfare practice perspective. *Child Welfare, 85,* 2, 215–241.

Marsiglia, F., & Booth, J. (2015). Cultural adaptation of interventions in real practice settings. *Research on Social Work Practice, 25*(4), 423–432.

Masten, A. (2011). Resilience in children threatened by extreme adversity: Frameworks for research, practice, and translational synergy. *Development and Psychopathology, 23,* 493–506.

Masten, A., & Reed, M. (2002). Resilience in development. In C. Snyder & S. Lopez (eds.), *Handbook of positive psychology* (pp. 74–88). New York, NY: Oxford UP.

Mathie, A., & Cunningham, G. (2002). *From clients to citizens: Asset-based community development as a strategy for community-driven development.* Occasional Paper Series, No. 4. Antigonish, NS: Coady International Institute.

Mattison, M. (2000). Ethical decision making: The person in the process. *Social Work, 45*(3), 201–212.

Maynard, S., Campbell, E., Boodhoo, K., Gauthier, G., Xenocostas, S., Charney, D., . . . Gill, K. (2015). From policy to practice: Implementation of treatment for substance misuse in Quebec primary healthcare clinics. *Healthcare Policy, 11*(2), 86–101.

McCloskey, D., McDonald, M., & Cook, J. (2013). Community engagement: Definitions and organizing concepts from the literature. Retrieved from http://chl.berkeley.edu/images/stories/conference/f6%201%20community%20engagement%20-%20definitions%20and%20organizing%20concepts.pdf

McGovern, J. (2015). Living better with dementia: Strengths-based social work practice and dementia care. *Social Work in Health Care, 54*(5), 408–421.

McKenzie, J., Neiger, B., & Thackeray, R. (2009). *Planning, implementing, and evaluating health promotion programs: A primer* (5th ed.). San Francisco, CA: Pearson.

MedBroadcast. (n.d.). Adolescent suicide. Retrieved from https://medbroadcast.com/condition/getcondition/adolescent-suicide

Mental Health Commission of Canada. (2015). *Informing the future: Mental health indicators for Canada.* Ottawa, ON: Mental Health Commission of Canada.

Mental Health Commission of Canada (2019). What we do: Children and youth. Retrieved from https://www.mentalhealthcommission.ca/English/what-we-do/children-and-youth

Merrill, G. (2013). Assessing client dangerousness to self and others: Stratified risk management approaches. Retrieved from https://socialwelfare.berkeley.edu/sites/default/files/users/gregmerrill/Assessing%20client%20dangerousness%20to%20self%20and%20others%2C%20stratified%20risk%20management%20approaches%2C%20Fall%202013.pdf

Messinger, L. (2006). Social welfare policy and advocacy. In D. Morrow & L. Messinger (eds.), *Sexual orientation & gender expression in social work practice*: Working with gay, lesbian, & transgender people (pp . 427–459). New York, NY: Columbia UP.

Meyer, J.H.F., & Land, R. (2003). Threshold concepts and troublesome knowledge: Linkages to ways of thinking and practising. In C. Rust (ed.), *Improving student learning—Theory and practice ten years on* (pp. 412–424). Oxford, UK: Oxford Centre for Staff and Learning Development.

Minkler, M., & Wallerstein, N. (2012). Improving health through community organization and community building: Perspectives from health education and social work. In M. Minkler (ed.), *Community organizing and community building for health and welfare* (3rd ed., pp. 37–58). New Brunswick, NJ: Rutgers UP.

Mitchell, C. (2007). *Effective techniques for dealing with highly resistant clients* (2nd ed.). Johnson City, TN: C.W. Mitchell.

Morin, B. (2017, September 13). Where does Canada sit 10 years after the UN Declaration on the Rights of Indigenous Peoples? *CBC News.* Retrieved from https://www.cbc.ca/news/indigenous/where-does-canada-sit-10-years-after-undrip-1.4288480

Morley, C. (2003). Towards critical social work practice in mental health: A review. *Journal of Progressive Human Services, 14*(1), 2003.

Morris, S., Fawcett, G., Brisebois, L., & Hughes, J. (2018*). Canadian survey on disability reports: A demographic, employment and income profile of Canadians with disabilities aged 15 years and over, 2017.* Ottawa, ON: Statistics Canada.

Morrow, D. (2006). Sexual orientation and gender identity expression. In D. Morrow & L. Messinger (eds.), *Sexual orientation & gender expression in social work practice*: Working with gay, lesbian, bisexual, & transgender people (pp. 3–17). New York, NY: Columbia UP.

Muir, N., & Bohr, Y. (2014). Contemporary practice of traditional Aboriginal child rearing: A review. *First Peoples Child and family Review, 9*(1), 66–79.

National Aboriginal Health Organization. (2007). *Cultural competency and safety: A First Nations, Inuit, and Métis context & guidelines for health professionals.* Presented at The Royal College of Physicians and Surgeons of Canada: Advisory Committee—First Nations, Inuit and Métis Health Education in PGME & CME. Retrieved from https://www.saintelizabeth.com/getmedia/80178789-0554-4895-8f02-0b47a1ce992a/Cultural-Competency-and-Safety-A-FNMI-Context.pdf.aspx

National Survey of Children's Health (2011). Data query from the Child and Adolescent Health Measurement Initiative, Data Resource Center for Child and Adolescent Health website. Retrieved from http://www.childhealthdata.org

Navaneelan, T. (2017). Suicide rates: An overview (Statistics Canada Catalogue no. 82-624-X). Retrieved from https://www150.statcan.gc.ca/n1/pub/82-624-x/2012001/article/11696-eng.htm

Neckoway, R., Brownlee, K., & Castellan, B. (2007). Is attachment theory consistent with Aboriginal parenting realities? *First Peoples Child & Family Review, 3*(2), 65–74.

Nester, J. (2016). The importance of interprofessional practice and education in the era of accountable care. *North Carolina Medical Journal, 77*(2), 128–132.

New South Wales Department of Education. (n.d.). Referrals. Retrieved from https://share.tafensw.edu.au/share/file/2a995212-86ee-4e14-a573-088cd99490cf/1/CIV%20Youth%20Work%20Online%202010.zip/CIV%20Youth%20Work%20Online%202010/knowledge/referrals/referrals.htm

Newfoundland and Labrador Association of Social Workers. (2018). *Standards of practice for social workers in Newfoundland and Labrador.* St. John's, NL: Newfoundland & Labrador Association of Social Workers.

Ng, L., Bampton, C., Stevens, S., & Woods, P. (2017). The infant observation task as a tool in psychiatric practice. *Australasian Psychiatry, 25*(3), 236–238.

Nova Scotia Mental Health Services. (2017). Involuntary Psychiatric Treatment Act. Retrieved from https://novascotia.ca/dhw/mental-health/involuntary-psychiatric-treatment-act.asp

O'Donnell, V., Wendt, M., & National Association of Friendship Centres. (2017). *Aboriginal Peoples Survey, 2012: Aboriginal seniors in population centres in Canada.* Ottawa, ON: Statistics Canada.

Office of the High Commissioner for Human Rights. (2018). Human rights dimension of poverty. Retrieved from https://www.ohchr.org/en/issues/poverty/pages/srextremepovertyindex.aspx

O'Hara, A., Weber, Z., & Levine, K. (2016). *Skills for human service practice: Working with individuals, groups, and communities* (2nd ed.). Don Mills, ON: Oxford UP.

O'Leary, D., & Majic, L. (2018). Here's what Canada's first National Anti-Poverty Plan needs. Retrieved from https://www.hilltimes.com/2018/07/18/heres-canadas-first-national-anti-poverty-plan-needs/151332

Ontario Human Rights Commission. (n.d.). Questions and answers about gender identity and pronouns. Retrieved from http://www.ohrc.on.ca/en/questions-and-answers-about-gender-identity-and-pronouns

Packard, T. (2017). Tactics for successful organizational change in a youth and family services agency. *Children and Youth Services Review, 81,* 129–138.

Palmer, J. (2018). Picturing health: health advocates for Indigenous communities in British Columbia, Canada. *Lancet, 391*(10131), 1660–1673.

Park, J., Goode, J., Tompkins, K., & Swift, J. (2016). Clinical errors that can occur in the treatment decision-making process in psychotherapy. *Psychotherapy, 53*(3), 257–261.

Payne, M. (2014). *Modern social work theory* (4th ed.). New York, NY: Palgrave Macmillan.

Pearson, M. (2012). Multiple intelligences, eclecticism and the therapeutic alliance: New possibilities in integrative counsellor education. *BeyondSCAPE: Possibility and Necessity in Counselling and Psychotherapy Education.* Art Conference Papers, 36. Retrieved from https://researchonline.nd.edu.au/arts_conference/36/

Plumb, J., Bush, K., & Kersevich, S. (2016). Trauma-sensitive schools: An evidence-based approach. *School Social Work Journal, 40*(2), 37–60.

Preston, S., George, P., & Silver, S. (2014). Field education in social work: The need for reimagining. *Critical Social Work, 15*(1), 57–72.

Pritzker, S., & Lane, S. (2014). Field Note—Integrating policy and political content in BSW and MSW field placements. *Journal of Social Work Education, 50,* 730–739.

Quintana, S., Chao, R., Cross, W., Hughes, D., Nelson-Le Gall, S., Aboud, F., … Vietze, D. (2006). Race, ethnicity, and culture in child development: Contemporary research and future directions. *Child Development, 77*(5), 1129–1141.

Ramsden, I. (1992). *Kawa whakaruruhau: Guidelines for nursing and midwifery education.* Wellington, New Zealand: Nursing Council of New Zealand.

Rappaport, J. (1987). Terms of empowerment/exemplars of prevention: Toward a theory for community psychology. *American Journal of Community Psychology, 15*(2), 122–148.

Reamer, F. (2013). *Social work values and ethics* (4th ed.). New York, NY: Columbia UP.

Reamer, F., & Nimmagadda J. (2017). Social work ethics in India: A call for the development of indigenized ethical standards. *International Social Work, 60*(1), 182–195.

Regehr, C., Bogo, M., Donovan, K., Lim, A., & Anstice, S. (2012). Identifying student competencies in macro practice: Articulating the practice wisdom of field instructors. *Journal of Social Work Education, 48*(2), 307–319. http://doi.org/10.5175/JSWE.2012.201000114

Regehr, C., Stern, C., & Shlonsky, A. (2007). Operationalizing evidence-based practice: The development of an institute for evidence-based social work. *Research on Social Work Practice, 17,* 408–416.

RELIESS. (2012, October). Local development and the social economy in urban Quebec—Community Development Economic Corporations. Retrieved from https://ccednet-rcdec.ca/sites/ccednet-rcdec.ca/files/cdec_va.pdf

Richards, S., Donovan, S., Victor, C., & Ross, F. (2007). Standing secure amidst a falling world? Practitioner understandings of old age in responses to a case vignette. *Journal of Interprofessional Care, 21*(3), 335–349.

Richmond, C., & Cook, C. (2016). Creating conditions for Canadian Aboriginal health equity: The promise of health public policy. *Public Health Reviews, 37*(1), 1–16.

Rivera, F., & Erlich, J. (1998). *Community organizing in a diverse society* (3rd ed.). New York, NY: Pearson.

Robinson, M., Cross-Denny, B., Lee, K., Werkmeister Rozas, L., & Yamada, A. (2016). Teaching note—teaching intersectionality: Transforming cultural competence content in social work education. *Journal of Social Work Education, 52*(4), 509–517.

Rogers, C. (1961). *On becoming a person.* Boston, MA: Houghton Mifflin.

Rogers, C.R. (1956). Client-centered approach to therapy. In I.L. Kutash & A. Wolf (eds.), *Psychotherapist's casebook: Theory and technique in practice.* San Francisco: Jossey-Bass.

Rogers, C. R. (1980). *A way of being.* Boston, MA: Houghton Mifflin.

Rønningstad, C. (2018). Us and them: First-line management and change resistance. *Nordic Journal of Working Life Studies, 8*(2). 5–22.

Rosen, A., & Proctor, E. (2003). Practice guidelines and the challenge of effective practice. In A. Rosen & E. Proctor (eds.), *Developing practice guidelines for social work intervention: Issues, methods, and research agents* (pp. 1–16). New York, NY: Columbia UP.

Rossiter, A., Walsh-Bowers, R., & Auclair, R. (1998). Introduction: Critical perspectives on applied ethics. *Canadian Journal of Community Mental Health, 17*(2), 5–13.

Rostosky, S., Black, W., Riggle, E., & Rosenkrantz, D. (2015). Positive aspects of being a heterosexual ally to lesbian, gay, bisexual and transgender (LGBT) people. *American Journal of Orthopsychiatry, 85*(4), 331–338.

Rothman, J., & Tropman, J.E. (1987). Models of community organizing and macro practice perspectives: Their mixing and phasing. In F. M. Cox, J.L. Erlich, J. Rothman, & J.E. Tropman (eds.), *Strategies of community organization: Macro practice* (pp. 3–25). Itasca, IL: Peacock.

Roy, P., Tremblay, G., & Duplessis-Brochu, E. (2017). Problematizing men's suicide, mental health, and well-being. 20 years of social work innovation in the province of Quebec, Canada. *Crisis, 39*(2), 137–13.

Royse, D., Dhooper, S., & Lewis Rompf, E. (2012). *Field Instruction: A Guide for social work students.* White Plains, NY: Longman.

Sackett, D., Rosenberg, W., Gray, J., Haynes, R., & Richardson, W. (1996). Evidence based medicine: What it is and what it isn't. *British Medical Journal (Clinical Research Ed.), 312*(7023), 71–72.

Schmitz, C., Stinson, C., & James, C. (2010). Reclaiming community: Multidisciplinary approaches to environmental sustainability. *Critical Social Work, 11*(3), 83–95.

Schön, D. (1987). *Educating the reflective practitioner: Toward a new design for teaching and learning in the professions.* Jossey-Bass Higher Education Series. San Francisco, CA: Jossey-Bass.

Schulz, W. (1994). *Counselling ethics casebook.* Ottawa, ON: Canadian Guidance and Counselling Association.

Scott, C. (2016). How French Canadians became white folks, or doing things with race in Quebec. *Ethnic and Racial Studies, 39*(7), 1280–1297.

Sethi, B. (2015). Education and employment training supports for newcomers to Canada's middle-sized urban/rural regions: Implications for social work practice. *Journal of Social Work, 15*(2), 138–161.

Shaw, I. (2012). *Practice and research.* Aldershot, UK: Ashgate.

Shebib, B. (2017). *Choices: Interviewing and counselling skills for Canadians* (6th ed.). Toronto, ON: Pearson.

Sherr, M., & Jones, J. (2014*). Introduction to competence-based social work: The profession of caring, knowing, and serving.* Chicago, IL: Lyceum Books.

Shlonsky, A., & Benbenishty, R. (2014). From evidence to outcomes in child welfare. In A. Shlonsky & R. Benbenishty (eds.), *From evidence to outcomes in child welfare: An international reader* (pp. 3–23). New York, NY: Oxford UP.

Smith, C., Fluke, J., Fallon, B., Mishna, F., & Decker Pierce, B. (2018). Child welfare organizations: Do specialization and service integration impact placement decisions? *Child Abuse & Neglect, 76*, 573–582.

Smith-Osborne, A. (2007). Life span and resiliency theory: A critical review. *Advances in Social Work, 8*(1), 152–168.

Souffrant, K. (2019). Standing up to injustice: Professor Cindy Blackstock on moral courage. Retrieved from https://mcgill.ca/arts/article/courage-act-face-injustice

Sovet, L., DiMillo, J., & Samson, A. (2017). Linguistic identity and career decision-making difficulties among French-speaking Canadian students living in an Anglo-dominant context. *International Journal for Educational and Vocational Guidance, 17*(3), 269–284.

Statistics Canada. (2017). Aboriginal peoples in Canada: Key results from the 2016 census. Retrieved from https://www150.statcan.gc.ca/n1/en/daily-quotidien/171025/dq171025a-eng.pdf

Staub-Bernasconi, S. (2012). Human rights and their relevance for social work as theory and practice. In L. Healy & R. Link (eds.), *Handbook of international social work: Human rights, development, and the global profession* (pp. 30–36). New York, NY: Oxford UP.

Steen, J., Mann, M., Restivo, N., Mazany, S., & Chaple, R. (2017). Human rights: Its meaning and practice in social work field settings. *Social Work, 62*(1). 9–17.

Stokes, J. (2019). Substance use decision-making—Are clinicians using the evidence? *Journal of Social Service Research, 45*(1), 16–33.

Substance Abuse and Mental Health Services Administration (SAMHSA). (2018). Adverse childhood experiences. Retrieved from https://www.samhsa.gov/capt/practicing-effective-prevention/prevention-behavioral-health/adverse-childhood-experiences

Swift, J., & Callahan, J. (2010). A comparison of client preferences for intervention empirical support versus common therapy variables. *Journal of Clinical Psychology, 66*(12), 1217–1231.

Swift, J. K., Callahan, J. L., & Vollmer, B. M. (2011). Preferences. *Journal of Clinical Psychology, 67*(2), 155–165.

Swift, J., Derthick, A., & Tompkins, K. (2018). The relationship between trainee therapists' and clients' initial expectations and actual treatment duration and outcomes. *Practice innovations, 3*(2), 84–93.

Tam-Tham, H., Nettel-Aguirre, A., Silvius, J., Dalziel, W., Garcia, L., Molnar, F., and Drummond, N. (2016). Provision of dementia-related services in Canada: A comparative study. *BMC Health Services Research 16,* 184–193.

Taylor, A. (2018). Case and systemic advocacy at the Nelson Advocacy Centre. *Perspectives, 40*(1), 22–23.

Taylor, B. (2010). *Professional decision making in social work practice.* Exeter, UK: Learning Matters.

Taylor, C. (2004). Underpinning knowledge for child care practice: reconsidering child development theory. *Child and Family Social Work, 9,* 225–235.

Thomas, J. (2016). Adverse childhood experiences among MSW students. *Journal of Teaching in Social Work, 36*(3), 1–21.

Thunderbird Partnership Foundation. (2019). First Peoples Wellness Circle. Retrieved from https://thunderbirdpf.org/about-tpf/first-peoples-wellness-circle/

Trevithick, P. (2008). Revisiting the knowledge base of social work: A framework for practice. *British Journal of Social Work, 38,* 1212–1237.

Trocmé, N. (2016). Still in critical demand? *Canadian Social Work Review, 33*(1), 141–146.

Trotter, C. (2015). *Working with involuntary clients: A guide to practice* (3rd ed.). New York, NY: Routledge.

Truth and Reconciliation Commission of Canada. (2015). *Truth and Reconciliation Commission of Canada: Calls to action.* Winnipeg, MB: Author.

Tucker, E. (2014, January 10). 5 occupations in high demand amid Canada's surprising job losses. *Global News.* Retrieved from https://globalnews.ca/news/1074649/5-occupations-in-high-demand-amid-canadas-surprising-job-losses/

Turcotte, M., & Schellenberg, G. (2007). *A portrait of seniors in Canada: 2006.* Ottawa, ON: Statistics Canada, Social and Aboriginal Statistics Division.

Turner, D. (2016). "Only connect": Unifying the social in social work and social media. *Journal of Social Work Practice, 30*(3), 313–327.

Uggerhøj, L. (2011). What is practice research in social work—Definitions, barriers and possibilities. *Social Work and Society International Online Journal, 9*(1).

UN News. (2007, September 23). United Nations adopts Declaration on Rights of Indigenous Peoples. Retrieved from https://news.un.org/en/story/2007/09/231062-united-nations-adopts-declaration-rights-indigenous-peoples

United Nations. (2007). Frequently asked questions on the Declaration on the Rights of Indigenous Peoples. Retrieved from https://www.un.org/esa/socdev/unpfii/documents/FAQsindigenousdeclaration.pdf

University of Manitoba. (2018). Ongomiizwin. Retrieved from http://umanitoba.ca/faculties/health_sciences/indigenous/institute/background.html

UNTERM (2010). Community development. Retrieved from https://unterm.un.org/UNTERM/DGAACS/unterm.nsf/WebView/526C2EABA978F007852569FD00036819

Vaicekauskienė, V. (n.d.). Workshop 3. The importance of team approach in social work. Retrieved from http://www.journals.vu.lt/STEPP/article/view/8513/6384

Wankah, P., Couturier, Y., Belzile, L., Gagnon, D., & Breton, M. (2018). Providers' perspectives on the implementation of mandated local health networks for older people in Quebec. *International Journal of Integrated Care, 18*(2), 1–17.

Watkins, C. (2014). The supervisory alliance as quintessential integrative variable. *Journal of Contemporary Psychotherapy, 44(*3), 151–161. http://doi.org/10.1007/s10879-013-9252-x

Wattie, C. (2017, February 12). How social worker and activist Cindy Blackstock does self-care. *The Globe and Mail.* Retrieved from https://www.theglobeandmail.com/life/relationships/how-social-worker-and-activist-cindy-blackstock-does-self-care/article33998628/

Wayne, J., Raskin, M., & Bogo, M. (2010). Field education as the signature pedagogy of social work education. *Journal of Social Work Education, 46*(3), 327–339.

Webb, S. (2001). Some considerations on the validity of evidence-based practice in social work. *British Journal of Social Work, 31,* 57–79.

Webb, S. (2015, August). *Professional identity and social work.* Keynote presentation at the 5th International conference on sociology and social work, Chester UK. Retrieved from http://www.chester.ac.uk/sites/files/chester/WEBB.pdf

Weiss-Gal, I. (2016). Policy practice in social work education: A literature review. *International Journal of Social Welfare, 25,* 290–303. http://doi.org/10.1111/ijsw.12203

Weiss-Gal, I., & Peled, E. (2009). Publishing voice: Training social workers in policy practice. *British Journal of Social Work, 39,* 368–382.

Wells, L., Ferguson, J., & Interdepartmental Committee on Family Violence and Bullying. (2012). *Family violence hurts everyone: A framework to end family violence in Alberta [A source document].* Calgary, AB: The University of Calgary, Shift: The Project to End Domestic Violence.

Wells, M., Maschi, T., & Slater, G. (2012). Integration of research and practice: Innovations and challenges in social work programs. *Social Work Education, 31*(3), 331–346.

Wesley-Equimaux, C., & Calliou, B. (2010). *Best practices in Aboriginal community development: A literature review and wise practices approach.* Banff, AB: The Banff Centre. Retrieved from http://communities4families.ca/wp-content/uploads/2014/08/Aboriginal-Community-Development.pdf

Whitfield, K. (2018). A case study exploring the implications of one Alberta rural community's experience with planning their own hospice care. *Journal of Rural and Community Development, 13*(1), 1–12.

Wilkin, L., & Hillock, S. (2014). Enhancing MSW students' efficacy in working with trauma, violence, and oppression: An integrated feminist-trauma framework for social work education. *Feminist Teacher, 24*(3), 184–206.

Wilkins, D. (2017). Using Q methodology to understand how child protection social workers use attachment theory. *Child and Family Social Work, 22,* 70–80.

Wing Sue, D. (2017). The challenges of becoming a white ally. *The Counseling Psychologist, 45*(5), 706–716.

Wong Y., & Vinsky J. (2009). Speaking from the margins: A critical reflection on the "spiritual-but-not-religious" discourse in social work. *British Journal of Social Work, 39*(7), 1343–1359.

Wood, Donna E. (2013). The Canada Social Transfer and the deconstruction of pan-Canadian social policy. *Vibrant Communities Calgary.* Calgary, AB.

Wronka, J. (2008). *Human rights and social justice: Social action and service for the helping and health professions.* Thousand Oaks, CA: Sage.

Yeager, K., & Bauer-Wu, S. (2013). Cultural humility: Essential foundation for clinical researchers. *Applied Nursing Research, 26*(4), 251–256.

Yee, J. & Dumbrill, G. (2016). Whiteout: Still looking for race in Canadian social work practice. In A. Al-Krenawi, J. Graham, & N. Habibov (eds.), *Diversity and social work in Canada* (pp. 13–37). Don Mills, ON: Oxford UP.

Zhang, K. (2016). French speaking on the situation of multiculture and nationalism in Quebec during 1980–2010. *Procedia—Social and Behavioral Sciences, 236,* 219–224.

Zimmerman, M. (2013). *Interview guide for evaluating DSM-5 psychiatric disorders and the Mental Status Examination.* East Greenwich, RI: Psych Products Press.

# Index

# Q

# R

# S